CYPRUS AND THE BALANCE
OF EMPIRES

ART AND ARCHAEOLOGY FROM JUSTINIAN I
TO THE CŒUR DE LION

AMERICAN SCHOOLS OF ORIENTAL RESEARCH
ARCHEOLOGICAL REPORTS

Kevin M. McGeough, Editor

Number 20

Cyprus and the Balance of Empires:
Art and Archaeology from Justinian I to the Cœur de Lion

CAARI MONOGRAPH SERIES 5

CYPRUS AND THE BALANCE OF EMPIRES

ART AND ARCHAEOLOGY FROM JUSTINIAN I TO THE CŒUR DE LION

Edited by

CHARLES ANTHONY STEWART,
THOMAS W. DAVIS,
and ANNEMARIE WEYL CARR

organized by

THE CYPRUS AMERICAN ARCHAEOLOGICAL RESEARCH INSTITUTE

AMERICAN SCHOOLS OF ORIENTAL RESEARCH • BOSTON, MA

Cyprus and the Balance of Empires:

Art and Archaeology from Justinian I to the Cœur de Lion

edited by

Charles Anthony Stewart, Thomas W. Davis, and Annemarie Weyl Carr

Cover: Chalice with Tyche Personification of "The City of Cyprus," from the Avar Treasure Hoard, Vrap (Albania). Gold. 8th–9th century, possibly made in Cyprus. The Metropolitan Museum of Art, New York, acc. no. 17.190.1710. Image copyright © The Metropolitan Museum of Art / Art Resource, NY.

The American Schools of Oriental Research © 2014

ISBN 978-0-89757-073-2

Library of Congress Cataloging-in-Publication Data

Cyprus and the balance of empires : art and archaeology from Justinian I to the Coeur de Lion / edited by Charles Anthony Stewart, Thomas W. Davis, and Annemarie Weyl Carr ; organized by the Cyprus American Archaeological Research Institute.
   pages cm. -- (Archeological reports / American Schools of Oriental Research ; number 20) (CAARI monograph series ; 5)
 Includes bibliographical references and index.
 ISBN 978-0-89757-073-2 (acid-free paper)
1. Cyprus--Antiquities. 2. Cyprus--Civilization. 3. Art, Cypriot--History. 4. Architecture--Cyprus--History--To 1500. 5. Material culture--Cyprus--History--To 1500. 6. Cyprus--Relations--Byzantine Empire. 7. Byzantine Empire--Relations--Cyprus. 8. Cyprus--Religious life and customs. I. Stewart, Charles Anthony. II. Davis, Thomas W., 1956- III. Carr, Annemarie Weyl.
DS54.3.C9317 2014
956.93'01--dc23
           2014013742

Printed in the United States of America on acid-free paper.

Contents

List of Illustrations

- Was there ever a Cypriot "insularity"?
- How were the policies of Damascus and Constantinople manifested within Cypriot society?
- Can we detect settlement patterns and population decline and growth?
- How was the island governed?
- Are there signs of a unique Cypriot identity?
- Where does the ceramic and numismatic evidence lead?
- What impact did iconoclasm have on the church and its relations with the Byzantine Empire?
- How did the Crusades economically impact Cyprus in the twelfth century?

Naturally, such grand questions were not fully answered. Each paper, however, provided new and unpublished data; and when grouped as a whole, a larger picture of the period emerged that challenged earlier perceptions.

The conference was first conceived by Thomas W. Davis, the former director of CAARI, in 2006. At that time, the Schaefer Library was adding the Stylianou Collection of Byzantine books, and several medievalists were conducting research at CAARI. Earlier, he had organized the "Medieval frescoes of Cyprus" conference in October 2005, which opened up the possibilities of having a larger, broader conference on material culture. So Tom asked me, a Fulbright fellow at the time, to put together a proposal. Annemarie Weyl Carr, a CAARI trustee and foremost expert on Byzantine Art, quickly joined in the preliminary discussions. In time we asked Helena Wylde Swiny to join our Organizing Committee. Eventually the Planning Committee was formed, spearheaded by Vathoulla Moustoukki and Evi Karyda, which was given added assistance by Doria Nicolaou and Phodoulla Christodoulou.

We initially planned to have a five-day conference in the summer of 2009, consisting of 24 speakers. Because of the global economic downturn in 2008, the conference was delayed and our original sponsors could no longer fund us. And yet the CAARI director was tenacious, and in the summer of 2010 the conference came to life again with new energy, thanks to the encouragement of Mr. Constantinos S. Loizides. New realities forced the committee to reduce the number of participants by half. Nevertheless, we believed the abbreviated schedule could still represent key facets of Byzantine material culture.

Since the conference would now coincide with the 50th-year anniversary of the Republic of Cyprus, we highlighted the contribution of Cypriot scholars to Byzantine archaeology, such as Athanasios Papageorghiou and A.I. Dikigoropoulos. And we asked Professor Demetrios Michaelides, an internationally renowned archaeologist and a Cypriot, to provide the opening keynote lecture. His enlightening presentation recounted the *Agioi Pente* (Yeroskipou) excavations, which revealed a complex pilgrimage site dating from the sixth through eighth centuries. This was a superb opening lecture since it touched on all the issues that subsequent papers addressed: material culture, economics, trade, burial practices, religious beliefs, architectural development, artistic production, etc.

The morning presentations opened with Tom Davis' lecture on the historiography of archaeological research on Byzantine Cyprus. This provided an overview of the methods of past scholars, setting the context for the following papers. Professor Claudia Rapp prepared a lecture on the development of bishop-saints in Cyprus from the fourth century, and how this tradition would continue to play an active role in shaping Cypriot society, politics, and cultural practices. Unfortunately, Claudia could not attend due to illness; rather graciously, Professor Paul Stephenson (Durham University) offered to read Professor Rapp's paper — and he did so quite eloquently, despite the short notice.

Professor Marcus Rautman gave us a synopsis of the field surveys of the Troodos region and how these allowed us to glimpse trade, settlement, and investment patterns in early Byzantine Cyprus. Afterwards, Brooke Shilling illustrated how Byzantine literature and theology could assist us in interpreting a great masterpiece — the apse mosaic of the Panagia Angeloktisti (Kiti). To conclude the morning session, Dr. Michael Metcalf elucidated how numismatics and sigillography have clarified settlement patterns between 649 and 965, when the Arabs had a presence on Cyprus.

The afternoon session began with Dr. Eleni Procopiou's important lecture on the vast pilgrimage shrine located at *Katalymmata ton Plakoton* (Akrotiri Peninsula). This formerly unknown

7th-century settlement was persuasively linked to the activities of the famous Cypriot, St. John the Almsgiver, Patriarch of Alexandria. Next, Professor M. Tahar Mansouri gave a dynamic presentation regarding the Arabic source material for the study of Cypriot history; his main thesis challenged our previous understanding, arguing that the Arabs did not see Cyprus as a conquered territory, but rather as an "independent tributary" within the Byzantine Empire. Afterwards, I discussed the development of Cypriot Byzantine architecture and their significant place in medieval art history.

The evening session focused on the visual arts of Cyprus during the Byzantine period. Professor Sophocles Sophocleous provided a survey of icons which have been attributed to the Early Byzantine Period. He gave reasons based on stylistic grounds, and the pitfalls and benefits of such an approach. Afterwards, Dr. Maria Parani discussed the daily life of Byzantine citizens, as reconstructed through the material culture, historical sources, and depictions in surviving frescos. And to conclude the conference, Annemarie Weyl Carr delivered an intriguing lecture on the development of the Blessed Virgin Mary's image in Cypriot frescos, unequaled in the rest of the Byzantine Empire.

The conference laid the foundations for this book, but the result is much more than a published proceeding. Additional excavation data and new research over the past two years have been incorporated within the chapters. And there are three significant changes that should be noted. First, Dr. Vasiliki Kassianidou kindly analyzed an artifact featured in Dr. Parani's presentation. Her subsequent investigation is included here as an Appendix to Chapter 10. Second, due to unforeseen circumstances, Brooke Shilling was unable to include her paper here. This disappointment resulted in a third change, which bears further explanation. Our committee had originally planned for Dr. Tassos Papacostas to participate in our conference, but he was unable due to the revised schedule. Later, when we submitted our proposal for publication, an anonymous reviewer of the ASOR's Archaeological Report Series mentioned that Dr. Papacostas should have been included. Naturally we agreed. It just so happened that Annemarie Weyl Carr and Gudrun Bühl had organized a work-shop at Dumbarton Oaks, Washington, DC, called "Cyprus from Byzantium to the Renaissance," in conjunction with the Smithsonian Institution's exhibit *Cyprus: Crossroads of Civilizations* (September 29, 2010 through May 1, 2011). Fortunately, Dr. Papacostas was able to participate at that time, where he gave an insightful paper called "Decoding Cyprus from Byzantium to the Renaissance." And so we invited him to prepare that paper for this volume. Though at first glance his topic seems to fall outside this book's timeframe, actually it underscores how "Byzantine" culture on Cyprus continued to flourish, even after it was no longer part of the Byzantine Empire; moreover, he explained how Cypriot spirituality would have influence *outside* the island.

The Organizing Committee hopes that this publication will continue discussions initiated by the conference. Collegial dialogue among the various disciplines is necessary for formulating metanarratives and conveying the significance of Cypriot archaeology. While the data is unique to the geographical context, it touches on issues pertaining to the wider Islamic, Byzantine, and Latin world, and the temporal transition between the Late Roman and Medieval periods. We also believe that this volume highlights Cyprus' changing roles, sometimes at the center and at other times the periphery, but always reflecting the wider world.

From my personal perspective, I also see this volume as a "monument" to Thomas Davis' tenure as CAARI director from 2003 to 2011. That was a particularly momentous era for archaeological research on Cyprus, when there was a renewed hope for a solution to the island's political and geographical division. In April 2003 travel restrictions were eased, so for the first time in 30 years international scholars could reevaluate the sites, frescos, and architecture in the northern areas. Tom Davis worked tirelessly in exploring all the possibilities how such a reconciliation would impact antiquities laws and archaeological practices. He witnessed how northern Byzantine sites were still being desecrated and pillaged, and the urgent need to protect and preserve them. This motivated him to encourage Byzantine scholarship and conferences within the Republic of Cyprus. He also mentored numerous junior scholars, such as myself, how to observe the

Department of Antiquities' protocols while studying the entire island. As a result, during these years, a new picture of Byzantine Cyprus arose. We began to see a very wealthy center, in both its agricultural produce and artistic output, keeping in mind that it was sometimes influenced, and sometimes isolated, from the surrounding continents. With a dominant Byzantine culture, the Cypriots were able to tolerate numerous non-Greeks and religious views within their shores, especially those of Armenians, Georgians, and Latins. The most beautiful aspect that emerged, at least to my modern eyes, was that Byzantine Cyprus was an island undivided.

As this book was being prepared another historic episode was taking place. Recently, the Menil Collection honored their agreement with the Church of Cyprus and returned the Lysi Byzantine frescos to the island. These had been the largest and most complete Byzantine artworks in North America. Their story should never be forgotten. As a result of the 1974 war, thieves plundered the wall frescos from the church of Agios Themonianos in Lysi, Cyprus. Eventually, these made their way on the international black market. In 1984, Domenique de Menil recognized both their significance and questionable provenance. In an unprecedented act of magnanimity, Mrs. De Menil contacted the rightful owners, the Church of Cyprus, and agreed to purchase and restore the frescos on their behalf.

As a result, the frescos were put on full display in a unique chapel — a *chef-d'œuvre* itself — designed by Françoise de Menil. The chapel was located in Houston, Texas, and situated between the campuses of the Menil Collection and the University of St. Thomas. Over the years, thousands of visitors were able to experience the mastery and power of Cypriot art — people who would never have traveled to Cyprus. Moreover, the frescos also kept alive the issue of the looting of archaeological sites in northern Cyprus, putting pressure on politicians to pass legislation in order to ward off vandals and thieves. On a more personal note, my university office was two doors down from the chapel. Every semester I would bring students there to study these masterpieces. I was struck by how these frescos moved my students in ways that went beyond mere political or academic curiosity, but provoked transcendent experience. Great art is not passive. Over the years, Americans developed a relationship with these saintly figures, and they ceased to be mere pigmented plaster, but transformed into persons that actively spoke and comforted.

I would smile when my students referred to the Theotokos fresco as "Our Lady," with the same reverence as my Cypriot friends call her "Panagia." So I was not surprised to see all the tears and solemn faces, when the Menil chapel was deconsecrated in March 2012. Such a momentous occasion was officiated by His Eminence Demetrios, Orthodox Archbishop of America, and Rev. Demosthenes Demosthenous (representative of the Church of Cyprus). They too felt the sincere emotional impact on our all-American cosmopolis; in other words, the fresco departure was experienced more like a divorce rather than a de-accessioning. And so, at this event, Americans were able to understand, to a small degree, the kind of pain that Cypriots feel when their antiquities illicitly leave their shores.

Scientific research of a bygone civilization might seem relevant to only a select few academics. However, the Menil episode highlights the vital intersection between scholarship, politics, and modern spirituality. Archaeology powerfully exerts its influence on us and future generations. It is with this in mind that this CAARI monograph is presented.

Charles Anthony Stewart
Houston, Texas

Acknowledgments

The conference and this publication were made possible through the generosity of Constantinos S. Loizides, The Piraeus Bank Group, Ambassador Frank C. Urbancic (The Embassy of the United States, Nicosia, Cyprus), Elizabeth Kassinis and Alan Davis of the United States Agency for International Development (USAID), Council of American Overseas Research Centers (CAORC), the Trustees of the Cyprus American Archaeological Research Institute, Friends of Archaeology (Houston), and the University of St. Thomas, Houston.

Success depended on the dedication and effort of the Planning Committee, who we sincerely thank: Vathoulla Moustoukki, Evi Karyda, Helena Wylde Swiny, and Phodoulla Christodoulou.

Likewise, we are grateful for these individuals who provided additional assistance prior to, during, and/or after the conference: Ambassador Raymond C. Ewing, Joseph A. Greene, R. Scott Moore, Bernard Knapp, Demesticha Styliani, Vasiliki Kassianidou, Charalambos Bakirtzis, Demetra Papanikola-Bakirtzis, Maria Hadjicosti, Pavlos Flourentzos, Despos Pilides, Marina Solomidou-Ieronymidou, Doria Nicolaou, Nicholas Coureas, Chris Schabel, Brooke Shilling, Paul Stephenson, Jonathan Cohen, Frank Garrod, Ruth Keshishian, Alexis M. Clark, Anna Michael "Ka Anna" Moustoukki, and Diana Constantinides. A special thanks is also extended to Andrew McCarthy, current director of CAARI.

Other individuals contributed to this publication in an indirect way, especially in how the intellectual material was framed: Gudrun Bühl, Susan de Menil, Kristina Van Dyke, Amy Papalexandrou, Glenn Peers, Dominic Aquila, Bernard Bonario, and Rev. George Hosko.

Several institutions and individuals provided permissions to reproduce artworks, for which we are grateful: the Department of Antiquities of Cyprus, the Byzantine Museum (Nicosia), the A. Pisidllides Collection, and the Monastery of St. Catherine (Sinai, Egypt).

To the 2011 CAARI board of advisors, we are thankful: Chris Christodoulou, Achilleas Demetriades, Constantinos S. Loizides, Manthos Mavrommatis, and Efthyvoulos G. Paraskeviades. We appreciate all the Trustees at the time who encouraged this project: William S. Andreas, Clay Constantinou, Nancy J. Corbin, Lillian Craig, Takey Crist, Thomas J. Dodd, Steven Falconer, Ellen Herscher, Ioanna Kakoulli, Ann-Marie Knoblauch, Charles L. Perry, Nancy Serwint, Brian Shelburne, Alan H. Simmons, Joanna S. Smith, Stuart Swiny, Michael K. Toumazou, Gisela Walberg, F. Bryan Wilkins, Frederick A. Winter, Birgitta Lindros Wohl, and Robert J. Wozniak.

Much gratitude is also extended to Professor Kevin McGeough, Kevin Cooney at ASOR, and Susanne Wilhelm at ISD, and the entire team of anonymous peer-reviewers who encouraged and helped shape this volume.

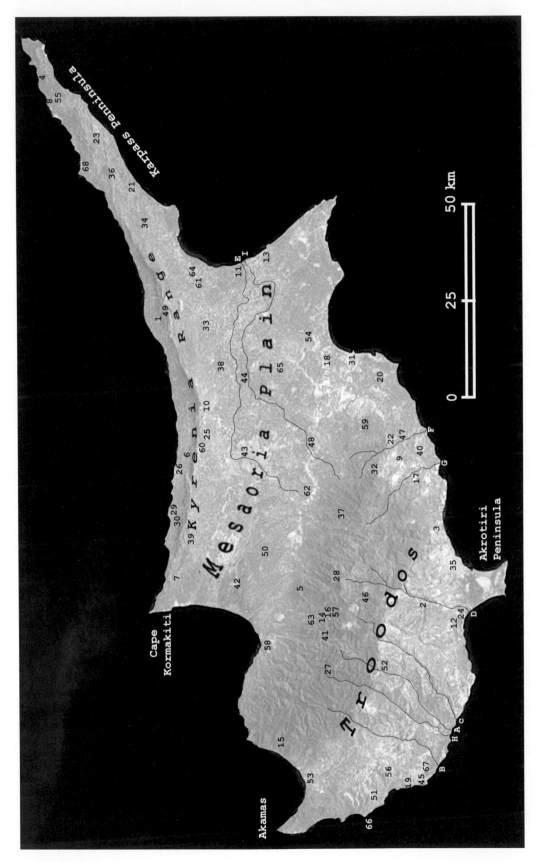

Map of Cyprus. Numbers indicate key sites mentioned in this volume (C. A. Stewart).

MAP KEY

1	Akanthou	36	Lythrankomi	**River Deltas**	
2	Alassa	37	Machairas Monastery	A	Dhiarizos River
3	Amathous	38	Marathovouno	B	Ezousas River
4	Aphendrika	39	Margi	C	Khapotami River
5	Asinou	40	Maroni	D	Kouris River
6	Bellapais	41	Monastery of Agios Ioannis Lampadistis	E	Pedhieos River
7	Cape Kormakiti			F	Pentaschoinon River
8	Carpasia (Karpasia)	42	Morphou	G	Vasilikos River
9	Choirokitia	43	Nicosia (Leukosia)	H	Xeros River
10	Chytroi	44	Ornithi	I	Yialias River
11	Constantia (Salamis)	45	Paphos		
12	Episkopi	46	Pelendri		
13	Famagusta	47	Pentaschoinon		
14	Galata	48	Perachorio		
15	Gialia	49	Pergaminiotissa		
16	Kakopetria	50	Peristerona		
17	Kalavasos	51	Peyia		
18	Kellia	52	Philousa		
19	Khlorakas	53	Polis (Arsinoë, Marion)		
20	Kiti	54	Pyla		
21	Koma tou Gialou	55	Rizokarpaso		
22	Kophinou	56	Saint Neophytos Enkleistra		
23	Koroveia	57	Saint Nicholas tis Stegis		
24	Kourion (Curium)	58	Soloi (Soli)		
25	Koutsovendis	59	Staurovouni		
26	Kyrenia (Kerynia)	60	Sychari		
27	Kykko Monastery	61	Syncrasis		
28	Lagoudera	62	Tamassos (Politiko)		
29	Lambousa (Lampousa)	63	Temvria		
30	Lapithos (Lapethos)	64	Trikomo		
31	Larnaka (Kition)	65	Tremithous (Tremithoussia)		
32	Lefkara				
33	Lefkonoiko	66	Yeronissos Island		
34	Livadia	67	Yeroskipou		
35	Limassol (Neapolis)	68	Yialousa		

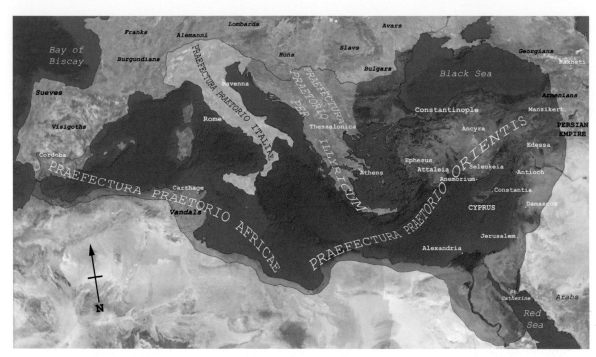

Map of the Byzantine Empire by the end of the reign of Justinian I (AD 565) (C. A. Stewart).

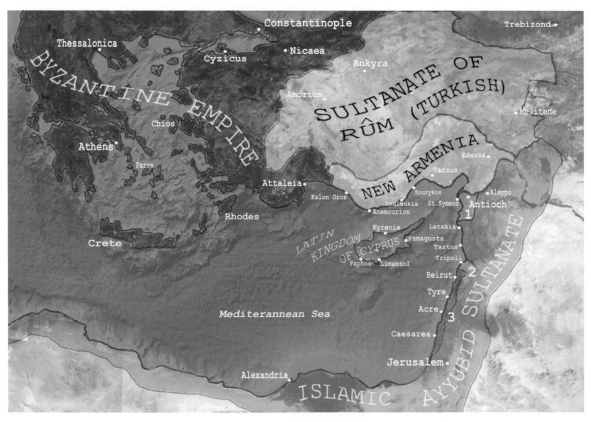

Regional map showing political divisions by the year 1200. The Crusader Latin States are noted as: 1. Principality of Antioch; 2. County of Tripoli; 3. Kingdom of Acre (C. A. Stewart).

Chapter 1

The Significance of the Basilica at *Agioi Pente* of Yeroskipou

by Demetrios Michaelides

Archaeological evidence in the area of Yeroskipou begins in the fourteenth century BC and continues without any major interruptions up to the third century AD.[1] There follows a hiatus that leads to the most famous monument of Yeroskipou, the church of Agia Paraskevi, first built in the eighth/ninth century (fig. 8.10).[2] This gap, even though seemingly accidental, could not be bridged due to the lack of archaeological evidence ascribable with certainty to the Early Christian period. The only exception was a series of marble *spolia* reused in the fabric of the church of Agia Paraskevi, and others that used to lie in the church yard. A few years ago, most of these were used for decorating the new enclosure wall of the church, while others have disappeared. These clearly originate from an earlier structure or structures, and it was assumed that this was a predecessor of the present church. Small-scale investigations by the Department of Antiquities, however, have failed to locate such a structure.[3] The excavations at *Agioi Pente* have filled the Early Christian lacuna in Yeroskipou's history and probably explain the origin of at least some of these *spolia*.

The area north of Yeroskipou, in particular the localities *Lakxia* and *Asproyi* (also known as *Chrysochoraphon*, meaning the Field of Gold), have long been celebrated for their necropoleis, especially those of the Late Bronze age, rich in pre-cious and exotic grave goods.[4] Equally well-known are the Hellenistic tombs of the area, which have yielded very high-quality offerings.[5]

No later remains were known in this area until 2002, when the opening of a new road north of the town brought to light vestiges of Early Christian structures in this and the adjacent locality of *Agioi Pente*. Heavy machinery bulldozed away everything in its way, adding to the destruction already wrought by ploughing and tomb robbing.

After the intervention of the Department of Antiquities, the road-works were interrupted and the brief investigation that followed was supervised by the then Archaeological Officer for Paphos, Dr. Eustathios Raptou. Some of the discoveries were widely reported in the daily press, especially the mosaic floors and an important tomb. The burial is lined entirely with enormous slabs of Proconnesian marble, a unicum for Cyprus, and preserves the bronze fittings that held the marble in place, as well as the iron bars that carried the weight of the large stone blocks that sealed it. The tomb contained a small golden reliquary (*encolpion*) and apparently remnants of textile.[6] Soon after, at the invitation of Mr. Tassos Kouzoupos, Mayor of Yeroskipou, the Archaeological Research Unit of the University of Cyprus undertook the systematic excavation and study of the remains.[7] The project is still on-going.

area, while two floors survive more or less intact. All appear to have been decorated with polychrome geometric motifs of the so-called rainbow type and had no figured decoration.[20]

Of the two floors surviving *in situ*, the southernmost one (figs. 1.8 and 1.9), adjacent to the already discussed structure with the ossuaries, is rectangular, measuring about 5.25 by 2.65 meters. Within a frame of intersecting circles forming quatrefoils, three large medallions with inscriptions are set on a trellised background. The central medallion is framed with a rarely-used ornament having the appearance of overlapping conical discs, which, as A.-M. Guimier-Sorbets has shown, is a late and not fully-understood interpretation of the three-dimensional bead and reel motif.[21] By contrast, the medallions on either side are framed with a common rainbow cable. The tesserae are of local limestone, but there are also some cut from Proconnesian marble, which are used for the blue of the frames of the inscriptions, while a few glass tesserae highlight the frame of beads around the central inscription. The medallions face south and thus not towards the basilica (for which *see infra*). They have a white background and the central and right-hand ones are written with red tesserae, the left-hand side one with grey/black tesserae. A difference is also noted in the white background, which is of a different quality and hue from the rest of the white used in this floor, leaving little doubt that this medallion was restored in antiquity.

All three inscriptions are passages (with frequent spelling mistakes) from the Psalms. On the left, there is verse 15 of Psalm 117:

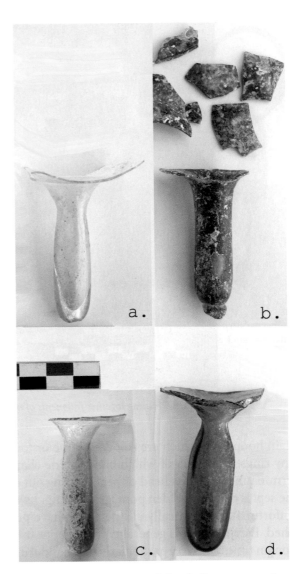

FIG. 1.7   *The lower parts of plain hollow stem type glass lamps (Peter Cosyns).*

† ΦΩΝΗ
ΑΓΑΛΙΑϹΕ
[Ω]Ϲ ΚΕ ϹΟΤ
[Η]ΡΙΑϹ Ε(Ν) Ϲ
[Κ]ΗΝΕϹ ΔΙ
ΚΕΩΝ †

(Φωνὴ ἀγαλλιάσεως καὶ σωτηρίας
ἐν σκηναῖς δικαίων)

The voice of rejoicing and salvation is in the tabernacles of the righteous

The inscription in the central medallion is verse 20 of the same Psalm 117:

† ΑΥΤΗ
Η ΠΥΛΗ ΤΟ
Υ ΚΥΡΙΟΥ ΔΙΚ
ΕΟΙ ΕΙϹΕΛΕΥ
ϹΟΝΤΕ ΕΝ
ΑΥΤΗ †

(Αὕτη ἡ πύλη τοῦ κυρίου, δίκαιοι
εἰσελεύσονται ἐν αὐτῇ)

FIG. 1.8   *The southern mosaic with the Biblical inscriptions (D. Michaelides).*

FIG. 1.9   *Detail of the central and left medallion of the southern inscription (D. Michaelides).*

"This is the gate of the Lord
into which the righteous shall enter"

Lastly, the third inscription from verse 2 of Psalm 28, on the right, reads:

† ΠΡΟϹΚΥ
ΝΗϹΑΤΕ
ΤΩ ΚΥΡΙ
Ω ΕΝ ΑΥΛ
Η ΑΓΙΑ ΑΥ
ΤΟΥ †

(Προσκυνήσατε τῷ κυρίῳ ἐν αὐλῇ ἁγίᾳ αὐτοῦ)

"Worship the Lord in His Holy court"[22]

The position and the more elaborate frame emphasize the importance of the central inscription: "This is the gate of the Lord into which the righteous shall enter" (Ps. 117: 20). This verse, in fact, was popular in mosaic floors of the Eastern Mediterranean, especially the Holy Land.[23] The dating of many of these examples is not absolutely certain but falls in the period from the fifth to the eighth century, with most examples ascribed to the fifth and sixth centuries. Of significance is the fact that most of these, as well as inscriptions in stone and other media with the same passage, are often associated with entrances and are even inscribed above gates (of public buildings and city walls) and on door lintels and thresholds; the most famous example being the one over the original main gate of the Monastery of Saint Catherine on Mount Sinai, where the passage is preceded and followed by verses from Exodus (3, 6, and 14).[24]

The use of the inscription in the left medallion, "The voice of rejoicing and salvation is in the tabernacles of the righteous" (Ps. 117: 15) is rare, but it is already known in a mosaic example from Cyprus. It is found in a *tabula ansata*, together with two other Biblical quotations, within the entrance of the sixth-century *diakonikon* of the Episcopal Basilica at Kourion.[25] The full verse does not appear in Antonio Felle's catalogue, but he does mention three instances from Egypt, where only the latter part of the verse: "in the tabernacles of the righteous" is used.[26] All three are of funerary character: two are inscribed on stelae and one on a plaque, something particularly interesting in view of what will be said below.

I have failed to find an exact parallel for the third inscription "Worship the Lord in His Holy court" (Ps. 28:2).[27] Furthermore, I have not come across the combined use of even the first two inscriptions from anywhere else and, as Dr. Leah Di Segni has proposed, a link between the three inscriptions on the Yeroskipou floor "is perhaps the reference to the church as the temple of God (Ps. 117:15) / gateway to the kingdom of heavens (117:20) / kingdom of heavens (Ps. 28:2), if the 'tabernacles of the righteous' are understood in the sense indicated" by the three epitaphs from Egypt.[28] In this sense, one could associate all three inscriptions with pilgrimages or visits to sacred places, while at least one of them has a funerary use as well. When the mosaic was first discovered,

FIG. 1.10   *The burials under the southern mosaic (D. Michaelides).*

I was rather puzzled by this and by the fact that this is the one inscription that was clearly remade in antiquity. As will be seen, later discoveries provide a possible, even though still perplexing, clue.

Given that the mosaic had a couple of large lacunae and a fair amount of detached tesserae, I decided to clean and record it and then rebury it for protection. During the cleaning of the largest lacuna, however, it became evident that under part of the mosaic there lay a tomb covered by two large stone slabs, one of which had a funnel-like hole blocked with a small flat stone. The mosaic was thus lifted and the tomb investigated.[29]

The human remains in the tomb were in an extremely poor condition (fig. 1.10). Two distinct skeletons were discernible during excavation, lying side by side on a floor made of large terracotta tiles. Frances Lee has identified these individuals

FIG. 1.11   *The northern mosaic being prepared for lifting (S. Christodoulou).*

as males of a middle or mature age, but she has also isolated the even poorer remains of a third person lying between them. This was a smaller individual who may have been a female. Three broken glass vessels in one of the corners near the skulls were the only grave goods: a bright green juglet, the lower part of a hollow stemmed lamp, and a small vessel. Although broken and incomplete, there is little doubt that they were placed there intentionally.

A dark patch at chest level between the two large skeletons proved to have been caused by a concentration of 19 bronze coins.[30] Only seven of these can be identified and they belong to different emperors, from Constans II of the mid-fourth century to Marcian of the mid-fifth. The coin spread lay immediately under the afore-mentioned funnel-like hole and, for this reason, I am of the opinion that the coins do not form the content of a now decayed cloth or leather pouch, but were dropped into the tomb through this hole. However, the question remains: at what point? After burial and before the tomb was covered by the mosaic? Or later, when people, driven by the memory of some important persons buried there, broke the mosaic — hence the lacuna — and made the perforation on the slab? In this sense, but still providing

no answer, it is worth pointing out that the tomb lies at the very edge of the room and mostly under the medallion with verse 15 of Psalm 117 ("The voice of rejoicing and salvation is in the tabernacles of the righteous"), which, as mentioned already, was remade in antiquity and bears an inscription that is used in three epitaphs on Egypt.

The second mosaic (fig. 1.11) is practically square, measuring 3.40 by 3.25 meters, and extends to form a small rectangular threshold.[31] It has a wide framing band where a triple guilloche forms adjacent octagons, all decorated with patterns characteristic of the so-called "rainbow style." A plain band marks out the centrepiece decorated with a black and white checkerboard, which is not only plain but also seems rather incongruous in its rainbow setting — despite the fact that it must have been a lot more striking originally, given that the centers of the white squares were decorated with colored glass tesserae, which have now largely perished. The rest of the tesserae are of local limestone, save the grey/blue ones, which are made of Proconnesian marble.

The irregularities observed around the central checkerboard and the different color palette suggested that this did not belong to the original mosaic but had been remade at some later point in the floor's history. Other factors, in particular its alignment with the marble-lined tomb, also suggested that the mosaic was probably overlying another tomb. For this reason it was decided to lift this mosaic as well. The bedding under the centerpiece was quite distinct from that of the rest of the floor and corresponded with the top of a rectangular, stone-built shaft, having approximately the dimensions of the central panel.[32] The rather loose soil with which it was filled was removed, and three large stone slabs were found sealing the shaft at a depth of about 75 centimeters. Around 40 centimeters below these, there was a plain stone sarcophagus with a lid made of a single large slab of Cypriot *marmaron*.[33]

The burial inside the sarcophagus lay at a depth of about 1.5 meters below the mosaic. The human remains were invisible, since they were covered with dark-colored remains of decomposed cloth, but careful cleaning revealed a badly-preserved skeleton and some personal items of the deceased. The skeleton, in an extended position, was that of a mature woman, over the age of 45, with extremely bad osteoporosis and a noticeably curved spine (fig. 1.12). The woman was, in fact, suffering from Pott's disease (*malum Pottii*). This is extra-pulmonary tuberculosis, which in this case is evidenced by a huge osteolytic lesion (the result of pus formation and bone destruction) on the 12th thoracic vertebra. This, together with the already mentioned possible case of tuberculosis in one of the ossuaries is precious evidence indeed, because although tuberculosis was widespread in antiquity, it is very rarely traceable, since it attacks the bone in only about 7% of the cases.[34]

Near the skull there was a silver *otoglyphis* (a scoop for cleaning the ears), which the woman must have worn in

FIG. 1.12   *The burial under the northern mosaic during cleaning, with the otoglyphis and the pendants in situ (D. Michaelides).*

FIG. 1.13   *Three golden pendants (Department of Antiquities).*

FIG. 1.14 *Remnants of cloth covering the skeleton, before treatment (Eleni Loizides).*

her hair like a hairpin. Three golden pendants were found near the neck (fig. 1.13). One is ring-like and very plain. The other is a small spherical *bulla*, and the third is a rectangular reliquary *encolpion* containing well-preserved remnants of wood (another piece of the Holy Cross?).[35] This is very similar to the *encolpion* found by the Department of Antiquities in the nearby marble-lined tomb,[36] and both are decorated with the Christogram, a cross combining the letters Chi-Rho symbolising Christ, as well as the apocalyptic letters A and Ω. I have not managed to find close parallels for this *encolpion*, nor date it satisfactorily. The few fragments of pottery found in the fill of the shaft down to the tomb, including sherds of a Late Roman 3 amphora, give a general fifth to sixth century date.

The remnants of cloth, some of them still preserving their red color (fig. 1.14), even though small, are quite important since ancient textile rarely survives in Cyprus. The examination of a small sample revealed at least five distinctly different textile structures, reflecting the woman's sophisticated clothing: a cream-coloured cloth of plain weave; a reddish brown cloth of plain weave; a cloth with twisted warp threads or leno; a plied, two-stranded thread or fine cord; and a red fabric with gold "thread." Also interesting is the fact that, in the sample examined, the fibers themselves have

perished and what survives is a pseudomorph of the original.[37]

The presence of these burials and ossuaries was a sure indication of the existence of a basilica in the vicinity. In the search for this, the area north of the excavated zone was investigated, where a series of badly preserved rooms were located. The surviving stumps of walls are roughly built, using recycled building material and objects, including quern stones and a large Hellenistic cippus. Judging by the finds in them, these rooms were most likely workshops or annexes, probably monastic and associated with the basilica.

Several types of Late Roman fine wares were found in this area, including very good examples of dishes of Cypriot Red Slip Ware, one of which was found upturned over a spread of coins of the Emperor Heraclius (610–641). Also of note is a large concentration of shells of the large freshwater bivalve *Chambardia rubens*, which does not live on Cyprus and was probably imported from the Nile.[38] These shells were exported around the Eastern Mediterranean (Cyprus included) already during the Bronze Age.[39] Although in later times some of them might have been used as exotic food items, they seem to have been more prized as exotic objects and served as special offerings in graves and sanctuaries. Their role in the context of Early Christian Yeroskipou is difficult to define, but their silvery mother-of-pearl, fragile though it is, does bring to mind the innumerable baptismal spoons, crosses, and other such souvenirs (made of harder shells) that, in later times and to this day, the faithful bring home from the Holy Land or other pilgrimages.

Other interesting finds from this area, which was relatively undisturbed by the bulldozers, include a varied series of cooking wares, most importantly hand-made and related vessels in stratified sequences. These offer a good case for investigating the initial stages of the development

FIG. 1.15 *Plan of the site showing the remains of the basilica (Athos Agapiou).*

of the cooking/coarse wares manufacture, from wheel-thrown to hand-formed, in the transitional period from Late Roman times (sixth–seventh century) to the eighth century — a transformation that eventually led to the fully-developed hand-formed production of medieval Cyprus.[40] There is also an absolutely amazing variety of pithoi of all sizes and many different fabrics. As far as I am aware, such a rich collection of Early Christian pithoi has so far not been found anywhere else on the island. Other objects of daily use include a bronze funnel,[41] probably to be associated with the commonest find in the area, namely amphorae, the most frequent types of which are Late

Roman 4 ("Gaza"), Late Roman 5/6 ("Palestinian"), and, above all, Late Roman 1.[42] As for the dating of this part of the site, the majority of coins are of Emperor Heraclius (610–641), while Smadar Gabrieli suggests that some of the cooking wares might be even later, bringing the date perhaps well into the eighth century.

Another obvious place for the basilica was the area in front of an apsed recess, which contained traces of a destroyed tomb. This, however, was the most disturbed part of the site, and two trial trenches showed that the deposit consisted of excavated soil and modern rubbish re-deposited and compacted there by the mechanical excavators.

FIG. 1.16 *The remnants of one of the stylobates of the basilica emerging under the baulk (D. Michaelides).*

FIG. 1.17 *Nail for fixing veneering onto the wall (Eleni Loizides).*

It was only when this deep contemporary deposit was removed that the very last traces of the basilica were eventually located (fig. 1.15). Not much survives; only some poor traces, which, however, are enough to offer a glimpse of the old glory of the building. This was a three-aisled structure with, perhaps, an extra aisle on the south.[43] The semi-

circular recess turned out to be the central apse of the basilica, with the marble tomb to its south and the tomb of the woman with Pott's disease to its north. The southern stylobate (fig. 1.16)[44] is fairly well-preserved, but only some small fragments of the columns of *cipollino rosso*[45] and the capitals of Proconnesian marble survive. The tiny fragments of the capitals are not dissimilar to some of the *spolia* around the church of Agia Paraskevi at Yersokipou, and this is, perhaps, an indication of the origin of some of them. There are no other architectural marbles and only small fragments of ecclesiastical furnishings of marble survive. These include the lower part of a pedestal of *greco scritto* and, most importantly, several pieces of offering tables. These were found both in the bema area and the presumed narthex of the basilica and are of both the circular and *sigma*-shaped type. There is also one fragment of the much larger and less common variety equipped with semicircular recesses.[46] All the evidence indicates that the marble objects and fittings from this building were removed from the site either to be re-used or to end up in lime kilns.

The marble wall veneering had the same fate. Several small fragments of local and imported stones and marbles come from the slabs that once lined the walls. Further evidence for this is provided by a fair number of a particular type of bronze nails found in the bema area (fig. 1.17). These have a characteristic T-shaped profile and a flattened head, and were used for fixing the slabs of marble veneering onto the walls. The veneering also included champlevé reliefs, a form of decoration popular in the fifth and sixth centuries, especially in Syria and Cyprus.[47] Two important examples survive. One depicts a bird,[48] a common theme in this kind of decoration, but the other is most unusual. It is a small panel (fig. 1.18) depicting a roundel with a stylised cross, accompanied by the inscription: †ΚΥΡΙ]ΟΣ ΕΜΟΙ†/ †ΒΟΗΘΟΣ†. This is the beginning of Psalm 117: ὁ Κύριος ἐμοὶ βοηθός, [οὐ φοβηθήσομαι τί ποιήσει μοι ἄνθρωπος] ("With the Lord on my side I do not fear. What can man do to me?"), which was already known in Cyprus, used in the threshold of a mosaic floor in the so-called Byzantine House in Paphos.[49] The scooped-out background of this panel preserves considerable remains of the red-colored substance (not analyzed yet) that once filled it. Other forms of wall decoration reflecting the old glory of the building are fresco fragments with vegetal and geometric motifs, and very scanty remains of wall mosaic.

FIG. 1.18 *Champlevé panel with Cross and Biblical quotations (Eleni Loizides).*

Despite the tragic destruction of this site, I believe that what little does survive affirms that the remains at *Agioi Pente* of Yeroskipou present great interest. This completely unknown Early Christian site has given Yeroskipou its earliest basilica and its first mosaic floors, which, moreover, add three new examples to the rather poor corpus of Early Christian mosaic inscriptions of Cyprus. The champlevé plaque preserves a fourth new inscription. It is also the first time that an undisputed association of floor mosaics with burials outside

the main roof of a church has been established in Cyprus.[50] Further study of the pottery and other finds also promises to shed light onto the little-known period post-dating the beginning of the Arab Invasions of Cyprus.

The two tombs on either side of the apse — the marble-lined tomb and the tomb of the woman suffering from Pott's disease — clearly belonged to very important persons. The architectural relation of these rooms to the basilica is not yet clear. There is no doubt, however, that the most prestigious sector of the basilica, namely the main apse, once housed the tomb of an even more important religious personage of the early Church of Cyprus. Unfortunately, this is also the spot that suffered most from the recent interventions on the site.

NOTES

1   I would like to thank Charles Anthony Stewart, Tom Davis, and the Organizing Committee for inviting me to give the keynote address at this conference.

2   For an account of the archaeology of Yeroskipou, see Michaelides 2008; for Agia Paraskevi, see Foulias 2008.

3   The investigation of the tetraconch structure appended to the southeast corner of the church did not locate the anticipated tomb (Papageorghiou 1989: 108). Other small-scale investigations, the most recent in 2007, also failed to locate any earlier structure in the immediate vicinity of the church (Raptou 2007a; Foulias 2008a: 66; and note 26).

4   Nicolaou 1983; see also Karageorghis 1965: 248–50, figs. 29–31; Maier and Karageorghis 1984: 104, figs. 88–91; and Maliszewski 1997: 71.

5   These include the finest Magenta ware vessel (in the shape of a female head) so far found on the island. On the vessel and Magenta ware in Cyprus, see Michaelides 1991; 1994; and 1997.

6   The tomb is unpublished, but see Chotzakoglou 2005: 727 and Raptou 2007b: 697. For photographs of the tomb, see Michaelides 2008b: fig. 67 and Michaelides 2013: fig. 1.

7   Despite the enormous problems that the interruption of the road works and the adjacent development would cause, in a courageous move, Mr. Kouzoupos insisted on the systematic investigation of the area and invited the University of Cyprus to undertake it. The necessary excavation permit was granted by the then Director of the Department of Antiquities, Dr. Sophocles Hadjisavvas, and was later renewed by his successors, Drs. Pavlos Flourentzos and Maria Hadjicosti, to all of whom I extend my thanks. Above all, however, I would like to express my deep gratitude to the Mayor and the Municipal Council of Yeroskipou, not only for the invitation to undertake the excavation, but also for the financial support they have generously provided over the years. Needless to say, this work would not have been possible without the open-handed funding and support of the University of Cyprus, and the good work of the students and my assistant at the excavations, Ms. Skevi Christodoulou.

8   The study of several groups of finds is already complete or well under way. I would like to thank the following collaborators for their important input towards the understanding of the site and for providing me with preliminary reports from which I have culled a lot of the information that follows. They include, in alphabetic order: Pamela Armstrong for the fine wares; Peter Cosyns for the glass; Smadar Gabrieli for the cooking wares and the pithoi; Anthi Kaldeli for the amphorae and the statistical analysis of the finds; Frances Lee for the human bones; Marie-Christine Marcellesi for the coins; and Diana Wood Conroy and Adriana Garcia for the textiles. The undersigned is responsible for the jewelry and the mosaics.

9   Hitherto published reports and studies on the excavations at *Agioi Pente* include Michaelides 2003; 2004; 2006; 2008a; 2008b: 49–55; and 2013: 87–95. On the pottery, see Gabrieli, Jackson and Kaldelli 2007: 795 and the already mentioned brief references in Chotzakoglou 2005: 727 and Raptou 2007b: 697.

10 For the cave and the worship of the Agioi Pente, see Foulias 2008b: 99–100. See also Tsiknopoulos 1971: 214.

11 A general view of the ossuaries is published in Michaelides 2008b: fig. 63.

12 For tuberculosis, see the burial of a woman under the second (northern) mosaic, *infra.*

13 I would like to thank Marie-Christine Marcellesi for the preliminary coin reports from which this information has been extracted. I would like to also extend my thanks to Eleni Loizidou for her patient work cleaning the coins and all the other metal objects from the excavation.

14 A buckle is illustrated in Michaelides 2013: fig. 2a.

15 See Michaelides 2008b: fig. 77.

16 For more examples of earrings from these excavations, see Michaelides 2013: fig. 3.

17 For Cypriot examples, see Pierides 1971: 47, pl. XXXII.8; Nicolaou 1990: 119, XXXII.d; and Karageorghis 2011: 163, attributed to the Roman period. For more examples and a correct dating to the 5th–7th century, see Coche de la Ferté 1957:

emphasizes the continuities between the pre-raid centuries and the Byzantine resurgence in the tenth century. Art historians display the same theoretical approach regarding the term *Early Byzantine*, as employed by, for example, Susan Boyd (a long-time researcher at Dumbarton Oaks).[5] This perspective anticipates the flowering of Byzantine art and culture during the eleventh and twelfth centuries on Cyprus and highlights its precursors in the artistic assemblage of earlier centuries. With the exception of Metcalf, most of these scholars are focused on the visual arts and built resources.

Early Christian is the primary choice of terms for ecclesiastical historians and architectural historians, who use the term to discuss fourth-century basilicas on Cyprus.[6] A.H.S. Megaw, who directed the colonial Department of Antiquities from 1935 to independence, uses *Early Christian* or *Christian Period* to discuss archaeological sites and remains from the fourth to the seventh century.[7] This terminology is an ideological/theoretical compromise, recognizing the watershed nature of Christian dominance in the archaeological architectural record, while still seeing continuities in the material culture with the past. The terminology reflects a focus on the change in the architectural assemblage, particularly the appearance of ecclesiastical basilicas, and is therefore urban-focused. Megaw may be using the term because of his own architectural interests, and this usage may have roots in the attempt to distinguish through nomenclature between "Christian" ecclesiastical basilicas and earlier Roman civic basilicas. Likewise, archaeologist Charalambos Bakirtzis uses the term to describe rock-cut tombs from an "Early Christian settlement" at Peyia.[8] The majority of the tombs are marked by Christian symbols, so the terminology appears to have cultural as well as chronological meaning for Bakirtzis.

Most contemporary field archaeologists, particularly field surveyors, use the term *Late Roman* to designate this particular era.[9] This reflects a material-oriented approach with a bias towards rural settlement sites where the material continuities across the Constantinian divide are more pronounced. The term is associated with Peter Brown's articulation and advocacy of the concept of *Late Antiquity*, but is also quite distinct. *Late Roman* assumes cohesion of the society and politics under a centralized Roman system, whereas *Late Antiquity* emphasizes imperial decay and fragmentation.[10]

Scholars who study the Byzantine heartland of Anatolia use the reign of Justinian as the breakpoint between the Late Roman and Byzantine periods.[11] Syro-Palestinian experts use historical markers as brackets: they begin the Byzantine period with Constantine and then switch to the early Islamic Period (or Umayyad) after 638 when Jerusalem fell to the Arabs.[12] For Cyprus, the archeological record provides a clear marker for the beginning of Christian dominance with the mid-fourth century earthquakes on the island.[13] Following these events, none of the major pagan shrines were rebuilt at that time; instead, Cyprus witnessed an explosion of church construction, evidencing the social transformation facilitated by the earthquake devastation.

THE COLONIAL PERIOD

When the first academic studies of Byzantine material culture arose in the late nineteenth century, they focused on the imperial cities, such as Thessaloniki, Ravenna, and Constantinople.[14] The Greek isles were seen as provincial and less significant to the study of the Empire. And yet, travel and general surveys such as Robert Curzon's *A Visit to the Monasteries in the Levant* (1849) and James Fergusson's *A History of Architecture in All Countries* (1874) helped establish the importance of eastern Mediterranean coastlands as places for artistic innovation. Ironically, it was Camille Enlart's pioneering study of Cypriot Gothic architecture that first showcased the richness of Cyprus' medieval monuments, though he only discussed Byzantine constructions in passing.[15]

The first monographic study of Cypriot Byzantine monuments was carried out in 1895 by Jakov Smirnov (1869–1918), a young teacher who later became one of the most influential Russian art historians.[16] Smirnov traveled to Cyprus in search of its early Byzantine mosaics and their relationship to literary sources. Though his account was more descriptive than explanatory, he provided valuable information on the Panagia Angeloktistos (Kiti) and Panagia

Kanakariá (Lythrankomi) with original ground plans and photographs. Smirnov was not interested in Byzantine archaeology *per se*, but the survival of sixth century mosaics.

Earlier in 1890, the first systematic archaeological excavation of a Byzantine monument took place at the cathedral of Agios Epiphanius, Salamis-Constantia.[17] The excavators at the time did not realize they were uncovering one of the most important Byzantine monuments on the island. They noted its large expanse and centralized location, and found clear evidence of destruction by fire. Their plans and excavation reports are still important resources for our understanding of a provincial Byzantine capital. It was much later that George Jeffery would correctly identify the site as the remains of the church commissioned by the famous fourth-century archbishop, St. Epiphanius.[18]

By 1900, the field of Byzantine archaeology was still in its infancy, with most scholarly interest focused on architectural monuments. However there was a gradual interest developing regarding objects. O.M. Dalton's pioneering work on Byzantine artifacts showcased the fine craftsmanship and beauty of early medieval Cyprus.[19] The Lambousa Treasures (also known as the "First" and "Second" Cyprus Treasure) — a stunning collection of Late Antique ecclesiastical silver from the north coast of Cyprus — appeared on the antiquities market in the late 1890s and the first decade of the twentieth century.[20] Split between the Metropolitan Museum in New York, the British Museum, and the Cyprus Museum, the Lambousa Treasures alerted the scholarly world to the quality and richness of the surviving material record of Byzantine Cyprus. These scholarly developments outside Cyprus would influence how the British government approached the historic monuments in its keeping.

In 1903, the colonial administration hired George Jeffery in a new position known as the "Government Architect." Earlier, he had traveled to the Near East to assist in the construction of St. George's Anglican Cathedral in Jerusalem. So it was natural that Jeffery found the architectural history of the island intriguing. As a result he developed, and then assumed, the title of "Curator

of Ancient Monuments"— a position he held until 1936. This was a powerful appointment, in which he influenced the permissions for archaeological excavations, policies on the antiquities trade, the establishment public museums, and the preservation of monuments. Unfortunately, the financial resources that he could call upon were pitifully inadequate.[21] Jeffery was mainly interested in Gothic architecture of the island, but he realized he could not improve upon Enlart's publication. Perhaps that is why he decided to specialize on the Byzantine monuments. Despo Pilides, during her research on Jeffery's diaries, uncovered evidence that he was deeply concerned for the preservation of Byzantine architecture. He was alarmed at the rate in which historic churches were being torn down and unrecorded by the current Orthodox population of Cyprus in order to build "modern churches."[22] Regardless of Jeffery's motives, we can consider him the first Byzantine architectural historian on the island.

In 1916, Jeffery presented a lengthy paper at the Society of Antiquaries in London entitled "The Earlier Byzantine Churches of Cyprus."[23] This important survey identified the basic typology found on the island and recorded many important buildings that no longer survive. Unfortunately, this seminal work was accompanied by narrow subjectivities, which belied his understanding of the Orthodox religion, Byzantine architecture, and the dating of historic buildings. For example, concerning the sixth-century mosaics at the Panagia Angeloktisti (Kiti) and the Panagia Kanakariá(Lythrangomi), Jeffery declared, "[they] doubtless belong to the same series and age as the great school of mosaic art at Bethlehem and Jerusalem of the eleventh–twelfth centuries." It is difficult, even by the standards of his day, to justify this error. We might excuse Mr. Jeffery for his ignorance of art history, since he lacked formal education in the discipline, but his comments also reflect an imperialist disdain for eastern aesthetics. In this same lecture he stated that Cypriot Byzantine frescos were "rude decoration in crude primary colours…such primitive attempts at pictorial art." This distaste was carried over into his analysis of the architecture, which he concluded "betrayed a clumsy unscientific idea of construction." These opinions seem rather odd today, since we consider these some of the greatest masterpieces of all time. And yet, how else could Jeffery judge material culture, which he had already assumed was produced by, what he called, the "half-savage peasantry" of Byzantine Cyprus?

Although we can easily dismiss Jeffery's imperialist snobbery, he did have a lasting effect on Cypriot archaeology. His position in the colonial government gave him the power to influence and shape the discourse on Byzantine architecture. Even the British Governor of Cyprus, Sir Ronald Storrs, recognized Jeffrey's incompetence when he wrote:

> [Some of our officials]…have been here too long, a few have passed their entire (and wearily prolonged) careers within the Island, as often as not in key positions. To name but one, not of the first importance, the Director of the Museum is far better qualified to occupy than to administer the shelves of which he has been in nominal charge for the past quarter of the century.[24]

And yet, Jeffery's greatest achievement was his 1918 publication *A Description of the Historic Monuments of Cyprus*, which surveyed and catalogued many Byzantine sites for the first time. This brought Byzantine Cyprus to the attention of English-speaking scholars, just as Enlart's work notified the French community. Fortunately, in time many other British scholars would challenge Jeffery and recognize the significance of the Byzantine frescos on Cyprus.

In the early 1930s, Harold Buxton (the Bishop of Gibralter), Vivian Seymer (a Lieutenant Colonel at the time), and William Buckler (a specialist in ancient Roman inscriptions and civic law) traveled through Cyprus visiting the historic monuments, including the painted churches of the Troodos. As a result they published the first scholarly study of Byzantine frescos on Cyprus.[25] These scholars held views that contrasted sharply with their colleague Jeffery. Buxton expressed that Byzantine Cyprus had "remarkable paintings…nothing comparable to this had I ever seen…first the coloring, then the vigour of the drawing, then the sense of mystical reflection which the interior with its unique

painting inspires, seemed to rivet one to the spot." Likewise, Seymer concluded: "Artistically speaking, the painting is in the full flower of the Byzantine style."[26] Most scholars today would agree with these sentiments.[27]

While these English visitors became intrigued with Cyprus, Greek archaeologists were also interested in the material culture. Georgios M. Soteriou (1880–1965), a professor of history of the University of Athens and director of the Byzantine and Christian Museum, was invited by the Church of Cyprus to provide an architectural survey of the island in 1931. Upon his arrival, Soteriou hired Cypriot architects J. Pericleous and Theophilus Mogabgab to draw elevations and plans, along with C. Papaioannou to photograph the Byzantine monuments. Soteriou's preliminary report was published in a 1931 article, "The Early Christian and Byzantine Remains of Cyprus" in the *Report of the Athens Academy*.[28]

Soteriou believed that the remains of Cyprus held the key to understanding the development of Byzantine architecture as a whole. Therefore he planned a more comprehensive two-volume study. The first tome would contain plans and photographs, while the second volume would consist of texts on history and dating. In 1935, the first volume *The Byzantine Remains of Cyprus* (*Τα Βυζαντινά Μνήματα της Κύπρου*) was published.[29] It included well-drawn architectural plans and high-quality photographs for the time. Scholars anticipated the second volume but were disappointed when Soteriou died in 1965, leaving no trace of a manuscript. It would be left to another generation of scholars to provide a broader architectural history. A.H.S. Megaw was one such scholar.

Megaw (1910–2006) was already trained as an architect when he moved to Cyprus in the 1930s after receiving a post in the British government. He was later appointed as the second Director of the Department of Antiquities from 1936 to 1960, following J.R. Hilton (who replaced Jeffery in 1935).[30] Megaw had earlier worked in Greece, studying Byzantine architectural decoration, and was confident in filling the shoes of his predecessor Jeffery. He began excavating and restoring the island's Christian monuments and, following Soteriou, hired both Pericleous and

Mogabgab to assist him. At the same time he aided Joan du Plat Taylor in the excavation of the multi-component site of Agios Philion in Carpasia.[31] He maintained an interest in standing architecture as well, excavating monuments such as Agios Mamas in Morphou while it was being repaired.[32] Megaw left his position at the Department of Antiquities when Cyprus gained independence. He subsequently became the Director of the British School at Athens, where he continued to study Cypriot and Byzantine architecture.

Byzantine archaeology on Cyprus under Megaw's guidance generally was in step with archaeological research in neighboring countries.[33] Medieval archaeology in North Africa, Syria, Palestine, and Jordan primarily focused on the elucidation and study of built resources and standing ruins, although some excavations at major sites sampled this period (Jerash in Jordan, Beth Shean in Palestine, etc.). The primary aim of such excavations was chronology-building to elucidate political history, the recovery of floor plans, and the identification of the structures. This reflected the desires of the Western European and American intelligentsia to construct a sweeping metanarrative of Western civilization. The relatively low level of expense involved in excavation in the Eastern Mediterranean world also encouraged international archaeology in the region.

On Cyprus, at the major urban archaeological site of Kourion, Byzantine material was both unanticipated and *unwanted*. The excavations began in 1934 under the auspices of the University Museum of the University of Pennsylvania. The driving force behind the excavation was a wealthy amateur, George McFadden, who paid most of the cost of the excavation out of his own pocket.[34] McFadden wanted to excavate a classical site that was on the seacoast. The University Museum wanted displayable items. Bert Hodge Hill, the former Director of the American School in Athens, was brought in to provide a professional veneer. He obtained the permit from the colonial government, but warned the University Museum Director that, "we should not…expect 'finds' in great number and good preservation, since we should have to do with an exposed city site." He was pleased to note that "Curium would probably…not bring us down

into Byzantine times at all," allowing quick access to museum-quality objects from Classical times.[35] Ironically, no Classical remains were uncovered at the city site; one of the most important discoveries by McFadden's team was the so-called House of Eustolios, a fifth-century town home with a Christian-themed mosaic that mentions the name of Christ. To his credit, McFadden insisted on keeping all of the floor mosaics *in situ,* an attitude that was at odds with the prevailing colonialist mentality of the day, and counter to the museum's wishes.[36]

After the disruptions of World War II, the Department of Antiquities expanded and Megaw hired young native Cypriots: Vassos Karageorghis for field archaeology on ancient sites and Andreas Dikigoropoulos for standing monuments on medieval sites. In the course of his career in the Department, Dikigoropoulos examined and/or excavated over twenty-five Early Christian and Byzantine Churches in Cyprus between 1948 and 1959. He was a pioneer in the study of lead seals and Byzantine numismatics on Cyprus. Moreover, together with Hector Catling, Dikigoropoulos developed early methods of field survey on Cyprus which identified scores of archaeological sites, including Byzantine and medieval settlements. Two results of this survey were published, including the 1958 rescue excavation of a Byzantine kiln discovered in 1955.[37]

Dikigoropoulos would continue the excavations of the Cathedral of Agios Epiphanios in 1954, which had begun in the previous century. He would discover the important remains of a multiple-domed basilica in the cathedral annex, as well as the late seventh-century ramparts. These findings further supported his earlier theories regarding the "period of the Arabic raids" on Cyprus. He subsequently studied Byzantine history under Professor Joan Hussey (1902–2006) at Oxford University, where he received his doctorate in 1962, completing his dissertation entitled "Cyprus 'betwixt Greeks and Saracens,' A.D. 647–965"—the seminal work on the subject. For personal reasons, Dikigoropoulos left the Department of Antiquities in 1959 and worked for a short time at Dumbarton Oaks, Washington D.C., where he continued to research Byzantine sigillography and numismatics.[38]

INDEPENDENT CYPRUS

At the time of Independence, Cypriot Byzantine archaeology had achieved substantial progress, but much remained to be done. Dikigoropolous' work at Salamis and the identification of the urban basilica at Kourion by McFadden pointed to fruitful lines of research that would lead to a better understanding of urban basilicas and their immediate surroundings. The Department's work on rural ecclesiastical sites provided a good picture of the spread of Christian architecture, but examination of the accompanying village life had barely begun. The continuing need for stabilization and restoration of Byzantine mosaics and frescoes continued to be a major priority of the Department as it had been under the Colonial administration.[39] Dumbarton Oaks was invited to continue its collaboration with the Department of Antiquities which began earlier in 1959. A multidecade project resulted which did much to bring the magnificent frescos of the Middle Byzantine churches to an international audience.[40]

In 1962, the Department hired Athanasius Papageorghiou to replace the outgoing Dikigoropoulos. Previously, Papageorghiou had studied theology at the University of Athens, and later undertook coursework with famous art historian André Grabar at the University of Paris. In time, Papageorghiou would emerge as the island's foremost specialist in Early Christian and Byzantine art, excavating many key sites, such as the early basilica at Marathovouno and the Apsinthiotissa Monastery.[41] During the 1960s, his initial findings and theories were published in the ecclesiastical journal *Απόστολος Βαρνάβας*. Unfortunately, this periodical was not widely circulated outside Cyprus and largely overlooked by the international community.[42] His chief contributions to Byzantine archaeology are his entries within the *Μεγάλη Κυπριακή Εγκυκλοπαίδεια*, published in 1985 (and revised in 2011), which documented hundreds of monuments. Papageorghiou became Director of the Department in 1989, a position he held until he retired in 1991.

In the 1960s, the Department of Antiquities under the directorship of Vassos Karageorghis began to reexamine Byzantine basilicas in their urban context with the help of foreign missions. For example, at Salamis-Constantia, French archaeologists excavated a second large basilica, the Campanopetra, dating to the late fifth century and reflective of a robust, prosperous, urban Christian population.[43] Also the Department of Antiquities began work on a newly discovered basilica at Amathous, located below the acropolis, outside of the urban center.[44] Around the same time, Papageorghiou re-examined the Panagia Limeniotissa basilica at Paphos harbor, first discovered in 1939.[45] In 1966, a French Canadian team began to work at Soloi, where they uncovered a major urban basilica that would later yield a valuable inscription providing vital epigraphic evidence of the impact of the Arab raids on Cyprus.[46] Megaw returned to independent Cyprus and directed the re-excavation of the main urban basilica of Kourion.[47] The discovery of the magnificent mosaics of Roman Paphos in the 1960s forcefully reminded scholars that Cyprus in the fourth century was a rich and cosmopolitan province, integrated into the eastern Mediterranean cultural world. The mosaic of Achilles, laid in the fifth century, demonstrated that the earthquake destruction in the fourth century did not terminate the sophisticated urban culture of Cyprus.[48]

The Department continued to examine individual churches and ecclesiastic sites outside the Late Antique cities. Papageorghiou excavated sites such as the Basilica of Agia Trias in Yialousa, churches at Ktima, Lysi, and the monastery of Agios Herakleidos at Politiko-Tamasos (undertaken when the present church was being restored). These excavations usually focused on recovering the floor plan and trying to determine the date of their construction phases.[49]

Eventually, researchers began to expand their archaeological focus beyond ecclesiastical remains. In Salamis, in the area of the Campanopetra, the French excavators delved beyond the churches and uncovered a large urban villa, the "Huilerie," which they interpreted as the bishop's residence.[50] The area continued to be occupied after the Arab raids began and provided valuable information on the once archaeological "Dark Age" from the late seventh to the tenth century. Likewise, Megaw led a major excavation at the Byzantine/medieval fortress site of Saranda Kolones in Paphos.[51] At Kourion, an elegant early Byzantine house was also excavated, the so-called "Triclinium House."[52] These findings began a trend in which archaeologists contextualized major monuments, from the Byzantine structure within the city, and from the city to the Byzantine countryside.

The *coup d'état* against Cypriot President, Archbishop Makarios III (1913–1977), in July 1974 led to the invasion and occupation of northern Cyprus by the Turkish army. This was catastrophic for Cyprus' archaeology and cultural heritage. Since that time, no internationally-condoned archaeological excavations have been undertaken in the areas outside the direct control of the Republic of Cyprus. A few Turkish archaeologists and Turkish Cypriot scholars have undertaken excavation and survey work in the northern areas of Cyprus, but these are not published, at least by international standards, and have been condemned by UNESCO and academics throughout the world. As a result of the looting and destruction of Byzantine art during (and after) the war, Papageorghiou expended much energy protecting the antiquities from the black market through his publications and diplomacy with foreign governments. In time, he became a leading expert on the damage and destruction of the Byzantine heritage in the areas under the control of the Turkish Cypriot community.[53] Nevertheless, numerous churches have been severely vandalized and artworks have disappeared. The United States government has responded by imposing emergency import restrictions on Cypriot antiquities and church-related objects.[54]

In the meantime, the study of Byzantine Cyprus and its archaeology received a strong boost towards recovery with the opening of the first international archaeological research institute in Nicosia. With the strong support of the American Ambassador, William Crawford, The American Schools of Oriental Research (ASOR) approached the government of the Republic of Cyprus for approval of the proposed "Cyprus Archaeological Research Institute." The new center was to follow the model of the other two ASOR schools, the American Center for Oriental Research (ACOR) in Amman and the long-established Albright

Institute for Archaeological Research (AIAR) in Jerusalem, and functions as both a research center and as a logistics base for excavations. The Cyprus Government requested the addition of "American" in the title, and, in 1978, the new center became the *Cyprus American Archaeological Research Institute,* known to all as CAARI.[55] When CAARI was founded, Cyprus lacked a research university and an academic program for archaeological training. And so CAARI functioned as the archaeological academic center for the island until the Archaeological Research Unit of the University of Cyprus was created in 1991. Since that time, CAARI has continued to host hundreds of international Byzantine scholars, especially those interested in field surveys and urban space.

Urban archaeology after 1974 focused on the Byzantine cities in the south of Cyprus, at Kourion, Amathous, and Paphos. These investigations greatly increased our understanding of the urban world of Cyprus from the fourth to the seventh centuries. These results added a focus on material culture and brought Cypriot archaeology into the theoretical model of Late Antiquity. The Department of Antiquities, under the direction of Demos Christou, launched a long-term examination of the forum area at Kourion. Christou excavated a small urban church built in the ruins of the bath complex after the massive earthquake of 365 destroyed the city. Also in the early 1990s, he excavated a newly discovered beachfront basilica destroyed at the time of the Arab raids.[56] The Department excavated the lower city at Amathous where Pavlos Flourentzos eventually expanded their investigations to include the Byzantine neighborhoods between the acropolis and the Roman forum. Moreover, Papageorghiou continued to work in Paphos, uncovering the massive late fourth-century Christian basilica of Chrysopolitissa, which became the site of a later Gothic church. The Arabic graffiti on the columns from Chrysopolitissa and from the basilica of Limeniotissa documented the presence of an Arab garrison in the late seventh century, which has opened the possibility of further Umayyad archeological research on the island.[57] David Soren, of the University of Arizona, reopened one of McFadden's old trenches on the Kourion acropolis and spent four seasons excavating the "earthquake house"—an urban neighborhood destroyed by the earthquakes between the years 365 and 370.[58] This work provided a snapshot of the material culture of that specific moment in time. Likewise, in the 1990s, Danielle Parks began excavation of the Amathous Gate cemetery at Kourion, providing valuable evidence on the Late Roman, post-quake population of Kourion.[59]

Despite this new work, the sub-discipline of Byzantine archaeology remained overshadowed by discoveries in other archaeological periods. In 1987, Tim Gregory summarized the state of understanding in the field in bleak terms: "It is ironic that one of the least understood periods in the history of Cyprus is also one of the most recent…thus, when compared with the classical or the Bronze Age, our knowledge of Byzantine and medieval Cyprus is woefully inadequate."[60] Such a conclusion could not be drawn today, as exemplified by the work of scholars who have contributed to this volume. The economic recovery of Cyprus after the events of 1974 was fueled by rapid development in the south. Fortunately, the development coincided with the survey "revolution" in Eastern Mediterranean archaeology. Multi-disciplinary surveys became powerful tools for locating, identifying, and understanding ancient landscapes and settlement patterns. The Canadian Palaepaphos Survey (CPSP), begun in the 1970s by David Rupp, was a pioneer in modern surveys on Cyprus. In recent decades, international and Cypriot archaeologists have conducted many regional surveys which have recovered a wealth of data regarding Late Roman settlement.[61]

The Late Roman world has become a more complex picture thanks to survey data. The last twenty years have seen a number of targeted projects, such as Marcus Rautman's work at Kalavasos-*Kopetra* (part of the larger Vasilikos Valley Project of Todd and South), and Sturt Manning's rescue work at Maroni.[62] More recently, Scott Moore, Bill Caraher, and David Pettigrew have conducted a survey specifically targeting the Late Roman world at Pyla-*Koutsopetria*.[63] Significant rural Byzantine settlements have also been detected at Prastio-*Mesorotsos* along the Kouris and Dhiarizos river valleys by Andrew

McCarthy and his team of researchers.[64] All these surveys have dramatically increased our knowledge of settlement patterns and land use. Also, field surveys have led to innovative methods of study of Byzantine material culture. For example, Rautman's use of neutron activation analysis in the study of ceramics on Cyprus has opened many new avenues of research for the next generation of Byzantine scholars.[65] Likewise, Cornell University's Tree-Ring Laboratory, under the directorship of Peter Kuniholm and Sturt Manning, has been collecting Byzantine wood samples on Cyprus, which will provide scholars with a network of fixed dates. In other words, eventually scholars will be able to match Byzantine sites on Cyprus with other monuments throughout the eastern Mediterranean.[66]

Like field survey, rescue archaeology has become a major force in 21st-century archaeology around the world. In Cyprus, Byzantine monuments are usually exempt from this category. However, recent construction projects at the *Palaion Demarcheion* and St. George's Hill have uncovered large sections of medieval Nicosia.[67] These findings will certainly rewrite our knowledge of Byzantine urban settlement when they are fully published. Another important component of the island's rescue archaeology is found within the University of Cyprus. The development of the Archaeological Research Unit under the guidance of Demetrios Michaelides bodes well for the future of Byzantine archaeology. Michaelides' rescue operation at Yeroskipou is a textbook example of recovering as much data as possible from a damaged site.[68] Associated with rescue archaeology are the renovation projects of churches, which are continually revealing earlier Late Roman and Byzantine foundations and fresco painting.[69]

These new discoveries still have the ability to astound us and underscore the complexity of Byzantine Cyprus. The uncovering of the pilgrimage site at *Katalymata ton Plakoton* on the Akrotiri Peninsula was completely unexpected. Its *tau*-shaped basilica with a well-preserved mosaic floor is unlike anything ever excavated on the island before. A small portion of the mosaic had been previously located by Frank and Anthea Garrod of the Western Sovereign Base Archaeology Society. The Department of Antiquities anticipated a small rescue operation; instead, Dr. Eleni Procopiou has carried out a thorough excavation revealing the magnificent seventh-century martyrium (as reported here in Chapter 6). The surrounding settlement, when excavated, will certainly shed new light on Cyprus' connection to Byzantine Egypt.

Archaeological light on the Byzantine period, and specifically the so-called "Dark Age" from 647–961, has come slowly and much remains unpublished.[70] A well at Amathous, Arab activity at the beachfront basilica at Kourion, and the documented presence of the Arab garrison at Paphos have begun to fill this gap.[71] Field surveys have not contributed as much as they should have. Tim Gregory understood this to be an archaeological issue, not a historical one: "The problem must be in part our inability to recognize the local pottery of this age thus leading to the virtual disappearance of the period from the archaeological record."[72] Targeted excavations are needed of known Byzantine sites. Village churches, with evidence of Byzantine frescos or architectural fabric are a good place to begin this targeted approach. As already mentioned above, recent field surveys already have provided glimpses into new vistas for research. Unfortunately, some of the most interesting urban resources (Salamis, Carpasia, Lambousa, Soloi) are in the illegally-occupied area of northern Cyprus.

The CAARI leadership has recognized that the Institute can contribute to the lifting of this scholarly darkness. The addition of the Stylianou Collection and the Anatolian Archaeology Collection to the Schaffer Library continues to make CAARI a leading repository of resources on Byzantine archaeology on the island. Past and current research fellows affiliated with CAARI have examined various aspects of post-Roman Cyprus.[73] Collaboration between international and Cypriot scholars remains strong. The future of Byzantine research on Cyprus looks very bright.

NOTES

1   The study of cultural identity is an important component of archaeological research. However, unlike other bygone civilizations, issues surrounding "Byzantine identity" are often politically charged in contemporary scholarship. This is due to the way scholars use the term. Among Greek-speaking scholars the term "Byzantine" is often used to describe contemporary Greek Orthodox culture on Cyprus, as well as in other eastern European countries, which is not only active but thriving in our times. Most English-speaking scholars historicize the term "Byzantine" to denote the Eastern Roman Empire prior to 1453; for Greek culture after 1453, the term "Post-Byzantine" or simply "Greek Orthodox" is preferred. We must keep this distinction in mind as we organize archaeological materials: for historical Constantinopolitan views of Cyprus, see Mango 1976c: 1–13; for Byzantine self-identity see Mango 1980: 1–5 and Rapp 2008: 127–47; for Byzantine Cypriot identity, see Demosthenous 2007: 153–66, and Stewart 2008: 183–97; see also Kaldellis 2007: 42–172 and James 2010: 2–5.

2   Runciman 1990; Wharton 1991.

3   Metcalf 2009; Dr. Metcalf confessed that another factor in his choice of dates was that he liked the symmetry of 700 years from 491 to 1191 (spoken at CAARI, Nicosia, 6 January 2011).

4   Michaelides and Bakirtzis 2010: 207–13.

5   Boyd 1999: 49–62. A popular tourist guide to the built monuments by Gwyneth der Parthog (2006) uses Early Byzantine and Middle Byzantine, with 843 AD marking the divide.

6   For example, Vera von Falkenhausen (1999) who used the term for the 4th and 5th centuries.

7   Megaw 1955.

8   Bakirtzis 1999: 35–41.

9   Winther-Jacobsen 2010 provides a good summary of the recent survey projects that recovered Late Roman material.

10   Brown 1978; Bowersock and Brown 1999.

11 For example, the classic surveys of the English scholar David Talbot Rice begin to distinguish Justinian's reign as "Early Byzantine." This clarified the categorization of O.M. Dalton (1925), who included "Early Christian Art" with "Eastern Christian and Byzantine Archaeology." This can be compared to the earlier influential surveys by the American scholar Walter Lowrie (1901), who preferred to classify all "Byzantine Art" within the category of the "Early Church." These British and American scholars were heavily influenced by the nomenclature developed by the German art historian Joseph Strzygowski (1862–1941).

12 Stern (2008) begins the period in 324, when Constantine gained sole control over the Roman Empire.

13 Davis 2010: 3–14.

14 The late nineteenth century saw a burst of studies on Byzantine monuments, for example Pulgher 1878, Unger 1878, Byzantios 1890, and Richter 1897) For a general history of the first Byzantine archaeological studies see Kleinbauer 1992.

15 Enlart 1899; it must be noted that Enlart's focus on medieval architecture on Cyprus was preceded by the pioneering work in E.G. Rey's publication of 1871 and E. L'Anson and S. Vacher's monograph of 1883.

16 Smirnov 1897; at the time, Smirnov was working as a private tutor; two years later he would become curator of medieval and Renaissance materials at the State Hermitage Museum in St. Petersburg.

17 Arthur et al. 1891: 59–198.

18 Davis 2010: 3–14.

19 O.M. Dalton 1911.

20 Merrillees 2009: 1–15; this is a lively and informative account of the machinations of museums collectors and looters who played a part in the late 19th- to early 20th-century antiquities market.

21 Smirnov 1897: 1–93.

22 Pilides 2009: 31–32.

23 Jeffrey 1915–16: 111–34; 1928: 344–49.

24 Georghallides 1985: 46.

25 Buxton et al. 1933: 327–50; Buckler 1933: 105–10; 1946: 61–65.

26 Buxton et al. 1933: 328–32.

27 Stylianou 1997: 114–40; Carr and Nicolaides 2013.

28 Soteriou 1931: 477–90.

29 Soteriou 1935.

30 Rouerché 2001: 163; the first Director, Hilton, was also trained as an architect. His authority was challenged by the local colonial establishment (especially by Rupert Gunnis) and undercut by the governor. He resigned after a few ineffectual months.

31 Du Plat Taylor 1980: 152–216; Du Plat Taylor and Megaw 1981: 209–50. Joan Du Plat Taylor (1906–1983) was a pioneering archaeologist in underwater archaeology. She, along with medieval scholars like Gertrude Bell (1868–1926) and Ella Armitage (1841–1931), demonstrated that near eastern archaeology extended beyond "the old boy's club." Her work on Cyprus was fundamental in how archaeology would be recorded and archived in the Department of Antiquities. At Carpasia, Plat Taylor and Megaw concentrated their excavation on the immediate surroundings of the church and sampled the extensive Late Roman remains. The impetus for the excavation was to repair the medieval church, which led to the discovery of the remains its 5th-century predecessor.

32 Megaw 1958a; Megaw's report is contained in an unpublished manuscript on file at the State Archive of Cyprus. A copy exists in the archives of CAARI. The Ciborium restoration project at Agios Mamas, undertaken at the request of the Bishop of Morphou, includes a plate of the plan of Megaw's work and a discussion; Remsen 2010.

33 Frend 1996.

34 Davis, forthcoming. McFadden graduated from Princeton with a degree in English and had no background at all in Byzantine art or archaeology. His death by drowning occurred before any of the material from the site was published.

35 Bert Hill to Jayne, Feb 8, 1934; letter in the University Museum's Kourion Archives (University of Pennsylvania).

36 Davis, forthcoming; in contrast to McFadden, the 1930s Antioch excavations, led by a consortium of American and European museums, took half of the discovered mosaics out of Syria.

37 Catling and Dikigoropoulos 1970: 43–59; Catling 1972: 1–82.

38 A.I. Dikigoropoulos died in 2005, after publishing a few, but very important articles (see the Secondary Source Bibliography). He maintained his friendship with Megaw and was active in carrying out research on Byzantine monuments, like Staurovouni Monastery, but these were never published. It should

be noted that much of the information in this paragraph was communicated to Charles Anthony Stewart by Dikigoropoulos' daughter, Merope, in Nicosia on the 15th of June 2007.

39 A perusal of the *Annual Report of the Director of the Department of Antiquities* throughout the 1960s provides many examples of the strong commitment of the Department to the restoration of churches.

40 Carr 2008: 95–103; Mango 1969: 98–104.

41 Papageorghiou 1963 a/b.

42 These important articles were apparently overlooked in some notable studies on Byzantine architecture in Cyprus (Curčić 1999, 2000; Wharton 1988), but acknowledged in others (Megaw 1974; Papacostas 1999).

43 Roux 1998: 17.

44 *Annual Report of the Director of the Department of Antiquities for 1965*, 1966: 13.

45 Dikigoropoulos 1961: 230; Karageorghis 1968: 351, 1969: 564–66; Papageorghiou 1969: 82–88, 1996: 6, 55.

46 Gagniers and Tinh 1985; this project was terminated prematurely by the Turkish invasion in 1974. The inscription, which had been uncovered that summer, has since disappeared. USAID funded the cleaning and stabilization of the basilica mosaics and published a full record of the visible mosaics; no further excavation was undertaken by the USAID team (Neal 2010).

47 Megaw et al. 2007; this was published posthumously. Megaw also reported on the results of McFadden's work in the 1930s, which remained unpublished.

48 Davis 2010: 3–14.

49 See the Secondary Source Bibliography under Papageorghiou.

50 Argoud et al. 1980.

51 Megaw 1971: 117–46; Rosser 1985: 81–97.

52 Christou 2008.

53 Committee for the Protection of the Cultural Heritage of Cyprus 1998; Papageorghiou 2010.

54 Knapp and Antoniadou 1998: 13–43; the Memorandum of Understanding was reaffirmed on the 10th of July, 2012, and extended to include the ecclesiastical and ritual ethnological material of the Post-Byzantine period, c. 1500–1850 AD. This was significant legislation that has influenced other countries to protect their Byzantine patrimony.

55 Davis 2008: 16–20.

56 Christou 2008; despite the numerous publications on Kourion's archaeological remains, it does not represent the quantity of data which has actually been excavated.

57 Dikigoropoulos 1940–1948: 94–114; Papageorghiou 1964b: 152–58, 1986–1988: 167–75; Mansouri 2001; Kyrris 1994–1998: 185–236; Christides 2006.

58 Soren and James 1988.

59 Parks 1996; 127–33; 1997: 271–76; Parks, Given, and Chapman 1998: 171–85; Parks and Chapman 1999: 259–67; Michael Given will be publishing the final report.

60 Gregory 1987: 199.

61 Winther-Jacobsen 2010.

62 Rautman 1998; 2003; 2007; Manning et al. 2002.

63 Caraher, Moore, Noller, and Pettigrew 2007: 293–306.

64 McCarthy et al. 2009.

65 Rautman, Gomez, Neff, and Glascock 1993; 1995a; 1995b; 1996; 1999; 2002; it should be noted that Rautman was the first American archaeologist to have worked on Cyprus whose expertise lies in Byzantine material culture.

66 Manning and Bruce 2009; Ousterhout 2008; 32, note 42.

67 Violaris 2004: 69–80; Pilides 2002: 181–200.

68 Michaelides 2004: 185–98; see also Chapter 1 in this volume.

69 Specific reparations and discoveries are too numerous to list here. They are listed every year in the *Annual Report of the Department of Antiquities Cyprus*. But it should be mentioned that the most spectacular discoveries in recent years have been the crypt of Agios Athanasios Pentaschoinitis (at Agios Theodoros village) by Giorgos Philotheou and nearby the Mazotos baptistery by Giorgos Georgiou.

70 Recent scholarship has avoided using the terms "Dark Age" or "Condominium Period," so it is used here for rhetorical flair. Charles Anthony Stewart has advocated instead the term "Period of Neutrality," whereas D.M. Metcalf calls it the "Treaty Centuries."

71 Aupert and Flourentzos 2008: 311–46; Dikigoropoulos 1961: 230; Papageorghiou 1969: 82–88; 1996: 6, 55.

72 Gregory 1987: 200.

73 In recent years, CAARI has facilitated and supported several Byzantine scholars. Just to name a few: Brooke Shilling was the Kress Foundation

Fellow from 2010–2011, studying Early Byzantine mosaics on the island; in 2008, Professor Richard Rutherford was the CAARI Senior Scholar in Residence and Fulbright Fellow, who researched the Early Christian and Byzantine baptisteries; Charles Anthony Stewart was pre-doctoral Fulbright Fellow and CAARI O'Donovan Fellow from 2005–07 focusing on the architecture of the so-called "Dark Ages;" and the late professor Danielle Parks was a CAARI National Endowment for the Humanities Fellow from 2000–2001, specializing in Late Roman burial practices.

Chapter 3

Christianity in Cyprus in the Fourth to Seventh Centuries: Chronological and Geographical Frameworks

by Claudia Rapp

Since ancient times, Cyprus' location in the Eastern Mediterranean, combined with its rich natural resources, has determined its role as a crossroads where people from different regions converge. The shortest distance to the mainland is to the north, where the coast of Cilicia is only 69 kilometers away.[1] Syria is almost twice as far, 110 kilometers, while Egypt is at the greatest remove, 420 kilometers. For anyone setting out towards the north from Egypt, Cyprus was a convenient first stopping point. The same is true for travelers from the coast of Syria or Palestine on their way to the west, whether to North Africa, Sicily, Rome, or even locations in Western Europe. Throughout history, these established lines of north–south and east–west traffic brought not only traders and merchants, but also visitors and, at times, invaders. Many of them left their mark and contributed to the unique tapestry that constitutes Cypriot culture.

Much has been said about Cyprus as "a crossroads, a melting pot, a meeting place of east and west," as Cyril Mango pointed out in his important article "Chypre, carrefour du monde byzantin."[2] Rather than viewing Cyprus as a point of convergence, this study proposes a supplemen-tary approach by assuming a viewpoint that is anchored on the island itself. It aims to invoke the south-eastern Levant as a maritime region with its own cultural and political cohesion and Cyprus as its focal point. In the first part, I will investigate Cyprus' connections to the neighboring mainland regions in the north, west, and south.[3] Regardless of whether these contacts originated in Cyprus or had Cyprus as their destination, the aim will be to highlight the role of the island as a center of activity. A related question is whether there prevailed a specific sense of regional identity on Cyprus, articulated through the assertion of a particular historical tradition. In the second part of this chapter, I shall pursue this question in the context of the growth of Christianity on the island, and highlight how hagiography and the cult of saints played an important role in bolstering Cyprus' unique role in the history of Byzantium. The chronological end point of this investigation is the Arab invasions of the mid-seventh century which changed the previous political and religious parameters.[4]

Ever since the days of the first apostles, Christianity has been propagated through the movement of people, ideas, and texts. On Cyprus, the progress in the Christianization of the population and the eventual Christianization of literary culture can be divided into three chronological tranches, each of which may be associated with a major figure: the first century with the apostle Barnabas, the late fourth century with Epiphanius, bishop of Salamis-Constantia, and the early seventh century with Leontius of Neapolis, a prolific author of saints' *Lives*.

When Christianity first came to Cyprus, the island had been under Roman rule for about a century, after the Romans wrested it from the Ptolemies of Egypt in 58 BCE.[5] At first administered as part of the province of Cilicia, it became an independent senatorial province in 22 BCE. After the reorganization of the provinces under Diocletian and Constantine, Cyprus formed part of the Diocese of Oriens, which had its headquarters in Antioch. The island boasted numerous important pagan cults, most prominent among them those of Aphrodite in Paphos and of Zeus in Salamis. It was also home to a very numerous Jewish population, which in 115 staged a dangerous revolt against Roman rule.

From the earliest days, as reported in the Acts of the Apostles, Cyprus had a strong association with Christianity. The geographical reference point of this association was Antioch, the largest urban center within easy reach of Cyprus and, after the administrative reforms of the late third/early fourth century, the administrative capital of the Prefecture of Oriens. Next to Jerusalem, Antioch was also a focal point for the nascent Christian movement. It was at Antioch where the term 'Christians' was first applied to Jesus' disciples. When the Christian mission expanded from Jews to Gentiles, this too occurred in Antioch, and it was Cypriots, along with men from Cyrene in North Africa, who preached the message of "good news" (εὐαγγέλιον) to non-Jews. These three locations, Antioch, Cyrene, and Cyprus, were also the destinations for the followers of Jesus when they scattered after the martyrdom of Stephen in Jerusalem.

Cyprus was thus one of the earliest regions to generate and to receive Christian preachers — long before Athens, Rome, or Alexandria, let alone Constantinople. The leading figure in the mission to the island was Barnabas. Himself descended from a wealthy Jewish family in Cyprus, he had lived among the hellenized inhabitants of the Roman province of Palaestina when he joined the followers of Jesus. He was present in Antioch when the Christian community consolidated itself, and his name is the first to be mentioned among the teachers and prophets there.[6] In 46/7, Barnabas set out from Antioch on a missionary journey to Cyprus, accompanied by Paul, who at that time was still his protégé,[7] and John Mark, who was a close relative.[8] Hackett suggests that Barnabas may have befriended Paul while they were both pursuing their education at Tarsus — an attractive hypothesis, given the geographical proximity of Cyprus to the Cilician coast.[9] They arrived in Salamis and began preaching "in the synagogues of the Jews," apparently with little resonance, until they finally made their way to Paphos. There, in the presence of the proconsul Sergius Paulus, they engaged in a disputation with the Jewish "magician" Bar-Jesus. Paul was so enraged by this man's obstinacy that he insulted him and struck him blind — a miracle that resulted in the immediate conversion of the proconsul and established the miracle-working apostle in a leadership role among the disciples. From a historical perspective, it is doubtful that one man's embrace of the new religion, no matter how high his political position, would have led to a widespread acceptance of Christianity. Indeed, a few years later, Barnabas is reported to have paid another missionary visit to Cyprus, again accompanied by John Mark, but after parting ways with Paul.[10] This second mission to Cyprus, too, seems to have remained without significant impact at the time. As we shall see below, however, this period would be glorified in retrospect, in written legends of the fifth century, as a major stepping stone in the Christianization of the island.

By the time of the episcopate of Epiphanius in the late fourth century, Christianity had not only gained large numbers of adherents, but the Christian Church had also established a dense network of bishoprics. This trend becomes evident already at the beginning of the fourth century. Among the regions whose bishops were in attendance at the Council of Nicaea in 325, Cyprus was the only island.[11] According to official documents, it was represented by two bishops, Gelasius of

Salamis and Cyril of Paphos, and other sources report the attendance of bishop Spyridon of Tremithous.[12] By the year 400, Cyprus had no less than fifteen bishops,[13] all of equal rank, within a territory of 9,250 square kilometers, about three-fifths the size of Connecticut. Such density of episcopal sees without apparent hierarchy among them (such as the designation of *metropolitan* or *chorepiskopos* would indicate) is not known from any other region in the Early Byzantine Empire except on its fringes, such as on the island of Sicily and among the Christian Arabs.[14] It should be added, however, that since the late fourth century, the see of Salamis-Constantia was commonly regarded as the most important bishopric.

At the Council of Nicaea, Spyridon of Tremithous made a particular impression. He is singled out in the Latin *Ecclesiastical History* of Rufinus of Aquileia as deserving of special mention for his miracles of immobilizing thieves and of making his virgin daughter pronounce from her grave where she had safeguarded some money. Particularly noteworthy was the fact that Spyridon remained a shepherd even after his ordination — hence the distinctive iconographic feature of his headgear in the form of a shepherd's cap. His reputation as a wonder-worker was such that the fifth-century ecclesiastical historians Socrates and Sozomen devote short chapters to him. The former was writing in Constantinople, the latter had access to local informants from Cyprus.[15] These historians mention his attendance at Nicaea, although his name does not appear in the list of signatories of the Council.

In Epiphanius' time, monasticism was becoming an important force in Egypt and Palestine, which led to closer ties between Cyprus and these regions. Hilarion, a monastic leader from the environs of Gaza, came to Cyprus to seek respite from his popularity and died there a few years later in 371, as we know from the Latin account of his life written by Jerome. Conversely, many men and women from Cyprus traveled to Egypt to visit the holy men and to benefit from the healing shrines, especially that of Cyrus and John in Alexandria. Epiphanius himself was a product of this monastic tradition that was taking root in Egypt and Palestine and from there spread

to Cyprus. According to the *Vita* that was composed some time in the second half of the fifth century, he was a converted Jew from Palestine. It was under the tutelage of Hilarion, who was then still active in the environs of Gaza, that he received his monastic formation, which he later deepened through an extended visit to Egypt. By a concatenation of unrelated circumstances — the *Vita* mentions divine intervention in the form of a shipwreck — Epiphanius was in 367 elected as bishop of Constantia, as the city of Salamis had been re-named under Constantius II.[16]

Epiphanius held the episcopate for almost four decades, until his death in 402 or 403. He became a prominent figure in ecclesiastical politics because of his unrelenting stance against heresies of any kind. A prolific author, he expressed his zeal for the maintenance of doctrinal purity in his two most famous works, the *Panarion*, a "medicine chest" of antidotes against the sting of heresies which are compared to poisonous animals, and the *Ancoratus*, which offered a firm "anchor" of faith in the mainline orthodox tradition. His activities on behalf of the preservation of Orthodoxy occasioned journeys to Rome, Jerusalem, and Constantinople. His work as an author covered an even larger radius of contacts: clergy in Antioch during the Meletian schism, Basil of Caesarea in Cappadocia as a correspondent in matters of theological disagreements,[17] and "the presbyters Acacius and Paul, archimandrites, or abbots, in Chalcis and Beroea in Coelesyria,"[18] who requested his composition of the *Panarion*.

A more tangible monument credited to his name is the large basilica in Salamis-Constantia. At the time of its construction, it was one of the largest churches in all of Christendom. With dimensions of 58 by 42 meters, it was only slightly smaller than the Sion Basilica in Jerusalem, but surpassed in size Santa Sabina on the Aventine in Rome and Saint Demetrius in Thessaloniki. The church interior was divided into five aisles, including a niche where Epiphanius was buried. There would have been additional space along the narthex and outer circumference of the nave, the location for the catechumens during the period of preparation for their baptism.[19] While they were not yet full members of the community, these

Christians-in-the-making were only permitted to follow the liturgy from a distance and were dismissed at a certain moment prior to the celebration of the Eucharist. This same arrangement is very clearly visible in the basilica at Kourion on the southwestern shore of the island, which dates from the early fifth century. In search of similar architectural features on the neighboring mainland, scholars disagree on the patterns of influence. Delvoye sees parallels to Pamphylia and Cilicia, as well as Constantinople and Ephesus, but decidedly no connection to Antioch.[20] Megaw, by contrast, remarks that the same distinctive architectural features as in Kourion and Salamis-Constantia are also present in church architecture in Syria, including the region of Antioch, indicating a shared culture with regard to liturgical practice and ecclesiastical architecture.[21] However that may be, the spatial accommodation for new converts in these two Cypriot churches indicates that the most rapid increase in conversions to Christianity occurred after the reign of Constantine, in the course of the fourth century — a pattern that Keith Hopkins has shown to prevail throughout the Empire.[22] This had important and far-reaching consequences for the production of Cypriot hagiography, as we shall see later.

The radius of Epiphanius' activities extended well beyond his birthplace in Palestine and the location of his monastic perfection in Egypt. As bishop of Salamis-Constantia, he took a stance in the internal divisions in the church of Antioch in order to support the appointment of Paulinus to the episcopate and a few years later attended a council in Rome where this dispute was the subject of further discussion. Near the end of his life, as an octogenarian, he traveled to Constantinople after Theophilus of Alexandria had brought to his attention that John Chrysostom was not only harboring Origenist thought, but also sheltering a small group of prominent Egyptian monks of Origenist persuasion. The geographical scope of Epiphanius' efforts on behalf of orthodoxy thus encompassed the entire Mediterranean, although he displayed a particular concern for the ecclesiastical affairs of Antioch and Alexandria. From this vantage point, Cyprus can indeed claim its rightful place alongside the major cities of the early Byzantine Empire,

as it does on an early medieval gold chalice found at Vrap (Albania, not far from ancient coastal city of Dyrrachium), now in the Metropolitan Museum in New York. The chalice, which is depicted on the title of this volume, bears the slightly misspelt inscription "City of Cyprus (πωλης κυπρος)" next to the "City of Constantinople," the "City of Rome," and the "City of Alexandria."[23]

At Epiphanius' ordination to the episcopate in 367, only bishops from Cyprus participated. This fact, along with similar episodes, was invoked as precedent at the Council of Ephesus in 431 when the claims of the Patriarch of Antioch to authority over the church in Cyprus were rebuked and the ecclesiastical independence of the Cypriot church was affirmed.[24] With this decision, the reach of the Patriarch of Antioch no longer extended to the island, although it remained under the administrative authority of the Praetorian Prefect for the Diocese of Oriens. A renewed attempt to submit the church in Cyprus to the Patriarchate of Antioch, by Peter the Fuller, was averted in around 478 by the timely discovery of the relics of S. Barnabas. They were found near Salamis-Constantia, the body of the apostle uncorrupted as a sign of his holiness, with a copy of the Gospel of Matthew on his chest — tangible proof for the apostolic origins and hence the right to independence of the see.

The discovery of relics of the apostolic era seems to have enjoyed a particular fashion in the fifth century. The Latin version of the *Apocalypse of Paul* reports the miraculous discovery in Tarsus of a box containing the sandals of the Apostle Paul and a copy of his *Apocalypse* during the reign of Theodosius II in 420. The immensely popular text has a complex history in the languages of the Christian Orient and in Latin, while the original Greek does not survive, except in a condensed version. The earliest suggested date for this Latin version are the final years of the reign of Theodosius II who died in 450.[25] We might well ask whether the *inventio* of Barnabas' body only a few decades later, also accompanied by a relevant codex, was more than just coincidence, especially in view of the geographical proximity of Cyprus to Cilicia and the fact that Barnabas was accompanied on his first missionary journey to the island by Paul, who was a native of Tarsus. A tale of this nature would have traveled fast, regardless of distance and language barriers. It might have made the Cypriots receptive to an analogous miraculous discovery on their own soil that would enable them to press the advantage of their apostolic roots.

The presence of Barnabas' relics proved the island's apostolicity, thereby forever invalidating Antioch's claim to be superior in rank.[26] As Francis Dvornik has shown, the notion that an episcopal see could claim precedence and authority over others based not on the political importance of the city, but on its historical connection to one of Christ's apostles, was first promoted by Rome and only slowly gained currency in the East in the late 440s. The bishops of Antioch seem to have been particularly receptive to this idea.[27] By tangibly reinforcing the connection of the island with the Apostle Barnabas, Cypriot bishops did more than merely assert their independence from the city on the Orontes — they beat the Antiochenes at their own game.

Cyprus thus became the first church in Christendom to be granted autocephaly — a frequently invoked point of pride for the Cypriot church.[28] Curiously, the term 'autocephaly' does not appear to be employed at that time in any kind of writing. It is present neither in the Acts of the Council of Ephesus that report the proceedings and their outcome, nor in any other work of the fifth century. The first author to use this word is Theodore Lector in the late fifth or early sixth century in the context of his report on the miraculous *inventio* of the relics of Barnabas during the reign of the Emperor Zeno. "For this reason," he says,"the Cypriots achieved it that their metropolis [i.e., Salamis-Constantia] became autocephalous and no longer under the authority of Antioch."[29] Even more curiously, the *Notitia Episcopatum* (*List of Bishoprics*) that is attributed to Epiphanius of Salamis-Constantia, but in reality is a work of the eighth or ninth century, contains a separate entry for "autocephalous archbishoprics" which lists 34 sees, but does not include Cyprus — a possible nod to chronological accuracy and the avoidance of anachronism on the part of the compiler.[30]

During our third chronological tranche, the seventh century and the time of Leontius of Neapolis, the connections of Cyprus with Palestine remained strong, while those with Egypt gained further importance. This was the time when Cyprus became a major site within the context of large geopolitical shifts.[31] For five centuries, the coastal regions of the Eastern Mediterranean had enjoyed stable and tranquil times under the Roman Empire. But that would change dramatically and with lasting consequence in the second decade of the seventh century, when the Sasanian Empire, the age-old adversary of the Roman Empire to the East, began to pursue an aggressive policy of attack and invasion that eventually threatened even Constantinople itself. By 614, the Sasanians had brought Jerusalem under control, after wreaking havoc and inflicting unspeakable bloodshed in its rich churches and many monasteries. By 619 they had advanced as far as Alexandria. The human toll was enormous. Waves of refugees fled to Cyprus, while those who remained depended on humanitarian assistance sent by others.

One of the charitable benefactors was John, the Patriarch of Alexandria, who, as we shall see shortly, had his own ties to Cyprus. It must have seemed like a divinely ordained miracle when the Emperor Heraclius in 628 was able to bring the Sasanian Empire to its knees after six years of military campaigns in which he personally led the troops. His victory is celebrated in the famous David Plates, which were found at Lambousa in Cyprus and are now divided between Nicosia and New York.[32] They depict scenes from the life of David, prominently featuring his slingshot fight as a young boy against the giant Goliath and his anointing by Saul as King, the latter an unmistakable parallel to the dynastic change brought about by Heraclius' deposition of the Emperor Phokas in 610.

Among those who sought refuge on island of Cyprus from the Sasanian invasions was John, at the end of his tenure as Patriarch of Alexandria. As the wealthy son of the governor of the island and a prominent citizen of Amathous, he owed his appointment to this important ecclesiastical post in Egypt — a key province of the Byzantine Empire and the bread basket of its capital — to his close association with Heraclius and his cousin Niketas after the two staged their successful coup d'état against the emperor Phokas in 610.[33] John's patriarchate of Alexandria was distinguished by the justice and charity which he extended to the men and women of his city and to refugees from the Persian invasions alike, and which brought him into conflict on more than one occasion with Niketas, who had been appointed as the civil governor of Egypt. John's ties to Cyprus remained as strong at the end of his patriarchate as they had been prior to it. He adorned his home town in Cyprus in several ways: as a benefactor, he contributed to the beautification of the city's many buildings and even constructed a church dedicated to Saint Stephen,[34] and as a word-smith, he composed a literary monument to its fourth-century bishop Tychon, in the form of a *Vita*.[35] His association with Tychon extended even after his death, as he was buried in the chapel of that saint in Amathous and was commemorated on the same feast day.[36]

John the Almsgiver, as he would become known, was himself immortalized in an exceptionally colorful and detailed piece of hagiographical literature by the pen of a fellow Cypriot, Leontius of Neapolis. The author purportedly based himself on the oral account of a certain Menas, a former treasurer of the saintly Patriarch with whom he struck up a conversation on a visit to the healing shrine of Cyrus and John in Alexandria, a sanctuary which attracted many pilgrims from Cyprus in search of a cure.[37] Leontius claims to be continuing and updating an earlier account (that is no longer extant in its original form) by John Moschus and Sophronius, monastic companions from Palestine, who had met the Patriarch during a pilgrimage to Egypt, in the course of which Sophronius, like Leontius, visited the shrine of Cyrus and John in Alexandria. They also passed through Cyprus at some point between 614 and 619. John Moschus would later depict their journeys in the *Spiritual Meadow,* and Sophronius would acquire unfortunate fame as the Patriarch of Jerusalem at the time of the Arab invasions of the 630s.[38] The *Vita* of the Alexandrian patriarch in continuation of the work of John and Sophronius was not the only piece of hagiography from Leontius' pen. In addition, he composed a *Life of Spyridon,* the shepherd-bishop of Tremithous of the early fourth century, and a *Life of Symeon the Fool,* who lived a crazed life of

sanctity in disguise among the citizens of Emesa in Syria.[39] Leontius' geographical purview as an author thus extended well beyond Cyprus to Syria and Alexandria.

This leads me to the second part of this chapter, regarding the chronological and geographical framework and outlook of Cypriot hagiography. Recent scholarship has begun to pay attention to issues of identity, whether of individuals, groups, or political entities. Identity can either be attributed by another or assumed by the self. The only time in Byzantine writing (inasmuch as it is accessible in the *Thesaurus Linguae Graecae*) that Cypriots were identified as an *ethnos,* a distinct "people" or even "nation," occurred in the twelfth century, in the *Chronicle* of John Scylitzes.[40] In his discussion of a local revolt in Cyprus that occurred under Constantine IX Monomachus, he labels the rebels as "the Cypriot people (ἔθνος ἅπαν τῶν Κυπρίων)," thereby implying that the uprising was understandable, if not justified, because of the distinct identity of the islanders.

The meager results for an ascribed identity of the Cypriots is counterbalanced by richer evidence regarding the assumed identity of these men and women. Expressions of a saint's cult, whether chapels or churches, epitaphs on tombs or donor inscriptions, or indeed saints' *Lives,* all can serve the same function as regional histories: they feature the most prominent citizens in action and encapsulate the city's collective historical memory in order to project this image to posterity.[41] But when did these traditions begin in Cyprus? And what historical and local concerns do they reveal?

In answer to these questions, we have to turn to the period just after Epiphanius' episcopate, which was equally precedent-setting in its disregard for the authority of Antioch as in its efforts to accommodate unprecedented numbers of converts in the large basilicas. For it is in the course of the fifth century that the Cypriots were creating a written record of their own Christian traditions that indicates a strong sense of local pride. The vehicle for this articulation is the cult of local saints and the composition of hagiographical works. This observation is not new. It has been shown for all the regions of Christendom how the cult of local saints can rally a community around a common cause, attract commerce, generate donations, and bolster the authority of the clergy that presides over the annual celebrations at the shrine. The history of local cults is accessible to us in tangible form in the representations of saints on frescoes and icons, and in the shrines where they are commemorated. In written form, it is also preserved in calendars of saints, which commemorate the anniversary of their death and mention little else except their Christian credentials (as martyr, bishop, etc.). More detailed sources are the panegyric speeches delivered to an appreciative audience on the anniversary of the saint's death, or the written hagiographies that enjoyed wider circulation.

What is new and unique to Cyprus is the fact that the vast majority of its saints that are celebrated in Byzantine hagiography had the rank of bishop. This has been observed with regard to the fresco decoration in Cypriot churches by Doula Mouriki, and elaborated with regard to the hagiographical record by Vera von Falkenhausen.[42] There may have been martyrs and confessors among them in the pre-Constantinian period, and some of them may have distinguished themselves as great ascetics and miracle-workers, but the fact remains that all the Cypriot saints residing in Cyprus who are attested in the hagiographical record until the seventh century were in charge of communities of Christians.[43] Whether this is further confirmation of the striking absence of hierarchy among the Cypriot episcopate that was noted above, or whether it is the result of the selective reporting by a remarkably large number of prolific hagiographers in Cyprus, is a question that has to remain unresolved.

Epiphanius is something of an involuntary trendsetter in this regard, too. When his *Vita* was composed, supposedly by his disciples Polybius and Sabinus, but really — as I have argued elsewhere — in the third quarter of the fifth century, hagiographical writing was still in its infancy.[44] It was only a century earlier that Athanasius of Alexandria had composed the first piece of hagiographical biography with the *Life of Antony of Egypt,* whom he depicted as a hermit monk in the desert after rejecting the world and its temptations. By contrast, Epiphanius was among a very small

group of men who were believed to have attained personal sanctity through their episcopate, in daily contact with the world rather than in withdrawal from it. This group included the important bishops Porphyry of Gaza in the East, and Martin of Tours, Ambrose of Milan, and Augustine of Hippo in the West — all of whom were honored with hagiographies in the fifth century. In keeping with the conventions of hagiography, Epiphanius is depicted as an extraordinary miracle-worker who engages with powerful pagan individuals and whose spectacular deeds lead to mass conversions. The enormous basilica associated with his name bears witness to the large number of newly-minted Christians at that time. The *Vita* functions in a similar way as a local history: it points to buildings and highlights the activities of the good and great, especially if they join the church and become benefactors for the common good.

The sudden blossoming of Cypriot saints' *Lives* in the mid-fifth to seventh centuries coincides with a general trend in the flourishing of hagiography throughout the Byzantine Empire. But it is also tied to an important moment in local history, when the church in Cyprus was asserting its independence against the claims of the Antiochene see. What better way to defy the encroachments of a powerful neighbor than to assert local independence by recourse to historical precedent both in the apostolic age *and* during the continued struggle against paganism in the fourth century? In both periods, the protagonists can be shown to be defiant in the face of political authority and successful in besting their adversaries with the effect of generating many conversions. Hence the two historicizing clusters of Cypriot hagiography, the first one around Barnabas and his followers, Auxibius[45] and Heracleides,[46] the second one relating to saints of the fourth century, including Spyridon, Tychon, and Epiphanius.[47]

For almost two centuries, the only hagiography produced in Cyprus would be devoted to Cypriot saints, all of them bishops (including Barnabas, whose Laudatio by Alexander the Monk was probably composed during the reign of Justinian).[48] While it is undeniable that each city on the island would have cultivated great pride in its local saint, the hagiographers also make it

cal references, but not in works of hagiography; Yannopoulos 1983: 79–83. See also Thonemann 2012: 257–82; Rapp 2012: 291–311.

42 Mouriki 1993: 238–45; Falkenhausen 1999: 21–33.

43 The only exception is George of Choziba, a native of Cyprus who followed the example of his brother Heracleides — a name with great historical resonance on the island — and became a monk in the Holy Land, although one of their uncles was the abbot of a monastery in Cyprus. His *Vita* was composed by his disciple Antony, a fellow-Cypriot, soon after the saint's death in around 635; Antony of Choziba, *Vita sancti Georgii,* ed. Houze 1888: 95–144, 336–59. For the most recent treatment of this text, see Olster 1993: 309–22.

44 Rapp 2005: 18.

45 Deun and Noret 1993: 139–202; Noret 1986: 445–52.

46 Nau 1907: 125–36; Halkin 1964: 133–69; Esbroek 1985: 115–62.

47 The apostolic and sub-apostolic age in Cyprus are also well-represented, with a total of 11 saints, in liturgical calendars or short commemorative texts in the *Synaxarion;* Janin 1953: col. 793; cf. Delehaye 1907.

48 Alexander Monachus, *Laudatio Barnabae,* ed. Kollmann 2007: 51–60.

49 Usener 1907: 122–23.

50 Leontius of Neapolis, *Vita et miracula sancti Symeonis Sali,* and *Vita S. Johannis Ellemosynarii;* Arcadius of Constantia, *Vita Symeonis stylitae iunioris in monte;* Arcadius, Bishop of Tremithous, *Laudatio S. Georgii,* martyred in Palestine.

51 Cameron 1992: *passim.*

Chapter 4

The Troodos in Twilight: A Provincial Landscape in the Time of Justinians

by Marcus Rautman

It is an honor to recognize the Republic of Cyprus on the occasion of its 50th anniversary, and also the Department of Antiquities on its 75th. Twenty-five years ago, the Department held another symposium with the related theme of "Cyprus between the Orient and the Occident." For that event Peter Megaw assessed archaeology's contribution to understanding the seventh to ninth centuries on the island, with the goal of dispelling some of the gloom surrounding this "dark age" of contested memory. More recent reviews by Athanasios Papageorghiou and Michael Metcalf have added breadth and detail to our picture of Cyprus during these critical years, while also underscoring the limits of present knowledge.[1]

My intention is more modest, and focuses on what recent research can tell us about the countryside of this island province in the sixth and seventh centuries.[2] The transitional character of this time appears in the erosion of familiar, long-established structures of Late Roman life and the emergence of seemingly different cultural traditions. I use the term "provincial" without prejudice to describe the impact that mainland empires exerted on local lives during an era of sweeping political realignment. This perspective builds on Hector Catling's

caution, repeated by Robert Merrillies at that earlier gathering, that "Cyprus is a land whose history is bound to be involved with those of the countries by which she is immediately surrounded: she should not be viewed from one direction alone, for this distorts what we see." It also reminds us of deeper continuities, both local and regional, that can endure over long intervals of time.[3]

The development of Cypriot archaeology over the last century necessarily reflects modern social realities as much as its geographic setting.[4] The island's continuing political division has ensured that systematic fieldwork has continued mainly in the south, across the slopes, foothills, and valleys of the Troodos Mountains (fig. 4.1). Excavations have been initiated or expanded at a number of places along the south coast, while publication of interrupted expeditions in the north has continued as well. Surface surveys have been carried out, and often reported in detail, in many parts of the island, and as a result Cyprus has become one of the most intensively sampled parts of the ancient world. The integrative, diachronic study of landscapes, a contribution of Anglophone archaeology in the 1980s, is usually driven by prehistoric interests, yet has produced much information about later phases

FIG. 4.1   *The Troodos Mountains, eastern branch of the Kouris valley, near Agridia (Photo: C.A. Stewart).*

of Cypriot history. Viewed from this sweeping chronological perspective, the long century spanning the reigns of the two Justinians (i.e., Justinian I, 527–565, and Justinian II, 685–711) occupies a kind of twilight between classical antiquity and the Middle Ages.

The dozen or so cities of Roman Cyprus have claimed most of the attention of classical authors and modern historians. Once seats of Iron Age kingdoms, these ancient urban centers were, in Hellenistic and Roman times, newly monumentalized and joined by a coastal road, reflecting outside interests in efficiently administering the island and extracting its natural resources.[5] Not all of these places were of comparable size, nor did they benefit equally from Roman rule, but several would have been known to the first Justinian as historical *poleis* of enduring significance. The provincial capital at Salamis, refounded in the mid-fourth century as Constantia, featured the customary range of administrative and public buildings, with a theater, gymnasium, baths, and two large churches among the best-documented monuments. Amathous, Kition, Kourion, Paphos, and Soloi presented similarly impressive urban tableaux with extensive residential quarters, entertainment and recreation facilities, and, in some cases, timber-roofed basilicas — urban landmarks that were built and embellished by sponsors well aware of mainland trends. The size and appearance of the smaller *poleis* of Arsinoë, Carpasia, Chytroi, Kyrenia, Lapithos, and Tamassos are far less clear, despite the contributions of topographic research and limited excavation, and to this group the sixth-century *Synekdemos* of Hierokles adds three more: Kirboia, Ledra, and Theodosiana.[6] Urban life must have varied tremendously from place to place, no less than on the mainland, yet the available evidence suggests that many of these cities continued to thrive well into the seventh century. One of the few literary works of the period, the *Life of Symeon the Fool,* was apparently composed within a prosperous urban milieu by Leontius of Neapolis in the 640s. Despite the effects of brigandage, drought, earthquakes, and plague, many Cypriot cities remained places of consequence until the Arab campaigns of the mid-seventh century.[7]

Exploration of smaller settlements, mainly along the south coast, has broadened this picture of insular prosperity beyond the neglect of contemporary observers. Today known only by their current toponyms, these secondary centers or satellite towns varied widely in size but clearly had social and economic significance in Late Antiquity.[8] The sprawling townsite at Pyla-*Koutsopetria* exemplifies this level of settled life. The site lies about 10 kilometers east of Larnaka, near the presumed coastal roadway and with access to a shallow harbor. Systematic reconnaissance and remote sensing by the Pyla-*Koutsopetria* Archaeological Project (PKAP, 2003–2010) have traced the extent of late Roman habitation across the coastal plain as far as the plateau of *Vigla* and *Kokkinokremos,* over a total area of 40 hectares. Visible surface remains include equipment for agricultural processing, mortared walls, residential structures, and a great deal of pottery. Excavations carried out by Maria Hadjicosti (1993, 1999) have identified several buildings, including one or more basilicas that were decorated with *opus sectile* floors, painted walls, gypsum moldings, and marble furnishings.[9]

Recent survey of the Akrotiri peninsula has brought attention to several substantial Late Roman settlements located one to two kilometers from the coast. One vast habitation area encompasses the neighboring localities of Pano and Kato Katalymata. Another major settlement lies about three kilometers to the west at Katalymata ton Plakoton, where building debris and pottery cover an area of 25 hectares. Interesting structures at the site are being excavated and studied by Eleni Procopiou, and are described in this volume. The growth of these mid-size settlements coincides with evidence of more intensive land use and occupation across the peninsula.[10] Offshore prospection by the Institute for Nautical

Archaeology (INA, 2003–2009) has found extensive scatters of Late Roman transport jars near Cape Zevgari and Dreamer's Bay. The presence of these amphorae, mainly of LR1 but also LR4 types, suggests local residents developed strong commercial ties with coastal Cilicia, north Syria, and Palestine in the sixth and early seventh centuries.[11]

These substantial agricultural settlements contrast with the cluster of public buildings at Peyia-*Agios Georgios* on Cape Drepanum, 20 kilometers west of Paphos. Excavation by the Department of Antiquities in 1949–1953 revealed a group of three basilicas that were built, extensively furnished with Proconnesian marble, and paved with polychrome mosaics over the course of the sixth century. More recently the Aristotle University of Thessaloniki (since 1991) has explored a bath complex and tombs of the same period. The site's maritime orientation is suggested by the conspicuous bluff-top location facing Yeronissos Island, as well as by the material splendor of its buildings. A marble ambo from one of the basilicas specifically mentions the *naukleroi,* who may have been local participants in seagoing traffic between Egypt and the Aegean. By contrast, survey of the surrounding countryside has found few traces for agricultural activity or habitation. Most of interaction seems to have been with Paphos and other places along the coast.[12] This string of cities and secondary towns constitutes the maritime facade of a rich and varied landscape that had supported local economies for centuries (fig. 4.2). Pliny the Elder and Strabo, in the first century, and Ammianus Marcellinus, in the fourth, mention the island's abundant resources and productivity.[13] Copper is known to have been worked in Chalcolithic times and was widely traded in the Late Bronze Age. Principal exports in classical and later antiquity included timber, cereals, oil, and wine, which were accompanied by a broad range of almonds, figs, fruits, herbs, and minerals. Writing in the mid-sixth century, John Lydus includes Cyprus among the most affluent provinces of the late empire.[14]

The key element in organizing the countryside itself was the small, nucleated settlement or village comprising houses, an administrative center, and one or more churches. Contemporary sources use a variety of terms to designate such

FIG. 4.2   *The Cypriot countryside above Kalavasos.*

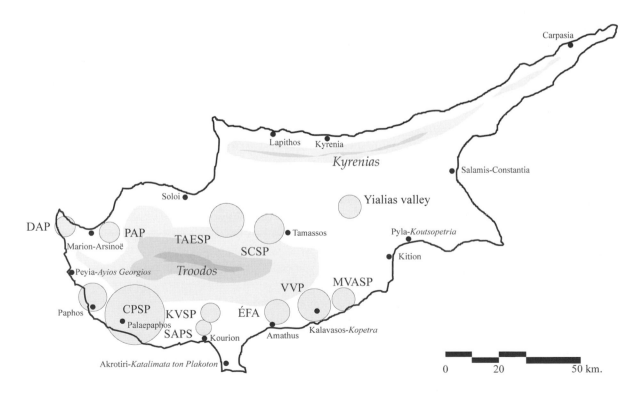

FIG. 4.3   *Map of Cyprus with late Roman cities and surveys discussed in the text.*

non-urban communities, ranging from the modest κώμη, κωμύδριον, χωρίον, and προάστειον to the larger κωμόπολις and μετροκώμη. Despite their inconsistent use and uncertain meaning, such terms nevertheless indicate the growing importance of rural settlements in the empire's fiscal and ecclesiastical organization.[15] Few such places have been systematically explored in Cyprus, but their numbers may not have differed greatly from the nearby mainland. In nearby Cilicia and Syria, for example, it has been estimated that cities typically included 20 to 30 village-like settlements within their dependent territory. Rural habitation sites identified in the field generally average two to five hectares in extent and appear at distances of two to four kilometers; the most distinctive features of the larger ones are agricultural processing equipment, permanently occupied dwellings, and two or three churches.[16] A comparable assessment of Cyprus in the sixth century suggests that its 12 to 15 major *poleis,* of which at least ten lay along the coast, formed only the most visible part of a habitation network that would have included at least 250 villages. An equally conservative estimate of 100 families per settlement would yield a minimum village population of 125,000, to which should be added farmers and shepherds who occupied scattered hamlets, farmsteads, and seasonal shelters. By this same reasoning one could assume that as many as 500 rural churches were in service around the year 600.[17]

The abstraction of literary accounts and demographic conjecture assumes tangible form through field reconnaissance and salvage excavation (fig. 4.3). Cyprus occupies a special place in the development of Mediterranean field survey, and over the last 60 years many parts of the island have seen extensive exploration.[18] The earliest systematic investigations took place in the mid-1950s, when Hector Catling initiated the survey branch of the Department of Antiquities. Focusing on the coastlands and northern slopes of the Kyrenia mountains, Catling noted a broadly dispersed network of villages, hamlets, and farmsteads whose occupation spanned the fourth and seventh centuries. Additional reconnaissance by Sophocles Hadjisavvas has extended this web of activity into the environs of Salamis-Constantia.[19]

For practical reasons, recent investigation of the Cypriot countryside has concentrated on the wooded slopes and lower valleys of the Troodos range. Present landforms and vegetation patterns have evolved in important ways over the centuries, yet cautious investigation has been able to differentiate sub-regional patterns of settlement within this complex terrain.[20] Concentrating on the massif's north-central slopes and foothills, the Sydney Cyprus Survey Project (SCSP, 1992–97) and the Troodos Archaeological Exploration Survey Project (TAESP, 2000–2004) have documented an extensive network of activity based largely on agriculture and mining. The abundance of surface artifacts near ancient Tamassos (modern Politiko) suggests that the city offered both a gathering point for local products and a central market for imported goods. The extensive occupation of the lower Karkotis valley, by contrast, appears more specifically directed to supplying the vast mining complex at Skouriotissa as well as urban Soloi on the northwest coast. Smaller activity areas at higher elevation seem to have functioned as satellite camps for extracting and smelting copper, or for their support.[21]

The rugged land on the west side of the Troodos, which in places drops sharply to the sea, appears to have been less densely occupied from Hellenistic through Late Roman times. A modest number of widely dispersed farmsteads and small villages, rarely more than one to two hectares in extent, have been located by the Polis-*Pyrgos* Archaeological Project (PAP, 1992–2000) in the hills overlooking Marion-Arsinoë (modern Polis) and Khrysokhou Bay. Reconnaissance of the western Akamas peninsula by the Danish Akamas Project (DAP, 1989–1994) noted a similarly sparse pattern of small agricultural settlements and pastoral encampments scattered across this remote region. Excavations at the site of Agios Kononas identified several houses and a small basilica that were built near a stone quarry. The buildings were occupied from the later fifth century onwards and gradually abandoned in the early 600s.[22]

A different, more extensive late Roman presence has been observed south of the Troodos, where the terrain relaxes into broad valleys and the fertile coastal plain. Occupation of the

FIG. 4.4   *The Vasilikos valley, looking north toward Kalavasos from* Kopetra.

region expanded with the rise of Paphos, which served as the island's provincial capital and main port in Hellenistic and early Roman times.[23] Reconnaissance of the Ezousas, Xero Potamos, Dhiarizos, and Khapotami river valleys by the Canadian Palaepaphos Survey Project (CPSP, 1979–1991) traced the growth of rural settlement, mainly in the form of farmsteads and small villages of one to two hectares in area, through late Roman times. Exploration of the Kourion environs by the Sotira Archaeological Project Survey (SAPS, 1997) and Kouris Valley Survey Project (KVSP, 2007–2008) has documented a similar network of rural activity that lasted well into the 600s.[24] Pavlos Flourentzos' excavation of a small basilica and associated structures at Alassa-*Agia Mavri* provides a glimpse of local village life in the early seventh century.[25]

These distinct sub-regions of the Troodos — the northern slopes, the rugged western hills, and the coastlands to the south — offer complementary perspectives of rural life in Late Antiquity.[26] Despite differences in location, topography, and climate, the broad agreement of data across western Cyprus suggests that habitation expanded through Late Antiquity and reached its greatest extent around the middle of the sixth century. The density of rural settlement trailed off over the following decades, rather earlier on the remote western slopes than in areas farther east. After 650, the material record appears sharply reduced everywhere, leaving little that is certain by the time of the second Justinian, and even less for centuries afterwards. Explicitly recognized or not, nearly all surveys have encountered the challenge of an implausibly empty landscape, stemming from the seeming invisibility of post-Roman material culture and the limits of empirical inquiry.[27] Written accounts add little to our understanding of the later seventh and eighth centuries, setting episodes of bad news — coastal violence, massacres, and forced relocations — against a meager background of reliable information. Literary sources, like the eighth-century *Life of Demetrianos,* mention the persistence of some villages, churches, and festivals, but generally leave the countryside in the dark until the Byzantine re-conquest of the mid-tenth century.[28]

Looking closer at another part of the Cypriot countryside may not resolve this longstanding problem but offers an instructive perspective of it. The lowlands to the southeast of the Troodos,

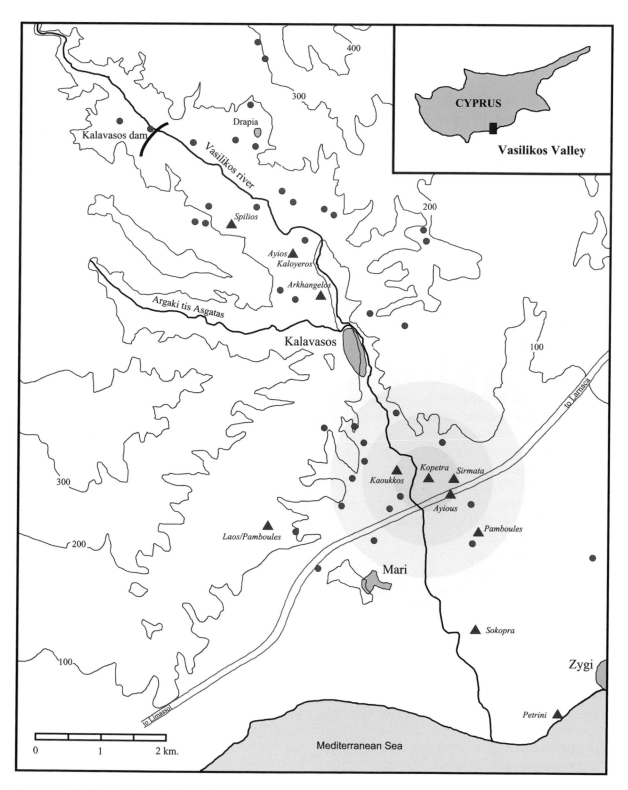

FIG. 4.5 *Vasilikos valley, distribution of primary (triangles) and secondary (circles) late Roman occupation sites.*

beyond modern Limassol, have long appeared among the most productive parts of the island. A series of parallel rivers drain the eastern slopes through chalky valleys before entering the broad coastal plain. Long-term investigation of this area has traced complex patterns of land use and occupation over the span of eight millennia. Three recent surveys of adjacent river valleys have found evidence for extensive occupation in prehistoric and early historical times, when the area probably lay within the territory of Amathous. Exploration of the ancient city and its environs by the French School of Athens (EFA, since 1975) has found small scattered settlements of Hellenistic date, which apparently dwindled in number during the first centuries CE before expanding again in the fifth to seventh centuries.[29] Similar results have been reported by the Maroni Valley Archaeological Survey Project (MVASP, 1990–1997). Intensive sampling of the valley floor has noted widespread activity in Roman times, when a series of minor sites were established along the coast and lower plain. The small basilica excavated at Maroni-*Petrera* illustrates the nature of local settlement in the sixth and early seventh centuries.[30]

More detailed information about long-term patterns of land use and occupation comes from the Vasilikos Valley Project (VVP, since 1976). Extensive field-walking in the valley has observed pronounced activity during the Neolithic period, the Late Bronze Age, and later antiquity (fig. 4.4).[31] The demands and benefits of Roman provincial administration apparently stimulated the growth of villages and farmsteads in the first two centuries CE. Two areas are of particular interest are a

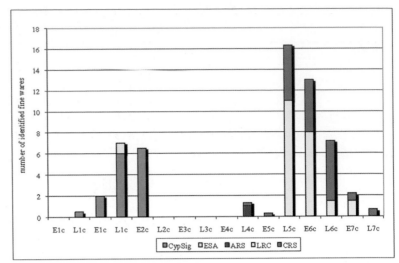

FIG. 4.6   *Kalavasos*-Spilios, *chronological distribution of dated survey pottery (n=57).*

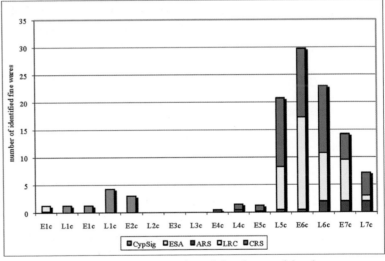

FIG. 4.7   *Kalavasos*-Ayious, *chronological distribution of dated survey pottery (n=107).*

group of small settlements (including *Petra* and *Spilios*) that developed around copper mines in the upper valley, and another (especially *Ayious* and *Pamboules*) that occupied a low plateau overlooking the river and coastal plain. After a time of apparent recession, widely noted elsewhere, activity rebounded in the fifth to seventh centuries. Late Roman pottery has been found at more than 50 locations in the VVP survey area, including two-thirds of the early Roman sites (fig. 4.5). Several of these grew into places of significant size and complexity. As was the case in the Late Bronze

FIG. 4.8   Kalavasos-Kopetra, *looking east from the Vasilikos river plain.*

Age, renewed interest in copper mining clearly benefited inhabitants of the upper valley, but also those living between mines and sea, close to the coastal roadway from Amathous to Kition (figs. 4.6–4.7). Smaller activity areas typically appear at intervals of one-half to one kilometer, near arable fields, pastures, and the coast.

Late Roman activities are clearest along the valley's eastern ridge, at the neighboring sites of *Ayious, Pamboules,* and a new settlement that developed at *Kopetra.* Survey and excavation by the Kalavasos-*Kopetra* Project (KKP, 1987–1995) documented a mid-size village, about four hectares in extent, which flourished here from the later fifth to mid-seventh century (fig. 4.8). The presence of stone basins, presses, and weights reflects the importance of agricultural processing by local residents. Excavation of different parts of the site found domestic units that were paved with gypsum slabs, had neatly plastered walls, and were covered by tile roofs. Recent trial excavations carried out by the Department of Antiquities in 2008 confirmed that similar structures, presumably domestic in purpose, indeed covered much of the ridge. The most substantial buildings identified by the KKP

were three churches. A 21-meter-long basilica, built near the northern edge of settlement (Area V), dates to the early sixth century. Within a couple generations, a second, 17-meter-long church had been constructed about 200 meters to the south (Area II; fig. 4.9). By the early 600s, a third basilica of comparable size stood at the center of a small monastery atop the nearby hill of *Sirmata* (Area I; fig. 4.10). Taken together, these three village landmarks track the area's economic expansion and the prosperity this brought local residents.

The churches at *Kopetra* and *Sirmata* reflect close contact with Amathous and other urban centers in the sixth century. As the earliest known churches in the valley, they imply that the spread of Christianity in Cyprus, well-attested in cities by the fourth century, may not have been uniform across the island. They also illustrate how external architectural ideas, such as the columnar basilica with its complex liturgical requirements, were received by a vernacular tradition (fig. 4.11). The practical difficulties faced by local builders can be seen in the way they fashioned slender cylindrical piers of mortared gypsum fragments and fieldstones, a process that makes an inherently pre-

FIG. 4.9 *Kalavasos*-Kopetra, *Area II, looking west.*

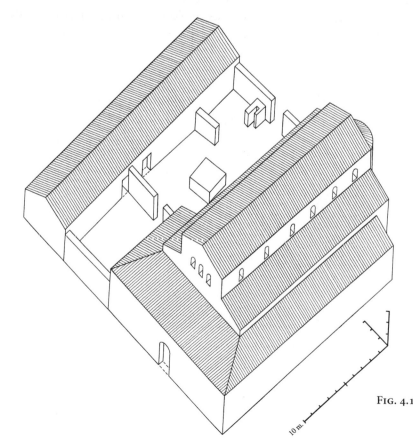

FIG. 4.10 *Kalavasos*-Sirmata, *reconstruction of monastic complex in the early 7th century.*

FIG. 4.11 *Kalavasos*-Sirmata, *basilica looking east.*

FIG. 4.12 *Kalavasos*-Kopetra, *Area II basilica, gypsum plaster relief of Virgin and Child.*

carious structural form even less stable.[32] Elegant plaster capitals, moldings, and decorative details at the south basilica seem to be the work of craftsmen brought from Amathous or even Constantia. Plaster fragments of baskets, birds, and quadrupeds suggest a lively church interior crowded with ornament. A small relief of the Virgin and Child, presumably made on site in the later sixth century, documents the remarkably swift diffusion of a metropolitan image into the Cypriot countryside (fig. 4.12). The sanctuary of the north basilica was paved with *opus sectile*. Geometric mosaics appear in the south lateral chapel and bema of the south church. Both buildings saw fine mosaics of polychrome glass with gold and silver accents in the semidome above the altar.[33]

Beyond their cultural contribution, the *Kopetra* basilicas provide essential information about economic and social life. Each of these monumental buildings offers a clear example of stationary investment — the setting aside of material wealth by a patron for purposes of public display and spiritual reward.[34] Beyond the cost of construction, these three churches were showcases for elite decorative materials scarcely known elsewhere in the valley: *opus sectile* paving, floor and vault mosaics, and moldmade plaster sculpture.[35] All three churches continued to function through the mid-seventh century, which increases the cumulative investment in maintenance and staff for an operational total of about 250 years.[36] One of these patrons, *Menelaos*, is known by a box-type monogram incised on a marble table at the south basilica. Presumably such sixth-century donors belonged to an emerging village elite, perhaps members of local families, but more likely drawn to the countryside from Amathous or another urban center. At the same time, the continued building of churches at Amathous and elsewhere shows that Cypriot cities remained viable places of private *euergetism*, even during times of widespread municipal decline.[37]

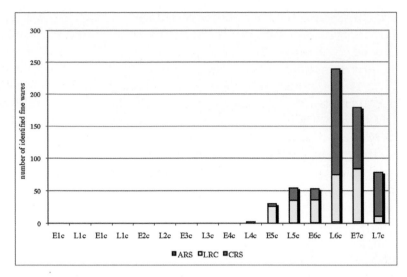

FIG. 4.13 *Kalavasos-*Kopetra, *chronological distribution of dated survey pottery (n=636).*

More specific information about rural lifeways comes from survey and excavation pottery from *Kopetra*.[38] Much of this takes the form of basins, jars, and storage *pithoi*, which seem to have been made of local clays and were intended for everyday household use. About half of the total assemblage is made up of transport amphorae, which brought agricultural commodities (mainly oil and wine) from across the Mediterranean, principally Cilicia, Syria, and Palestine, but also Egypt, the Aegean, and North Africa. Considering that some amphorae were likely used to redistribute or export goods, those remaining at the site document a lively consuming economy. The variety of imported, thin-walled, mass-produced cooking wares attests to the circulation of pans, casseroles, and pots from across Cyprus, Palestine, and Cilicia.

The variety of tablewares found at *Kopetra* offers essential evidence of local activities. Not only are the fine wares of Late Antiquity well-studied in their chronological and typological complexity, but as luxury items they reflect market availability and consumer choice. Nearly a third of all fine pottery at *Kopetra* consists of African Red Slip (ARS) and Phocean Red Slip (PRS) wares, which came from Tripolitania and west Asia Minor, respectively. The largest share is Cypriot Red Slip (CRS) ware, which seems to have been made in western Cyprus near Paphos.[39] The abundance of fine pottery reflects its daily use at village tables, along with glass vessels for eating, drinking, and lighting. The variety of this imported dining service demonstrates a growing demand for objects of modest luxury, which apparently served for social display beyond functional necessity. In this respect the purchase of glass and ceramic tablewares can be understood as a form of stationary investment on the level of the individual household. The material, decoration, and scarcity of such objects would have justified their cost mainly at places of long-term residence.[40]

Fine tablewares and other datable artifacts record *Kopetra*'s emergence between the late fifth and seventh centuries as one of the main settlements in the area (fig. 4.13). Local soils suited the raising of kitchen gardens as well as market crops, with the mid-valley location offering access to fields, quarries, and traffic along the coast. Perhaps 100 families lived at *Kopetra*, directly benefiting from this economic activity and investing their wealth in churches, houses, and furnishings. The nearby sites of *Ayious* and *Pamboules* had been occupied in early Roman times and, like *Kopetra*, plainly flourished in Late Antiquity as well (compare fig.

4.7). By around 600, this cluster of settlements had become the valley's principal market for local products and imported commodities.

The Vasilikos valley clearly documents the rural prosperity brought about by the political and economic integration of Cyprus within the late empire. Imperial policies encouraged the development of closer ties between the island and the Aegean in the later fifth and sixth centuries, which had tangible benefits for both regions. State-sponsored traffic between Constantinople and Alexandria, on the one hand, and along the Cilician coast, on the other, assured reliable access to wider markets for island products like Cypriot Red Slip ware and the oil, wine, and cereals that accompanied them. Justinian's creation in 536 of the *quaestura exercitus*, intended to provision troops posted along the Balkan frontier, brought Cyprus into even closer contact with Caria and the east Aegean islands, which experienced similar economic expansion in the sixth and early seventh centuries.[41] Such fiscal arrangements would have stimulated commercial and social traffic in many forms, from long-distance exchange and pilgrimage to coastal cabotage. The short-lived Persian successes of the early 600s may have interrupted trading contact with the East, but would also have increased the island's strategic importance, as well as its economic dependence on the capital.[42]

The long-term consequences of these provincial dynamics become apparent in the mid-seventh century, when the Arab campaigns left Cyprus in a state of political limbo between Constantinople and Damascus.[43] The disruption of prevailing routes of communication and exchange would have been clear everywhere but was especially acute in coastal cities, secondary towns, and market villages, whose residents turned of necessity from raising specialized surplus crops to meeting subsistence needs. The resulting contraction of rural habitation appears across the island but with special clarity in the Vasilikos valley. Prosperous settlements like *Kopetra* would have been plainly visible from the coast, making them vulnerable targets in insecure times. Most of the buildings here were found to have experienced burning or other structural damage around the middle of the century. The discovery of multiple

bodies in a cistern at *Sirmata* clearly documents an episode of intentional violence and desecration of place.[44]

The limited signs of later activity are equally informative. The narthex crypt at *Sirmata* was repaired, and small hearths and a bread oven were set up around the nearby courtyard. Two hundred meters to the west, two small chapels were built at east end of the south basilica. Evidence for dating this reoccupation consists of a coin of 659/60 and several distinctive types of pottery: late examples of Cypriot and African Red Slip wares, a jug with paddle-smoothed walls, LR1 and LR13 amphorae in Cypriot fabric, and thick-walled hand-made vessels (fig. 4.14). The coin and tablewares suggest that some degree of contact with Amathous and the wider empire continued after the Arab attacks of 649 and 653. The amphorae and cooking pots, by contrast, may have originated within the Vasilikos valley.[45]

One would expect many of these features of the later seventh century to be present elsewhere in the Cypriot countryside, even if they are not always recognized as such. Limited production of Cypriot Red Slip ware seems to have persisted until about the year 700, and some mainland imitations may have continued even longer.[46] Most of the late products of Cypriot Red Slip and African Red Slip workshops are sturdy dishes, plates, and basins, which could be mended and remain in use long after their manufacture.[47] Similar flat-bottomed, paddle-smoothed jugs have been reported in seventh-century or later contexts on the mainland.[48] LR1 and LR13 amphorae are known to have been manufactured at multiple (and sometimes even the same) sites across the east Mediterranean into the eighth century.[49] Storage *pithoi* and roof tiles of any period tend to be stationary objects with a long lifespan. Hand-made cooking pots have been found by survey and excavated in seventh-century contexts from the Akamas and Paphos to Kourion, Maroni, and Constantia.[50] Recent work on the mainland confirms the lingering currency of some of these wares in territory that remained under nominal Byzantine control. Surveys and excavations in Cilicia, Pamphylia, and Pisidia report evidence for rural habitation amid signs of wider retrenchment.[51] Late forms of red-slipped

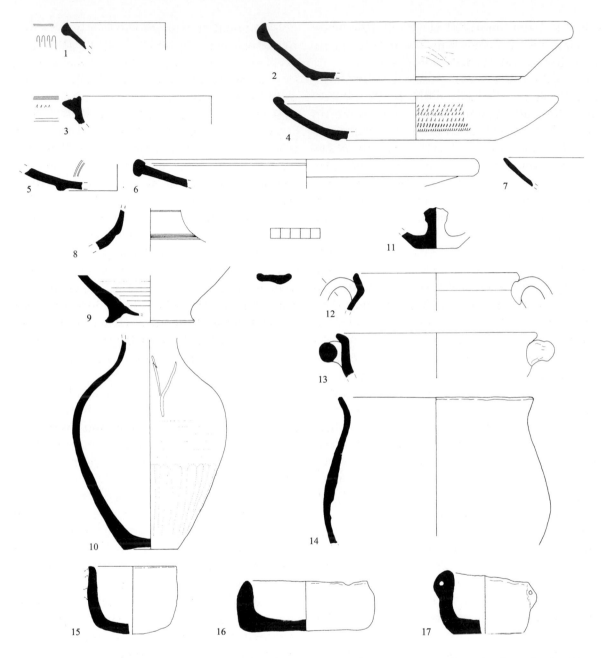

FIG. 4.14 Kopetra, *Area II, representative pottery from late occupation: 1 (Rautman 2003, no. II-16-2), 2 (no. 20), 3 (no. II-16-1), 4 (no. 34), 5 (no. 73), 6 (no. 74), 7 (no. 83), 8 (no. II-3-1), 9 (no. 126), 10 (no. 128), 11 (no. 140), 12 (no. 187), 13 (no. 189), 14 (no. 197), 15 (no. II-2-1), 16 (no. II-12-1), 17 (no. II-13-1).*

pottery, globular amphorae, and non-standard cooking pots appear in seventh- to ninth-century contexts at coastal Limyra and inland at Sagalassos.[52] Interestingly, not all of these wares turn up in Umayyad levels in Syria, Palestine, and Egypt, where a picture of continued habitation is emerging as well.[53]

The importance of these transitional ceramics is emphasized by what surveys in Cyprus rarely find: sites with clearly diagnostic material of the eighth to ninth centuries. Constantinopolitan Glazed White Wares, globular amphorae, and lead-glazed cooking pots may be uncommon at urban sites but are exceptional in the countryside.[54] Isolated reports of coins and lead seals emphasize their scarcity outside coastal cities. In the vicinity of the Vasilikos valley, for example, an early eighth-century Umayyad *fals* is said to come from Kophinou, about twelve kilometers northeast of Kalavasos. Additional examples may yet be reported, like the 30 to 40 or more unpublished seals allegedly found nearby.[55] After 50 years of systematic reconnaissance, however, it appears that such material played a limited role in rural lifeways, which continued well enough without them.

More convincing circumstantial evidence of rural activity may be the presence at the same locations of identifiable artifacts dating both before the eighth century and after the ninth century. A similar gap, in third- to fourth-century material, has been widely noted at Roman sites that were also inhabited during Late Antiquity.[56] While not all such locations were continuously occupied over this interval, in many cases their significance seems to have been remembered by later inhabitants.[57] It is possible to argue that this persistence of place through the eighth and ninth centuries varies with location and increases when moving inland, reflecting flight from coastal hazards during insecure times. Survey of the lower Mesaoria plain found signs of medieval activity at only 10% of late Roman sites, compared to about 20% in the Vasilikos survey area, nearly 30% in the Palaipaphos vicinity, to perhaps 40% in the Yialias valley.[58] Alternatively, these data may indicate the narrowing of island-wide variations in settlement density, which was greatest near coastal cities, towns, and market villages, to more sustainable, sub-regional levels that were less dependent on the networks of empire.[59]

The interruption of reliable routes of commercial and fiscal exchange in the later seventh century, combined with taxes due to both Constantinople and Damascus, would have encouraged many Cypriot families to revaluate household economies and live closer to their base of subsistence. As noted on the mainland, the transformation of traditional settlement patterns around this time created new habitation entities of variable appearance and function. Some of these hybrid formations seem to have abandoned the model of nucleation in favor of corporate identities, ecclesiastical as well as fiscal, which could extend over a dispersed population.[60] Without fixed centers of investment, habitation would appear markedly less evident on the ground. Small cultivators may have moved seasonally among scattered holdings, setting up buildings to provide shelter rather than to serve as social landmarks. Pastoral households probably relocated over even wider territory throughout the year. In the absence of centrally produced durable goods, local utility wares, wooden vessels, baskets, and the like would have claimed a greater role in daily routines. Such lives cross the threshold of material visibility only when their activities become stationary, and are repeated by generations of rural inhabitants addressing recurring needs.[61]

Rural lives in antiquity are among the most challenging for us to understand, the most resistant to external interference then and observation now. Our view of the Cypriot countryside, however incomplete and eroded by the years, suggests a landscape whose inhabitants adapted constantly to urban interests and outside powers. Closer ties with the mainland in the sixth century fostered economic growth, social complexity, and stationary investment in settlements that depended on efficient commercial networks and were unsuited to their absence. Earthquake, famine, plague, massacre, and deportation — all these touched many lives, especially along the coast, but of wider consequence may have been the realignment of imperial authority and the networks of interregional exchange it had made possible. As elsewhere in the east Mediterranean, the persistent if less conspicuous occupation of the Cypriot countryside after the seventh century should be sought on the level of local communities, in their ongoing response to the shifting balance of empires.

NOTES

1 Megaw 1986; Papageorghiou 1993; Metcalf 2009.

2 Our knowledge of rural life in late Roman Cyprus rests on the contributions of many people, archaeologists, surveyors, artifact specialists, and student volunteers, as well as the hospitality of landowners across the island.

3 Catling 1980: 24. For cultural implications of the island's provincial status, compare Megaw's (1974) use of the term and concerns raised by Ćurčić 2000: 8.

4 Karageorghis 1985; Roueché 2002; Iakovou 2004.

5 Mitford 1980 remains a valuable overview.

6 Papageorghiou 1993; Gregory 2001. The Peutinger Table, as revised c. 400, suggests the most important of these were Salamis, Paphos, Soloi, Kyrenia, and Tremithous; see Talbert 2010: 89–90.

7 Yannopoulos 1983; Cameron 1992; Chrysos 1993; Krueger 1996: 4–11; Metcalf 2009: 346–51.

8 For the growing importance of such settlements across the empire, see Brandes and Haldon 2000: 147–50; Morrisson and Sodini 2002: 179–81.

9 Christou 1993: 70–72; Hadjisavvas 2000: 692–93; Caraher et al. 2005, 2007; Caraher, Moore, and Pettegrew 2008: 85–88.

10 For survey of the Akrotiri peninsula, see Sollars 2005: chapter 4 and fig. 4.20. The martyrium is discussed by Procopiou (this volume).

11 For coast activity, see Leonard and Demesticha 2004; Leidwanger 2005, 2007.

12 Bakirtzis 1995, 1997, 2001; Michaelides 2002: 43–56; Raptes and Vasileiadou 2005. The environs of the site have been explored by Sollars 2005: chapter 6. The density of Roman settlement on the coastal plain increases as one approaches Paphos; see Hadjisavvas 1977; Rupp 1997; Baird 1985: 346. For maritime traffic, see Giangrande et al. 1987; Leonard and Demesticha 2004.

13 Pliny, *Naturalis Historia* 18.12.67–68); Strabo, *Geographica* 14.6.5; Ammianus Marcellinus, *Res Gestae* 14.8.14.

14 *De Magistratibus reipublicae Romanae* 2.29; Michaelides 1996: 144–46; Papacostas 2001: 111–12.

15 Brandes and Haldon 2000: 148–50; Lefort 2002: 275–76; Morrisson and Sodini 2002: 177–84; Laiou 2005: 36–38; compare with Veikou 2009: 44–47, for the complexities of differentiating levels of rural settlement in Greece.

16 For Lycia, see Elton 2006: 239–40; for Cilicia, see Varinlioğlu 2008.

17 Such estimates build on inconclusive discussion of the island's population and the effects of plague, immigration, war, and deportation in the 6th and 7th centuries. For a recent assessment, see Metcalf 2009: 400–402.

18 For a recent overview of archaeological survey in Cyprus, see Iakovou 2004; for its contribution to the study of late antiquity, see Caraher, Moore, and Pettegrew 2008: 82–84.

19 Catling 1972: 4–5; 2008: 201–9; Cadogan 2004. For additional observations see Hadjisavaas 1991; Killian 2008: 92–95. The problem of distinguishing settlements by size and function of surface artifacts is discussed by Winther-Jacobsen 2010.

20 Christodoulou 1959; Thirgood 1987. For recent assessments of the Troodos region and the impact of landscape change on archaeological visibility, see Deckers 2005; Butzer and Harris 2007.

21 R. S. Moore in Given and Knapp 2003: 277–82; Graham, Winther-Jacobsen, and Kassianidou 2006; Given, Corley, and Sollars 2007; Winther-Jacobsen 2010: 73–100.

22 Adovasio et al. 1975: 349; Maliszewski et al. 2003. Survey and excavations by the DAP are reported by Fejfer 1995; Fejfer and Hayes 1995.

23 Hadjisavvas 1977; Rupp 1997.

24 For the results of the CPSP, see Rupp 1986: 35–39, table 1, fig. 3; compare with Sørensen and Rupp 1993: figs. 58 and 60. For discussion of the Kourion environs, see Swiny and Mavromatis 2000; Sollars 2005; Jasink 2010: 38–39.

25 Flourentzos 1996; for comparative analysis of the mortuary remains, see Harper and Fox 2008: 16–18.

26 Comparing data among projects is complicated by varying objectives, methods, resources, and field conditions, but can constructively identify points of agreement as well as discrepancy; Rautman 2004: 191, 211–12; Iakovou 2005.

27 Gregory in Given and Knapp 2003: 283–84; compare with recent discussion of the wider problem in Pettegrew 2010.

28 Metcalf 2009: 425–97; for the *Life of Demetrianos*, see Ryden 1993: 197–202.

29 Petit, Péchoux, and Dieulafait 1996: 176–79, plan 20; for the survey area and several sites with late Roman pottery, see Briois, Petit-Aupert, and Péchoux 2005.

30 Manning et al. 2002: 7–16, 77–79.

31 Todd 2004 and forthcoming.

32 Rautman 2003: 45–53. Compare Papageorghiou 1963 for the use of similar materials in the 5th- or 6th-century basilica at Marathovounou. Traditional Cypriot building methods are discussed by Wright 1992.

33 For architectural sculpture and mosaics, see Rautman 2003; for their Cypriot context, Korol 2000.

34 The economic dimension of rural churches in the east Mediterranean is explored by Bowden 2001; Elton 2006; Dunn 2007: 103–4; and Sweetman 2010.

35 The VVP field survey reports only a few isolated tesserae and stone fragments. For mosaic and *opus sectile* floors in other Cypriot churches, see Michaelides 1988, 1993; Hadjichristophi 2000; for wall and vault mosaics, Korol 2000. Carved and form-cast plaster sculpture is best known at the House of the Oil Press at Salamis; see Argoud, Callot, and Helly 1980. The south basilica at *Kopetra* offers the most extensive remains from a church on the island.

36 Founded in the early 6th century, the north basilica functioned for about 125 years. The south basilica's primary phase of use (c. 575–650) was followed by limited reoccupation of its sanctuary and south chapel. Parts of the *Sirmata* complex (c. 600–650) saw limited reoccupation as well.

37 Rautman 2003: 109–11. For recent work at Amathous, carried out by the Department of Antiquities (1975–2006) and the French School of Athens (since 1980), see Aupert 1996: 61–65; Lehmann 2005; Flourentzos 2008.

38 Pottery from *Kopetra* is presented in Rautman 2003: 162–215.

39 For discussion of Cypriot Red Slip's area of production, see Rautman 2003: 164–65; Lund 2006: 214; Meyza 2007: 17–20. Western Cyprus remains the most likely source for the ware, which apparently spawned a number of regional copies.

40 For red-slipped tablewares as a facet of Romanization, see Poblome and Zelle 2002: 276–81; the same might be said of domestic silver plate, whose (portable) intrinsic value is offset by the need for (stationary) security.

41 Bakirtzis 1995, 1997; Morrisson and Sodini 2002: 191–92. For the role of Cilicia in fiscal traffic, see Iaconi 2010. Recent work on Rhodes is presented by Deligiannakis 2008; for Kos, see Diamanti 2010; Poulou-Papadimitriou and Dimioumi 2010. For east Mediterranean sailing routes, see Arnaud 2005: 216–23.

42 Bowersock 2000: 18–21; Rautman 2003: 257–58.

43 Cameron 1992; Chrysos 1993. The dates and consequences of the Arab campaigns are reviewed by Metcalf 2009: 395–418.

44 Rautman 2003: 71.

45 For late contexts at the south basilica, see Rautman 2003: 102–9. For the handmade cooking wares, see Rautman 1998. Production of LR1 and LR13 amphorae at nearby Zygi-*Petrini* is discussed by Manning et al. 2000; Demesticha 2003.

46 For late production of Cypriot Red Slip, see Hayes 2007: 435–36; Meyza 2007: 97–82; Armstrong 2009. A conjectured Umayyad garrison at Paphos from 653/63 until 680/83 (suggested by Megaw 1986: 513–16; compare Metcalf 2009: 412) would have ensured stability for local workshops as well as access to coastal markets in southern *Bilad al-Sham*. The fabric and shapes usually associated with western Cyprus are scarce after c. 700, both on Cyprus (e.g., Hayes 2003: 502–6; Gabrielli, Jackson, and Kaldelli 2007: 796) and the mainland (e.g., Reynolds 2003: 726). Production of a Pamphylian version of the ware may have continued into the 8th century; see Armstrong 2006, 2009.

47 Vroom 2003: 282–83; Peña 2007: 246–49; Winther-Jacobsen 2010: 111–30. Compare average sherd weights for fine wares at *Kopetra* in Rautman 2003: 164–66, table 5.3; see 188 no. 68 for a repaired early 6th-century African Red Slip bowl (form 93) found in a 7th-century context.

48 Vionis, Poblome, and Waelkens 2009: 156–58.

49 For Cyprus, see Touma 2001; Demesticha 2003. For Cilicia, see Ferrazzoli and Ricci 2010. For Kos, see Poulou-Papadimitriou and Didioumi 2010.

50 In general, Rautman 1999; 2003: 175–76. For Paphos and Yeroskippou, see Gabieli, Jackson, and Kaldelli 2007: 795–96; for examples at Maroni-*Petrera*, see R. Tomber in Manning et al. 2002: 52; for Kourion, see

Hayes 2007: 437, 446; for Constantia, see Diederichs 1980: 33.

51 Armstrong 2006: 24–26; Vanhaverbeke et al. 2009; Varinlioğlu 2008: 312–16.

52 Vroom 2007; Vionis, Poblome, and Waelkens 2009.

53 Sodini and Villeneuve 1992; Lewin and Pellegrini 2006; Walmsley 2008; Haldon 2010.

54 Hayes 1980: 379–80; 2003: 502–6, 511–14 for 8th- to 9th-century material excavated at Saranda Kolones in Paphos. For rural surveys, see Gregory 1993: 157; Gregory in Given and Knapp 2003: 283–84. Medieval pottery in the Vasilikos valley is discussed by B. J. Walker in Todd, forthcoming.

55 For the Kophinou *fals,* see Metcalf 2009: 178, and 587 for seals from the vicinity of Kalavasos.

56 Lund 1993: 141; 2006: 213–15; Rautman in Todd, forthcoming.

57 Compare Given 2007: 146.

58 Catling and Dikigoropoulos 1970: 57–60; Megaw 1986: 505–6; Rautman 2003: 261–62, based on Hadjisavvas 1991, Gregory 1993, Lund 1993, Catling 1982, and Todd 2004.

59 Compare recent discussion of rural settlement in south Greece in Pettegrew 2010: 226–27.

60 Such transitional entities in Epirus are discussed by Veikou 2009: 43–44.

61 For the viability of rural households, see Lefort 2002; Dunn 2007: 104–9; for their visibility, see Hardy 2010. Compare the discussion of rural economies in Ottoman Cyprus by Given 2000, 2007.

Chapter 5

The North–South Divide
in Byzantine Cyprus:
Some Evidence from Lead Seals and Coins

by D. M. Metcalf

Fifty years ago, our ideas about the governance of Cyprus during the so-called "condominium centuries" (better called the "treaty centuries") from 688 to 965 were based on such few and exiguous written sources, accompanied by such limited archaeological information, that Dikigoropoulos was able to suggest that the Cypriots at that time were essentially self-governing.[1] They viewed the iconoclast rulers with disfavour, but asked the emperor to send them an imperial servant to help them manage their affairs. This rather implausible picture has been and is being radically redrawn through the systematic study of lead seals, and through a closer examination of the numismatic evidence. The first half of the eighth century in particular was a time of great changes for the province. Also, we are beginning to acquire the material evidence which allows us to appreciate that conditions were not uniform throughout the island. There was a north–south divide, in terms of the exercise of military and political power, and also in terms of foreign trade, which we need to bear in mind when we are attempting to construe the written sources.

Our assessment of the "treaty centuries" should be based obviously on all the available evidence, whether documentary or archaeological, but in this chapter I am concerned only to draw attention to what coins and lead seals can contribute — which would otherwise be more or less unknowable. An attempt will be made to isolate and summarize a dozen disparate arguments concerning the governance and the economic trends in Cyprus, mainly in the period following the Arab invasions and running on into the "treaty centuries."[2] For convenience, the separate topics are numbered. How far their evidence is cumulative or mutually reinforcing is a matter for careful judgement in the context of all the evidence.

1.

The distribution map (fig 5.1) shows a north–south contrast as regards to stray finds of coins from the years 688 to 965. The find-spots of Byzantine coins, marked by crosses, are found in most parts of the island, especially the northern coastlands. But with the Islamic coins, marked by dots, they are mainly confined to the southern coastlands, especially the Paphos district. A comparable map of finds of lead seals would tell very much the same story, with a remarkable cluster of eighth-century Byzantine lead seals from a site near Polis, and

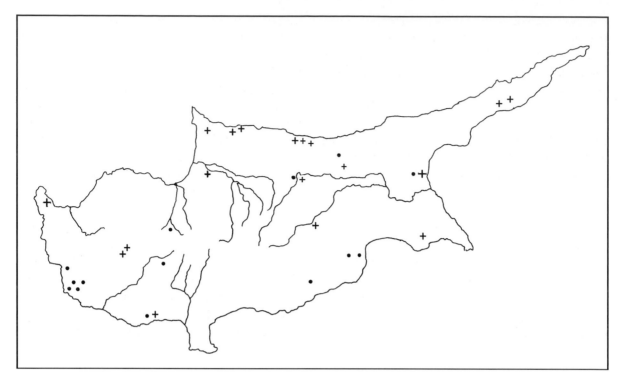

FIG. 5.1   *Findspots of coins from 688–965. Key: crosses = Byzantine coins, dots = Islamic coins.*

various other finds in the northern coastlands (e.g., in and around Kyrenia and
also at Constantia).[3] Besides Lambousa
and Constantia, the quantity of finds on
record is much less in the north, and the
material from the "treaty centuries" makes
up a significantly higher proportion of the
total than is the case in the south. Islamic
lead seals are relatively very few in Cyprus,
but they are (again) largely confined to
the southern coastlands, especially the
Paphos district and with Nicosia as an outlying
provenance.[4] The two distribution patterns help
to confirm each other. More finds, both of coins
and of lead seals, would certainly be welcome
in order to thicken up the distribution patterns,
especially as regards the occupied north. I believe,
however, that the tendency is already clear and is
very unlikely to be nullified by future discoveries.

FIG. 5.2   *Lead seal of Theodoros,* Kleisourarch; *Metcalf 2004: cat.
no. 212. Not to scale.*

2.

Whereas any argument from within-sample contrasts in distribution patterns is at root statistical
in character, and is to that extent relative, being

based on probabilities, the existence of lead seals
of a Byzantine official called a *kleisourarch* (fig. 5.2)
is absolute evidence. It reveals administrative provision against a perceived threat, and of an internal
frontier which lay, we need not doubt, along the
line of the Pentadaktylos range.[5] The *kleisoura*
(checkpoint or mountain pass), which it was this
official's responsibility to guard, was presumably in
the vicinity of St. Hilarion castle, and his task was
to be watchful for any attempted military raid on
Kyrenia launched from the Mesaoria. His duties
may have extended also to the other passes further east. So far as we know at present, there was

a *kleisourarch* only for a relatively short period in the late eighth or early ninth century; that is, we know of only one individual, Theodoros, who held the post. That could, of course, change as new finds come to light.

3.

In 649, Mu'awiya, the Muslim governor of Syria and future caliph, invaded Cyprus causing great material damage and loss of life. He no doubt besieged the walled cities and breached their defences. On withdrawing, he carried away many of the able-bodied into slavery. In 649 and again in 650, he also besieged Aradus off the coast of Syria using siege engines. In 653, Mu'awiya invaded Cyprus again.[6] The Soloi inscription describes the second invasion as "more lamentable than the preceding one." An even greater number of people were killed or led away prisoner. The Arab historian al-Baladhuri says that the second invasion was punitive, launched because the Cypriots had broken the treaty conditions of AH 32 (652) by supplying the Empire with ships. Now in 649, Mu'awiya would surely have seized any Cypriot ships that were riding at anchor. Does that mean that the remaining Cypriots had been building ships in 649–52, and if so, whereabouts in Cyprus? Presumably on the north coast, which had access to timber and was that much closer to the naval protection of the Kibyrrhaiote squadron. Unlike the Muslim conquest of Syria and Palestine, Mu'awiya did not conquer Cyprus on any permanent basis; the honours were shared, because he was not able to hold the northern coastlands. From there the Cypriots fought back. For several decades their ambition, backed by the central government, was to restore the status quo.

4.

Valuable as it is, the Soloi inscription, which was set up in 655, tells only one side of a complex and evolving story in which regional differences play their part. There is a major conflict of evidence between the pitiful accounts of death, destruction, and enslavement in the mid-seventh century and the evidence of lead seals, which shows that in the succeeding decades the governance of the province was conducted energetically by the archbishop and his suffragan bishops, and by a cadre headed by a score or more of civic notables with the senatorial dignity of *illoustrios*. Exact dating in relation to key historical events is always the "Achilles' heel" of sigillographic evidence, but by fortunate chance we dispose of a substantial archive of at least 157 lead seals of which the date (to within a few years) is secure. That is simply because it included a considerable number of lead seals with the distinctive monogram of Archbishop Epiphanios II, whose dates we know. It also included many more of the *illoustrioi* Petros and Stephanos, the latter certainly belonging to Constantia.[7] It is not known exactly where the archive was found, but very probably in the north — at a guess, possibly at Lambousa (Byzantine Lapithos). Or it may have belonged, for example, to the bishop of Soloi. It was abandoned at a date around 690 to 695, which coincides with the historical occasion of the transfer of Cypriots with their archbishop to the mainland.

Extrapolating from the fixed point of lead seals of Epiphanios II, we can construct a series of the lead seals of earlier archbishops. Prior to Arkadios (most of the lead seals with that name are arguably of Arkadios II) there are very few specimens, and one's impression is that the volume of sealed correspondence, far from declining, increased dramatically after the Arab invasions.[8] What is true for the archbishops is probably also true for the lead seals of their suffragan bishops, and even of secular officials as well. We must suspect that the volume of sealed correspondence followed the same trajectory as with the archbishops. Most, but by no means all, of the surviving seals originated in the north.

From the cities of the southern coastlands, especially Amathous and Khlorakas, there are plenty of lead seals of similar date to those in the archive, but they belonged to other named bishops and *illoustrioi*. That amounts to clear evidence that the dispersal of these varieties of lead seals was regionally restricted, that is, to Amathous and its diocese or to Paphos and its diocese.

In spite of the Muslim invasions, the traditional style of governance by church and state was resumed in the second half of the seventh century throughout the island. To an extent that Dikigoropoulos misjudged, Cyprus was full of

FIG. 6.1   *Akrotiri Peninsula, Cyprus (red square on insert). The* Katalymata ton Plakoton *site is marked in the red ellipse (1). Other areas marked in red indicate settlements of the Late Roman/Early Christian period, charted during the Archaeological Field survey (1954–2010): (2)* Kato Katalymata; *(3)* Pano Katalymata; *(4)* Shillastasia; *(5) Arkosykia. © 2012 Google, © 2012 DigitalGlobe, © 2012 GeoEye.*

centuries. These brief archaeological projects have given us a glimpse of the significant material culture that has yet to be systematically excavated in the Akrotiri Peninsula.

The current excavations at *Katalymata ton Plakoton,* which is located in the western part of the peninsula, revealed a monumental ecclesiastic complex of the Early Byzantine period. At this point, only the western part has been uncovered, which we have labeled "Building A" (figs. 6.2–6.4). It is a T-shaped structure, measuring 36 meters in width by 29 meters in length (excluding the protruding apse to the west), and is most likely not the main church of the complex. Nevertheless, it has the form of a three-aisled transept basilica, with a continuous side corridor (περίστωον) surrounding the main aisle. This corridor begins at the east

side-entrances and terminates at the north and south perimeter of a raised platform (ἐξέδρα).[7] This podium is the focal point of the entire structure, located where the transept arms intersect, measuring 10 meters in length by 7.80 meters in width. At the north end flanking the nave, we uncovered a possible portico and an adjacent hall. On the southern end, five other adjacent rooms were discovered.

The excavation exposed a type of wall construction which has not been recorded in other archaeological publications. First, the builders laid the foundations using carved and irregular stones together with mortar. Then wooden slats were placed on either side of the wall, forming a rectangular mold. Next, the builders poured plaster on top, binding the stones together. The stones were positioned so as to not touch the molds, resulting in

FIG. 6.2 *The result of the excavation from 2007 to 2009 at Aktrotiri*-Katalymata ton Plakoton.

FIG. 6.3 *The limits of the 2010 excavation at Aktrotiri*-Katalymata ton Plakoton.

denominations of ten, five, and six *nummi* (figs. 6.12—6.13), from the mints of Carthage and Alexandria, dating to the first decade of the reign of Emperor Heraclius, most probably before the conquest of Alexandria in 617. These coins can be regarded as the *terminus ante quem* for the construction date of the monument. Moreover, a *terminus post quem* coin has been found at the northwest corner in the foundation trench, 1.23 meters below the floor level, which is dated to 616 AD (fig. 6.14). A few well-preserved coins, uncovered during the recent 2012 excavation season, indicate a short period of use up to the year 641.

At the east side of the southern transept there was, in the center of the aisle wall, a small rectangular niche. Adjacent to this niche was discovered a small reliquary cover of marble. In figure 6.15 an arrow indicates the find spot at ground level. We can assume that the location and congruent shape of the reliquary cover indicates it once rested within the wall niche. This artifact, as well as the burials in the apses, underscore the funerary character of the entire structure, and hence its function as a martyrium.

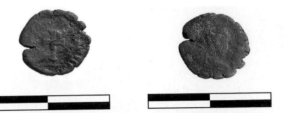

FIG. 6.12   *Reverse and obverse of a 5-*nummi *bronze coin (N6) from the larnax. Carthage mint, Heraclian reign, before 617.*

FIG. 6.13   *A 6-*nummi *bronze coin (N9) from the larnax. Alexandrian mint, Heraclian reign, before 617.*

FIG. 6.14   *Obverse and reverse of a half* follis *(20-*nummi*) bronze coin (N5) from the foundation trench of the west wall of the north transept arm (1.23 meters below floor level). Thessaloniki mint. (B)-616.*

FIG. 6.15
Niche in the center of the east wall of the south branch, close to which the small reliquary marble cover was found.

FIG. 6.16 *The raised central area (platform) at the crossing of the branches.*

THE CENTRAL PLATFORM (ἐξέδρα)

The raised central area, or platform (fig. 6.16), terminates in an apse at its western end. The apse is semicircular internally and polygonal on the exterior. Within the conch of that apse there is a smaller semicircle with the same diameter as the other aisle apses (2.25 meters). This area was surrounded by an ambulatory paved with trapezoidal marble plaques according to the traces preserved on the mortar substratum.

The sides of the platform were demarcated with low parapets, similar to a chancel screen. The western end of the parapet was built and decorated with marble revetments. In the central area, the base of a monolithic chancel is preserved. The chancel had fallen *in situ* along with a small pillar. In the center of the transenna (i.e., a large marble slab that formed part of the screen) was

carved in low relief a perforated monogram of Jesus Christ (Chrismon). A so-called "Chrismon cross" is formed when the iota (Ι – Ἰησοῦς) lies above a cross, which is above the chi (Χ – Χριστός) (fig. 6.17). A wreath surrounds the Chrismon cross and is flanked by crosses connected by curvilinear sprouts ending in ivy leaves. The entire composition is framed by a border of three concentric fillets. The chancel is a well-known type, widespread throughout the Empire in the late fifth and sixth centuries.[12] Examples are known from Constantinople, Italy, Asia Minor, mainland Greece, the Aegean Islands, the Balkans, Libya, Tynesia, Palestine, and elsewhere.[13]

Within the platform were two low benches along the north and south parapets (fig. 6.18). These probably functioned as seats or tables. Moreover, the parapet did not extend along the entire length of the platform. Flush with the

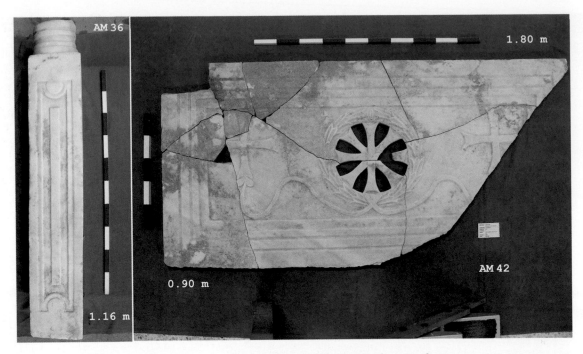

FIG. 6.17   *Marble pillar and transenna. From a chancel found fallen* in situ *close to its base.*

benches were openings on each side, indicating free communication with the center aisle of the transepts, where additional table bases were discovered beside columns (mainly at the east colonnade).

The platform was also demarcated by the crossing square, where the colonnades of the nave and transepts converge. At the corners are preserved four complex (Γ or T-shape) supports, forming a square of 6.15 meters. In the middle of the eastern end, the threshold is preserved, leading to an axial corridor of 3.65 meters in length. This formed the official entrance to the platform from the nave, and was opposite the central opening of the *tribelon*, which connected the structure to the other parts of the complex.

The platform served as the focal point of the whole structure. It was clearly emphasized for use by the clergy, who would perform services relating to the main saint's relics

FIG. 6.18   *Red areas highlight the foundation of benches along the sides of the platform (ἐξέδρα).*

FIG. 6.19 *The corridor attached to the east side of the platform (ἐξέδρα).*

arrangement (τρίστωον) of each transept arm. First, the celebrant was directed through the narrow corridor in the center aisle when he entered or exited (fig. 6.19). Second, after arriving at the platform, the clergy had access to the central apse and the transept arms through the openings in the chancel screen.

The floor of the martyrium was completely covered in mosaics. Most of the designs are abstract geometrical patterns. There are also many prominent representational forms with symbols like the so-called "Shield of David"[15] (placed in the central aisle of the north transept arm, fig. 6.21), a pair of gourds (or zucchinis), and a pair of Persian/Parthian shoes (τσαγγία).[16] These are contained within eight squares in the walkway leading to the threshold of the platform (figs. 6.19 and 6.22). The gourds can be interpreted as a symbol of the ignorance of nations according to the Prophecy of Jonah and, when paired with the Parthian shoes, perhaps symbolize warnings of destruction, as that of Nineveh, in relation to the Persian invasion of the Byzantine Empire at the time.[17] Another key image is in front of the semicircle of the central apse, which shows two stags drinking the water of life from a vine in a *cantharus*—a symbol of Jesus Christ (figs. 6.20–22).[18]

LITURGICAL FUNCTION

It is necessary to excavate the entire complex in order to specifically define the liturgical function of the architectural components. However, some preliminary interpretations can be discussed, since it is clear that the structure of "Building A" functioned as a martyrium and was attached to an atrium (as uncovered during the last two seasons). The martyrium had a podium that accommodated a particular liturgy; surrounding this was

within the apse and the other saints in the transept. Large quantities of table fragments, along with the benches in the transept and the sides of the platform, indicate ceremonies concerning offertory gifts. A preliminary suggestion is that such furnishings could be identified as "side altars" (παρατραπέζια), which were used, according to the primary sources, as secondary tables for offerings during a "pre-sanctifying service." Upon these surfaces would be placed Eucharistic bread and wine (πρόσφορον, νάμα), or they would be used in the blessings of other gifts (i.e., wine, oil, wax, honey, stone, and loaves; οἶνον, ἔλαιον, κῆρον, μέλι, ὠπόρας, και εὐλογίαι), and the pieces of consecrated bread for distribution later to individuals not present during the liturgy.[14] Other furnishings included the *mensae martyrum* (τράπεζαι μαρτύρων), which were used for funerary offerings and the veneration of saints.

Furthermore, the architectural layout facilitated ceremonial movement by the Π-shape

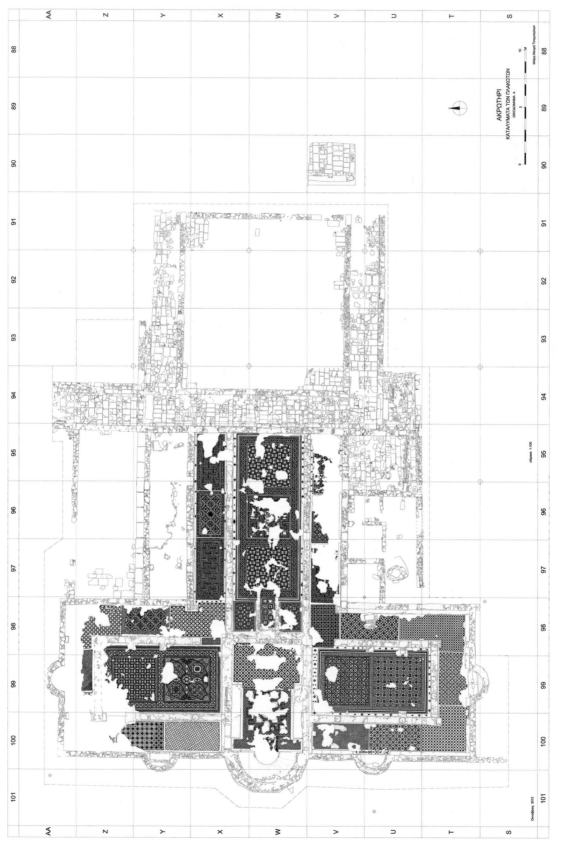

Fɪɢ. 6.20　*The plan of the floor mosaics (plan in progress).*

a peristyle arrangement (περίστωον), allowing the whole congregation to participate. As such, the podium is probably a bema used during the celebrations marking the feast of the saint(s) to whom it is dedicated. Moreover, it is probably neither the only bema in the complex nor the main one, since the martyrium's apse is pointing westward. Usually basilicas are oriented toward the east, and so the implication is that another ecclesiastical structure lies nearby, but has not yet been uncovered.

In liturgical terms, the services officiated in "Building A" can be identified with the Synaxis (Σύναξις[19]), that is, the congregational assemblies known also as the Catechumen's Liturgy (Λειτουργία Κατηχουμένων[20]) including the preparatory blessings of the offerings (εὐχαί προθέσεως). This ritual is known mainly from the Divine Liturgy of St. Mark (Alexandrian Rite) and must not be confused with the *offertorium* (πρόθεση-προσκομιδή), when the oblation of the consecrated bread and wine arrives at the altar.[21] Instead, the martyrium ceremonies were probably precursors to the rituals in which bread, wine, and oil were consecrated, similar to blessings like the later *Artoklasia* (Ἀρτοκλασία), which takes place during vespers on the eve of great feasts or, most likely, when the pre-sanctification of gifts is performed.

Moreover, these ceremonies were connected with incensation rites (εὐχή θυμιάματος), as described in the initial stages of the Divine Liturgies of St. James and St. Mark, before and during the Introitus (also known as the Lesser Entrance).[22] This indicates a very close relationship with the liturgical practices of the Eastern Churches, as exemplified by the Levantine Divine Liturgy of St. James and the Egyptian liturgical tradition of St. Mark.[23] These forms are still in

FIG. 6.21   *(above) The mosaic panels of the central aisle of the north transept arm. The "Shield of David" lies at the center; the so-called "Seal of Solomon" (knots) decorate the corners opposite the almond rosettes.*

FIG. 6.22   *(below) The mosaic decoration of the corridor in the central aisle of the "nave" leading to the platform (ἐξέδρα).*

use today in the monastic Typikon of Lite (Λιτή) and especially in the Holy Sepulcher services in Jerusalem which follow the monastic typikon.[24]

In the Eastern Liturgies, the service for the preparation or pre-sanctification of the offerings and the Lesser Entrance represented Jesus Christ offering himself as sacrifice.[25] This symbolism was influenced by the renovation of the Byzantine rite, which was actually a conflation and synthesis of the "cathedral office" of the Hagia Sophia in Constantinople with the liturgical rites of Jerusalem and its monasteries. The formation of a glorious Lesser Entrance, when the celebrant enters the nave, has been traced to the new emphasis and symbolism placed on the *Sanctus* hymn (Τρισάγιον) in the seventh century. It has been suggested that the *Sanctus*, known also as the *Hymn of Victory* (τὸν ἐπινίκιον Ὕμνον), with its Trinitarian ideology was a response to Monophysitism and was introduced into the Liturgy by Emperor Justinian.[26] These changes had additional historic significance, when the remnants of the True Cross were translated to Constantinople in 614 by Patrikios Nikitas. Because the Eastern Liturgies were influencing how the Byzantine Liturgy was evolving at this time, this has considerable importance for our interpretation of the *Katalymata ton Plakoton* monument.[27]

It is difficult to designate a precise term for this new sacred area within the martyrium, being particular to this location. It is generally accepted that similar spaces in earlier structures facilitated the initial stage of the Divine Liturgy,[28] before liturgical changes were made at the western areas, near the main entrances and narthex, or at the sacristy (σκευοφυλάκιον), as in the case of Hagia Sophia at Constantinople and at a diaconicon (διακονικόν),[29] which are often associated with martyria.[30]

The raised areas within such spaces are specifically designated for the clergy and are called the *exedra* (ἐξέδρα), embracing throne (ἀσπαστικὸν), and *mutatorium* (μυτατώριον).[31] *Mutatoria* were secondary bemas located within the narthex, where the patriarch and/or the emperor in Constantinople stood following the Sung Office before the Great Introitus. In the provinces, such as in Cyprus, a bishop, abbot, or secular archon, would occupy this space.[32] Also, the patriarch or

bishop performed the ceremonial dressing of the sacred vestments in the same area.[33]

Unfortunately, the primary sources are vague regarding the specific functions of the atrium and narthex during the first stage of the Liturgy and the Sung Office (that is, the Λιτή and Ἀσματική ἀκολουθία as recorded in either monastic or parish typika). But the archaeological evidence in late sixth- or early seventh-century Cyprus, as at "Basilica A" in Peyia, Soloi Cathedral, and the port basilica of Kourion, indicate that all the pre-Introitus services were practiced in a peristyled area, just before entry into the nave.[34] It would seem that these ceremonies were still communal events well into the seventh century, though we cannot be certain.[35] The archaeological evidence in other regions is complicated by the fact that there are such a wide variety of church ground plans, some with atriums and narthexes, and many without.[36]

In summary, the *Katalymata ton Plakoton* martyrium seems to have provided congregational space where the initial stages of the Divine Liturgy, such as the Sung Office, were performed. In Cypriot basilicas these were held in spaces close to the atrium, such as the diaconicon at Kourion, and corresponded with the function of the narthex or sacristy at the Hagia Sophia in Constantinople. "Building A" was designed both as a martyrium and a liturgical space, following the function and symbolism of the Eastern Liturgies. As such, it acquired a glorious character analogous to the Holy Sepulcher complex in Jerusalem, where the congregational basilica was connected to the Anastasis Rotunda by a courtyard or atrium.[37] In fact, Jerusalem's influences in the liturgy and the ecclesiastical architecture of Cyprus have been noted before, especially in the fifth-century church of the Campanopetra, located at the capital city of Salamis-Constantia.[38] However, the development at *Katalymata ton Plakoton* is quite different due to its later date and its association with the Egyptian Divine Liturgy of St. Mark.

THE MARTYRIUM OF ST. MENAS AT ALEXANDRIA

The *Katalymata ton Plakoton* structure has striking similarities to the Martyrium Basilica of Abu

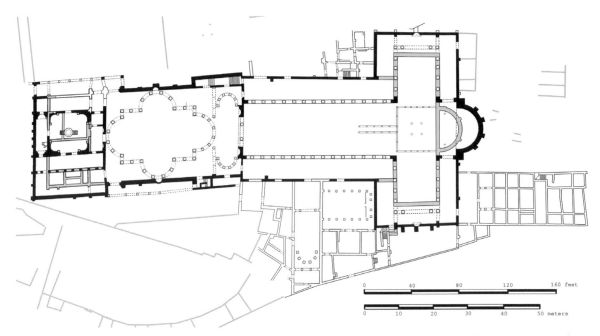

FIG. 6.23   *Ground plan of Abu Mena (Egypt), 5th-century transept basilica. Black areas are the first phase of the original basilica. Grey sections are later renovations. Redrawn by C.A. Stewart after Grossman (1989).*

Mena (fig. 6.23). This structure is located in the region known as the Ikingi Maryut, 45 kilometers southwest of Alexandria (Egypt). Most scholars agree that it dates to the Justinianic Period.[39] The relics of St. Menas were housed here, attracting pilgrims from all over the region. In time, it became one of the largest sacred sites outside the Holy Land. In 616, it was abandoned due to the Persian invasion, but later restored in 641. Its main sanctuary, like the *Katalymata ton Plakoton* martyrium, had the form of a three-aisled transept basilica, with its aisles serving as a continuous side corridor surrounding the main aisle. Likewise, it had a raised platform in the center of its crossing. More conspicuously, Abu Mena has small niches in its transept's north and south walls flanked by pilasters — just as we uncovered at the *Katalymata ton Plakoton*. Other similarities are the pilasters that jut outward, demarcating the nave from the transepts. Of course, the differences are also obvious. Besides its much smaller scale, the Cypriot structure is an ancillary building "oriented" westward, rather than being the main sanctuary. Nevertheless, their close relationship regarding design and function is beyond doubt.

It should be mentioned that Abu Mena belonged to a long tradition of three-aisled transept basilicas. The form goes back to the Constantinian martyria of the Holy Apostles in Constantinople and St. Peter's in Rome; the type was repeated throughout the fifth and sixth centuries, such as the famous martyria of St. Demetrios in Thessaloniki, Katapoliani in Paros (first phase), the Church of the Prophets, Apostles, and Martyrs at Gerasa, the cruciform basilica of Thasos and Dalmatia, etc.[40] This particular type was modified for vaulting by Emperor Justinian's architects, at the Early Byzantine phases of the influential cruciform martyrium of St. John the Theologian at Ephesus, the Church of Holy Apostles at Constantinople, and the Katapoliani at Paros.[41]

As Anastasios Orlandos observed, Abu Mena's design is quite similar to St. Demetrios in Thessaloniki.[42] They both have a continuous wooden roof and a continuous side corridor surrounding the main aisle. The use of such corridors would have facilitated the traffic of pilgrims around the relics located in the crossing square. In Constantinople, the closest parallel form was the main church of the Blachernae constructed by Justin I (518–527) and, in Jerusalem, the Justinianic rebuilding of the Church of Nativity in Bethlehem (532), although their transept colonnades were semi-circular in plan.[43] In all these cases, the transept basilica, as well as the cruciform design, were inextricably connected to their use as martyria.[44] The *Katalymata ton Plakoton* site is the only monument in Cyprus that we know of which belongs to this wider architectural phenomenon.

PRELIMINARY INTERPRETATION

Because our excavation has only uncovered a fraction of the entire site, any suggested interpretation at this point is tentative. Nevertheless, sufficient data has been uncovered to lead us beyond mere speculation. As mentioned above, the Akrotiri peninsula was known to Roman geographers as the seaport of the city of Kourion.[45] However, the historical sources do not mention any large-scale settlement or pilgrimage site in the area. Therefore, it was surprising that our excavation revealed such a remarkable ecclesiastical monument with large dimensions, innovative liturgical practices and architectural features, and expensive decoration.

While archaeological field surveys on the Peninsula have identified five sites which flourished in the same period as the *Katalymata ton Plakoton*, none of them were recorded in any written source (fig. 6.1).[46] There is an oral and literary tradition regarding how St. Helena and Duke Kalokairos established the monastery of St. Nicolas of the Cats on Akrotiri in the fourth century.[47] Although the current monastery is not earlier than the fifteenth century, the tradition reflects the importance of the Peninsula for the Imperial navy in relation with the area's ports, settlements, and ecclesiastical monuments during the Byzantine Period. Moreover, the tradition seems related to other references to the Holy Cross in the area, such as the relics (κάνναβος) now housed in the Monastery of the Holy Cross at Omodhos. A significant number of Middle and Late Byzantine sites are known throughout the Peninsula.[48] These are related to its harbors and shrines. In fact, the most prominent toponym for the major archaeological sites of the peninsula is the word "Katalymata," from the verb *καταλύω*, which means "to stay for a while" or "to lodge."

The Peninsula lies within the sphere of the municipal boundaries of three major bishoprics — Kourion, Neapolis (now Limassol), and Amathous. Based on ecclesiastical tradition, the western area of the Peninsula would have been under the ecclesiastical jurisdiction of the Bishop of Kourion and, later, of Neapolis. However, in terms of history, the city of Amathous would have played a more leading role in the area as the capital of a provincial district encompassing the southern coastline. Its harbor (which in that period was moved westward towards the Peninsula, near Neapolis) served a strategic role protecting the entire island from maritime threats arising from Egypt.[49] It is important to keep in mind that Neapolis is located just 10 kilometers (6.5 miles) from the *Katalymata ton Plakoton*. In fact, a few seventh-century documents describe the region around Amathous, providing material for a plausible explanation of how the martyrium site came into being.

The chief account comes from the *Life of St. John the Almsgiver,* which was written by Leontios, Bishop of Neapolis (Cyprus), in the middle of the seventh century. The *Life* describes the historical context of John, the Patriarch of Alexandria, who was originally born in Amathous where his father lived as governor of Cyprus. The *Life* contains significant information about how the Patriarch John constructed a "divine church" in the city's vicinity between the years 617 and 619:

> After the Persian armies had completely laid waste the whole of Syria, Phoenicia and Arabia, and among various cities, these sinners still threatened Alexandria itself. And then the holy man [Patriarch John], having found this out by God's help, that a murderous plot was being hatched against him, sailed away to his native country, Cyprus.
>
> Now a general, one Aspagurius by name, had been sent to Constantia in Cyprus but had not been admitted into the town. So he prepared himself for war against its citizens, and they began arming themselves against him. And they were just on the point of engaging in this slaughter of each other when the all-admirable John, the disciple of the God of Peace, intervened and induced both parties to seek reconciliation. He succeeded in bringing them to terms.

He [Patriarch John] once received relics from Jerusalem of Stephen, the first martyr, and of James the brother of our Lord. So he built a divine church (θεϊόν οἶκον) in the name of this first great martyr, and having made a list of all his belongings he generously dedicated them to this church.

Isaac, who was general at that time, betrayed the city of the Alexandrians (to the Persians) and then fled for refuge to Cyprus. There he found the most holy Patriarch and formed a murderous intrigue against him, intending to kill him on the Monday before Palm Sunday. The saint was informed of this and therefore stayed at home and received no one, and thus by God's providence he was miraculously saved from this deadly attack. But the author of this plot, the miserable Isaac, by the just judgment of the unsleeping providence of God was savagely set upon by some men and murdered on the very day on which he had planned death against the righteous Patriarch.[50]

The *Katalymata ton Plakoton* complex can be identified as this particular "divine church," built to house the relics of the Protomartyr Stephan and St. James (the Son of Adelphotheos). Because of its size and significance, Patriarch John dedicated it to the Protomartyr Stephan and gave his personal fortune for its construction and maintenance as a foundation, most likely monastic in nature.

In the context of this passage, where war and invasion are the main themes, the mention of this ecclesiastical building is rather curious. Moreover, these relics are not Alexandrian or Cypriot, but originally rested at famous sanctuaries in Jerusalem.[51] We know that the Persian invasion forced priests and other clerics to flee from the Holy Land in 614. John Moschos (ca. 550–619), the Patriarch Sophronios of Jerusalem (560–638), and 7,500 people found refuge in Alexandria due to its merciful Patriarch John.[52]

Relics were translated as Christians abandoned their churches before the advancing Persian army. Most likely, the Judean refugees would have moved again and resettled in the Amathus vicinity

with the Patriarch John, when he and his parishioners left Alexandria due to the Persian occupation of Egypt in 617. If so, this relocation would go far in explaining why the account of Jerusalem's relics in the *Life* was awkwardly inserted between the Persian invasion and the flight of refugees from Alexandria to Cyprus. Moreover, we know that the Patriarch John had also received a piece of the Holy Cross from John, Bishop of Tiberias.[53] Perhaps this was the same relic sent by Patrikios Niketas to Constantinople in 614, as mentioned above. Moreover, it is unlikely that Patriarch John would have left behind his monastic flock or the Patriarchate's holiest relics, such as those at Abu Mena.[54] And so, Cyprus came to house both refugees and some of the most sacred Palestinian and Egyptian relics. This might also explain why Patriarch Sophronios of Jerusalem is in Cyprus in 619 when Patriarch John died; at that time, he wrote a funeral inscription that was placed on John's grave.[55]

There are several reasons why we can associate the *Katalymata ton Plakoton* structure with part of the complex described by Leontios as the "divine church" where the relics of St. Stephan and St. James were placed. First, the dating and location of the *Katalymata ton Plakoton* monument coincide with the place and time described in the text. Second, the building has typological characteristics similar to the famous martyrium of Abu Mena, which dates earlier to the sixth century (fig. 6.5). The relics of Stephan had to be enshrined in a special building type (martyrium) in order to signify their sacredness and accommodate pilgrims. Third, it is obvious that the *Katalymata ton Plakoton* structure was indeed a martyrium. There was special care taken for its design, which literally housed (οἶκον) at least six relics of saints (or other privileged persons). When considering these factors together, we can place the *Katalymata ton Plakoton* within the historical context of Emperor Heraclius' wars against the Persians.

After many churches and monasteries were destroyed by the Persians, the merciful Patriarch and his assistants, having the support of the Imperial navy, transferred the clergy and some of their flock to the island. It is recorded that he left all his personal fortune to care for and maintain them.[56] This was not a political decision; it was an act of compassion displaying the saint's spiritual love for his flock and his brothers. And yet, such virtue compelled the Emperor and his officials to also assist, since Heraclius (through his cousin General Niketas in Egypt) consciously propagated his image as a Christian Pious King (Εὐσεβής Βασιλεύς). Heroic images are testified in the seventh-century poetry of George Pisidia, who tried to rally citizens in supporting the war effort.[57] The *Katalymata ton Plakoton* martyrium was part of this political framework, probably designed, built, and maintained by refugees who brought with them the ransomed relics of the Holy Land, Syria, or/and Alexandria. Some of the other relics in the complex might have been, if not holy relics, remains of war heroes who perished during the Heraclian "Crusade" against Persia.[58]

HISTORICAL CONTEXT

The Byzantine Empire began to wane in the first half of the seventh century. The Persian invasion and the occupation of Syria (610–613), Palestine (614), and Egypt (619), and the Avar-Persian alliance (which led to the siege of Constantinople in 626) indicated that the Empire needed both a martial and spiritual revival.[59] After much prayer (and taxation) Heraclius was able to turn the tide. While his troops successfully defended the capital, he recaptured most of the eastern provinces, marching triumphantly into Jerusalem with the relics of the Holy Cross (630). It would have seemed, to the average Byzantine citizen, that these wars were burdened by, if not the result of, the tribulations caused by heresies (Nestorianism, Monophysitism, and the later versions, Monothelistism and Monoergetism), as well as the conflicts with the Jews in the eastern provinces and Egypt. The later appearance of the Arab Muslim army (634) would be an explosive culmination of the cultural tensions of the previous decades.

Heraclius' utilization of Cyprus was crucial to his successful thirty-year reign. The island's leadership, being one of the most reliable and loyal supporters of the Heraclian administration, facilitated the restructuring of the eastern defenses while implementing cultural initiatives.

Although the documentary sources only provide circumstantial evidence, the archaeological material is more substantial. For example, Heraclius established at the island's capital, Constantia, an imperial mint to issue coinage.[60] This investment stimulated the local economy, while facilitating payment to soldiers stationed in the wider region. Moreover, the archbishop at Constantia was selected specifically by Heraclius to bring about religious reform to the region. In 643, a synod was convened at Constantia for the systematic implementation of Monotheletism — which was ultimately rejected.[61] Several years earlier, in 619, Heraclius had instructed Kyros, the bishop of Edessa (Syria), to go to Cyprus and learn how to interpret ecclesiastical books.[62] Besides indicating that Cyprus was a center of learning and education, it shows that the Emperor had very close ties to the Cypriot Church and intimately knew of its resources.

Besides the strategic role of the Cypriot Church, there was also a profound religious movement taking place on the island. This is exemplified by several accounts that describe visions of Cypriot saints. In one story, Ioannis, a Monophysite monk from Egypt, arrived in Cyprus after the Persian invasion in 619. He found other Monophysite priests and monks already there who welcomed him into their community. But soon afterwards, Ioannis had a miraculous vision of St. Epiphanius, the fourth-century archbishop of Cyprus. The saint encouraged him to reconsider the traditional doctrines, and eventually Ioannis was compelled to reject Monophysitism.[63] This represents how the authorities of the Church of Cyprus, as represented by St. Epiphanius, could influence and successfully reinstate Monophysites into Orthodox doctrine. Perhaps Heraclius himself understood how the Church of Cyprus could assist him in healing these cultural wounds and, in turn, strengthening the unity of the Empire.

Heraclius made many enemies in Constantinople, having violently dismantled the administration of the previous Emperor Phocas, though he was quite unpopular. Naturally, the aristocratic Blue Party, who had supported Phocas, was suspicious of the Heraclius' agenda and undermined his programs. Therefore Heraclius depended on his provincial (i.e., non-aristo-cratic) allies in North Africa and Cyprus, who assisted him since the beginning of his reign. The emperor would maintain a close relationship with his trustworthy general, Niketas (his cousin and father-in-law from his later second wife), and the family of a provincial district governor of Cyprus, which included John (now known as St. John the Almsgiver).[64]

While he was still just a priest in Cyprus, John was recommended by Niketas to sit on the throne of the Alexandrian Patriarchate. He would have been seen as the most trustworthy and compe-tent person to restore the prestige of the Egyptian Church — which was, at that time, an Orthodox community surrounded by Monophysitism. Recent archaeological research along the south-ern coast of Cyprus, especially at Amathous, has revealed a wealthy and flourishing society where St. John the Almsgiver grew up prior to his arrival in Alexandria.[65] Apparently, Niketas was convinced that John was competent and had the necessary charisma for such a momentous task as chief spiri-tual leader of the Egyptian people.

This relationship was maintained by the close collaboration between the regional general, Niketas, and the Cypriot governor. This coordi-nation was manifested in the restoration of the defense system in the area, including the instal-lation or rebuilding of southern naval bases, such as at Cape Drepanon and, perhaps, at Cape Gata on the Akrotiri Peninsula. On the northern coast, the city of Carpasia was fortified with curtain walls surrounding the naval port, which was also refur-bished. This coincides with the construction of Amathous' fortification walls at the summit of the acropolis overlooking the harbor towards Egypt.[66] Amathous would have been a key stronghold for consolidating Heraclius' authority in Egypt when his forces were being reorganized in 609–610.[67] These martial construction projects coincided with a type of spiritual renaissance led by St. John the Almsgiver, who sponsored the establishment of monasteries and charities.[68]

As the Patriarch of Alexandria (from 610 to 617), John worked for the redemption of hostages, prisoners, and captives of the Persian invasion and their resettlement.[69] This is how he earned the sobriquet "the Almsgiver." Besides physically ministering to the people, he venerated the holy relics of Christianity as sources of strength and solidarity, at a time when their society and culture was being persecuted. For instance, he actively res-cued or ransomed holy relics, such as the fragment of the Holy Cross.[70] As a result, Niketas and John became imperial partners, achieving a sense of unity in the region, especially in a cultural sense.[71]

Patriarch John continued his ministry after arriving in Cyprus. One of the first things he did was recommend Theodoros for the posi-tion of Bishop of Amathous. This was significant, because, apparently, Theodoros — one of his main assistants — was expected to continue the projects started by the Patriarch after his death in 619.[72] New settlement sites arose, and older cities expanded under their leadership. For example, at Kalavasos two new basilicas and a monastery were established in a formerly rural area.[73] At Cape Drepanon, three basilicas were built that served ships sailing between Europe and Africa.[74] At Alassa, the Agia Mavri Basilica was constructed in the middle of a new settlement.[75] A seventh-century monastery was recently uncovered also at Pyla-*Koutsopetria* by Dr. Maria Hadjicosti.[76] And most likely, the newly-discovered basilicas located under the Panagia tou Kampou (Choirokitia) and Panagia (Kofinou) date from the early seventh century (figs. 6.24–26).[77] Admittedly, these monu-ments are unrecorded in historical sources, and we are left to conjecture their significance. Perhaps one of these sanctuaries sheltered the Orthodox Bishop of Edessa, Pavlos, who in 619 visited the island, as mentioned by the Nestorian chronicler Jacob.[78] What is clear is that a meaningful pattern does emerge in terms of archaeology. It seems hardly coincidental that this expansive church-building campaign, along with the need for new settlements and monasteries, arose slightly before and after St. John the Almsgiver and other refugees arrived on the island.

Naturally, the population of the Eastern prov-inces must have sought escape from the Persian armies. It is plausible that areas nearer to the Byzantine navy were safer, such as the coastlands of Asia Minor, North Africa (until 617), and pos-sibly the southeastern Aegean islands.[79] However,

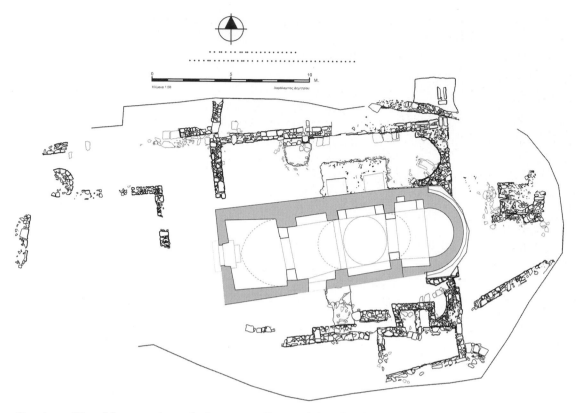

FIG. 6.24   *Plan of the excavation at the Panagia tou Kampou (Choirokitia). Light grey is the 11th-century domed-hall church built above the remains of the 7th-century basilica.*

FIG. 6.25   *Excavation at the Panagia tou Kampou (Choirokitia). South aisle.*

FIG. 6.26 *Excavation at the Panagia tou Kampou (Choirokitia). North aisle.*

much more research is needed to support such a theory. In the future, archaeologists should try to distinguish seventh-century settlements from other periods, and determine whether their development was related to seismic activity, war, and other factors related to population movements. Already there are some promising cases. For instance, at Gortyna (Crete) scholars have identified the expansion of the fortress and the city, along with new churches and a monastery on the Acropolis.[80] On Telendos island (near Kalymnos), there is some indication that both the Galatiani fortress and Agios Konstantinos were constructed in the early seventh century.[81] Other sites, such as the Agia Irene complex in Arnitha (Rhodes) and the Byzantine phase at Emporio (Chios), could very well belong to the wider phenomenon of population resettlement in the region.[82] If such a broad migration occurred, it would have led to the exchange of ideas and skills that would have influenced artistic style and technique.[83] Perhaps this was manifested in the so-called "Greek-Oriental" style found in the artworks at Cappadocia.[84]

We know that refugees fled even further west. Populations, mainly from Asia Minor, seemed to settle in Constantinople along with their holy relics, leading to the establishment of new churches or monasteries to house them, like that of St. Theodore of Sykeon.[85] In 619, the plague spread to Constantinople and other areas of the Empire. This outburst might have been spread due to the movement of a considerable amount of people from the war front—a fact testified by the archaeological material, at least in Carthage.[86]

When we step back and look at the entire historical picture, we see Cyprus' role at the center of these activities. The primary sources indicate a short period of life for several refugee settlements and their associated structures. There is no doubt that the time between the initial Persian incursions and the establishment of new sites was affected quickly by the rise of Islam, just a few years later. The restoration of holy sites in Palestine after 630, and elsewhere, testifies to a slight recovery by the Christian populations that remained behind or by those who returned.[87] However, their influence and affluence would never achieve their former state. The *Katalymata ton Plakoton* martyrium, with its short period of use, is the best-preserved monument that literally commemorates this dynamic transitional period.

SUMMARY

For the past five years the Department of Antiquities of Cyprus has been conducting systematic archaeological research at the site of *Katalymata ton Plakoton* on the Akrotiri Peninsula — a formerly unknown settlement. The foundations of a monumental cultic area, with floor mosaics and a burial shrine, have been uncovered. Inscriptions and coins date the complex to the early-seventh century. This time period and geographical location is significant, since it can be linked to sites mentioned by the contemporary writer Leontius, bishop of Neapolis (Cyprus). It is certain that this particular shrine was associated with refugees fleeing Palestine and Egypt due to the Persian siege and conquest (617–618). Though the excavations are far from complete, already our preliminary work has shed much light on Cyprus and its crucial place in the Byzantine Empire.

NOTES

1   Swiny 1988a, 1988b; Simmons, Held and Reese 1989; Sondaar 1986.

2   Strabo, *Geographica* 14.6.3–5; Ptolemy, *Geographia* 5.13; Herodotus, *Historiae* 5.113. Incidentally, it is from this ancient designation that the current toponym "Akrotiri" is derived, since the Modern Greek word for "promontory" is ἀκρωτήριο. Strabo wrote "Κουριὰς ἄκρα χερσονησώδης, πόλις Κούριον ὅρμον ἔχουσα…" Moreover, the *Stadiasmus maris magni* recorded: "Ἀπὸ τοῦ Κουριακοῦ ἐπὶ Καργαίας στάδιοι μ´, Ἀκρωτήριον ἐστιν ἔχον λιμένα, ὕφορμον καὶ ὕδωρ," ed. Müller 1855–1882: 302, 502. Forty stadia was about 7.5 kilometers (each stadium is 600 feet or 188.88 meters); Kountoura 1996. The distance between the two areas (Kourion and Kargaias) is within the limits of the Peninsula; Leonard 1997. In later publications of Ptolemy's *Geography* (and in other medieval maps), the current salt lake area is depicted as a gulf open to the east, which was most likely the main port; Chatzēpaschales and Iakovou 1989: 82, figs. 25–26.

3   Étienne de Lusignan (1573) wrote: "Curias era città anticamente & Regale, temporanea delle altre, al tempo delli noue Re: & questa è appresso allamarina, discosto da Arsenoe tre leghe. Fù edificata da gli Argiui, quando re gnauano in Cipro, avanti che fusse fabricata Paffo vecchia, circa glianni del mondo 3600 avanti l'avvenimento dí Christo 1595" (fol. 7r , 7v) and "…dunque il Re Crasso ouer Argo prese l'Isolas, & edifitò la città, hora il Casal Accathu, & la città di Piscopia detta Curias…" (fol. 35v). The later French translation adds: "L'an du monde deux mil trois cents quarante & deux, Crasse, ou comme les disent, Arge, Roy des Argives, passa de Cilicie avec une armee en Cypre, & aborda un rivage plein d'arbres, où y avoit un petit bois fort espez. Là ils edifierent une ville, & l'appellerent Actes de Argives, qu'on nomme pour le iourdhuy le village d'Accanthou" (91v). See the Modern Greek translation by S. K. Perdikēs (2004: §20).

4   References regarding a harbor of the Late Bronze Age in the vicinity of Asomatos village, north of the Salt Lake, are the result of confusion with the Late Bronze Age site in Kyrenia District by the same name; Swiny 1982: 166; Blue 1997: 37; Catling 1962: 149.

5   Leonard 1997: 179, fig. 13; Ault and Leonard, forthcoming; see the list of sites below, note 48.

6   I.e., Royal Air Force (Great Britain) and Western Sovereign Base Area; Procopiou 1997; 2006: 118–19.

7   The term ἐξέδρα (exedra) is the term applied by Eusebius regarding the Tyros Basilica (Pallas 1954:

470–82). It is translated here in English as "podium," which describes a raised area within a church, usually demarcating the bema (sanctuary).

8 The type of the Corinthian capital is well-known in the area already at the fifth century (e.g., Kourion Basilica, Agios Tychon) and has its origin at the Proconnesus workshops; Asgati 1995: 269–71, figs. 5–6. It is not clear if these capitals were carved and imported to Cyprus specifically for this monument. The preserved ionic-like bases have a wide variety of dimensions, and there are some differences in the form of the abacus between the small fragments, both of which indicate the possibility of being in secondary use.

9 Regarding the relationship of the domed central plan with martyria, see Grabar 1949: 97, 99–100.

10 I base the possibility of a wooden dome/tower (ξυλότρουλλος) over the crossing square according to Orlandos' criteria (1994: 183–87, figs. 148, 151). The Ilissos basilica belongs to his "category d" roofing system. See also Soteriou 1920a; Chatzēdakēs 1948; Laskaris 2000: 368–72, 655, fig. B.7; Varalis 2001: 413–14; Markē 2002: 164–65, 170–71. For the domed-cruciform, wood-roofed basilicas, see also Pallas 1976–1977: 50–51; 1981: 15–24. Regarding the original structure of the Holy Apostles, see Eusebius, *De Vita Constantini* 4.58.

11 For the libation perforations, see Laskaris 1996: 313.

12 This chancel type is known from 5th-century contexts (Stoufi-Poulimenou 1999: 108–13) and has its origin in the Proconnesus workshops; Sodini 2006: 224. The *Katalymata ton Plakoton* chancel, as far as I know, is the only known example with a perforated Chrismon cross. The wreath with the sprouts has its origin in ancient funeral iconography, symbolizing one's lifetime and the hope for everlasting life after death. The theme passed to the iconography of Early Christian graves and sarcophagi already in the first centuries of Christianity as a symbol of the victory over death; Pallas 1969: 131; Markē 2005: 85; Koch 1998: 464, fig.2. The wreath combined with the Chrismon cross symbolizes the triumph of Jesus Christ over death and his resurrection; Stoufi-Poulimenou 1999: 109–13; Laskaris 2000: 420–22, 506–10, 699, fig. D.11; Markē 2006: 181. The motif is common during the reign of Constantine I and his successors, when it was adopted as symbol of Imperial power. Mrs. Poulimenou suggests that it

is a triumphal representation of Jesus Christ, and that the wreath is an expression of the fact that Jesus Christ is the source of life. The two free crosses on each side, at a lower level in relation with the Chrismon cross, receive life and, in turn, victory from the triumph of Jesus Christ, signified in the center. Most probably their presence has no relation with dogmatic expressions, but rather symbolizes the triumph of the Church and its unity under the two primary apostles Peter and Paul.

13 Here I list comparable examples from 19 distinct regions. (1) Constantinople: Hagia Sophia (563), where a simplified variation is used in a window panel within the holy bema. In that chancel there are crosses neither in the wreath nor within the sprouts; Guidobaldi and Barsanti 2004: 141, fig.10). (2) Marmara region (Turkey): the closest example to the Akrotiri chancel was found at the village of Yenice, but not *in situ*; Mango and Ševčenko 1973: 271. (3) Novigrad (Istria, Croatia): a Chrismon cross was placed within a disk rather than a wreath; Jurković 1998: 1122, 1126, fig.1. Also, two fragments of a chancel with a Chrismon cross in a medallion (dated to the Justinianic period) are found at Pula Cathedral, itself dated 4th–5th-century; Vicelja 1998: figs. 3–4. (4) Rome (Italy): San Clemente, where a chancel screen displays a monogram of Pope John II within a wreath, dated 533–535; Guidobaldi 2000: fig. 5; 2002: 1484, fig. 1. (5) Ravenna (Italy): Sant'Apollinario in Classe, now in the Ravenna Museum, showing the Christ monogram within the wreath; Guidobaldi 2000: fig. 106. A chancel from San Vitale exhibits the same motif, but sprouts two crosses, just like the *Katalymata ton Plakoton* chancel; Guidobaldi 2000: 685, fig. 397; Farioli 1969: cat. nos. 135–42, figs. 128–34. (6) Marzaremi (Sicily); Kapitän 1969: 128; 1980: 85–87, 90–91, figs. 9, 11–12. (7) Attica (Greece): at the Church of Taxiarchis at Kouvaras there is a chancel embedded within the wall from the Early Christian phase; Orlandos 1928–1933: 169, fig. 3. Another similar fragment is housed in the Byzantine Museum of Athens; Pazaras 1977: 42, 7.12b. (8) Thebes (Greece): at Basilica A in Nea Achialos, dated to the end of the 5th or the 6th century: Soteriou 1929–1930: figs. 90–91; Lazaridis 1970: pl. 53; at Basilica A in Nicopolis: Philadelpheus 1918: 35, fig. 2; at Olympus: Kotzias 1952: 111–12, fig. 11; at Amvrakikos (Kefalos): Barla 1965: 83–84, fig. 5); at

Sikyon Basilica: Orlandos 1933: 83, dr. 2; 1994: 514, fig. 6; Stoufi-Poulimenou 1999: fig. 129. (9) Peloponnese (Greece): the Lechaion Basilica at Corinth, dated to the second half of the 5th century: Pallas 1958: pl. 102b; at Provantinos (Tegea), from the second half of the 5th century: Orlandos 1973: 103–4, with references to more examples. (10) Macedonia (Greece): at Thessaloniki, the early basilica to the east and below St. Sophia: Drosogianni 1963: 238–40, pl. 269d; the external area of St. Sophia: Pazaras 1977: 41–42, VI.11b; Agios Demetrios basilica, second half of the 5th century: Soteriou and Soteriou 1952: 171–72, pl. 47d; Pazaras 1977: 32–33, pl. II, 3b; Rotonda of St. George: Pazaras 1977: 44, X.17b; Basilica B at Philippi, middle of the 6th century: Hoddinott 1963: pl. 56b has an isolated Chrismon cross on a fragment from the south apse; Lemerle 1945: 16, 32, 39, fig. 99, pl. 75; the second phase of the extramural Basilica at Philippi dated to the 6th century: Pelekanides 1955: 129, fig. 11, 152, fig. 33; Hoddinott 1963: fig.10; the "Loggos" Basilica A at Edessa: Stoufi-Poulimenou 1999: fig. 131; Michaelides 1963: 251–52; 1965: 475–76, pl. 593; 1968: 209–10, fig. 4, pl. 91b–c. This chancel varies from the other types since it has two cypresses beside the two crosses, and the circle encloses a flower rather than a Chrismon cross; Michaelides 1963: 212–14, fig. 9, pl.92b. (11) Crete (Greece): Kolokyntha of Lasithi and Pyrgi of Eleutherna, (Gortyna): Trygonaki 2004: 1152–53, 1157–58, figs. 11, 25–26. (12) Lesbos (Greece): Ypsilometopos Basilica: Orlandos 1929: figs. 18, 20, 24–25; note that figs. 18 and 20 omit the Chrismon cross, while fig. 24 has the wreath and cross, and fig. 25 omits the sprouts; at the Eressos Basilica, a wreath surrounds a cross: Orlandos 1929: 31–32, fig. 32; at Afenteli Basilica: Orlandos 1929: 46, figs. 48, 59. (13) Mytilini (Greece): Evangelides 1930–31: 13, fig. 7. (14) Rhodes (Greece): the motif decorated an Early Christian sarcophagus found in the mosque of Houdai-Mestzid in secondary use (now in the Castello interior yard): Orlandos 1948: 21–22; chancel fragments are known from Gennadi (from a sarcophagus in the mosque of the town) and Plemmyri: Orlandos 1948: 31, 36, 43–44, figs. 16, 26, 36; Stoufi-Poulimenou 1999: fig. 130. (15) Serbia: Suvodol Basilica: Hoddinott 1963: 192, pl. 56e. (16) Asia Minor: Chrismon cross in a disk depicted at St. John the Theologian in Ephesus: Soteriou 1924: 173; ambo screen located in the

Nicaea Museum: Sodini et al. 1998: 355, fig. 42. (17) Palestine: Mausot Jizhak, Hebron: Sodini et al. 1998: 305–6, fig. 5; the wreath includes a rosette instead of a Chrismon cross at Nessana, Beth Shan; moreover, at the synagogues these motifs have the mensa instead of the Chrismon cross: Foerster 1989: figs. 6–7, 10–11]. (18) Libya: Latrum (Apollonia): Duval 1989: 2787, fig. 30.j; Ward Perkins 1972: pl. 86, fig. 16; Tynesia: Baratte and Bejaoui 2001: 1447–48. (19) Cyprus: Campanopetra basilica at Salamis-Constantia: Roux 1998: figs. 155–56, 196–98, 202; Agios Philon at Carpasia, dated to the early 5th–7th centuries: Taylor and Megaw 1981: pl. 37, fig. 4, 52. 9 reconstruction phase of 620; Acropolis basilica at Amathous, where a small fragment with a Chrismon cross was reused in the *opus sectile* floor dated to 653–680, while a wreath with a concave shield of David has ivy sprouts: Pralong 1994: figs. 15, 20; at the Monastery of St John the Chrysostom in Koutsoventis, where a chancel with the Chrismon cross and sprouts was recarved and reused as table: Mango et al. 1990: 72, fig. 46.

14   For the παρατραπέζια, see Trempelas 1997: 18–19; 1993: 144, 152; Galavaris 1970: 109–12; for *Mensae martyria*, see Soteriou 1942: 75–77; Chalkia 1991: 128–31.

15   In Cyprus, the only other known mosaic example of the "Shield of David" belongs to a renovation phase of the basilica of St. Philon at Carpasia dated to 620; Taylor and Megaw 1981: 237, 250, pl. 43; Michaelides 1993: 95, fig. 18f. It is tempting to entertain the possibility that this hexagram was linked to the biblical King David as early as the seventh century. If that were the case, then the symbol here could be indicative of the "New David"—a name given to Emperor Heraclius, recognizing his efforts against the Persian Goliath. The Byzantine writer Theophanes the Confessor wrote: "Ἡρακλείῳ ἐν τῇ ἀνατολῇ Δαυίδ," *Chronographia*, ed. Boor 1883: 335. Art historians have interpreted the representations on the "David Plates" as celebrating Heraclius' victories. These were silver dishes discovered in Lapithos, Cyprus, dating to the first half of the 7th century; Wander 1973: 89–104. The interpretation becomes even more interesting here when we notice the mosaic hexagram is combined with the cruciform knot, the so-called "Seal of Solomon" (*sigillum Salomonis*). The hexagram has a long history of use

by the Jewish, Christian, and Arab communities in the Middle Ages. However, exactly when the hexagram became associated with King David or Solomon is difficult to establish. It seems that the earliest historical connection dates from to the 13th century, though this probably reflects a much earlier tradition; Scholem 2007: 338.

16 Piccirillo 1993: 76–78.

17 Jonah 4:6–8; Trempelas 1993b: 78–85: Markē 2005: 86. St. Theodore of Sykeon, a contemporary and "advisor" to the Emperor Heraclius taught that "ἐὰν μὴ ἐπιστρέψωμεν καὶ μετανοήσωμεν πρὸς τὸν Θεόν, ὥστε διαλλαγῆναι ἡμῖν ὡς ἐπὶ τῶν Νινευϊτῶν, πάλιν ἐλεύσεται μετὰ δυνάμεως πολλῆς καὶ ἐρημώσει πᾶσαν τὴν γῆν ἕως θαλάσης;" Festugière 1970: 123–24.

18 Charalambous 2012: 217–21; a full analysis of the mosaics is being prepared by the author.

19 Trempelas 1993: 122–23.

20 According to the *Mystagogia* of St. Maximus the Confessor (d. 662), catechumens were seated in the nave during the reading of the Gospel; afterwards they were asked to leave before the litanies. Behind them, the doors of the *tribelon* were then closed. Maximus wrote: "Ἡ δὲ μετὰ τὴν Ἱερὰν ἀνάγνωσιν τοῦ ἁγίου Εὐαγγελίου, καὶ τὴν ἐκβολὴν τῶν κατηχουμένων γινομένη κλεῖσις τῶν θυρῶν τῆς ἁγίας τοῦ Θεοῦ Ἐκκλησίας, τήν τε τῶν ὑλικῶν δηλοῖ πάροδον…;" Cantarella 1931: chapter 15; see also Brightman and Hammond 1896: 527. In the Liturgy of St. James, the duration of the catechumens' service is longer, and they stayed in the nave until the beginning of Liturgy of the Faithful. They were asked to leave during the Great Entrance: "Μή τις τῶν κατηχουμένων, μή τις τῶν ἀμυήτων μή τις τῶν μὴ δυνάμενων ἡμῖν συνδεθῆναι Ἀλλήλους ἐπιγνῶτε, τὰς θύρας ὀρθοὶ πάντες;" Brightman and Hammond 1896: 28–41. In the *Apostolic Constitutions,* the Catechumens Liturgy began soon after the Lesser Introit. At this point, visitors (non-Christians) were asked to leave before the catechumens, and then the competents (candidates for baptism), followed by the energumens ("afflicted ones"). Before the entrance in the Liturgy of the Faithful, the penitents were dismissed, whereas those who had "obstacles" (i.e.,were "in sin") were not allowed to enter. It is unclear if, at the same moment, the catechumens were also dismissed then, or if dismissal took place

before the Burnt-Offering, when the doors were closed and guarded; Brightman and Hammond 1896: 3–13. The catechumens left the nave before the Great Entrance also in the Liturgy of St Mark; Brightman and Hammond 1896: 122. Likewise, this happened according to the texts of the Liturgies of St. Basil and St. John the Chrysostom from the 9th century onward; Brightman and Hammond 1896: 316.

21 For the position of, and movement within, the diaconicon, see Pallas 2007: 24–25 and Orlandos 1964–1965. For the distinction of two stages of prothesis, see Trempelas 1997: 18–19; Philias 2006: 177, nn. 203–4, 181–89; Pallas 2007: 28. Regarding the prothesis service (ἀκολουθία προθέσεως) before the beginning of the Divine Liturgy of St. Mark, see Phountoulis 2007: 11.

22 Concerning the use of incense offerings, see Pallas 1950: 275; 2007: 32–34; Taft 2004: 37, 150; Phountoulis 2007: 11, 17, 75; Dix 1945: 288–89; Hoddinott 1963: 30–31; Trempelas 1993a: 125; Stouphi-Poulimenou 1999: 147–59.

23 For the Divine Liturgy of St. James, see Brightman and Hammond 1896: 31–38. For the Divine Liturgy of St. Mark, see Trempelas 1997: 22 and Cuming 1990. The Matins (ὄρθρος) merged with the first stage of the Divine Liturgy as noted in the Alexandrian rite of St. Mark. This tradition also influenced the Early Christian architecture of Eastern Illyrikon; Varalis 2001: 534–36.

24 Pallas 1950: 284–86; Babić 1969: 11–14. These liturgies have continued to this day with slight variance. I had the chance to observe such ceremony personally on the 15th and 16th of August 1998 in Jerusalem.

25 S.Sophronii Patriarch Hierosolymitani, *Commentarius Litugicus,* ed. Migne, PG 87: 1860, 3389: "Ἐρτὸ γοῦν προσαγόμενον πολλοῖς ὀνομάζεται· καλεῖται γὰρ εὐλογία, προσφορά, ἀπαρχή, ἄρτος· εὐλογία μεν ὡς τῆς ἀραστῶν πρωτοπλάστων ἀναίρεσις· προσφορὰ δὲ ὡς ἐξ ὅλου τοῦ ἀνθρωπείου φυράματος, οἴα τῆς φιλοτιμίας τῷ θεῷ καὶ Κτίστη εἰς τὰ τῶν Ἁγίων Ἅγια προσηνέχθημεν· ἀπαρχὴ δὲ, ὡς πάντων τῷ Θεῷ προσενηνεγμένων, ὡς τὸν οὐράνιον ἄρτον παραδηλοῦν, τροφὴ ἡμῶν μεταλαμβανόντων γινόμενον."

26 Schulz 1997: 62–64.

27 Philias 2006: 184–89; *Chronicon Paschale,* ed. Migne, PG 92, 988–89. Concerning the influence of litur-

gical procession on church architecture, i.e., for the formation of the peristyle (περίστωον), see Chatzētryphonos 2004: 71–87.

28 For the stages of Holy Liturgy see Mateos 1963: 307; 1971: 34–126d; Babić 1969: 10–15; Mathews 1971: 138–47; Baldovin 1987; 1991: 3–27; Taft 1980: 105–15; 1980–1981: 49–52; 1992: 28–38; 1997: 204–5, 210–15; Donceel-Voûte 1998: 97–156. For the use of the atrium or narthex in the Liturgy before the Lesser Introit, see Strube 1973: 97–117; Mathews 1971: 111–15; Pallas 1950; Procopiou 2007: 419. Regarding Hagia Sophia in Constantinople, the Typikon states: "Γίνεται δὲ ἡ ἀκολουθία οὕτως. Ὑπομινήσκεται ὁ πατριάρχης καὶ εἰς οἷον ἂν ἐπιτρέψῃ ἀντίφωνον τοῦ ὄρθρου εἰσέρχονται οἱ ψάλται ἐν τῇ ἐκκλησίᾳ ἔσω, καὶ κατὰ τὸν δέοντα καιρὸν κατέρχεται ὁ πατριάρχης καὶ εἰσέρχεται εἰς τὸ θυσιαστήριον, καὶ μετὰ τὸ πληρῶσαι τὰ ἀντίφωνα γίνεται εὐχὴ τοῦ τρισαγίου καὶ ἄρχονται οἱ ψάλται ἐν τῷ ἄμβωνι τροπάριον ἦχος πλ.α´ Κύριε ἡμάρτομεν, ἠνομήσαμεν, προσπίπτομεν, ἐλέησον ἡμᾶς. Καὶ ἀνέρχεται ἡ λιτὴ ἐν τῷ Φόρῳ, καὶ δοξάζουσιν ἐκεῖσε, καὶ λέγει ὁ διάκονος τὴν μεγάλην ἐκτενῆ, καὶ εἶθ᾿οὕτως πάλιν ἄρχονται τὸ αὐτὸ τροπάριον καὶ εἰς τὸν Ἅγιον Θύρσον δοξάζουσιν οὕτως…ὁ δὲ ὄρθρος γίνεται εἰς μὲν τὰ Χαλκοπρατεῖα ἐν τῷ ἄμβωνι. Εἰς δὲ τὴν μεγάλην Ἐκκλησίαν ἐν τῷ νάρθηκι;" Mateos 1962: 130, 222. Moreover, the Washing of the Feet Service was officiated in the narthex of Hagia Sophia: "Ἑσπέρας δὲ, μετὰ τὰ ἑσπερινά, γίνεται ἀκολουθία τοῦ νιπτῆρος ἐν τῷ νάρθηκι;" Mateos 1963: 72, 308.

The stages of the Holy Liturgy changed in the 15th century; Pallas 1950: 284. This coincided with the establishment of infant baptism and the infrequency of adult conversion, and the allowance of penitents and women in menstruation to participate in the entire ceremony within the main church. Regarding these latter two groups, see Mathews 1971: 125–34, 138–47. Earlier, the narthex had already developed into a mainly funerary function: see, for instance, the sermons by Antiochean Patriarch Theodoros Balsamon (1214), who wrote: "οὐ γὰρ εἰσὶν οἱ πρόναοι κοινοὶ ὡς τὰ τῶν ἐκκλησιῶν προαύλια, ἀλλὰ μέρος αὐτῶν κατανεμηθὲν ταῖς γυναιξὶ ταῖς μὴ κωλυομέναις ἐκκλησιάζειν. Ὃς δὴ πρόναος, τόπος δευτέρας ἐστὶ μετανοίας, ὁ τῶν ἀκροωμένων λεγόμενος, ἀλλὰ ἔξωθεν αὐτοῦ προσκλαίειν. Ἔδει γοῦν τοὺς τοιούτους προνάους

εἰς οὓς οἱ τοιαῦται ἀκάθαρτοι γυναῖκες ἔμελλον ἵστασθαι, μὴ ἀναπληροῦν τόπον ἐκκλησιῶν ἐξ ὀρθοῦ, ὥστε καὶ ἱερεῖς μετὰ τῶν θείων ἁγιασμάτων διέρχεσθαι κατὰ τὸν χερουβικὸν ὕμνον, καὶ θυμιᾶν τοὺς ἐν τούτῳ ἴσως ὄντας τάφους καὶ ἁγίους καὶ τελευτὰς ἁγίων εὐχῶν ποιεῖν· ἢ κἂν μετὰ ἐπισκοπικῆς ἐπιτροπῆς τοὺς τοιούτους τόπους ἀφορίζεσθαι, ὥστε ἀπροκριματίστως ἵστασθαι ἐν αὐτοῖς τὰς ἀκαθάρτους γυναῖκας;" *Commentaria in B. Dionysii archiepsicopi Alexandrini Epistolam ad Basilidem epsicopum,* ed. Migne, PG 138: 465–68; Kallinikos 1969: 85–89, 579.

29 For changes at the Hagia Sophia, see note 27 above; for the diaconicon, see Orlandos 1964.

30 Donceel-Voûte 1998: 122–23. Martyria in the 5th and 6th centuries were located within narthexes and atria in mainland Greece and the Balkans. A characteristic case is the Basilica of Leonide in Lechaion at Corinth, dated at the end of the 5th and the beginning of the 6th century (521 or 552), where the martyrium lies between the atrium and the narthex; Pallas 1960: 146–47, fig. 1; 1963: dr. 1; 1977: 164–65; Laskaris 2000: 420–22, 670, fig. B.33. In Philippi, a peristyle pronaos was located at the west end with an apse between an atrium and a narthex; Lemerle 1945; Hoddinot 1963: figs. 80–81. In the Basilica A at Nea Achialos (Thebes), dated to the end of 5th to the 6th century, an apsidal formation in the west portico of the atrium had a liturgical role, although no elements relating to a saint's cult have been preserved; Soteriou 1929–1930: 36–37, pl. B. In North Africa, Early Christian churches have apses serving as martyria at the western end of the central aisle of the nave; Duval 1989: 2755, fig. 11; Donceel-Voûte 1995: 180; 1998: 122, figs. 15.1, 18.

31 Regarding the *exedra* and embracing throne, see Pallas 1954: 49–97; For the *mutatorium* in Constantinople, see Pallas 1950: 295–307; Strube 1973: 104; Mathews 1971: 108. In the provinces, see Sodini 1984: 460–62 and Gounaris 2000: 80–81. It is also referred to as place for *adlocutio;* Pallas 1950: 297; 1952: 122–23, 125. For a parallel example, Jelčić identified the side apses in the narthexes as *mutatoria* at a church Lovrečina, located in the northern part of the island of Brač in the Adriatic Sea (1979: 38–39). In its north apse, the springing of an arch (which separated the conch from the rest of the structure) is preserved. Another example was found in the

south apse (which was walled-in in later times), as well as a synthronon with a throne in the middle, indicating its use by the Bishop during the Divine Liturgy. A grave was also found in the foundations of the north apse. Many other examples of narthexes with side apses can be cited; for Egypt: Wessel and Restle 1966: 71, fig. 72, 75, fig. 5; for the Basilica in Gülbahçe (Asia Minor): Wessel and Restle 1966: 338, fig.3; Emporio Basilica at Chios: Wessel and Restle 1966: 958, fig.3; see also Balance et al. 1989: fig. 3, dr. 1; Karm Abu Mena: Wessel and Restle 1972: 1133–42; Grossman 1987: 172–73, pl. 5; Katapoliani of Paros: Orlandos 1965: 17, fig. 2; Korykos Basilica (Asia Minor): Orlandos 1994: 134, fig. 192; Hill 1996: fig. 17; Aphenteli Basilica, Lesbos: Orlandos 1994: 137, fig. 98; 1965: figs. 1, 7, 22; Apollonia Basilica in Cyrene: Duval 1989: 2763–64, fig. 3. In Cyprus, there are several examples: the Cathedral of Agios Epiphanios and the Campanopetra basilica at Salamis-Constantia, and Agia Trias at Yialousa; Papageorghiou 1970; 2002: fig. 17; Roux 1998: 77, pl. Ia; Gkioles 2003: 70, fig. 3; Chotzakoglou 2005: 468–69, 478. Soteriou suggested an Anatolian origin for these ecclesiastical structures (1920b: 36).

32 Later in the Middle Byzantine period, a Patriarch would be stationed in this space and was called an emphyteusis (ἐμφύτευσις).

33 Pallas 1950: 286, 291; Wessel and Restle 2005: 914, narthex.

34 For Peyia, see Megaw 1997: 351, fig. 7; for Soloi, see Gagniers and Tinh 1985; Neal 2009: fig. 3a; for Kourion, see Christou 1998: 51.

35 Concerning the relationship between the atrium, the Matins, and the procession of offerings in the Liturgy of the Faithful, see Pallas 1950: 279–89; Orlandos 1994: 95–96, 131–37; Gounaris 1999: 78, fig. 82.2–5, 7–8; Michel 2001: 18–23. It should be noted that the distinction of the role of atrium and narthex in the initial stages of the Byzantine liturgy is unclear; Varalis 2001: 455–56, 533–34. The problem lies with how the different rooms and areas within churches, like the diaconicon, were utilized. The function of most rooms was defined by their portable or perishable furnishings, which usually do not survive; Orlandos 1964–1965: 353–72.

36 There are some basilicas that have atria without narthexes, but these are found mainly in Rome and Palestine; Orlandos 1994: 94, 100.1–5, 7–8, 101.8–9;

Gounaris 1999: 79; Smith and Day 1989. The second phase of the civic complex church of Pella (Jordan), dated 525/550–614 AD is a good example; Michel et al. 2001: 19–20, figs. 65–66, 72, 74. This should be compared with the church at Gerasa (Michel et al.. 2001: figs. 200–201, 211, 249) and the south church at Basilica D in Kato Polis (Garičin Grad) (Hoddinott 1963: figs. 145–46; Varalis 2001: pl.38b). And there other examples: Arapai: Varalis 2001: pl. 48a; Negeb: Donceel-Voûte 1998: figs. 3.2–3, 4.3; and the Panagia Eleousa at Souvala (Greece): Pallas 1977: fig. 9.

37 Labbas 2009: 97.

38 Roux 1998: 245–51.

39 Grossmann 1984; 1989; 2007: figs. 6–7.

40 St. Demetrius: Bakirtzis 2002: fig. 1; Brouskari et al. 2008: 97–100; Paros Katapoliani: Orlandos 1965: 11–15, fig. 3; Church of Prophets, Apostles, and Martyrs of Gerasa: Crowfoot 1931: 30–31; Thasos port Basilica: Orlandos 1951: 52–56; Dalmatia: Dygge 1934; 1951.

41 Soteriou 1924: 205–18; Hörmann 1951; Thiel 2005.

42 Orlandos 1994: 178–79; Soteriou and Soteriou 1952: fig. 140.5; Ousterhout 2007: fig.4.

43 For the Blachernae, see Mango 1998: fig. 1; for Bethelehem, see Brouskari et al. 2008: 132–35.

44 Soteriou 1920a: 6–8; 1942: 72–75; Grabar 1972: 120–41; Laskaris 2000: 355–62; Balderstone 2007: 27–29.

45 Chatzioannou 1973: 314–15.

46 See notes 1, 2, 5, and 6, above, and note 48, below.

47 Étienne de Lusignan 1573: fol. 7r–8v; 1968: 19–20. The church of Agios Nikolaos of the Cats cannot be dated before the 14th century, and it is clear that the ruins of the monastery belong to the 14th through 16th century. The ruins which Camille Enlart saw to the south of the Katholikon in the late 19th century (which were restored by the Department of Antiquities after 1974) belong to the last phase of the re-establishment of the monastery by Bishop Makarios of Kition in the middle of the 18th century and not to the 16th century, as Enlart claimed (since he was unaware of the Kition codices); Enlart 1987: 348–52; Kyriazēs 1937: 96–131. The earliest written sources focus on the 16th century, when the Ottoman Turks forced the monks to abandon the monastery.

48 Here is a list of a known Byzantine sites at Akrotiri: A – St. Mark's Catacomb in the locality known as Agios Markos, which lies to the west of *Kato*

Katalymmata site (surveyed by E. Procopiou 11.5.2006).

B – Cave-Hermitage of Agios Sylas, close to the western side of Cape Zeugari in the locality *Agios Sylas* (surveyed by E. Procopiou 11.4.2006)

C – Ruins of an Early Christian church dedicated to Agia Iphigenia in the locality *Agia Phinia* to the west of *Agios Sylas* cave (surveyed by E. Procopiou 26.10.2005)

D – Vaulted Byzantine chapel of St. Demetrianos; Philotheou 2006: 132, fig. 4; Procopiou 2006: 125–26, fig. 29; 2008: 16.

E – A vaulted chapel of a 18th-century Katholikon, belonging to a ruined monastery dedicated to St. George to the north of the village of Akrotiri.

F – Ruined chapel of Agios Varas to the southeast of the Monastery of St. Nicolas (information provided by the Ecclesiastical Committee of Akrotiri).

G – The church of Panagia Galousa of an early Middle Byzantine date for the initial phase; Procopiou 2007: 191–218.

H – Ruins of Agios Eleutherios on the west bank of Kouris river close to the M1 road (information provided by the Ecclesiastical Committee of Akrotiri).

49　John of Nikiu, *Chronikon* 97.10, ed. R. Charles.

50　*Vita S. Johannis Ellemosynarii.* The English text is based on Elizabeth Dawes' translation. Here is the Greek transcription:

Τῶν περσικῶν οὖν στρατευμάτων ἄρδην ληϊσαμένων πᾶσαν Συρίαν, Φοινίκην τε καὶ Ἀραβίαν καὶ λοιπὰς ἄλλας πόλεις, ἠπείλουν οἱ ἀλιτήριοι καὶ αὐτὴν Ἀλεξάνδρειαν ἑλεῖν. Τότε δὴ θεόθεν γνοὺς ὁ ἅγιος ἐπιβουλήν τινα μελεττωμένην γενήσεσθαι κατ' αὐτοῦ φονικήν, ἐπὶ τὴν οἰκείαν πατρίδα Κύπρον ἐξέπλευσεν.

Ἀσπαγούριος δὲ τις τοὔνομα στρατηγὸς ἐπὶ Κωνσταντίαν τὴν κατὰ Κύπρον σταλεὶς καὶ μὴ δεχθεὶς παρὰ τῶν τῆς πόλεως, εἰς πόλεμον ὡπλίσθη κατ' αὐτῶν κἀκεῖνοι δὲ κατ' αὐτοῦ ἀνθωπλίζοντο· οἱ καὶ πρὸς τὸν κατ' ἀλλήλων φόνον ὅσον οὔπω χωρεῖν ὁμόσε ἔμελλον, εἰ μὴ προκαταλαβὼν ὁ τοῦ εἰρηνικοῦ μαθητὴς Ἰωάννης ὁ πανθαύμαστος ἀμφότερα τὰ μέρη πρὸς εἰρηνικὰς κατὰ καταλλαγὰς μετέβαλεν καὶ καλῶς συνεβίβασεν.

Ὁ αὐτός ποτε λείψανα δεξάμενος ἐξ Ἱεροσολύμων Στεφάνου τοῦ πρωτομάρτυρος καὶ Ἰακώβου τοῦ Θεαδέλφου θεῖόν τε δειμάμενος οἶκον ἐπ' ὀνόματι τούτου τοῦ μεγάλου πρωτομάρτυρος, τούτῳ πάντα τὰ ὑπάρχοντα αὐτοῦ καταγραψάμενος φιλοφρόνως ἀφιέρωσεν.

Ἰσαάκιος τοίνυν ὁ τότε στρατηγὸς τὴν Ἀλεξανδρέων πόλιν προδούς, φυγὰς τὴν Κύπρον κατέλαβεν· ὃς εὑρὼν ἐκεῖσε τὸν ἁγιώτατον πάπαν, συσκευὴν κατ' αὐτοῦ φονικὴν κατειργάσατο, ὅπως τῇ δευτέρᾳ τῆς πρὸ τῶν βαΐων ἑβδομάδος τοῦτον διαχειρίσηται.

Chatzioannou 1988a: 166; taken from Addendum A: Greek codex 349 at the San Marco Library (Venice), fol. 163v–202.

51　St. Stephen's relics were housed near Golgotha at the "greater church;" *Itinerarium Egeriae* 6.3, see ed. McClure and Feltoe: 53, n. 1, 81, n. 2. St. James' tomb was located on the Mount of Olives, presumably housed within a church; *Antonini Placentini Itinerarium* 16.1–2.

52　Leontius of Neapolis, *Vita S. Johannis Ellemosynarii*, ed. Chatzioannou 1988: 30. The abandonment of the Patriarchate is implied in the *Life of Saint Anastasios the Persian*. Soon after the saint's martyrdom in 627, his brothers tried to translate his relics to the monastery of St. Sabbas, east of Bethlehem, since that was where he was first tonsured. Afterwards, they arrived in Jerusalem and found nobody there except Bishop Elijah, who recounted that these circumstances were according to God's plan; Flusin 1992: vol. 2, chapter 2, pp. 100–101.

53　Leontius of Neapolis, *Vita S. Johannis Ellemosynarii*: 11.

54　Regarding the fate of other Christians in Egypt, an 11th-century source notes that St. John the Almsgiver left from Alexandria with just a remnant of his congregation ("…ἀνεχώρησεν ἐκεῖθεν οὐ μετὰ πολλῶν τῶν ὑπ' αὐτοῦ λαόν"); Nikon of the Black Mountain, *Taktikon* (Sinai.MS.Gr.436, folio 172).

55　Leontius of Neapolis, *Johannis Ellemosynarii*, ed. Migne, PG 87: 4009–10; Chatzioannou 1988: 180.

56　Regarding the destruction of monasteries, churches, and holy sites in the year 614, see Hirschfeld 1992: 16; Dauphin 1993: 46; Dauphin-Edelstein 1993: 53; Aviam 1993: 65; Tzaferis 1993: 77, 205; Patrich 1993: 113; Hirschfeld 1993: 152; Hizmi 1993: 163; Magen 1993: 174.

57　George of Pisidia's epic poems, like *In restitutionem S. Crucis, Expeditio Persica,* and *Heraclias,* combine classical themes with Christian values for the purpose of political propaganda. But there are other examples, like the Syrian *Alexander Legend.* There is a growing amount of scholarly literature on this subject. Reinink's article "Die Entstehung der Syrischen Alexanderlegende als Politisch-Religiöse Propagandaschrift für Herakleios' Kirchenpolitik" discusses this issue at length (1985: 263–81); Reinink 2002: 84–91. Also see the general summary by Regan 2006: 15, 105, 126; and, more recently, Chronopoulos 2010.

58 The possibility of honoring heroes is only a hypothesis. As far as I know, there are no such references in written sources. Regarding the characterization of Heraclius as a prototypical Crusader, compare the views of Regan (2006) with Kolia-Dermitzaki (1991). Since this chapter was written, excavations at the *Katalymata ton Plakoton* have uncovered tangible proof of Heraclius' political ideology manifested in the form of a terminus or stele. This object is being prepared for publication by Charles Anthony Stewart.

59 See the chronological table in Kaegi 2003: 325. John Haldon's *Byzantium in the Seventh Century* (1990) remains the standard historical and societal description of the period.

60 Grierson 1968: 41; Dikigoropoulos 1940–1948: 97; Hill 1940: 282–83.

61 Brock 1973: 299–346.

62 Chrysos 1999: 207.

63 Chrysos 1999: 207–8.

64 Festougière 1974: 261; Chrysos 1984: 61. See also the important study on this familial cohesion by Rapp (2004: 121–34).

65 Here I am referring to the three monasteries founded by St. John around Amathous before he became patriarch. The first is the Acropolis monastic basilica excavated by A. Pralong (1994: 411–55). The second is the Basilica of the eastern cemetery of Amathous excavated by M. Loulloupis; Chatzioannou 1988: 235–38. And, third, the small monastic basilica I have excavated in Yermasogeia over the Amathous river; Procopiou 2007c: 71. For a general overview of the archaeology of Amathous, see Aupert 1996.

66 For Carpasia, see Taylor and Megaw 1981: 250; for Amathous, see Aupert and Leriche 1994: 337, 340–41.

67 Chrysos 1984: 60–61; Dunn 1998: 797.

68 Pralong 1994: 455; Chatzioannou 1988. For the site known as the Prophet Eliah at Germasogeia, see

Procopiou 2007c: 71.

69 Festougière 1974: 350, 357–58.

70 Kaegi 2003: 91.

71 Kaegi 2003: 81.

72 Leontius of Neapolis wrote: "Περσῶν γὰρ τὸ τηνικαῦτα τὴν Σύρων γῆν πᾶσαν ληϊσαμένων, οἱ τὰς τούτων χεῖρας ἐκφυγεῖν δυνηθέντες, ὅσοι τε τῶν λαϊκῶν ἦσαν ἄρχοντες ὁμοῦ καὶ ἀρχόμενοι, καὶ ὅσοι τοῦ κλήρου αὐτοῖς ἐπισκόποις εἰς Ἀλεξάνδρειαν καταφεύγουσιν, οἷς πᾶσιν ὁ πλούσιος ἐκεῖνος καὶ ἀστεναχώρητος ἑστιάτωρ ἱλαρῶς καθ᾽ ἑκάστην ἐχορήγει τὰ πρὸς τὴν χρείαν, οὐ πρὸς τὸ πλῆθος βλέπων τῶν δεομένων, ἵνα τι καὶ μικρόψυχον ὑποστῇ, ἀλλὰ πρὸς τὸν ἀνοίγοντα χεῖρα καὶ παντὶ ζώῳ εὐδοκίας μεταδίδοντα. Ρασμιόζου δὲ τοῦ ἀρχιστρατήγου Χοσρόου, τοὺς σεβασμίους τῶν Ἱεροσολύμων τόπους δηώσαντός τε καὶ ἐκπορθήσαντος, ἐπεὶ τοῦτον ἤκουσεν ὁ τοῦ Θεοῦ ἄνθρωπος, καὶ ὡς πάντα τὰ ἅγια πυρὶ παρεδόθη, θρηνεῖ μέν ἐπίσης Ἱερεμίᾳ τὸ γεγονός, οὐ μέχρι δὲ τούτου τὸ συμπαθὲς ἵστησι, ἀλλὰ καὶ Κτήσιππόν τινα θεοφιλῆ ἄνθρωπον ἀποστέλλει χρυσίον αὐτῷ συχνὸν ἐγχειρίσας, σῖτον τε καὶ τροφὰς ἑτέρας καὶ περιβόλαια καὶ πρὸς τὴν αὐτῶν μετακομιδὴν ὑποζύγια πάμπολλα, ὁμοῦ μὲν τὴν ἐρήμωσιν κατοψώμενον, ὁμοῦ δὲ τοὺς ἐκ τῆς αἰχμαλωσίας περιλειφθέντας ἱκανῶς διὰ τῶν εἰρημένων ἀνακτησόμενον. Πρὸς τούτῳ καὶ Θεόδωρον Ἀμαθοῦντος ἐπίσκοπον καὶ Ἀναστάσιον τὸν τοῦ ὄρους τοῦ μεγάλου καθηγουμένου Ἀντωνίου καὶ Γρηγόριον Ρινοκορούρων ἐπίσκοπον ἐπὶ ἀναλήψει τῶν αἰχμαλώτων ἐκπέμπει, χρυσίον οὐκ εὐάριθμητον παρασχόμενος;" emphasis mine. Chatzioannou 1988: 176; from Appendix B: Paris Codex 1487, fol.134r–137r, 108–12.

73 Rautman 2003: 235–39.

74 Megaw 1974: 70–72; Bakirtzis 1995: 251.

75 Flourentzos 1996: 37.

76 Hadjicosti 1993: 70–72; Caraher et al. 2007: 293–306.

77 Excavations were conducted at the church of Panagia tou Kampou in Choirokoitia by the author in 2010. Its findings will be published in the forthcoming *Annual Report of the Director of Antiquities, Cyprus,* for the year 2010. The excavations at Panagia Kofinou were conducted recently (August–November 2011) by D. Demetriou under the supervision of the author, in the frame of the EU project "Eumathios Philokales." See the press release on the website of the Department of Antiquities: http://www.mcw.gov.

cy/mcw/DA/DA.nsf/All/DD5C629BC1C77E3F42257
8F60045652C?OpenDocument.

78 Chrysos 1999: 207.

79 For Asia Minor in general, see Sodini 2004; Koder
1998: 256. For the Pontus coast, Sivrihisar Dağlari
in Galatia, Kalykandos, and Isaurian coasts: Dunn
1998: 796–97. For Ankara and the reformation of
the defense system in the Anatolikon, Armeniakon,
and Cappadocia, and how these areas later emerged
as Themes (e.g., reinforcement of the fortress of
Smyrna), see Vlysidou et al. 1998: 39, 41, 225, 264.
For North Africa, see Tsafrir 1993: 332. Regarding
Crete, the island was generally in decline in the early
seventh century, and its population shifted to the
interior, such as the Pediada Bishopric's move to
Piscopiano; Chaniotaki and Marē 2004: 289. For
Cretan Early Christian architecture, see Platon 1955
and Varalis 2004.

80 Vita 2004: 474; Perna 2004: 548, 552–53; Ruggieri
1991: 265. Special attention should be given by future
excavators to the reexamination of the Vetranios
phase of reconstructions in the Metropolis Basilica
(Gortyna); Bormpoudakis 2004: 628–30.

81 Koutellas 1998: 94–95, 108–10.

82 For Rhodes, see Orlandos 1948: 32–35; 1957: 114–15;
for Chios, see Balance et al. 1989: 2–3.

83 Kaegi 2003: 154, 223, 278.

84 Thierry 1984: 318–20.

85 Kaegi 2003: 154; Ruggieri 1999: 191.

86 Kaegi 2003: 186–87.

87 Kaegi 2003: 197–98, 203, 207–8, 219; for Paphlagonia,
see Trombley 1998: 107, 112–13; for Agia Eirene in
the Antitaurus mountains and the Church of the
Archangel in the borderlands of Phrygia-Galatia see
Karač 1998: 969.

Chapter 7

Chypre et les Arabes avant les Croisades à la Lumière des Sources Arabes

par M. Tahar Mansouri

Chypre, une île à la croisée des chemins, occupant une place de choix dans la Méditerranée orientale ou ce que les textes arabes appellent, la mer de Syrie. Elle pointe le regard vers les rivages d'en face, sans jamais se détacher de la mer, la grande, et sans jamais s'éloigner de la mer Égée ni de cette mer qui la lie à l'Égypte.[1] Et comme l'a si bien écrit le Professeur Costas Kyrris, "L'emplacement géographique de Chypre à la croisée des routes entre le Proche Orient, l'Asie Mineure et l'Afrique, lui donne un atout stratégique exploitable dans tous les domaines, celui du commerce ou de la guerre ou encore pour d'autres activités."[2]

Cet emplacement a été exploité au début du VII siècle par Mu'awiya b. Abi Soufyan, alors gouverneur de la Syrie, pour convaincre le pouvoir central de Médine de la nécessité de conquérir l'île. Et c'est à partir de ce moment que se pose la question des rapports entre Chypre et Byzance d'un côté et les Arabes d'un autre. Quelles lumières les sources arabes peuvent-elles nous donner sur l'île de Chypre durant la période allant du milieu du VIIe siècle jusqu'à la veille des croisades? Trois éléments retiennent l'attention quant aux informations présentées dans les sources arabes: la présentation de l'île, la conquête arabe, et les relations qui ont suivi cet épisode.

LES DONNÉES RELATIVES À L'ÎLE

Le premier élément est l'explication donnée par les lexicographes quant au sens du nom de l'île. Ce nom en plus qu'il soit un nom de lieu il veut dire le cuivre de bon aloi ou le meilleur du cuivre en plus ce nom n'est pas semble-t-il pour les textes arabes un nom vide de sens puisqu'on nous dit que le cuivre de cette île est le meilleur. La première information que nous livrent les lexicographes se rapporte au nom de l'île. C'est un nom de lieu situé dans les marches syriennes et qui n'est pas d'origine arabe. On y ajoute un sens à ce nom — c'est le cuivre de meilleur aloi. Le cuivre chypriote est le meilleur.[3]

Au XIIe siècle les données relatives à la vie économique et sociale de l'île commencent à apparaître dans les sources arabes.

Le premier à nous donner une idée sur l'île est al-Idrisi. On y trouve cultures, bétails et arbres fruitiers. On y cultive la canne, de l'artisanat et le miel en abondance. En plus on extrait un métal appelé *al-Zaj* qui est exporté dans différents pays. C'est une île urbanisée car en plus des trois villes importantes, qui sont *al-Noumaysoun* (Limassol), *Laffqasiya* (Nicosie) et *Kryna* (Kyrenia), il y a des villages.[4] L'île de Chypre est souvent associée à l'île de Crète dont Ibn Hawqal vante les richesses et la diversité des produits agricoles dont notamment la soie, le lin, le blé, l'orge et différentes autres céréales et richesses diverses.[5]

En plus, les textes qui ont relaté la conquête de l'île, tel Ibn A'tham al-Koufi, nous disent que les Arabes quand ils ont envahi l'île, ils y ont trouvé des produits de luxe telle que la soie et la fourrure et d'autres produits de luxe qui ont permis d'avoir un butin important ayant permis de remplir les navires.[6]

Par ailleurs, on relate aussi une diversité de richesses résumé par l'un des soldats de la conquête; quand interrogé par le calife Othman, il répondit, "qu'on y trouve des rivières, des cultures, des arbres, de la vigne et une diversité de fruits. On y trouve des châteaux très hauts. Elle a aussi les chevaux, les mulets, les ânes, les ovins et les vaches en grand nombre."[7] Il ressort de ces descriptions l'image d'une île urbanisée et prospère de par son agriculture qui semble développée et son sol riche; ce qui justifie en quelque sorte l'effort consenti pour sa prise mais aussi le lourd tribut que les Chypriotes ont dû payer aux Byzantins et aux Arabes en même temps. C'est aussi comme si les sources rapportant une telle prospérité essayant de justifier a posteriori des actes qui pourraient être condamnables, surtout quand on apprend que les *fuqahā* (experts en droit islamique) se sont opposés au pouvoir central dans le traitement réservé aux habitants de l'île soupçonnés de transgresser le pacte qui les liait aux Arabes.

LA CONQUÊTE DE CHYPRE

Quand les Arabes ont conquis la Syrie, l'île de Chypre était une domination byzantine, très proche du nouveau domaine de l'Islam et qui semble facile à conquérir. Les textes arabes s'accordent pour insister sur la proximité géographique de l'île ce qui rend cette proximité à la fois un avantage mais aussi un danger. Mais de l'autre côté on montre le refus du pouvoir central à autoriser une telle opération. Le calife Omar b. al-Khattab s'est montré intransigeant quant à l'envoi de troupes pour conquérir l'île, allant jusqu'à menacer le gouverneur en cas de désobéissance. Cette décision califale s'est faite sous l'effet des conseils de 'Amrou ibn al-'As. Lesquels textes insistent aussi sur

la ténacité du gouverneur de Syrie pour mener une campagne navale contre Chypre. Mais ce n'est que sous le règne d'Othman que les conquêtes maritimes ont été engagées. La conquête de Chypre est en définitive une œuvre personnelle du gouverneur de Syrie plus qu'un choix du pouvoir central. Le nouveau calife a rappelé à Mu'awiya (602–680) la décision de son prédécesseur avant de lui accorder l'autorisation de mener campagne contre Chypre. Tout cela exprime la prudence avec laquelle la question de la conquête a été traitée au niveau du pouvoir central.

Une fois l'autorisation accordée, Mu'awiya a embarqué du port d'Acre,[8] avec beaucoup de navires — les textes n'avancent pas de chiffres précis — au printemps de 28 ou 29 AH (648–649), accompagné de sa femme et de certains compagnons du Prophète, dont Ubada ibn as-Samit avec son épouse Umm Milhan b. Haram.[9] Le résultat de l'expédition était en plus du butin important en hommes et en richesses, et en plus de la victoire sur la peur de la mer, c'est la signature d'un traité entre les Musulmans, les Chypriotes et les Byzantins par lequel l'île de Chypre devient tributaire à la fois pour les Arabes et pour les Byzantins. Le traité signé prévoit deux conditions pour son respect:

1. Le payement d'un tribut annuel dont le montant varie selon les textes de 7000 à 7200 dinars payables pour chacun des deux protagonistes: les Arabes et les Byzantins.

2. Informer les Arabes sur d'éventuelles expéditions byzantines et informer les Byzantins des mouvements des armées musulmanes.

L'île devrait se trouver dans une position de neutralité et de dépendance à l'égard des deux belligérants.

Cependant cette neutralité qui a fait l'objet d'une des clauses du pacte signé suite à l'expédition de Mu'awiya sera l'objet d'une discorde entre les pouvoirs musulmans successifs omeyyade puis abbassides et les habitants de l'île de Chypre et la cause d'interventions militaires répétées. L'une des actions menées contre l'île est la déportation de ses habitants. Quels en étaient les motifs et quelles étaient les réactions face à de telles pratiques?

LA POLITIQUE DES OMEYYADES

Pour mieux comprendre la politique des Omeyyades, il faut aller aux sources originales. Ci-dessous est que nous disent les textes.

Ibn Sallam rapporte les leçons suivantes :

> Quand al-Walid b. Yazid les a déplacés en Syrie, les *fuqahā* s'y sont opposés et ont vu dans cet acte une injustice et une énormité. Et quand Yazid b. al-Walid est devenu calife il les a rapatriés, les Musulmans ont été satisfaits de cet acte et l'ont considéré comme une justice rendue.[10]

Muhammad ibn Mousaffa (*sic*) al-Himsi a rapporté à propos d'al-Walid, qui a dit:

> Nous avons appris que Yazid b. Mu'awiya a dépensé de grosses sommes d'argent pour rapatrier les soldats stationnés à Chypre, et quand ils ont été rapatriés, les Chypriotes ont détruit leur ville et leurs mosquées.[11]

> Quand al-Walid b. Yazid les a déportés vers la Syrie, les Musulmans n'ont pas trouvé de précédent analogue, et les *fuqahā* l'ont condamné. Et quand Yazid b. al-Walid b. 'Abd al-Malik est devenu calife, il les a rapatriés à Chypre, les Musulmans ont apprécié son geste et y ont vu une équité.[12]

Selon le chroniqueur chrétien du Xe siècle, Agapius ou Mahboub al-Manbaji, d'expression arabe, dans sa chronique universelle intitulée *Kitab al-'Unwan* nous dit :

> al-Walid ibn Yazid fit déporter les Chypriotes de leurs foyers et de leur pays pour les installer à al-Mahour, qui est situé au bord de la mer, entre Tyr et Sidon.[13] Ensuite Yazid le Simple (le diminué) renvoya chez eux les Chypriotes que al-Walid avait déportés de leur pays.[14]

> En cette année [125 AH (742)] al-Walid b. Yazid a engagé son frère al-Ghamr b. Yazid b. 'Abd al-Malik, dans une expédition et

a mis la marine sous le commandement de al-Aswad b. Bilal al-Muharibi, et lui a ordonné d'aller à Chypre et demander à ses habitants de choisir entre le départ pour la Syrie et le départ pour Byzance. Une partie d'entre eux ont choisi d'aller en Syrie, al-Aswad les a transportés, et d'autres ont choisi d'aller à Byzance, ils s'y sont rendus.[15]

De ces textes on peut tirer quelques conclusions relatives à la fois à la politique de colonisation et aux techniques de domination adoptées par les Omeyyades face aux populations qui n'étaient forcément sous leur contrôle direct.

La technique adoptée est celle de la déportation. Celle-ci avait pour but:

1. Châtier les peuples insoumis. Le cas des Chypriotes est qu'ils n'étaient ni *dhimmis* (protégés), ni *harbi* (en état de guerre), mais des tributaires (*ahlou fidyatin*).

2. Créer une sorte de "no man's land" en Chypre ce qui aura tendance à priver l'armée byzantine de toute possibilité d'aide logistique sur l'île.

3. Déplacer ces populations de Chypre et les installer en Syrie, c'est aussi les couper définitivement de leur racines mais surtout transformer leur statut de celui de tributaire se contentant de payer une somme fixe une fois par an en *dhimmis* ayant l'obligation de payer les deux impôts obligatoires que devait un non-Musulman en terre d'Islam: la *jiziya* (capitation) et le *karaj* (impôt sur la fortune).

4. Mais aussi tenir une carte maîtresse dans la diplomatie ommeyyade, c'est celle d'utiliser cette population comme moyen de pression, si nécessaire face aux Byzantins.

Cependant, si ainsi était la politique officielle de l'état, la réaction populaire semblait être différente des intentions du pouvoir. Mais malgré la signature du traité, les raids arabes, prétextant assez souvent du non-respect de ce traité, vont continuer contre l'île.

En 32 AH (652), l'île de Chypre se range du côté byzantin en offrant de l'aide à son armée ce qui a été considéré comme une rupture du traité signé auparavant, alors Mu'awiya attaque l'île en 33 AH (653) ou en 35 AH (655),[16] qui se termine par la captivité d'une partie de la population chypriote qui sera ramenée en Syrie et remplacée par un contingent de 12,000 hommes originaires de la région de Baalbek, accompagnés de leur famille et pour qui on aurait construit une ville et des mosquées.[17] Et là en plus du changement de statut de l'île, on peut constater un double transfert de population entre l'île et le continent voisin. Rien n'est dit à ce propos quant à la coexistence entre ces peuples transférés, malgré leur volonté avec les populations locales sur leur terre d'exil.[18]

Quand Mu'awiya est décédé, son fils Yazid lui succéda ordonna de rapatrier les soldats que son père a installés à Chypre et aurait même ordonné la destruction de la ville qui leur a été construite.[19] A ce propos, les versions relatives à la destruction de la ville construite par les Musulmans divergent. La première version attribue l'ordre de la destruction au calife Yazid ibn Mu'awiya. Quant à la deuxième version, elle laisse aux Chypriotes la responsabilité d'avoir détruit la ville des Musulmans et leurs mosquées. Le rapatriement des soldats et des colons installés par Mu'awiya, et effectué par son fils, semble avoir coûté très cher au trésor de Damas, puisque Yazid aurait dépensé une somme importante a cet effet (*rasha malan 'adhiman dha qadrin Hatta aqfala jundu qubros*).[20]

En 107 AH (725), le Calife omeyyade Hisham ibn Abd al-Malik (724–743) a ordonné à Maymoun ibn Mihran, gouverneur des marches frontières du littoral, de mener une expédition contre Chypre.[21] Mais la décision la plus radicale sera prise par al-Walid ibn Yazid ibn Abd al-Malik (743–744) qui décida de déporter une grande partie de la population chypriote vers la Syrie "*ajla minhum khlqa 'adhiman.*" Al-Baladhuri cite un texte anonyme rapporté sous la rubrique, "on dit que al-Walid ibn Yazid a déporté parmi les Chypriotes un nombre important en Syrie les accusant d'un certain forfait qu'ils ont commis." Alors que Tabari rapporte une autre version différente qui consiste aux faits suivants:

En cette année [125 AH (742)] al-Walid b. Yazid a envoyé son frère al-Ghamr b. Yazid b. Abd al-Malik, en expédition à Chypre et a nommé à la tête de la marine al-Aswad b. Bilal al-Muharibi et lui a donné l'ordre d'aller à Chypre et laisser à ses habitants le choix entre l'émigration vers la Syrie ou vers le pays des Rums. Un groupe a choisi le voisinage des Musulmans, al-Aswad les a transportés vers la Syrie alors qu'un autre groupe a choisi l'émigration vers le pays des Rums, ils s'y sont rendus.[22]

Certes, Tabari présente ce fait comme un choix volontaire qui aurait été laissé au peuple de Chypre mais dont les conséquences sont graves si l'on croit les faits rapportés, puisque l'île semble avoir été dépeuplée. Et le but de tout cela c'est vider l'île de toute personne susceptible d'aider les Byzantins contre les Musulmans, ce qui est dans le cas contraire le même but pour les Byzantins.

LES RÉACTIONS

Seulement cette déportation n'a pas été acceptée et a été dénoncée à la fois par la population de Syrie et les *fuqahā* dans une réaction spontanée. Les textes nous disent que les gens ainsi que les *fuqahā* ont dénoncé une telle pratique. On trouve des termes forts dénonçant un tel acte:

ankara al-Nasu dhalika:[23]:
Les gens ont dénoncé un tel acte.

Istaqta'a al-muslimuna dhalika:[24]
Les Musulmans n'ont pas trouvé un précédent à cet acte pour procéder par analogie.

Ista'dhamahu al-Fuqaha:[25]
dans le *fiqh* et dans la langue *Ista'dhama* c'est à la fois un jugement et une dénonciation.[26]

Istafdha'a al-Fuqahau dhalika:[27]
al-Fadha'a c'est l'horreur ce qui permet de dire que les fuqaha ont jugé une telle déportation comme un acte horrible.

Les Chypriotes ne sont pas des *dhimmis* et ne sont pas de ennemis — ils sont tributaires, *"ahlu fidyatin,"* ils payent un tribut aux Musulmans.

Le pouvoir reconnaissant ses erreurs s'est trouvé dans l'obligation de procéder à un double transfert de population. D'un côté ce sont les Chypriotes qui devaient être rapatriés, et de l'autre ce sont les Syriens qui devaient être ramenés en Syrie. En dépit du sentiment de satisfaction général affiché dans les textes qui ont relaté les faits en écrivant *"wa astahsana al-nasou dhalika,"* on remarque un certain regret quant aux agissements du pouvoir. D'abord pour des considérations morales et jurisprudentielles et ensuite parce que l'opération était coûteuse.[28]

Si la raison de la déportation semble-être l'intelligence des Chypriotes avec Byzance, leur retour était dicté par une obligation de conformité à l'esprit des lois défendu par les *fuqahā* et la dénonciation d'un acte jugé irresponsable et contraire à la *shari'a*. C'est que ces *fuqahā* représentaient un contrepoids à l'autorité et exprimaient le point de vue de ce qu'on pourrait appeler les "intellectuels" de l'époque. Leur position a infléchit le pouvoir politique et a obligé le Calife à faire marche arrière.

Bien évidemment une telle position de la part des *fuqahā* pourrait se comprendre à la lumière de deux éléments. Le premier est le rôle qu'ils commençaient à jouer — cette catégorie de gens qui n'ont d'autre pouvoir que celui de porter un jugement moral et religieux sur les actes du prince. Le deuxième est qu'un tel déplacement d'une population chrétienne en Syrie pourrait créer un déséquilibre ou du moins gonfler les rangs des chrétiens de la région si l'on sait qu'en plus des *dhimmis* qui y vivaient, il y a les Mardaites (*al-jarajima*) dans la région du Liban actuel.[29]

Il va sans dire que déportation coercitive était une pratique courante appliquée par les Omeyyades à l'égard des ennemis de l'extérieur aussi bien que ceux de l'intérieur. Elle était utilisée comme un moyen de domination de régions le plus souvent hostiles ou pour bannir des éléments: par exemple, le cas des habitants des zones frontalières parmi les chrétiens, les Mardaites ou tout simplement les opposants parmi les Musulmans qui n'étaient pas de la même obédience que les Omeyyades.

La Réaction des Fuqahā

En ce qui concerne le deuxième événement, c'était parce qu'il y avait une deuxième violation du traité qui liait les Chypriotes aux Musulmans. Tabari nous informe :

> Qu'en cette année [190 AH (805)] Harun al-Rashid a nommé Humayd b. Ma'yuf à la tête des zones côtières de l'Égypte et de la Syrie. Il a atteint Chypre, il a détruit, brûlé et pris en captivité 16000 personnes parmi ses habitants, il les a amenés à al-Rafiqa, où le juge Abû al-Bukhturi les a vendus, au prix fort selon leur statut dans leur île.[30]

Et là il ne s'agit plus de la déportation telle que pratiquée par la dynastie précédente, mais d'une sorte de prise de captifs destinés à la vente (*fay*).

Un autre événement intervient sous le règne du même calife Harun al-Rashid en 196 AH (811) et rapporté par Abou 'Oubaid ibn Sallam qui nous dit:

> Qu'il y a eu une trahison de la part des habitants de Chypre, qui est une île dans la mer, partagée entre les Byzantins et les Musulmans. Auparavant Mu'awiya a conclu avec eux un traité stipulant le payement d'un tribut égal aux Musulmans et aux Byzantins. Ils étaient les protégés des deux états. Ils ont été toujours ainsi jusqu'au moment où 'Abd al-Malik b. Salih était gouverneur des marches. Sous son autorité, ils ont commis un quelconque forfait, ou du moins certains parmi eux, ce que 'Abd al-Malik a estimé être une raison suffisante pour prouver la rupture du contrat.

> Et du moment que les *fuqahā* [exégètes] étaient nombreux, il a alors écrit à certains d'entre eux pour les consulter à propos de la légitimité de la guerre. Parmi ceux à qui il a écrit: al-Layth b. Sa'd, Malik b. Anas, Soufyan b. 'Uyayna, Mousa b. A'youn, Isma'il b. 'Ayyach, Yahya b. Hamza, Abou Ishaq al-Fazari et Makhlid b. Housayn. Ils ont tous répondu à sa requête.

Puis Abou ʿOubaid ibn Sallam rapporte:

> J'ai trouvé leurs lettres dans la chancellerie de ʿAbd al-Malik, j'en ai abrégé le sens de ce qu'ils ont voulu dire et auquel ils ont aspiré. Leurs opinions étaient divergeantes. Cependant ceux qui lui ont conseillé de respecter le pacte et de ne pas les combattre étaient plus nombreux que ceux qui lui ont conseillé la guerre.[31]

Bien au contraire, certains *fuqahā* ont cherché à légitimer leur connivence avec les Byzantins en disant comme Ismail ibn Ayyache "que les gens de Chypre sont vaincus et humiliés par les Rums, au lieu de les châtier il est de notre devoir de les défendre et de les protéger."[32] Les *fuqahā* dont al-Layth ibn Saad, al-Imam al-Aouzaʿi, Yahya ibn Hamza, Musa ibn Aʿyun, Malik ibn Anas, Abu Ishaq al-Fazari et Makhlid ibn al-Husayn se sont opposés à la décision du gouverneur des marches du Littoral visant à rompre leur traité et à les attaquer.[33] Le seul qui s'est montré favorable à un châtiment dure à l'égard des Chypriotes est Sufyan ibn ʿUyayna qui invoque la tradition du prophète qui a châtié les Mekkois qui ont soutenu ses ennemis parmi la tribu de Khuzaʿa, ou encore le châtiment infligé par ʿOmar aux juifs de Najran qui ont signé avec lui un traité par lequel ils ne devaient pas pratiquer l'usure. Quand ils n'ont pas respecté ce traité, ʿOmar a décidé de les bannir. Et à quelle Sufyan ajoute, "il y a un consensus que celui qui ne respecte pas un traité ne peut plus se protéger des représailles," et c'est selon lui le cas des Chypriotes.[34] Ainsi sur huit parmi les plus éminents docteurs de l'Islam de l'époque, seul un s'est montré favorable à la politique envisagée par le gouverneur.

Il va sans dire qu'une telle opposition massive des hommes de la loi a obligé le gouverneur à faire marche arrière. S'agit-il de l'émergence durant cette période d'une élite intellectuelle qui cherche à affirmer son pouvoir? Et peut-on parler d'une élite intellectuelle qui a voulu se donner le pouvoir de contrôler les actes du politique?

Dans tous les cas, la politique officielle vis-à-vis des peuples vaincus ou des peuples sans défense ne pas été toujours soutenue par l'élite socio-intellectuelle. Ce qui permet tout de même de nuancer l'esprit de guerre, qu'on attribue souvent au monde musulman, confondant textes et pratiques. Nous pouvons dire que les différentes prises humaines effectuées sur la population de l'île — en plus de ceux qui ont eu la possibilité de fuir vers Byzance — contribueraient largement à son affaiblissement démographique. La population capturée et déportée de son milieu originel ne semble pas avoir été prise en considération dans les échanges de prisonniers fréquents entre Abbassides et Byzantins. Même si au début du Xe siècle, Nicolas Mystikos, patriarche de Constantinople, a pris la défense des Chypriotes et écrivit deux longues lettres aux autorités de Bagdad, invoquant à la fois le traité de Muʿawiya et remarquant la régularité des Chypriotes dans le payement du tribut qui leur a été imposé depuis les premiers temps de l'Islam. Dans une lettre envoyée au Calife abbasside al-Muqtadir, Nicolas Mystikos lui rappelle que les Chypriotes se sont toujours acquittés de leur tribu depuis 300 ans.[35]

LA SCÈNE ET ÉTAPE POUR L'AVENIR

En conclusion, nous pouvons dire que l'île de Chypre reste un cas dans les relations entre Byzance et l'Islam, mais un cas qui aurait failli être appliqué à l'Afrique du nord selon les informations rapportées par certains textes arabes.[36] Cependant, durant tout le moyen-âge l'île de Chypre a joué à la fois le rôle de front entre Chrétienté orientale et Islam puis entre croisés et Musulmans. Elle sera une tête de pont pour les croisés vainqueurs puis un lieu de repli pour les croisés vaincus.

ABSTRACT

Arabic sources give us a range of information relating to the Arab presence on Cyprus. They record political aspects and types of relationships that existed between the island and the various Muslim domains. For example, one can read in the Arabic sources about the context of the conquest and partition of the island between Byzantine and Muslim powers, while at the same time maintaining that the neutrality of the Cypriots was observed. However, two main events marked this period.

The first event was the breaking of the treaty — whether actual or assumed — caused by Cypriots against the Arabs. The consequences of this alleged breach were the momentary deportation of Cypriots to Syria and the reactions that followed. This deportation was later canceled because of the position of the *fuqahā* (judges) who denounced Umayyad high-handedness and condemned the act. A second event took place during the reign of Harun al-Rashid, when the central powers faced opposition from the scholarly Islamic community. The case of Cyprus developed various legal theories relating to the perceived relationship or contact between Muslims and other populations. These two events shed some light on the internal organization of the island. They give us an idea about its economic conditions and the state of urbanism, especially by focusing on three major cities that seem to be at the top of the urban hierarchy: *Lafqosia* (Nicosia), *Al-Noumaysoun* (Limassol), and *Kyrnéa* (Kyrenia).

With all things considered, the Arabic sources seemed more interested in the status of the island and its relations with neighboring Muslim powers than its internal evolution. So this chapter highlights three general issues: (1) the conquest of the island by the Arabs; (2) the Umayyad policy towards Cyprus and the reactions of scholars regarding this policy; (3) the social, economic, and urban context of the island within the Arab world.

NOTES

1   [Editorial note] The body of this chapter retains the common French spellings for Arab historical persons. For the notes and the bibliography, it was decided to use transliterations commonly used in library databases. This seemed to be the best compromise for upholding the integrity of the French, while citing the source materials for English-speaking scholars.
Pour les textes arabes relatifs à Chypre, voir M. Tahar Mansouri, *Chypre dans les sources arabes médiévales* (Nicosie: Centre de Recherche de Chypre, 2001).

2   Kyrris 1996: 27.

3   Mansouri 2001: 17.

4   al'Idrīsi, *Nuzhat al-Mushtāq fī Iktirāq al-Āfāq*, ed. Mansouri 2001a: 39.

5   Ibn Hawqal, *Kitāb al-Masālik wa'l Mamālik*, ed. Mansouri 2001a: 34.

6   Ibn A'tham al-Koufi, *Kitāb al-futuh*, ed. Mansouri 2001a: 36.

7   Ibn A'tham al-Koufi, *Kitāb al-futuh*, ed. Mansouri 2001a: 39.

8   Qudama ibn Ja'far, *al-Kharaj wa sina'at al-Kitaba*, éd. M. H. al-Zubaydi 1981: 290; Mansouri 2001a: 241–42, et 32–33 de la traduction. Le Mausolée de Umm Haram est encore visible en Chypre au sud ouest de la ville de Larnaka, appelé "Hala Sultan Tekke." Il est considéré comme un lieu de visite pour les Musulmans ou un sanctuaire à visiter. Il suffit de voir les tombes avec inscriptions funéraires datant de l'époque ottomane pour s'en rendre compte; Papalexandrou 2008: 251–81.

9   Mansouri 2001a: 241–42; Aristeidou 1982.

10   Ibn Sallām, *Kitāb al-Amwāl*, ed. Mansouri 2001a: 223–28.

11 Al-Balādhuri, *Kitāb Futūh al-Buldān,* ed. Mansouri 2001a: 158.

12 Ibid.: 161.

13 Agapius of Manbij, *Kitāb al-ʿUnwān,* ed. Mansouri 2001a: 511.

14 Ibid.: 512.

15 Tabari, *Taʾrīkh al-Rusul waʾl Mulūk* VII, ed. Ibrāhīm 1960–1969: 227.

16 Tabari, *Taʾrīkh al-Rusul waʾl Mulūk* VII, ed. Ibrāhīm 1960–1969: 158; Ibn Taġrībirdī, *Al-Nujūm al-zāhirah* I, ed. Tarhān 1963–1971: 84–85. L'auteur résume al-Waqidi mais ne retient que la date de 33 AH (653). Mais nous pensons qu'il n'était pas possible pour Muʿawiya de s'attaquer à Chypre en 35 AH (656), parce que la situation dans le monde musulman ne le permettait pas et les troubles conséquents à la mort de ʿOthman en Dhu al-Ḥijjah la même année. La décision de contester le pouvoir d'Ali (à la bataille du Chameau), la demande de châtiment pour les assassins de ʿOthman, le conflit qui se prépare entre les Omeyyades et le nouveau Calife, signifie que Muʿawiya ne pouvait pas s'engager dans une guerre aux portes de sa province. D'ailleurs il signe dans la même période un traité de paix avec Byzance pour assurer ses arrières. Le danger n'est plus du côté de Chypre ou de Byzance, il est plutôt du côté de Kufa proche et déterminante pour son avenir et celui des siens.

17 Tabari, *Taʾrīkh al-Rusul waʾl Mulūk* VII, ed. Ibrāhīm 1960–1969: 158.

18 On peut comprendre que les Chypriotes n'attendaient que l'occasion pour se débarrasser de ces éléments étrangers, puisqu'à la suite du rapatriement des soldats musulmans, les Chypriotes ont détruit leur ville et leur mosquée.

19 Tabari, *Taʾrīkh al-Rusul waʾl Mulūk* VII, ed. Ibrāhīm 1960-1969: 158. Une autre version dit que les Chypriotes auraient détruit la ville qui a été construite par les Musulmans.

20 Al-Balādhuri, *Kitāb Futūh al-Buldān,* ed. Mansouri 2001a: 158.

21 Tabari, *Taʾrīkh al-Rusul waʾl Mulūk* VII, ed. Ibrāhīm 1960–1969: 40.

22 Ibid.: 227.

23 Al-Balādhuri, *Kitāb Futūh al-Buldān,* ed. Mansouri 2001a: 159.

24 Ibid.: 161.

25 Ibid.: 161; Ibn Sallām, *Kitāb al-Amwāl,* ed. Mansouri 2001a: 226.

26 Ibn Manẓūr, *Lisān al-ʿArab,* lettre ʾA, 1956–1955: 410. L'une des variantes de ce verbe est dénoncer: *Istaʿ dhama al-amar idha ankarahu.*

27 Ibn Sallām, *Kitāb al-Amwāl,* ed. Mansouri 2001a: 226.

28 Al-Balādhuri, *Kitāb Futūh al-Buldān,* ed. Mansouri 2001a: 158.

29 Ibid.: 183; Yaqut, *Kitāb muʾjam al-buldān* V, ed. Dār Ṣādir 1955–1957: 11, 22.

30 Tabari, *Taʾrīkh al-Rusul waʾl Mulūk* VIII, ed. Ibrāhīm 1960–1969: 320 et 322. Le prix de l'archevêque de Chypre a atteint 2000 dinars.

31 Ibn Sallām, *Kitāb al-Amwāl,* ed. Mansouri 2001a:, 223.

32 Al-Balādhuri, *Kitāb Futūh al-Buldān,* ed. Mansouri 2001a: 161.

33 Ibid.: 160.

34 Ibid.: 160.

35 Patriarche Nicholas I, *Epistulae,* ed. Jenkins and Westerink 1973: 3 et *passim*; cf. Ducellier 1990: 230; Hamidullah 1953: 7 (texte arabe) et 10 (traduction anglaise).

36 Mansouri 2001b: 2–10; Epalza 1991: 145–48.

Chapter 8

The Development of Byzantine Architecture on Cyprus

by Charles Anthony Stewart

In Cyprus there are over 200 Early Christian and Byzantine buildings either still standing or known through archaeology. This number is increased if we include those mentioned in historical sources but which do not survive. With this rather large data set, coupled with the island's well-defined boundaries, the architectural historian has a unique case study in typological development. Pioneers of Byzantine archaeology were puzzled by the surviving monuments. George Jeffery's seminal monograph concluded that Byzantine architecture on Cyprus "betrayed a clumsy unscientific idea of construction."[1] Characterizations like this persist today, leading to Cyprus' omission in general publications on Byzantine architecture. This chapter discusses how in recent years momentum is moving in another direction. Cyprus, as a small Byzantine province, was clearly influenced by the trends of the surrounding continents; and yet, the island also had rich resources and a deep building tradition which fostered local innovation.

BEYOND BINARY MODELS

In 1903 the British colonial government hired George Jeffery to manage and maintain the antiquities of the island. He held this position until 1936. As Dr. Despo Pilides uncovered in her research on Jeffery's diaries, he was alarmed how Byzantine monuments were being torn down in order to construct newer, more "modern" churches. Perhaps that is why he set out to write the first survey of Byzantine monuments of the island.[2] In 1916 he presented a lengthy paper at the Society of Antiquaries in London entitled "The Byzantine Churches of Cyprus." Unfortunately his survey exposed his lack of knowledge in Byzantine history, offering incorrect dates accompanied by imperialist opinions. For example, he described the Byzantine frescos of Cyprus as "rude decoration in crude primary colours…such primitive attempts at pictorial art" rendered by "half-savage peasantry."[3] In time Jeffery's harsh assessment of Cypriot frescos would be abandoned. We now celebrate them as masterpieces.[4] And yet Jeffery's disregard for its Byzantine architecture, which held such precious paintings, lingers on in scholarship. As the island's first Byzantine architectural historian, Jeffery set the tone for the succeeding generation. There is no doubt his opinions were formed by a colonial mentality.

Cyril Mango lamented that Byzantine architectural historians have held on to paradigms long after archaeology has shown those models to be obsolete.[5] One model that has dominated Byzantine research on Cyprus is the "binary model."

Naturally historians cannot ignore the linear prog-ress of time as our perception of *diachronical* events unfolds. Inherent in this term is the idea of pairings, such as "past and present," which logically leads to other dichotomies such as "cause and effect," "rise and fall," "formation and reformation," "golden age" and "dark age," etc. Temporal pairings are often correlated with spatial binaries, such as "center and periphery," "urban and rural," "eastern and west-ern," "capital and tributary," etc. Constructs such as these are useful in organizing and presenting our data.[6] However, we should keep in mind that these are merely rhetorical tools. Binary labels, in other words, are historians' constructs and not necessar-ily historical facts.

Binary terms are often laden with derogatory, erroneous judgments—like George Jeffery's. He seemed to be comparing Cyprus' *early* Byzantine architecture with its *later* Gothic buildings. This temporal dichotomy was conjoined with the spatial binary of "eastern / western." In Jeffery's day, architec-tural historians linked Latin scholastic architecture with the rise of modern "science"—therefore, in contrast, Byzantine architecture was "unscientific" by comparison.[7] If cosmopolitan Gothic architec-ture was located in the *urban* settings of Nicosia and Famagusta, then, by comparison, monastic Byzantine architecture was *rural* and constructed by "half-savage peasants."

Fortunately A.H.S. Megaw did not share the same opinions as his predecessor. When we exam-ine his entire corpus, we detect Megaw's historical perspective, cautious of his own subjective values. But because the quantity of Cyprus' Byzantine archaeology was immense, Megaw continued to use the binary model to help organize the material. In his influential 1974 *Dumbarton Oaks Paper* arti-cle, Megaw posed the question: *Was architecture on Cyprus Metropolitan or Provincial?* Of course, he was playing on the word *metropolitan*, which means both "urban" and, in a Greek Orthodox con-text, a bishop (or archbishop) below the rank of a patriarch. On the one hand, if Cyprus was "metro-politan" it could mean two things: first, either it was subject to the patriarch of Constantinople, or sec-ondly, that it was a large urban center. Historically, in both cases, it was neither. On the other hand, if Cyprus was "provincial," it would mean that its

architecture was subjected to, and depended on, the imperial capital of Constantinople. Such a lim-ited question necessarily corralled the reader to the narrow conclusion that Cypriot architecture was "provincial."

Megaw avoided elucidating what *provincial* signified: Did the builders have some training in Constantinople, or were the locals merely imita-tors of the imperial master-builders? How were typologies imported? And more conspicuously, why are there no clear Constantinopolitan archi-tectural types on the island? The reader was not given a chance to consider whether Cypriots could develop their own particular, insular architecture. Likewise, he did not allow us to ponder the influ-ence of the great schools of architecture of other metropolises of the region, such as Alexandria, Jerusalem, and Damascus. Instead, emphasis was placed on the cohesion of the Byzantine Empire and the importance of its capital.

Megaw's binary model reflected the political situation of his day. Fourteen years earlier Megaw was part of the British colonial government in Cyprus. At that time the most notable twentieth-century monuments on the island were designed by British architects and paid for by the colonial government with subsidies sent from London. In contrast, local building traditions were of timber and mud-brick with no significant native architects by imperial standards. Besides this, both Megaw and Jeffery originally came to Cyprus as colonial architects, and so their *raison d'etre* depended on the idea that imperial structures were superior to native ones. Moreover they witnessed the turbu-lent years of the twentieth century when Cypriots struggled for independence, often using violence against symbols of British colonialism, such as the burning of the imperial headquarters at Nicosia in 1931.[8]

The British Empire modernized the urban infrastructure and harbors, and introduced electricity and railways on the island. Economic benefits of being a member of the Empire —funding, military protection, and moderniza-tion—greatly outweighed what the island could provide by itself alone, especially after decades of Ottoman decline.[9] Naturally it was viewed that the charitable powers residing in London ushered the island into the modern world, mitigating insularity by connecting Cypriots to a global empire. To colonial historians it was reasonable to think that Constantinople played a similar role during the Middle Ages. This attitude was also reflected by the colonized Cypriots, who were not clamoring for autonomy, but *enosis* (unification) with Greece in order form a type of twentieth-century Byzantine Empire.[10] In other words, they accepted the British argument that Cyprus needed to be part of an empire, but they wanted a Hellenic one instead. The hectic years between 1960 and 1974 affirmed the British imperial view, when the young republic struggled internally, leading to the calamitous Turkish invasion. It must be stressed — I am *not* saying that colonial scholars conflated the "Byzantine Empire" with the "British Empire." I am saying that the binary opposition between imperial/provincial adopted in the twentieth century naturally reflected the current reality and influenced how medieval archaeology and history was interpreted by both British and Cypriot scholars.

As a result of these historical realities, the binary opposition between Constantinople (the imperial and global metropolis) and Cyprus (the provincial island) has been a rut that architectural historians have had difficulty escaping. For instance, Annabel Wharton closely followed Megaw's thesis, while insisting on the term "regional" as opposed to "provincial" architecture to avoid derogatory labels. But it is clear that her account makes Cypriot visual culture dependent on Constantinople, leaving the reader to ask the obvious question: if Cypriot architectural traditions were derived from imperial models, why did they have different masonry construction, scale, and typology? To Wharton, "regionalism" seemed to explain these differences.[11] Basic ideas and types were imported from the capital, but most aspects were lost in translation, due to the lack of skilled labor, materials, or understanding. As a result, *regional* was effectively synonymous with *provincial*, that is, crude, poor, naïve, or unscientific. As Slobodan Ćurčić stated:

> …regional style has at times been viewed
> as "provincial," created under particular
> insular circumstances that separated

Cyprus from the presumed fountainhead of creative thinking — the Byzantine capital … medieval Cyprus had developed certain distinctive traits, but that these earned it an inappropriate derogatory label, "provincial"… a judgmental meaning of inferiority.[12]

In response to this bias, Ćurčić offered an alternative model in his public lecture *Middle Byzantine Architecture on Cyprus: Provincial or Regional?*[13] His title is clearly referencing Megaw's earlier publication and accepts the notion that Cypriot monuments were not "metropolitan."

Ćurčić's model also advocated the term *regional* instead of *provincial*. He agreed that *regional* did not carry the same negative stereotypes, but went further and asserted that imperial architecture was actually shaped by innovations in the regions beyond the capital.[14] This marked an important paradigm shift in Byzantine architectural historiography regarding Cyprus. However in this context *regional* was still used within a binary model, which led to the negative value judgments in the first place. For example, it was proposed that "The label 'provincial' has stuck to these monuments with such tenacity that at times they appear to have been physically neglected… [Was] Cyprus…such a 'backwater' place, beyond the reach of Constantinopolitan architectural influence…?"[15] In his answer, Ćurčić claimed that the Cypriot churches were not "provincial," though he admitted that they demonstrate qualities less technically or aesthetically sophisticated than those of the capital. Implied in his question is the assumption that without "Constantinopolitan architectural influence" Cyprus would be a "backwater." And even with influence from the capital, Cypriot achievements in architecture would still be derivative.

Ćurčić's resolution retained the focus on Constantinople, while explaining the idiosyncrasies of Cyprus as vague "regional" developments — whatever that might mean.[16] In actuality, he and Wharton were asking the same limited question as Megaw, which led to the same assessment. The fact that all these scholars, including Jeffery, would spend considerable energy researching and puba.

b.

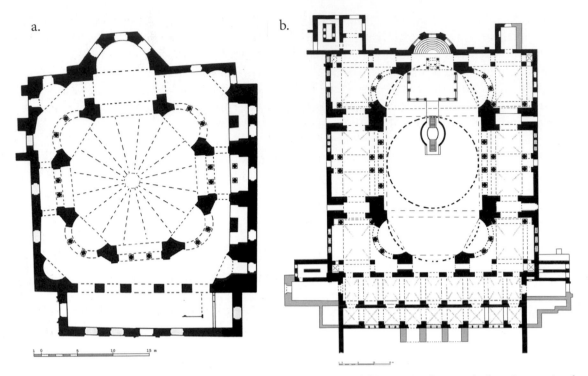

FIG. 8.1   *Ground plans: (a) Saints Sergius and Bacchus, built in 527, and (b) Hagia Sophia, 536; both in Constantinople. Grey areas are hypothetical. Not to scale.*

a.

b.

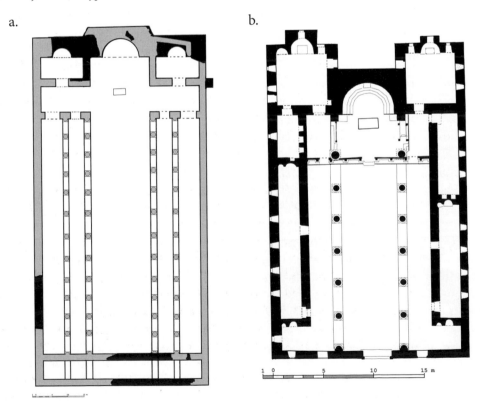

FIG. 8.2   *Ground plans: (a.) Nea Ekklesia, Jerusalem, 543 and (b.) St. Catherine's basilica, Sinai, after Manaphes 1990. Grey areas are hypothetical. Not to scale.*

lishing Cypriot architecture underscores that they recognized Cyprus' historic value to understanding general developments of Byzantine architecture. Simply put, their intentions were noble, but the old binary model rooted in twentieth-century imperialism was still an inadequate framework when applied to the island's monuments.

Not all architectural historians have used the binary model. The publications of Andreas Dikigoropoulos and Athansasios Papageorghiou represented a change in how Cypriot monuments were assessed. Perhaps, as native Cypriots, they were open to the possibility that their ancestors could develop their own architectural methods of design and construction sometimes influenced by, and sometimes isolated from, developments in the region and Constantinople. They, in a literal sense, provided the first post-colonial approaches to the discipline, fundamentally changing how we view the island's material culture after 1960. This was not deliberate. Instead, it seems that their methods were shaped by field archaeology rather than architectural history. In other words, they had no historical models to populate with data. They simply uncovered material. And what they discovered could not be accounted for by what was previously written. Below I provide a brief historical sketch of Cyprus' Byzantine architectural history based on their (and other's) archaeological work.[17]

EARLY BYZANTINE ARCHITECTURE (6TH–MID-7TH CENTURY)

The reign of Justinian the Great marks the beginning of the Early Byzantine Period. His building program was a watershed moment in architectural history, characterized by precise brick construction, innovative centralized plans, lofty vaults, and soaring domes. Saints Sergius and Bacchus and Hagia Sophia represent Constantinopolitan architecture at the height of its creative power (fig. 8.1).[18] And yet these developments were not reflected in Cypriot architecture at the time, and centrally-planned churches do not appear on the island for another five centuries. This should not surprise us, since none of the other eastern provinces of the Byzantine Empire exhibit Constantinople's innovative buildings. For example the Nea Ekklesia

(Jerusalem) and St. Catherine's (Sinai) were both commissioned by Justinian (fig. 8.2).[19] These were traditional basilicas conforming to typical forms of the area; besides the date and funding, they have nothing in common with the Justinianic architecture of Constantinople. Perhaps we can attribute this to "provincialism;" that is, that Byzantine Palestinians and Egyptians lacked skilled labor, materials, or understanding of the sophisticated imperial architecture. Of course, this is absurd, since the scale of these buildings and their lavish decor testify that expense or craftsmanship was not an issue. Simply put, it seems that the eastern provinces were not impressed with Justinian's revolutionary architecture.[20] We can assume that the clergy in Cyprus also held the same attitude in the sixth century, when the cathedrals of Salamis-Constantia, Paphos, and Soloi were rebuilt along traditional lines (figs. 8.3–8.4).

By the time of Justinian, the Cypriot Church was already four centuries old. Its autocephalous status was confirmed in 431, several years before the bishops of Jerusalem and Constantinople were recognized as patriarchs (451).[21] As an exarchy, the Church of Cyprus had the freedom to appoint its own bishops and developed its own practices — this included how it would express itself in the monumental arts. The Metropolitan Chalice (illustrated on the cover of this book) celebrates this exceptional status. Four tyches (personifications) are shown, labeled Rome, Constantinople, Alexandria, and Cyprus. The elevation of Cyprus to the level of these great metropolises can either be seen as an extraordinary example of artistic license or, more likely, an expression of cultural freedom and sense of identity.[22]

According to the sixth-century chronicler Hierokles, the fifteen largest cities in Cyprus each had a governing bishop.[23] Supervising them was the archbishop of Salamis-Constantia. Among these bishoprics, archaeologists have uncovered nine cathedrals. Between the fourth and sixth centuries, these cathedrals changed very little in their overall design: rectangular in layout, three eastern apses, three to five aisles separated by colonnades, and narthexes proceeded by atria. They were constructed with local limestone ashlars joined with lime mortar and covered with a wooden roof.

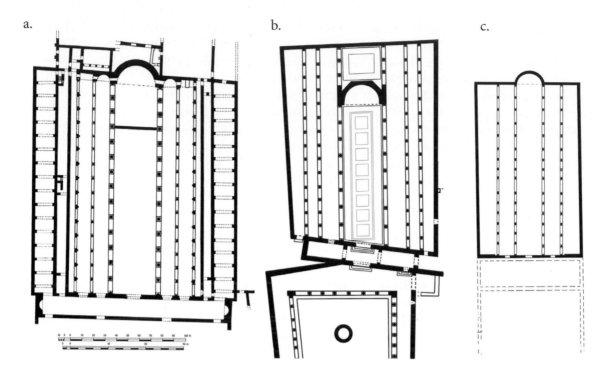

FIG. 8.3   *Phase 1 ground plans (by the mid-5th century); cathedrals of (a.) Salamis-Constantia, (b.) Paphos, and (c.) Soloi. To scale.*

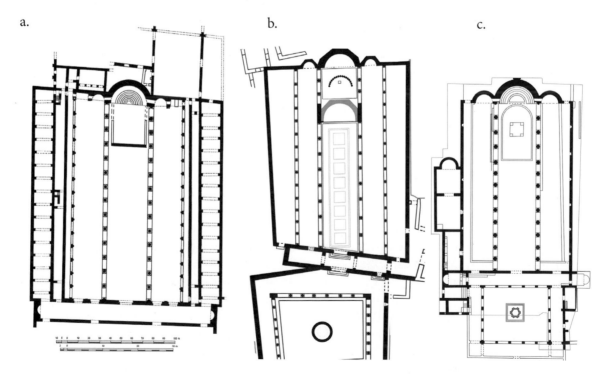

FIG. 8.4   *Phase 2 ground plans (by the mid-6th century); cathedrals of (a.) Salamis-Constantia, (b.) Paphos, and (c.) Soloi. To scale.*

Internal decoration consisted of imported materials, such as tesserae for mosaics and marble furnishings and columns. In the sixth century, the cathedrals at Salamis-Constantia, Paphos, and Soloi had their internal colonnades rebuilt to accommodate a larger congregation, coinciding with the installation of synthronons.[24] These slight changes reflected the contemporary ecclesiastical structures in the west, such as Constantinople and the Aegean, as well as the east, such as Palestine and Syria — but not entirely.[25]

In this Early Byzantine period, two characteristics developed that we find only on Cyprus. First, at the Cathedrals of Salamis-Constantia, Kourion, and Soloi, as well as the Campanopetra (Salamis-Constantia), there are two corridors on each side reserved for facilitating traffic to areas east beyond the apse.[26] As a result, the basilica's clerestory rose up over a complex of subsidiary buildings and courtyards to the east and west. Second, these basilicas have side-aisle apses flanking the central nave apse. This design originated in Palestine, as exemplified by the Gethsemane basilica of the Agony (Jerusalem) and Elusa Cathedral.[27] In Palestine these side apses were built within the eastern wall and do not extend beyond the wall. We see this feature first employed in Cyprus at the cathedral of Salamis-Constantia in the late fourth century; later it is implemented at Kalavasos-*Kopetra* (Area II).[28] By the fifth century, just about every Cypriot church was designed with these flanking apses jutting beyond the eastern wall. This signified that the internal sacred space would be recognized from the exterior. In Cyprus, the tri-partite layout of the bema was emphasized by passageways between the apses; this was first developed at the Cathedral of Salamis-Constantia, and is evident later at Soloi and the churches of Aphendrika.[29] These passages helped facilitate the transmission of the Eucharistic bread from the altar to the congregants in the side aisles. In other words, it seems that the side aisles served each sex; men occupied one aisle and women occupied the other.[30]

Basilica-building on Cyprus reached its zenith in the first half of the seventh century. Archaeology has provided us with a general picture of this development. Excavations at rural sites have uncovered several sixth- and early seventh-century village churches, which are scaled-down versions of the larger fifth-century urban cathedrals.[31] There was a general trend away from large centralized cathedrals, towards a plurality of smaller community churches, just a few yards away from each other. This pattern coincided with the gradual increase of coins and ceramic finds discovered in archaeological contexts.[32] We can interpret this in two possible ways: first, Christianity was initially established in the cities and gradually expanded into the once-pagan countryside; second, the development of suburbs is indicative of widespread prosperity in Cyprus, which led to population growth and settlement of virgin land. Of course, both interpretations are not exclusive of each other.

Regarding secular architecture, we have some of the most innovative Byzantine forms arising on Cyprus also in the first half of the seventh century. Waterworks at Salamis-Constantia, including the Grand Baths, aqueduct (running from Chytroi), and reservoir (known as the "Loutron") were completely renovated under the Emperor Heraclius, with the help of the island's powerful archbishops. Here we see the first systematic use of pointed arches and flying buttresses, fortunately dated by excavation evidence and inscriptions.[33] Several Byzantine houses have been excavated at Amathous and Salamis-Constantia, but these have not been published, except for the urban villa, known as the "Huilerie," where apparently a wealthy clergyman had lived.[34] Its stucco decoration was innovative, in the sense that it was mass-produced in molds and achieved a high level of sophistication mimicking marble reliefs. Other notable monuments built at this time include the city walls at Amathous, which were built in reaction to Monophysite raids from Egypt.[35]

SEVENTH-CENTURY TRANSITION

The era of expansive basilica-building on Cyprus ends by the eighth century. Archaeological evidence indicates that most churches were damaged around the year 650. This ushered in a 300-year period commonly called the "Condominium Period," which I would rather designate as "The Period of Neutrality." The island became a demilitarized zone between the Arab Caliphate

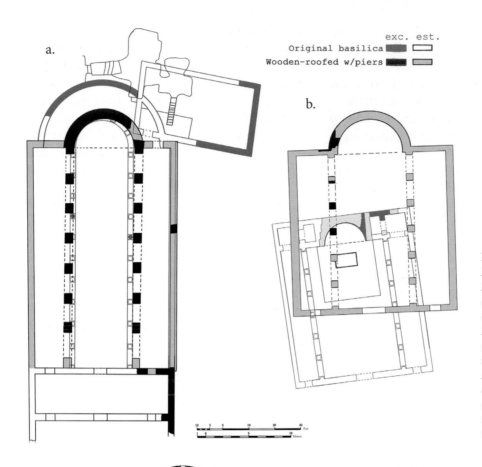

exc. est.

Original basilica ▮ ☐
Wooden-roofed w/piers ▮ ▮

FIG. 8.5
Phase 2 Wooden-Roof Basilica Ground Plans (Phase 1 faded): (a.) Cathedral Agios Heracleidos, Tamassos, (after Papageorghiou, see note); (b.) Agios Mamas, Morphou (after Department of Antiquities). To scale (exc. = excavated remains; est. = estimated reconstruction).

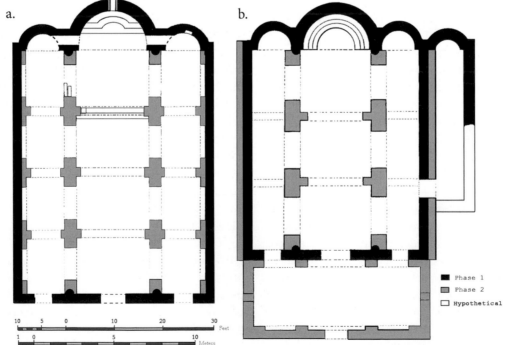

■ Phase 1
▮ Phase 2
☐ Hypothetical

FIG. 8.6 *Phase 2 Barrel Vault Ground Plans: (a.) Asomatos, Aphendrika, and (b.) Panagia Aphendrika (Sykhada); redrawn after Enlart 1899 and Megaw 1946. To scale.*

of Damascus and the Byzantine Empire. It was "Byzantine" in culture, but hardly governed as a "typical" province.[36] Controversy has surrounded the dating of this period's architecture. For many years, historians believed that no construction occurred during this period, though this notion seems quite strange today.[37] My doctoral research focused on this issue, finding that there is sufficient data to provide a reasonable chronology of development in this period.[38]

We have over 25 Early Christian and Byzantine monuments that are dateable based on coin, inscription, or documentary evidence.[39] Therefore we can securely date about 13% of the existing monuments. If we add other monuments which are dated based on the consensus of the fresco technique and style, our chronology becomes even more precise.[40] These dated monuments can be fixed on a timeline. Around these fixed points we can position the other 175 monuments based on comparable characteristics: construction techniques, materials, proportions, scale, furnishings, design, decoration, etc. One similarity is not enough; though when we have four or more similarities, we can place those monuments along the timeline, keeping in mind that development is both synchronic as well as diachronic.[41] This seems like a reasonable approach, as long we keep in mind that the framework is relative and can change with every new excavation.

After the original basilicas were destroyed, there seems to have been a widespread campaign to rebuild them. Some churches, like Soloi, were rebuilt as traditional columnar basilicas, while most were rebuilt as pier-basilicas. At Agios Herakleidos, which was the Cathedral of Tamassos, a martyrium basilica was constructed near a shrine above a subterranean tomb sometime in the Early Byzantine period (fig. 8.5a). Its apse was almost as wide as the entire basilica's width, like other contemporary martyria, such as San Lorenzo *fuori le mura* in Rome, built in the 580s.[42] At Tamassos, the basilica was rebuilt in the eighth century; its columns were replaced by square piers and the apse was entirely rebuilt on a smaller scale, presumably where the colonnade curved at the east end.[43]

Another example of this trend was uncovered in 1958, when the Department of Antiquities performed a series of trial trenches at Morphou (fig. 8.5b). Though it was not a complete excavation, they came up with an interesting series of developments. First, the original basilica — apparently of a Palestinian type — was destroyed. Over it was constructed a square-pier basilica of roughly the same size, but the builders did not utilize the earlier foundations.[44] Its apse and width were similar in proportions to the Tamassos cathedral. This might indicate that Morphou functioned as a cathedral, too; perhaps this site was once called Limenia, Kermia, or Kallinikos, which are recorded as significant historical sites, but were later renamed or abandoned.[45] This phase of construction exhibits continuity of the traditional basilica type. What changed was the use of piers constructed with local materials, rather than imported marble columns — a process that began earlier in the seventh century, as demonstrated at Marathovouno and the Kalavasos basilicas.[46]

THE PERIOD OF NEUTRALITY (650–965)

Within the Karpass Peninsula another architectural type emerged — the "barrel-vaulted basilica" — which, like the pier-basilica, maintained the earlier longitudinal form. Where they differ is that the new type had cross-shaped piers that supported barrel-vaulting (fig. 8.6). This particular method has no exact parallel in the rest of the Byzantine Empire and seems to have developed locally in the early eighth century.[47] At this time, the builders also had a peculiar manner of designing doorways: their jambs were narrower than the diameter of the arch (fig. 8.7). Further east, this method was well-known in later Abbasid architecture (fig. 8.8). There were practical advantages of constructing doors this way: the jambs served to support wooden centering for the round arch, minimizing wood use and construction time. While we could theorize a foreign influence or an immigrant population importing these techniques into Cyprus, it seems just as viable that Cypriot architects were working within the sphere of building trends within the wider region. And we must keep in mind that Umayyad and Abbasid architecture reflects building traditions of the local populations who were still culturally "Byzantine."

FIG. 8.7   *"Horseshoe-arch" doorways in the (a.) Panagia Kanakaria at Lythrancomi, (b.) Panagia Aphendrika at Sykhada, and (c.) Asomatos Church at Aphendrika.*

The barrel-vaulted church was related to another type — the "multiple-domed basilica" — which is the most distinctive type of Cypriot Byzantine architecture. All the evidence indicates that this design was first developed at the Cathedral of Epiphanius (Salamis-Constantia), where Dr. Dikigoropoulos in the 1950s discovered several distinct phases of building.[48] The first phase utilized the fourth-century annex, which served as a corridor connecting the southern aisles of the Cathedral to the baptistery (fig. 8.9a). The second phase occurred in the mid- to late seventh century, when the annex was rebuilt as a pier-arcaded basilica with an eastern apse and a synthronon (fig. 8.9b). Dikigorpoulos dated this phase based on a coin of Heraclius discovered in between this phase's *opus sectile* flooring near the synthronon and the earlier layer beneath. The third major phase took place in the early eighth century when the basilica was rebuilt with barrel-vaults in the side aisles and three domes along the nave (fig. 8.9c). This is the only church that shows clear evidence of how a pier-basilica was converted into a barrel-vaulted, domed church. Since we know what sixth- and tenth-century churches look like, along with their construction methods, we can place the domed phase at Agios Epiphanios somewhere in between, indicating an

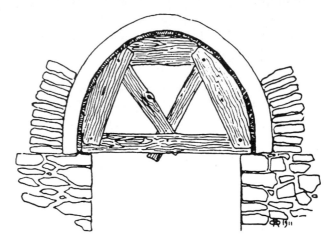

FIG. 8.8   *Hypothetical diagram illustrating how Abbasid builders constructed the "horseshoe-arch" portals at Al-Ukhaidir (Iraq) around 775 AD; from Reuther 1912.*

eighth- or ninth-century date.[49] It is a transitional structure, having the traditional basilica format of Early Byzantine churches, but combined with contemporary barrel-vaulting in the aisles and innovative domes along the nave's axis (fig. 8.10).

The experimental nature of Agios Epiphanios illustrates how a three-dome design was developed *in situ*, suited for this particular location. Methods used in redesigning this basilical structure were strikingly similar to how the barrel-vaulted churches at Aphendrika were built. In other words, it would seem that the "barrel-vaulted type" was developing within the same period when the "mul-

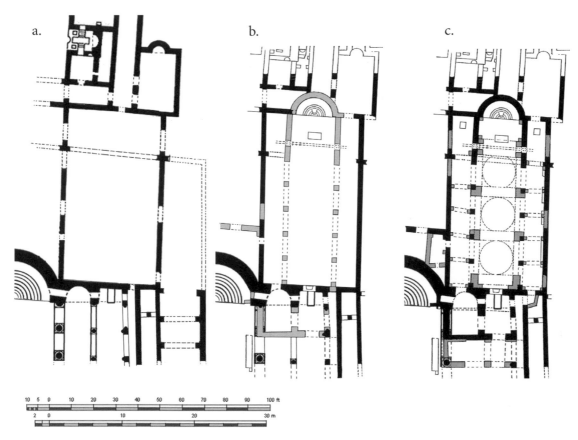

FIG. 8.9 *Ground plans of Agios Epiphanios, Cathedral of Salamis-Constantia: (a.) Phase 1 original annex, (b.) Phase 2 pier basilica, (c.) Phase 3 vaulted, multiple-domed basilica. Redrawn based on Dikigoropoulos 1961.*

FIG. 8.10 *Hypothetical reconstruction of the third-phase exterior of Agios Epiphanios, the Cathedral of Salamis-Constantia.*

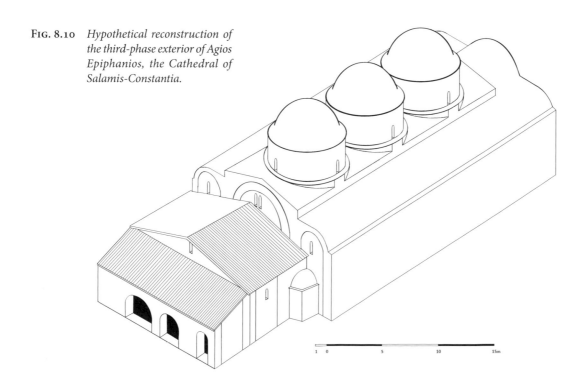

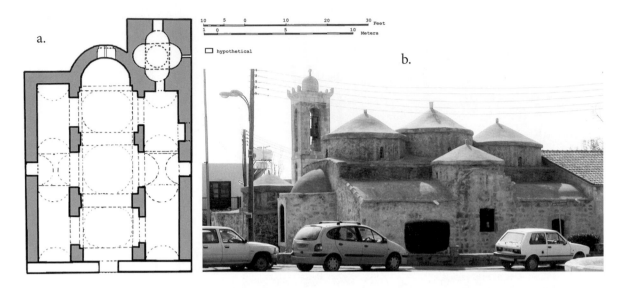

FIG. 8.11   *Agia Paraskevi, Yeroskipou: (a.) ground plan of original design; (b.) exterior photo looking southwest.*

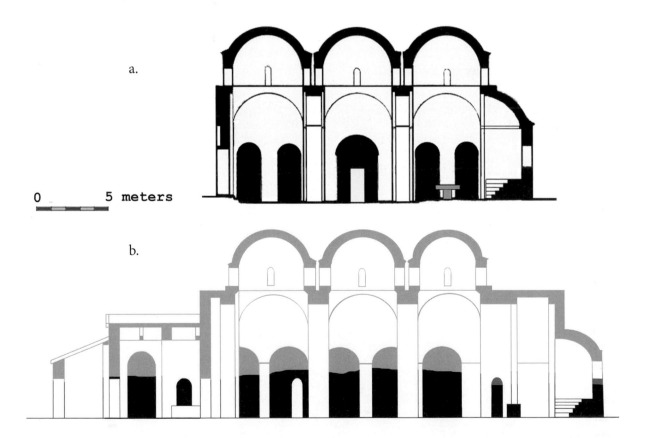

FIG. 8.12   *Elevations of (a.) Agioi Varnavas and Hilarion (Peristerona) and (b.) Agios Epiphanios (Salamis- Constantia). Faded areas are hypothetical. To scale.*

tiple-domed type" emerged. The latter typology would be adopted by other master-builders on the island.[50] For example the multiple-domed basilica at Yeroskipou, known as Agia Paraskevi, adopted the three congruent domes along the nave. It would also have characteristics of the barrel-vaulted type, such as cross-shaped piers and nine-bay layout (fig. 8.11). Further evidence of contemporaneity between the two types is found in the rare survival of fresco painting. As Andreas Foulias first observed, the aniconic fresco painting at Agia Paraskevi and the barrel-vaulted Agia Barbara (near Koroveia) are contemporaneous and belong to the eighth century (figs. 9.2–3).[51] The one difference between Agios Epiphanios and Agia Paraskevi is the latter's original barrel-vaulted transept; these were later replaced by domes, forming a five-dome variation.

The church of Agioi Barnabas and Hilarion (Peristerona) was rebuilt as a copy of Agia Paraskevi, and included the latter's domed-aisle transept in its design. And yet, the Peristerona church's form also can be traced to the original multiple-domed basilica of Agios Epiphanios. When we compare the elevations of the two buildings, we see that the proportions and scale were very similar to each other. The awkward side-aisle piers that divided the domed bays at Peristerona were architecturally superfluous, but reflected the structurally-necessary piers at Agios Epiphanios, which were remnants of the earlier wood-roof phase (fig. 8.12a–b).

Agios Barnabas (Salamis-Constantia) and Agios Lazaros (Larnaka) were the final manifestations of the "multiple-domed" type.[52] Their designs were based on the novel feature—the domed transept crossing. This concept was awkwardly experimental in the design at Agia Paraskevi, but was fully developed at Peristerona, showcasing wide arches and confident construction. The domed-aisle transept was preferable to the original design of the Salamis-Constantia Cathedral, because it allowed better visual and ambulatory communication between the nave and side aisles. And yet, the layout also maintained the characteristic, and perhaps "iconic," three-dome design. At Agios Barnabas and Agios Lazaros, their transepts are modular units, and repeated twice, creating structures with 21 bays. This is unlike any other

configuration in Byzantine architectural typology. And Agios Barnabas and Agios Lazaros would be the largest vaulted Byzantine churches on the island. Their scale and typology were not accidental. They were grand in order to impress and accommodate pilgrims visiting the relics of Barnabas and Lazarus — saints who were believed to be the founders of Cyprus' autocephalous church in the first century.[53] It is not a coincidence that this historical emphasis took place at the end of the Iconoclasm, when the island defied Constantinople in order to remain Orthodox. Based on their construction, design, and material, these churches must date to the ninth or early tenth century.

All four "multiple-domed" churches belong to a specific Cypriot type, showing solidarity with the archbishop of Salamis-Constantia, whose church was the prototype. The archbishop was called the "president" (πρόεδρος) of the island during the Period of Neutrality. Since secular Byzantine officials were disarmed, that is "neutralized," the Church played a vital role in the island's administration.[54] There is no reason why canon law (Πηδάλιον) could not be expanded to include secular regulations, enforced through anathema and social censure rather than corporal punishment. The ecclesiastic administration already paralleled the Roman diocese system in which the archbishop was the counterpart of the provincial governor. As such the cathedral of Agios Epiphanios became a symbol of the archbishops' spiritual and temporal authority, forming a sense of Cypriot identity apart from other Byzantine provinces.

The next type of building to emerge was based on these earlier developments. Cross-in-square churches were constructed beginning in the ninth century throughout the island. While these also can be found all over the Byzantine Empire in earlier contexts, the type need not have been imported to Cyprus. Technical achievements gained in the later multiple-domed basilicas, such as Agios Lazaros, could be altered to suit smaller congregations and monasteries. By truncating the multiple-domed design by removing the two westernmost bays, one obtains the cross-in-square with nine bays. The earliest of these were Agios Antonios (Kellia), dated to the ninth century by its earliest frescos, Panagia Angeloktisti (Kiti), and Agios Prokopios

a.

b.

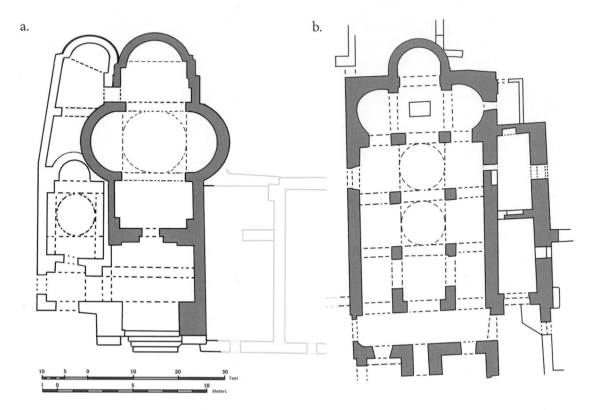

10 5 0   10   20   30
                                    Feet
1 0   5   10
                                    Meters

FIG. 8.13 *Sketched ground plans of (a.) the Georgian Monastery of the Panagia Chrysogialiotissa (Gialia), and (b.) the Staurovouni katholicon. To scale.*

(Syncrasis), dated to the tenth century by inscription.[55] All the surviving examples were constructed with square piers, except for Agios Georgios in Kyrenia Castle which was constructed with reused marble columns.[56]

BYZANTINE RECONQUEST (965–1090)

Archaeology over the past 35 years has shown that the Byzantine Reconquest of 965 did not radically change the material culture of Cyprus in the late tenth century.[57] Besides the grand fortifications in the Kyrenian Range, evidence is lacking for imperial investment on the island for over a century after reintegration. Eventually Cypriots witnessed an escalation of ecclesiastic building in villages and monasteries in the countryside, beginning in the late eleventh century. Common architectural types and styles found in Constantinople and mainland Greece are virtually absent on Cyprus beforehand. For example, only one church in Cyprus, Agia Triada at Koutsovendis, is built entirely of

brick.[58] Middle Byzantine architecture characteristically had exteriors decorated with undulating brick decor, tall lantern drums, mosaic interiors, ceramic tiles, and large twin or tripartite windows divided by marble mullions. These are unknown to Cyprus before the late eleventh century.

Of all the churches dated to the tenth century, only one is clearly connected to outside influence by historical sources. For the past five years, Georgian archaeologists under the direction of Dr. Iulon Gagashidre and Dr. David Mindorashvili, with the Department of Antiquities' George Philotheou, have been excavating the Georgian monastery at Gialia (fig. 8.13a).[59] The church was known as the Panagia Chrysogialiotissa and was a single-aisle, domed triconch structure.[60] This was a typical Georgian design, but its construction methods were not. By comparing the site to churches in Georgia, the excavators suggested that when Georgian monks came to Cyprus they had a blueprint, which was then given to local Cypriot builders who used local techniques and materi-

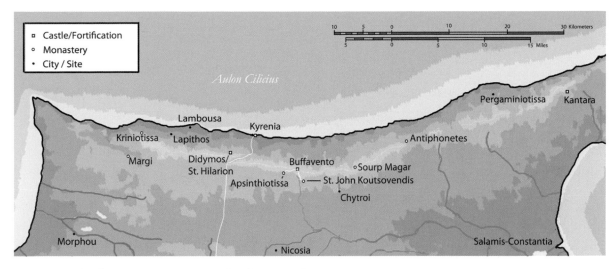

FIG. 8.14 *Map showing Kyrenia Mountain fortifications and monasteries.*

als.[61] This helps explain how Cypriot architecture could display both local and foreign characteristics. Perhaps Panagia Chrysogialiotissa was the inspiration for the original form of the sanctuary at Staurovouni (fig. 8.13b), which had a triconch design according to Jeffery's 1915 sketch. Moreover, the Staurovouni katholicon probably had a dome over its easternmost bay, forming a hybrid type, that is, a multiple-domed triconch basilica. These two structures represent how the Byzantine reconquest of Cyprus created a context in which monasticism could flourish and permit architectural experimentation.

IMPERIAL INVESTMENT AND MONASTIC GROWTH (1090–1191)

Beginning around the year 1100 Cyprus served as an important strategic base for Byzantine expansion eastward. Evidence of imperial investment is found in the northern Kyrenia Range, which overlooked the wide sea passage between Cyprus and Anatolia known then as the *Aulon Cilicius*.[62] Fortifications were constructed in the port of Kyrenia and in mountain passes, such as St. Hilarion Castle (Didymus) and Kantara, and at the summit of Buffavento (fig 8.14).[63] Much engineering, technical knowledge, and skilled manpower were needed for construction at such great heights, along cliff edges, utilizing narrow rocky paths. Buffavento Castle was built using materials and designs new

to the island (figs 8.15–16). The quality of the first-phase keep (*magna turris*) — a three-storied tower partially carved from the living rock — indicates that officials of high rank resided here.[64] Its portals and large window were constructed with imported bricks joined by thick mortar beds.

Associated with these fortifications are the most Constantinopolitan-looking churches on the island — known as the "octagon-domed" type — though these have no exact parallel outside the island.[65] Three of these survive in various states of repair (Agios Hilarion, Apsinthiotissa, and Antiphonetes), while two others were recorded by nineteenth-century drawings (Margi and Koutsovendis) but do not survive. We can assume that they were all katholicons of monasteries. Because we know when Agios Ioannis Chrysostomos at Koutsovendis was founded — around 1090 by a Palestinian Monk named George fleeing the Holy Land — we can date all the other examples to the same time period, though they may span several decades before or after.[66] It was hardly coincidental that the brick construction of nearby Buffavento castle is similar to the construction of the Koutsovendis monastery, since they are connected by a road and visible to each other (fig. 8.14). Besides, the small chapel at Agia Triada was commissioned by the imperial *doux* Eumathios Philokales, who was recorded at that time as a castle-builder.[67] At the nearby katholicon within St. Hilarion Castle

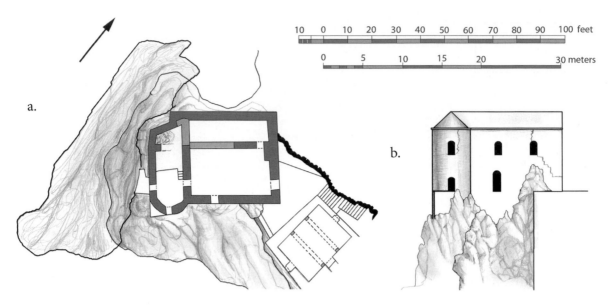

FIG. 8.15 *Buffavento Castle: (a.) ground plan of principal keep, i.e.,* magna turris *(first phase), (b.) reconstruction of keep's southeast façade.*

FIG. 8.16 *Buffavento Castle photographs: (a.) towards the northwest, (b.) surviving original brickwork in the window of the north wall of the keep.*

FIG. 8.17   *Domed octagon within St. Hilarion Castle: (a.) interior northwest wall pier, and (b.) interior view towards apse.*

FIG. 8.18   *Domed-Octagon within St. Hilarion Castle: exterior north wall.*

we see construction techniques not evidenced in other Cypriot churches before; for example, the *opus mixtum* (alternation between brick and ashlar courses) and the recessed brick technique within wide mortar beds (figs. 8.17–8.18). How did these construction techniques arrive here?

At St. Hilarion Castle it is not clear which came first, the fortification or the monastery. But like Buffavento, the katholicon here was inextricably connected to the defenses of the mountain pass. Since the barracks housed troops, we can assume that they were also the builders. Most likely all these castles were constructed by imperial marines, many of whom were Armenians, already familiar with constructing mountain fortresses on the opposite coast.[68] It seems plausible that they were also responsible for the construction of the affiliated monasteries, which explains their Constantinopolitan (i.e., non-Cypriot) qualities.

There once was a general consensus that the octagon-domed type of church was originally designed in Constantinople. As Dr. Tassos Papacostas argued, there are several other possible sources that may have influenced this type in Cyprus from abroad.[69] It is clear that the Cypriot examples are related to the developmental trends in Middle Byzantine architecture concentrated around the eastern Aegean.[70] For example, the Antiphonetes Church in Cyprus has barrel-vaults in the eastern corners going in a north–south direction on the inside,

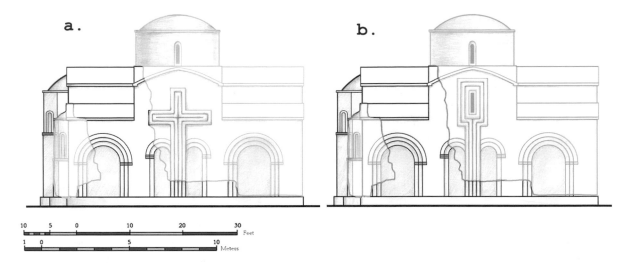

FIG. 8.24 *Agios Philon, Carpasia; (a.) hypothetical elevation illustrating cross relief; (b.) alternative elevation illustrating a molded window. Faded areas are sections that no longer survive.*

styles. And besides Armenia and Georgia, we know that Constantinople looked to many other places for inspiration. Fortunately the twelfth-century Byzantine writer Nicholas Mesarites provided a glimpse into the sources of imperial design. While marveling and praising a new monument — with arabesque *muquarnas* — in the Palace of Constantinople, he wrote:

> τὸ οἴκημα χειρὸς ἔργον οὐ Ῥωμαΐδος, οὐ Σικελικῆς, οὐ Κελτίβηρος, οὐ Συβαριτικῆς, οὐ Κυπρίου, οὐ Κίλικος, Περσικῆς μὲν οὖν…

> [This building is the work not of a Roman, nor a Sicilian, nor a Celt-Iberian (i.e., Georgian), nor a Sybartic (i.e., Apulian), nor a Cypriot, nor a Cilician (Armenian), but of a Persian hand…][88]

It does not matter that the architecture in question was not Cypriot — what matters is that Cyprus is mentioned amongst the truly great schools of medieval architecture. While we should not extrapolate too much from this list, we can assert that it defies the binary model of architecture and opens up a plurality of possibilities.

SUMMARY

The development of Byzantine architecture on Cyprus, therefore, is best understood within the context of specific local approaches to general regional trends. But what does *regional* mean here? Scholars can no longer use the term without defining their parameters. Regional affiliation shifted, based on the historical context: in the Early Christian period, "regional" means affiliation with Syria and Palestine; in the Early Byzantine period, it is the Aegean; in the early seventh century, it was Egypt and Palestine; and by the twelfth century, Constantinople and Anatolia. Over thirty years have elapsed since A.H.S. Megaw asked "Was architecture on Cyprus Metropolitan or Provincial?" Since then, archaeology and architectural research have led us to a more nuanced answer. Cyprus had important cultural centers, and so Cypriot master-builders could experiment with local building traditions, leading to innovation. Cypriots were also influenced by the surrounding provinces, and were, at specific points, crucial to the imperial agenda. It appears that terms such as *metropolitan* and *provincial* can both be applied to Cyprus at various times, depending on the shifting balance of empires.

NOTES

1 I sincerely thank all the scholars in the audience who provided their critique and suggestions for this paper during the conference, especially Nicholas Bakirtzis, Andreas Foulias, Michalis Olympios, Marcus Rautman, and Eleni Procopiou. I am grateful to Tassos Papacostas, who read over the draft of this paper and provided suggestions. It should be noted that we have diverging opinions on the date of some buildings.
Jeffery 1915–16: 116, 118.

2 Pilides 2009: 31–32.

3 Jeffery 1915–16: 124–25.

4 Carr and Morrocco 1991.

5 Mango wrote, "It cannot be claimed that historians of Byzantine architecture have been in the forefront of scholarly theory as compared to their colleagues who work in other periods and civilizations" (1991: 40).

6 The use of binaries to describe the ebb and flow of time goes back to the earliest historians, like Herodotus, and is inherent in ancient Greek and Latin language. Edward Gibbon's binary thesis of the *Decline and Fall of the Roman Empire* (1776–1788) was certainly influenced by historical constructs formulated in the Renaissance, especially by Petrarch's "Golden Age/Dark Age" paradigm, which, in turn, was inspired by classical Roman writers; Panofsky 1972: 5–34. Twentieth-century academics codified the binary system as a type of epistemology known as structuralism. This was applied to anthropology in Claude Levi-Strauss' *Anthropologie structurale* (1958). However, in art and architectural history, this approach was earlier developed by Heinrich Wölfflin's *Renaissance und Barock* (1888), *Die Klassische Kunst* (1898), and *Kunstgeschichtliche Grundbegriffe* (1915). Current archaeological hermeneutics, especially processualism and, to some extent, post-processualism, still have a predilection for binary classification; e.g., T. Champion's *Centre and Periphery: Comparative Studies in Archaeology* (1995) and M. Johnson's *Archaeological Theory* (2010).

7 The equation of Gothic sculpture with scholasticism is fully described by Panofsky (1951), but originated with the theories of earlier French scholars such as Jules Quicherat, Viollet le Duc, and Camille Enlart. In 1898, J.K. Huysmans summed up the view: "l'église [gothique] de Laon [a été la] paraphrase imagée de la théologie scolastique, la version sculpturale du texte d'Albert le Grand" (Chapter 10). For a recent critique of this thesis, see Croddy 1999: 263–72.

8 N. Crawshaw, *The Cyprus Revolt* (London: Unwin Hyman, 1978); Stavros Panteli, *A New History of Cyprus* (London: East-West Publications, 1988), 150 ff.

9 Tatton-Brown 2001; Varnava 2005: 167–86.

10 The Byzantine legendary hero Digenis Akritas became the symbol for Cypriot resistance, as illustrated by the EOKA declaration of 1955. The Kingdom of Greece, if it had united with Cyprus, would form a type of Panhellenic Empire, romantically viewed as a modern manifestation of the Byzantine Empire. For a Greek view, see Stefanidis 1999: chapter 7; for a British view, see Hill(1952: 488–568).

11 Wharton 1988: 53–90.

12 Ćurčić 2000: 7–8.

13 This lecture was published by the Bank of Cyprus Cultural Foundation, Nicosia, in 2002.

14 Ćurčić 2000: 9; Buchwald makes the same argument (1999: 209–15). In fact, both Krautheimer (1986) and Mango (1966, 1976a) were open to the idea that some novel architectural forms were developed in the provinces and then refined in Constantinople. Other publications, like Orlandos 1998 and Bouras 2006 still hold to imperial architectural dominance.

15 Ćurčić 2000: 12–13.

16 Ćurčić first applies the term *regional* in a 1999 article called "Byzantine Architecture on Cyprus." Without a clear definition, "regionalism" can mean many different things in archaeological literature. Wharton's study relegated Cyprus, as her title infers, to the *periphery* of architectural innovation. The term "regional" can lead to the same result.

17 In the past few years other Byzantine architectural histories have appeared, with varying degrees of scholarship, such as Papacostas 1999, Gkioles 2003, and Chotzakoglou 2005. Of these, Tassos Papacostas' work is the most analytical and insightful. Older architectural histories, e.g., Mastrogiannopoulos

cross (in brick) is also on the north-wall tympa-num at the Panagia Krina on the island of Chios, which connects the Aegean examples to this general development.

84 John Scylitzes, *Historiae,* ed. Thurn 1973: 409–12; Foss 1991. The sudden appearance, and hence significance, of "stepped-jambs" in Cyprus has been noted by both Tassos Papacostas (2006) and Eleni Procopiou (2007a) — both see a correspondence with structures in Armenian Cilicia.

85 Alpago-Novello et al. 1980: 299, 369, entry 83. It is not a coincidence that the molded cross at Agios Ioannis Chrysotsomos at Koutsovendis and the sculptural features at Agios Philon and Agios Hilarion are located on the north side of the churches facing the Cilician Sea. Perhaps the crosses served as apotropaic devices to ward off an attack from the coast.

86 This theory was the fundamental principle behind the pioneering publications of Joseph Strzygowski (1918).

87 Ćurčić does not provide a reference (2000: 16). He may be referring to a joint article by Thomas Mathews and Cyril Mango concerning the Panagia Kamariotissa (Constantinople). Mathews wrote, "[The] Panagia Kamariotissa with its combination of Greek-cross-octagon plus tetraconch argues a much stronger dependence on Armenia, for the combination of the two elements is as common in Armenia as it is unfamiliar in Byzantine circles. If there were lines of contact between Middle Byzantine architecture of Greece and earlier design ideas of Armenia, those lines could be expected to pass through Constantinople, where, closer to their sources, the plans would be received in a purer state. The absence of a narthex…tends also to strengthen this line of reasoning" (1972: 127); see also Mango 1976: 184–90. *Nota bene:* churches in Cyprus also do not have narthexes before the twelfth century. It should be mentioned that another church in Constantinople, St. George of Mangana, also must have been influential on other octagon-domed churches like the katholicon at Hosios Loukas; Mathews and Mango 1972: 132; see also Bouras 1977–1979: 21–32.

88 *Seditio Joanni Comneni* 44.35, dated to ca. 1150.

Chapter 9

Cypriot Icons before the Twelfth Century

by Sophocles Sophocleous

This chapter briefly examines a few icons that could be ascribed to the artistic activity of Cyprus before the twelfth century. Additionally, a critical reconsideration is provided regarding the levels of technique, style, iconography, and dating, to the extent that is possible, given that no physical or chemical analysis of these icons has been made so far. The term *icon* (εἰκών) is used in Byzantine sources referring to any religious image, but in this chapter the term is used in a more technical sense: portable wooden pictures painted in the encaustic or tempera technique. Also, it should be specified that the data used here for comparison and/or dating, especially the fresco murals, were based mainly on published material.[1]

From the Early Byzantine period (sixth to mid-seventh century), floor and wall mosaics survive in Cypriot churches and, in some cases, there is evidence for mural painting. Perhaps icons also existed in these churches made by the same workshops. The surviving artworks testify to external influence from Constantinople and the surrounding regions. One could refer to the floor mosaics discovered in various basilicas during excavations and the wall mosaics at the Panagia Kanakariá (Lythrankomi), Panagia Angeloktistos (Kiti), Panagia Kyra (Livadia), and others, which are mainly fragmentary.[2] A rare sixth-century wall-painting with the head of Christ over a Nilotic composition survived at the cistern known as the *Agiasma tou Nikodimou* at Salamis.[3] This heritage could hypothetically reflect the painting of icons at the time, even if these do not survive.

As far as the survival of portable icons from the Early Byzantine period is concerned, a supposition could be made about the *Acheiropoietos* icon from the homonymous monastery near Lambousa. The eastern areas of the fifth-century basilica are preserved, mainly the apse and part of the marble templon of the nave, as well as parts of the floor's *opus sectile*. This was incorporated into later building phases; in the sixteenth century, a new marble templon was added and, after a fire in the eighteenth century, an iconostasis was installed.[4] The *Acheiropoietos* icon depicted the Virgin and Child and was later covered by a gold-plated silver cover. By the eighteenth century, the icon was kept within the *diastylon* of the Early Byzantine marble templon (fig. 9.1).[5] Unfortunately, since the Turkish invasion of 1974 the fate of this icon is unknown, because the whole monastery became a military camp which forbids visitors. Nevertheless, even if this icon dates to the original construction of the Acheiropoietos monastery, or a later period,

FIG. 9.1   *Katholikon of the Acheiropoeitos Monastery near Lambousa. The icon of the Virgin with its gold-plated silver cover in the diastylon of the Early Byzantine templon and the later wooden-carved iconostasis as photographed by G. Soteriou in the early 1930s.*

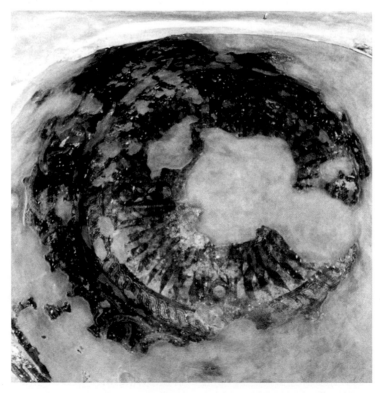

FIG. 9.2   *Church of Agia Paraskevi at Yeroskipou. East dome with aniconic murals. 8th/9th century.*

FIG. 9.3 *Church of Agia Barbara, near Koroveia. Aniconic ornament. 8th//9th century (Photo: C.A. Stewart).*

we know that in the eighteenth century the painting was damaged by Turkish invaders from Karamania when they burnt down the monastery and its library. This event is also recorded by the German traveler Heinrich Petermann who visited the monastery in 1851. He said that the burning of the monastery took place 90 years earlier, that is, in 1761.[6] At that time the iconostasis was repaired and on it was placed an inscription with the date 1765 underneath the icon. The remains of the earlier icon may have undergone a restoration, as in the case of the *Panagia Chrysaliniotissa* icon in Nicosia (see fig. 9.21). Besides this hypothetical *Acheiropoietos* icon, no other Early Christian or Early Byzantine portable icons are known on Cyprus.

THE ARAB RAIDS ON CYPRUS AND THE PERIOD OF ICONOCLASM

The Arab raids in Cyprus, which began in 649, led to Arab interference with the military, political, administrative, and economic affairs on the island.[7] In the year 668, a treaty was negotiated between the Emperor Justinian II and the Caliph Yazid bin Abd al-Malik in which Cyprus would maintain a neutral status between the Byzantine Empire and the Arab Caliphate. The taxes from the island would be shared by both powers. This situation would continue until 965, when the Byzantine Empire resumed full jurisdiction. Even with this treaty, the Cypriots had a precarious status and suffered devastating incursions and even population resettlement to overseas locations. Naturally, the development of art and painting was affected by these devastating events. This period also coincides with the iconoclastic controversy, which officially begun in 730 and ended in 843.

The information given in historical sources is sparse and piecemeal. But from the texts, it could be supposed that the island remained iconophile, continued its artistic traditions, and became a refuge for the monks from Asia Minor, while also serving as a place of exile for iconophiles banished from Constantinople.[8] Indeed, the ecclesiastical tradition attests that within these upheavals, icons themselves found refuge in Cyprus, and perhaps icon painters as well. The material remains show that aniconic decoration was applied in some churches, such as in the east dome of Agia Paraskevi (Yeroskipou) (fig. 9.2), the Panagia Kanakariá (Lythrankomi), and Agia Barbara (Koroveia) (fig. 9.3); these date from the eighth or ninth century.[9] The recently discovered mural in the chapel of Agia Athanasia (Risokarpasso) can also be ascribed to the first half of the ninth century.[10] Indeed, some figural wall paintings that survive from the tenth century, together with the rare portable icons of this period, could help form a better idea about the development of representational painting in general. For example, the Crucifixion in the Church of Agios Antonios at Kellia (fig. 9.4) and those in the chapel of Agia Solomoni at Koma tou Gialou (fig. 9.5a–d) are all ascribed to the tenth century; however, these could be earlier, since a comparable Crucifixion icon from the Sinai is dated to the ninth century.[11] Although they are not of the same workmanship, the aforementioned two murals have very dark outlines and contours, and are consequently characterized by flatness, stiffness, and overall lack of flexibility and volume. These characteristics appear also on some portable icons of this period considered below. The style at Agia Solomoni is very similar to contemporary murals in Syria and Lebanon, especially with those in the church of Mar-Charbel at Maad in Lebanon.[12] It is worth noting that new discoveries have potential to further clarify the period; for example, segments of non-figural wall paintings came to light during excavations of this period at the monumental shrine at *Agioi Pente* (Yeroskipou) and in the basilica of *Koutsopetria* (near Pyla).[13]

To the best of our current knowledge, at least three icons survived from this period (that is, from 650 to 965). The earliest one is that of Agia Marina from her church at Philousa, and today in the Byzantine Museum of Paphos (fig. 9.6a–c). The icon has been ascribed to the eighth or ninth century by some scholars and to the seventh or eighth century by others.[14] This rare relic is painted on the back side of a double-faced icon. The other side has a thirteenth-century painting of St. George, but it is not known whether this is a repainting over an earlier layer contemporary to St. Marina's image, since no research into this was made by its restorers. The female saint is reproduced full-body and strictly frontal in the *orans* position in a way that reminds one of the mosaic of Virgin Mary at *Panagia Kyra* dating to the first half of the seventh century. The background is green on the bottom half and dark blue on the top half. In the upper left corner the hand of God is extending

a blessing from the sky. Scenes from the martyrdom are well-preserved only on the left vertical border. The bottom border is decorated with foliage. The style of the painting could be described as if not "naïve," at least "very simplified" and frugal, conditioned by strong stylization and lack of plasticity and flexibility. Complete flatness in the rendering, accentuated by the strong black contours, abstracts the weight of the body and

FIG. 9.4   *Church of Agios Antonios, Kellia. Crucifixion, 9th century (Courtesy: Department of Antiquities, Cyprus, Photo: C.A. Stewart).*

a.   b.   c.   d.

FIG. 9.5   *Chapel of Agia Solomoni, Koma tou Gialou. Segments of murals sold abroad by the Turks after 1974. 9th century.*

FIG. 9.6   *Icon of Saint Marina from Philousa Kelokedaron and now in the Byzantine Museum of Paphos. (a.) full image of verso, (b.) detail of St. Marina being flayed, (c.) detail of portrait. 7th/8th century.*

FIG. 9.7   *Icon of* Blachernitissa *from the church of Panagia Phaneromeni (Nicosia) and now in the Byzantine Museum in Nicosia. Late 8th/early 9th century.*

suspends it within its background instead of placing it on the ground line. The dematerialization of the figure is achieved by means of flat, unshaded color for the flesh outlined in black contours. The dedicatory inscription mentioning a "✠ ΔΕ(ΗCIC) ΓΕΩΡΓΙΟΥ ΤΟΥ ΡΩΜΕΟΥ" (Prayer of Georgios Romeos) and the epigraphy of these letters seem to corroborate such early dating, perhaps even to the seventh century. The icon presents a series of common features with icons of the seventh and eighth centuries conserved at Mount Sinai, such as the flatness, the strong stylization, the distribution of the highlights on the garments, the dark background, and, more specifically, the technique of icon painting with tempera on wood, primed with a very thin coating of gesso and without cloth.[15]

The second portable icon from this period is the Virgin Orans with the medallion of Christ on her chest that qualifies her as a "Blachernitissa" type (fig. 9.7). It was found among the icons of the Church of Panagia Phaneromeni in Nicosia and is exhibited today in the Byzantine Museum of the Archbishop Makarios III Foundation.[16] This icon is painted, according to Athanasios Papageorghiou, with the encaustic technique.[17] It bears similar features found on the icon of Saint Marina and the

FIG. 9.8   *Icon of* Agiosoritisa *re-written as*
Agiomacherioritisa. *Monastery of Machairas.*
8th/9th century.

FIG. 9.9   Madonna di San Sisto. *Dominican convent Santa*
Maria del Rosario on Monte Mario, Rome. 7th
century.

Sinai icons, such as the dark background, consistent flatness, absence of figural weight, and the vivid black contours which define facial features and folds of the garments. It is commonly dated to the late eighth or early ninth century, that is, during the break between the two phases of the iconoclastic controversy.

The third icon preserved from this period is called the *Machairioritisa* (fig. 9.8), which is the *palladion* of the Machairas monastery.[18] The icon, which is usually concealed by its gold-plated silver cover, was uncovered and conserved in the late 1980s revealing a very precious relic dating before the tenth century. The iconographic type is that of "Agiosoritisa," according to the inscription "ΑΓΙΟCΩΡΙΤΗCΑ" on the upper half.[19] This epithet was later changed into "ΑΓΙΟΜΑΧΕΡΙΩΡΙΤΗCΑ" (i.e., *Agiomacherioritisa*), apparently to adapt the icon to the local cult tradition. According to legend, the icon was discovered by the hermits Neophytos and Ignatios around 1145 in the cave of the anonymous first hermit of the site. With a machete, the monks cut out a path from the thick blackberry

bushes concealing the entrance. The Greek term for *machete* is μάχαιρα (*machaira*), which provided the monastery's unique appellation.

If we assume this ecclesiastical tradition is correct, the alteration of the name into *Agiomacherioritisa* would have occurred after 1145, during the reign of Manuel I Komnenos (1143–1180). This emperor sponsored the creation of the first monastery here and endowed it with lands and privileges, which were reconfirmed by the Emperor Isaac II Angelos in between 1185 and 1195, based on a request by the Abbot Neilos.[20] In the icon, the Virgin is depicted in the usual manner of an *Agiosoritisa* gesturing in intercessory prayer. In the upper left corner Christ appears in a blessing pose. According to the first publisher of the icon,

FIG. 9.10 Santa Maria in Ara Coeli *at Campidoglio, Rome. Late 10th century copy of an earlier original.*

A. Papageorgiou, the face of the Virgin is painted with the encaustic technique.[21] Apart from the face, the icon received, according to the same writer, various repaintings during its history, but he does not specify whether there is a documented report on the restoration. The iconography and style of the icon, the typology of the physiognomic characteristics and the modeling of the face, as well as the epigraphy of the inscription all suggest a dating before the tenth century. This gives credence to the ecclesiastical tradition, which describes the icon's secret journey from Asia Minor to Cyprus during the Iconoclastic Period and the establishment of a cave hermitage for its protection.

The high quality of the icon's painting, especially the face, testifies that this is the work of a master trained in an artistic entourage under imperial or other aristocratic patronage in Constantinople. Of course, it had to be painted during a period which did not coincide with iconoclastic policy, most probably between 787 and 814, when there

was a hiatus between the first and the second phase of the iconoclastic controversy. The second phase finished in 843, and icons were definitely restored in the churches by this time.[22] Alternatively, the *Machairioritisa* icon could have been made after 843. In any case, it could not be dated on stylistic grounds before the beginning of the iconoclasm in 726/730, when the style, judging from the Sinai icons and others conserved in Rome, was quite different.[23] For instance, the *Madonna di San Sisto* is a seventh-century version of the *Agiosoritisa* kept in the Dominican convent of Santa Maria del Rosario on Monte Mario near Rome, and is quite different than the *Machairioritisa* on many levels (fig. 9.9).[24] In another Roman context exists an icon of the same type kept in the Church of Santa Maria in Ara Coeli at Campidoglio; the first church here was built by Greek monks in the sixth century, which Franciscans replaced with the present structure in the thirteenth century (fig. 9.10). This icon is assigned to the late tenth century and is believed to be a copy of an earlier original, attributed to the hands of Saint Luke himself. It came to Rome, according to tradition, from Jerusalem by way of the Church of the Theotokos Chalkoprateia in Constantinople.

The epithet "Agiosoritisa" is believed to have originated in the monastery of Blachernae in Constantinople, where a famous icon with this iconography was venerated in the chapel of Agia Soros. This cult seems to go back to the reign of the Emperor Marcian. In 451 his wife Pulcheria transferred, from Jerusalem to the Blachernae, the vestments (tunic and *maphorion*) of the Virgin originally kept in her tomb at the garden of Gethsemane.[25] The discovery of the *palladion* icon of Machairas monastery in Cyprus under its gold-plated silver cover in the late 1980s supports the theory that the epithet "Agiosoritisa" existed on icons of the Virgin with this iconographic type even before the 1040s, when lead seals with this image were made. Previously it was believed that these seals were the earliest documents of this image and epithet.[26]

Like the *Machairioritisa*, the important Cypriot icon known as the *Kykkotissa* (originally written Kikiotisa) has a similar monastic connection (fig. 9.11).[27] Unfortunately, its metallic cover, dated to 1795, which replaced an earlier one of 1576, has never been removed. According to the tradition, the icon is one of those made by the hand of Saint Luke and was donated to Kykko Monastery in Cyprus by the Emperor Alexios I Komnenos in the year 1092, or slightly after its foundation.[28] The iconographic type "Kikiotisa" existed in Cyprus, judging from the known documents, since the thirteenth century, if not from the late twelfth, and was disseminated from this monastery on Cyprus to wall frescos and portable icons known elsewhere.[29] The type itself appears on a Constantinopolitan icon at Mount Sinai, but without the epithet "Kikiotisa," dated by Kurt Weitzman to the second half of the eleventh century.[30] The presumed original *Kykkotissa* is respectfully kept on the iconostasis of Kykko Monastery and provokes scientific curiosity, because, if the original icon survived until today, it must date to at least the eleventh century, when the monastery was established, or perhaps even earlier.

FIG. 9.11   *The icon of* Kykkiotissa *at the Kykkos Monastery, covered by textile and gold plated silver.*

FIG. 9.12   *Church of Agios Antonios at Kellia. Detail of the Sacrifice of Abraham. Early 11th century (Courtesy: Department of Antiquities, Photo: C.A. Stewart).*

FIG. 9.13 *(a) Mural of St. Ignatius of Antioch, 11th century; (b) mural of St. Floros; both in the katholicon of Agios Nikolaos tis Stegis monastery, Kakopetria. 10th century (?).*

Another related icon of the Virgin is the *Agriotissa* from the monastery of Megas Agros which, according to the ecclesiastical tradition, came to Cyprus during the Iconoclastic Period from the monastery of Megas Agros in the Hellespont near Cyzicus.[31] Conservation of the icon in 1987 produced some evidence for the existence of a layer earlier than the twelfth-century layers, which, if the ecclesiastical tradition is correct, could possibly date to the era of iconoclasm.[32] Unfortunately, the earliest layer is not sufficiently visible for us to describe the iconography.

AFTER THE PERIOD OF ICONOCLASM

The reincorporation of Cyprus into the Byzantine Empire after the campaigns of Nicephorus Phocas in 965 heralded the Middle Byzantine Period, which lasted until the occupation of Cyprus by the Crusaders in 1191.[33] It was characterized by the official policy not only to fortify the island, but

also to endow it with churches and monasteries. Few frescoes can be ascribed to the tenth century, according to the dating proposed so far, and the same can be said for the eleventh century. To the tenth century are ascribed the aforementioned murals of Agia Solomoni and the Crucifixion at Agios Antonios of Kelia. Also the murals in the rock-carved chapel of Agia Mavra at Kyrenia are attributed the late tenth century (fig. 9.15b–c).[34] A mural icon of the Sacrifice of Abraham on the southwest pier at Agios Antonios (Kellia) (fig. 9.12) and the earliest layer of murals at Agios Nikolaos tis Stegis (Kakopetria), here exemplified by the bust of St. Floros (fig. 9.13b), have both been dated to the early eleventh century, but the evident stylistic contrast between them, especially between Abraham and St. Floros, suggests a reconsideration of their dating.[35] In the case of the anonymous master of Abraham, the flatness and the stylization issued from the linear treatment of the face by means of thin and calligraphic dark contours that are his most prevailing characteristics. In contrast, the mural of St. Floros and others of the same series at Kakopetria display an absence of stylization by means of contours. In fact, there was a clear endeavor for more or less successful illusionistic treatment, in order to confer plasticity and volume upon the figure, which suggests a dating perhaps to the tenth century and in the framework of the so-called "Macedonian Renaissance," characterized by painterly style and classicizing reminiscences from Greco-Roman Antiquity. In turn, it can also be proposed that the earlier layers at Agios Nikolaos tis Stegis, which have been dated to the early eleventh century, cannot all be attributed to the same painter or even to the same date, as illustrated by comparing, for instance, St. Ignatius of Antioch (fig. 9.13a) with St. Floros (fig. 9.13b).

The anonymous workshops of Kellia and Kakopetria may have also produced portable icons that did not survive. In the case of the wall frescoes at Agia Mavra at Kyrenia, an icon does exist that could be ascribed to the same stylistic trend, but not necessarily to the same workshop. It is the icon of Saints Minas, Victor, and Vikentios, conserved

FIG. 9.14   *Icon of Saints Minas, Victor and Vikentios. Larnaka, Bishop's Palace. Late 10th century.*

FIG. 9.15   *(a.) Detail of fig. 9.14 with the faces of Saints Minas, Victor, and Vikentios. Late 10th century; (b. and c.) Ascension mural in the chapel of Agia Mavra at Kyreneia, details of apostles. Late 10th century.*

a.   b.

FIG. 9.16   *Icon of Saints Kosmas and Damianos. Nicosia, Byzantine Museum. 10th century (Courtesy: The Byzantine Museum, Nicosia).*

in the Bishop's Palace at Larnaka (figs 9.14–15a).[36] The comparative study of these three figures with those of the Apostles in the Ascension at Agia Mavra (fig. 9.15b–c) permits an attribution of both works to the same stylistic trend of the late tenth century, when Agia Mavra is commonly dated in relation to Cappadocian churches.[37] The modeling of the faces, the haloes, and the garments are outlined by vivid black contours and by the contrast in the juxtaposition of the colors. The faces are characterized by vivid red cheeks, wide-open eyes framed in black contours, but enhanced on the lower part by strong white highlights. The wide thick highlights are also applied occasionally over the eyebrows. Thick black contours separate the hair from the faces. The hair is in most cases made of light chestnut color hatched with vivid dark lines. On these comparative grounds, this icon could be stylistically associated with the murals of Agia Mavra and ascribed to the late tenth century.

There is also a second icon that has been previously dated to the tenth century, which illustrates the *Agioi Anargyroi* ("Holy Unmercinaries"),

Kosmas and Damianos (fig. 9.16). It was found among the icons of Panagia Chrysaliniotissa in Nicosia and is today exhibited in the Byzantine Museum of the Makarios III Foundation.[38] The two saints appear surprisingly young, without facial hair, although they usually appear bearded and more mature in age within other paintings. They are frontal and their heads are surrounded by haloes with double lines on a gilded background. In the upper left corner Christ appears blessing them. This icon reflects the high quality of craftsmanship emanating from the capital during the tenth century. It is linked to Sinai icons, ascribed by Weitzman to Constantinople, on the level of the modeling of the faces, the chromatology, and also the special manner of distributing the shadows and lights.[39]

The icon of St. James the Persian (fig. 9.17a–b) is one example of an artwork with local Cypriot characteristics.[40] It was once housed in the thirteenth- or fourteenth-century church in the historic center of Nicosia, now in the United Nations buffer zone. When we compare the mod-

FIG. 9.17 *(a-b) Icon of Saint James the Persian from the homonymous church in Nicosia and now at the Byzantine Museum in Nicosia. 10th century (Courtesy: The Byzantine Museum, Nicosia); (c) Detail with the face of St. James the Persian from his icon in the Byzantine Museum of Paphos. Late 12th century.*

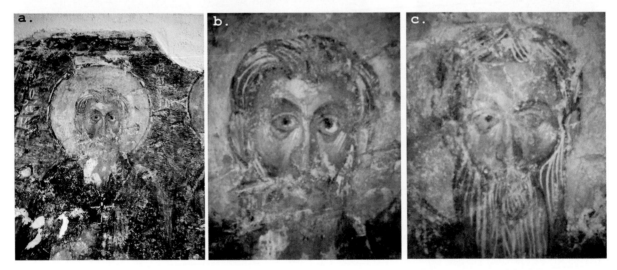

FIG. 9.18 *Details of the saints' faces in the hermitage of Agios Sozomenos at Potamia. (a) St. Sozomenos; (b.) detail; (c.) adjacent saint; now at the Byzantine Museum in Nicosia.*

eling of the icon's face with the murals of the tenth-century hermitage of Agios Sozomenos at Potamia (fig. 9.18a–c), it corresponds to a tenth-century dating and excludes the thirteenth century, which has also been proposed.[41] The icon has little to do with thirteenth-century style, as far as the technique, ornaments, modeling, the general aesthetics, and style are concerned. For instance, the large and wide-open ocular cavities lavishly enhanced by bright white flourishes, which also

highlight the forehead and the neck, are features completely alien to thirteenth-century style. There are strong local Cypriot connections to this icon, such as the typology of the letters of the inscription: "Ο ΑΓΙΟΣ ΙΑΚΟΒΟΣ Ο ΠΕΡΣΟΣ," instead of "ΠΕΡΣΗΣ," which is a peculiar Cypriot spelling for "Persian." Also, the foliage ornament on the upper frame and the prominent modeling of the face link this icon with the murals of the Agios Sozomenos hermitage at Potamia, dated to the

FIG. 9.19 *Part of an icon with apostles from the church of the Archangelos Michail at Lefkonoiko. Now in the Byzantine Museum. 11th c. (Courtesy: The Byzantine Museum, Nicosia).*

FIG. 9.20 *Icon of the Virgin flanked by Saints Luke and Lazarus. From the church of Panagia Angeloktistos, at Kiti, 11th century (?).*

tenth century. Finally, on an iconographic level, it could be theorized that this icon served as a model for the painting of St. James the Persian by Theodoros Apsevdis and his workshop, which is located at in the Church of Theoskepasti at Kato Paphos (fig. 9.17c). The fresco is dated to the end of the twelfth century and has particular elements of Theodoros Apsevdis' personal style, as well as the so-called Late and Post-Komnenian "mannerist" qualities.[42] For instance, the coiffure, red Phrygian bonnet, red chlamys, oblong face, pointed beard, ears, and the diagonal position of the spear over the right shoulder of the saint are among the elements that Theodoros Apsevdis adopted from a prototype.

The eleventh century also provides us with four icons that indicate both continuity and changes in style. The first example is the icon from the Church of the Archangel Michael at Lefkonioko, which

is now in the Byzantine Museum in Nicosia (fig. 9.19).[43] It is a surviving portion from a larger icon, perhaps of the Dormition of the Virgin. Three fragmentary figures of apostles are preserved, and the nose of a fourth appears on the right side. This icon is a sort of *sui-generis* work. The rendering of the faces has an elementary plasticity with expressive wide-open eyes; this contrasts with the garments which are completely flat, stylized and deprived of volume, resulting from the heavy dark lines marking the draperies. The black contours separate the hair from the red background, which isolates the figures from their physical space.

A second icon that possibly dates to the eleventh century is the enthroned Virgin with Child, flanked by Saints Luke and Lazarus from the Panagia *Angeloktisti* Church at Kiti (fig. 9.20). According to one scholar, the original layer of the icon dates to the thirteenth century, and the icon was completely repainted in the seventeenth, as well as in 1853.[44] However, it is worth noting that the restorer of the icon, in contrast, ascribes the original layer to the eleventh century.[45] This dating seems more plausible by a careful study of the modeling of the faces. The layer of 1853 has been transposed on a new wooden base and is exhibited in the church today as a separate icon. The layer of the seventeenth century is still on the icon and what is visible from the original icon are mainly the face of Christ and those of Saints Luke and Lazarus, while the face of the Virgin was repainted in the seventeenth century.

Another presumably eleventh-century icon is from the Panagia Chrysaliniotissa church in Nicosia (fig. 9.21). It has been restored in recent years, but its examination is still unpublished. The Virgin is holding the Child as a *Glycophilousa*, where their cheeks tenderly touch. Unfortunately, the condition of the icon, with its fragments assembled together on a newer wooden base and its missing portions, does not permit us to ascertain whether the iconographic type is that of *Kykkiotissa*. The icon has been repainted at least twice. According to

FIG. 9.21 *Icon of the Virgin Mary from the church of Panagia Chrysaliniotissa, Nicosia. Possibly late 10th/early 11th century with later repainting.*

a.

b.

FIG. 9.22 *(a) Icon of the Prophet Elijah from the Monastery of Agios Ioannis Lampadistis at Kalopanagiotis. (b) detail. Now at the Byzantine Museum in Nicosia. Possibly 11th century.*

the restorer, the original layer, from which only a part of the face of the Virgin has been uncovered, was made in the encaustic technique dating to the tenth or eleventh century.[46] We will have to wait, however, for the final publication with the results of the restoration in order to ascertain the main reasons for this dating.

The problem of dating arises also in the case of the Prophet Elijah icon from the Monastery of Agios Ioannis Lampadistis, now in the Byzantine Museum in Nicosia (fig. 9.22).[47] Although it has been dated to the thirteenth century since its first exhibition in the Museum, its technique and the style do not fit within the framework of that period, but rather bring to mind the eleventh-century Abraham fresco at Kellia (fig. 9.12).[48] Both artworks present a series of close similarities suggesting their dating to the same period, and perhaps even to the same artistic environment. They both have a bright red background, although it is almost completely missing today on the icon of the prophet Elijah. The use of the black contours distinguishes the beard from the flesh of the neck, the hair from the flesh of the face, and completely separates the neck from the garments. Stylization and expressiveness of the faces are strikingly similar in both artworks. Other elements are also quite analogous, such as the layout of the oblong faces, the outline of the beards with the slightly semi-circle contouring of the mouth, while leaving visible only the lower lip, as well as the round delineation of the chin. These similarities, the powerful but sufficiently elegant faces, almost deformed, together with the heavy black contours, could situate this icon in the eleventh century rather than the thirteenth, as suggested by the restorer.[49]

At the end of the eleventh century the Komnenian style, as it emanated from the capital of the Empire, was transplanted to Cyprus in accelerated rhythms. This was due to the strategic importance given to the island between the expansion of the Seljuk Turks in Asia Minor and the Crusaders on the Eastern Mediterranean coast.[50] The Byzantine Emperor Alexios I Komnenos fortified the island and appointed several *doux* (δουχ, i.e., dukes or governors) to Cyprus who were close to him, like Epiphanios Paschales, Eumathios Philokales, and Constantinos Katakalon. Until

the occupation of the island by the Crusaders in 1191, the *doux* governing Cyprus was either a member of the imperial family or closely related. They sponsored the building of monasteries and churches, and invited painters from the capital to decorate them with murals and icons. Around the year 1100 there are several well-documented examples. The monastery of Panagia Alypou was established by the *magistros* Epiphanios Paschales at the village of Geri outside Nicosia around 1091, though it no longer exists. A better known example is the chapel of the Holy Trinity and the octagonal *katholicon* in the Monastery of Agios Ioannis Chrysostomos (Koutsovendis).[51] The chapel of the Holy Trinity was founded by the Governor of Cyprus, Duke Eumathios Philokales, slightly after 1092, which was the date of his first appointment in Cyprus.[52] The high quality of these murals allows us to consider them as the most representative of Constantinopolitan paintings in Cyprus around 1100.[53] It is unfortunate that icons issued from this workshop have not survived.

Some years later, the murals were painted in the *katholicon* of the Monastery of Panagia Phorbiotissa at Asinou, dedicated by the *magistros* Nicephoros Ischyrios, the founder of the monastery in 1105/1106.[54] We see his portrait offering the model of the *katholicon* in the fourteenth-century repainting of the same subject underneath.[55] Icons that can be attributed to the same workshop have survived, such as the *St. John the Baptist,* now on display in the Byzantine Museum in Nicosia, and others.[56] These icons testify the new developments in icon painting in Cyprus around 1100. To the same master and his workshop are attributed also the murals in the Panagia Theotokos church at Trikomo. The artist was apparently a Constantinopolitan, or a Cypriot who studied in the capital, and flourished in Cyprus around the year 1105.[57]

All these examples of painting within Cyprus, showing both internal development and external influence, lead us to consider whether the island was an artistic center that influenced other regions. For example, the expansion of Cypriot icon painting around 1100 outside Cyprus is theorized by Kurt Weitzman. He assigned a group of icons in Mount Sinai to the Cypriot production of the early twelfth century.[58] Perhaps in the future, scholars might trace other examples of Cypriot painting techniques and iconography of the eleventh and early twelfth centuries in other parts of the Byzantine Empire, as has already been done for the late twelfth and thirteenth centuries.

CONCLUSION

In conclusion, perhaps the most certain thing we can say about the heritage of Cypriot icons dating before the twelfth century is that we have insecure dates. In this chapter, I have provided our best estimates so far, based mainly on stylistic analysis. These certainly need further confirmation and examination through:

◎   a more extensive comparative analysis with icons of other regions surrounding Cyprus, by scholars trained with a critical eye,

◎   a thorough scientific study of the icon materials (pigments, varnishes, woods and nails, gesso and the cloths in between the wood and the gesso) and techniques (treating wooden panels, brushstrokes, layers, gilding),

◎   detailed records, photographs, and published reports on the conservation/restoration of these icons by the restorers,

◎   and more systematic study of epigraphy.

These four parameters are very important for our future progress in understanding the chronological development of Byzantine painting technique, style, and iconography. This process would lead, most probably to a reconsideration of dates proposed so far, which are based solely on aesthetic, stylistic, and iconographic criteria. Already in 1975 Kurt Weitzman, when speaking about the Cypriot icons of the Middle Byzantine Period, brought this problem to the fore by stating: "Dating the few preserved icons is in some cases difficult and some of the dates proposed need further confirmation."[59]

One last thing must be said. In the past, the thirteenth century became a sort of "box" where every stylistically "strange" icon was placed. This unbalanced distribution of icons has provided us with a skewed line of development, conveying a very poor eleventh century, an abundantly rich twelfth century, an artificially inflated thirteenth century, and again an impoverished fourteenth century. This history needs reconsideration through further research. And yet chronological gaps will continue to challenge our understanding as to how Cyprus developed fresco and icon painting during and after Iconoclasm. Other factors, such as the scarcity of the surviving material and the aspects of local character, need also be considered. These can be obstacles in obtaining an accurate and valid comparison with examples in other regions. Nevertheless, the examples cited in this chapter provide us with a clear starting point.

NOTES

1   I express my thanks to Dr. Giannis Eliades, Director of the Byzantine Museum in Nicosia, for his kind allowance to use some digital photographs of items exhibited in the Museum.

2   Michaelides 1992: nos. 36–38, 42–47, 53–59; for the Kanakariá, nos. 67–68; for the Panagia Angeloktistos, 69–70; and for the Panagia Kyra, 71. For the fragment of an Archangel from Kourion basilica, see Megaw 1985b: 173–98, fig. 12.

3   Sacopoulo 1962; Sophocleous 1994: 12, fig. 5a; Chotzakoglou 2005: pl. 281.

4   Papageorgiou 1985: 96–97.

5   Soteriou 1935: pl. 145.

6   Petermann 1860; Papageorghiou 1985: 97; 2010: 109–16.

7   For more information on this, see Mansouri 2001 and Chapter 7 in this volume.

8 Such sources include the *Life of St. Stephan the Younger, Life of Saint John from Damascus,* and the *Life of the Nicephorus, Patriarch of Constantinople,* ed. Migne 1912: vol. 100: 1069–186, and vols. 94–96; Halkin et al. 1969: 1335. Regarding the imperial exiling of monks, such accounts are found in the writings of Theophanes the Confessor (*Chronographia,* AM 6262) and in the *Life of Saint Romanos the Neomartyr* by Stephen Mansūr, ed. Peeters 1911: 393–427.

9 For Agia Paraskevi, see Stylianou 1997: 384; Sophocleous 1994: 12 and fig. 5b; Chotzakoglou 2005: pl. 307; Foulias 2004: 123–45. For the Panagia Kanakariá, see Chotzakoglou 2005: pls. 308–9. For Agia Barbara, see Chotzakoglou 2005: pls. 302–3; Stewart 2010: 169–72, fig. 17.

10 Foulias 2011: 203–29, figs. 1–15.

11 For Agios Antonios, see Stylianou 1997: 437 (without an image); Spanou 2002: 23–25; Chotzakoglou 2005: pl. 324. The icon of the Crucifixion at Mount Sinai was dated by Kurt Weitzman to around the first half of the 9th century; Weitzmann 1976: no. B. 50; see also Corrigan 1995: 45–54. For Agia Solomoni see Papageorghiou 1974: 411–12; Sophocleous 1994: fig. 6; Chotzakoglou 2005: pls. 312–18 d; Papageorghiou and Eliades 2008: 34–35.

12 See for instance these examples: in the Cathedral of Bostra in Syria (Chotzakoglou 2005: pl. 319); one segment in the Museum of Damascus (Zibawi 1995: 38, fig. 13); and the Church of Mar-Charbel at Maad in Lebanon (Nordiguian and Voisin 1999: 316–23). See other examples in Sader 1987.

13 I express my thanks to Professor D. Michaelides for this information concerning his excavations at the site of *Agioi Pente,* as well as to Dr. Maria Hadjicosti for the information concerning her excavations at Pyla-*Koutsopetria.*

14 Papageorghiou 1991: 5, no. 2; 1996: pl. 91; Sophocleous 1994: no. 1a, 75 and 120–21; Gkioles 2003: 118; Chotzakoglou 2005: pl. 568. Some have even proposed a Middle Byzantine date; Ševčenko 1999: 150.

15 Weitzmann 1976: nos B.24, B.27, B.32, B.36.

16 Papageorghiou 1991: 3, no. 1; Sophocleous 1994: no. 2, 76, 123; Gkioles 2003: 118. Chotzakoglou 2005: pl. 567; Papageorghiou and Eliades 2008: 39.

17 Papageorghiou 1991: 5.

18 Papageorghiou 1991: 7, no. 3; Sophocleous 1994: no. 4, 77, 125; Gkioles 2003: 119. Chotzakoglou 2005: pl. 572.

19 Regarding the epithet "Agiosoritisa" and the "Virgin Hagiosoritissa," see N. Ševčenko 1991 and Nersessian 1960: 69–86.

20 *Rule of Neilos, Monastery of the Mother of God, Machairas,* ed. Thomas and Hero 2000: 3: 1126-–31.

21 Papageorghiou 1991: 9.

22 The Synod of 843 was convoked by Theodora, regent of her minor son, Emperor Michael III.

23 Weitzmann 1976: nos B. 1–5 and B. 9.

24 Belting 1996: pl. V.

25 The year 451 marked the Fourth Ecumenical Council at Chalcedon, where the theology around the Virgin Mary was discussed; Limberis 1994: 47–61. On the garments of the Virgin and their cult in Constantinople, see Shoemaker 2008: 53–74.

26 N. Ševčenko 1991: 2171.

27 Chrysostomos 1969: 27–28; Chotzakoglou 2005: pl. 566.

28 On the foundation and the history of the monastery, see Chrysostomos 1969: 8–11.

29 For the thirteenth-century date, see Sophocleous 1993: pls. 1–3 and 9–13; for the twelfth-century date, see for instance the *Kykkiotissa* painted on the late-twelfth century layer of murals in the Church of Agios Kirikos and Ioulitta at Letympou.

30 For the Sinai *Kykkiotissa,* see Weitzmann 1981: 48; Belting 1996: 288, figs. 174, 178, 293. Mouriki dates this icon to the first half of the twelfth century; 1990: 151.

31 Sophocleous 1992: 15–16, pls. 2–11; Chotzakoglou 2005: pl. 578.

32 Sophocleous 1992: 37.

33 The expedition in Cyprus was undertaken by the patrician Nikitas Chalkoutzis as mentioned by the written sources; Savvides 1993: 371–78.

34 G. Soteriou classified them as "Proto-byzantine wallpaintings," but they are, in fact, of a later date; Sotiriou 1935: pl. 62; Papageorghiou 1974: 412–13; Stylianou 1997: 451–55; Chotzakoglou 2005: pls. 320–23.

35 Agios Antonios: Stylianou 1997: fig. 260; Chotzakoglou 2005: pl. 338a. Agios Nikolaos tis Stegis: Stylianou 1997: figs. 19–21; Chotzakoglou 2005: pls. 325–26.

36 Sophocleous 2000: 132–33, no. 12.

37 Stylianou 1997: 452.

38 Papageorghiou 1969: 17; 1991: 8, pl. 4a–b; Papageorghiou and Eliades 2008: 44.

39 Weitzman 1976: nos B. 52, 54–56, 58.

40 The icon of Saint James the Persian was originally transferred to the Church of Agios Kassianos, and is now exhibited in the Byzantine Museum in Nicosia; Papageorghiou and Eliades 2008: 36. According to L. de Mas Lastrie, the Church of St. James was known as "Saint-Jacques de Commersarie" in late medieval texts; Papageorghiou 2010: 298.

41 Sophocleous 2000: 134–35, no. 13; Papageorghiou and Eliades 2008: 55. Doula Mouriki in her study on the thirteenth century icon painting in Cyprus does not consider such concepts and technical elaboration especially for the rendering of the faces; Mouriki 1986: 9–80.

42 Sophocleous 1994: no. 12b, 82 and 136; Papageorghiou 1996: 156, fig. 94; Corrie 1997: no. 75, 127–29; and Papageorghiou 1997: 107, no. 48b.

43 For the eleventh-century date, see Papageorghiou 1969: 16–17; 1976: 24–25, no. 1; 1991: 10, pl. 5; Papageorghiou and Eliades 2008: 49; for the thirteenth-century date, see Mouriki 1986: 47–48, fig. 54.

44 Spanou 2002: 134–35.

45 I express my thanks to Mr. Kostas Gerasimou, who restored the icon and provided me with this information.

46 I appreciate Father Demosthenes Demosthenous, who restored the icon at the Atelier for Conservation at the Archbishopric of Cyprus, for this useful information.

47 Papageorghiou 1976: 42–43, no. 10; 1991: 41, fig. 24; Papageorghiou and Eliades 2008: 57.

48 Spanou 2002: 25–26.

49 I express my thanks to Mr. Andreas Pharmakas, former conservator at the Department of Antiquities, for his information.

50 The Byzantine Emperor Romanos was defeated at Mantzikert in 1071 by the Seljuks, and the First Crusade lasted from 1096 to 1099.

51 Today a more recently-constructed chapel stands on top of the hill at Geri. The founder, *magistros* Epiphanios Paschales, offered a tenth-century *evangeliarion* to the Geri monastery on October 1091. This manuscript is conserved at the Municipal Library of Carpentras in France. On folio 277, the dedicatory inscription describes the Governor of Cyprus, Epiphanios Paschales; for the text of the inscription, see Papageorghiou 1984: 384; Galatariotou 2004: 57, 173. The Koutsovendis monastery was founded, according to a note in its Ritual Ordinance (Codex Paris. Gr. 402), by the monk Georgios, who became the first abbot. The inauguration of the monastery took place on the 9th of December, 1090; Mango, Hawkins, and Boyd 1990 and Papacostas 2008. The *katholicon* was demolished in the late nineteenth century.

52 Eumathios Philokales was appointed twice as governor of Cyprus, once from 1092–1103 and secondly from 1110–1118.

53 Stylianou 1997: figs. 273–76; Chotzakoglou 2005: pls. 345–74.

54 Stylianou 1963: pls. 8–11; Stylianou 1997: figs. 58–61.

55 Stylianou 1997: fig. 57.

56 For the icon of St. John the Baptist, see Papageorghiou 1969: 28; 1976: 26–27, no. 2; 1991: 12, pl. 6; Sophocleous 1994: 77, 126, no. 5; Gkioles 2003: 119; Papageorghiou and Eliades 2008: 48. For other, similar icons, see the icons of Archangel Michael and St. Spyridon, today in an American private collection, which came from Asinou; Vikan 1988; Chotzakoglou 2005: pls. 574–75. See also the Virgin with Child from the Monastery of Agios Ioannis Lampadistis at Kalopanagiotis; Gerasimou 2002: 242.

57 Stylianou 1997: figs. 294–97; Chotzakoglou 2005: pls. 412–23.

58 Weitzman 1975: 47–63, pls. 19–25.

59 Ibid.: 48.

Chapter 10

The Stuff of Life: The Material Culture of Everyday Living on Middle Byzantine Cyprus (11th–12th Centuries)

by Maria Parani

I saw an island that was not simply part of the world, but a whole world, containing all earthly grace.

These are the words with which the Constantinopolitan Nicholas Mouzalon, appointed archbishop of Cyprus by Alexios I Komnenos, described his first impressions upon his arrival in the island around 1107.[1] By that time, Cyprus had been part of the Byzantine Empire for nearly one hundred and fifty years, following its re-conquest in 965 by Niketas Chalkoutzes, the general of Nicephorus II Phocas. The unsuccessful revolts of Theophilos Erotikos in 1042 and of Rapsomates in 1092 did not constitute serious threats to Byzantine control over Cyprus, which remained a Byzantine province down to 1184, when a scion of the Byzantine imperial family, Isaak Komnenos, set himself up as an independent ruler of the island. Seven years later, Cyprus was irrevocably lost to the Empire when Richard the Lionheart conquered it on his way to the Holy Land in 1191.[2]

The Middle Byzantine period on Cyprus is generally acknowledged by modern scholars as an era of demographic, economic, and cultural recovery and growth, especially observable from the second half of the eleventh century onwards. Even the series of destructive raids against the island carried out by Renaud de Chatillion in 1155/6, by the Egyptian fleet in 1158, and by Raymond III of Antioch in 1161 has been interpreted by one historian as an indication of the island's wealth that made it an attractive target for raiding parties in search of rich and, apparently, easily obtainable plunder.[3] Be this as it may, it is this latter part of the Middle Byzantine period that offers the first signs of urban renewal on Cyprus after the end of Late Antiquity. While by this time the administrative center of the Byzantine province was the inland city of Nicosia, settlements of urban character began to develop anew on the coast. Kyrenia to the north apparently served as the principal port of entry for visitors and officials from Constantinople, while Paphos to the west and, especially, Limassol to the south seem to have carried the greatest weight of interregional and international traffic in pilgrims and commodities in the eleventh and, especially, the twelfth century. As for Famagusta, which in Lusignan times (1192–1474) would rise to become Cyprus' major port, it too seems to have had its modest beginnings during the period under discussion.[4] In addition to the development of towns and cities and, perhaps, partly in correlation to it, there is also some archaeological and written evidence to suggest a concomitant revitalization of the Cypriot countryside, though questions relating to the actual beginnings of this phenomenon and the nature, extent, and distribution of new settlement need to be elucidated further by future archaeological research.[5] The foundation of a number of important rural monasteries, some endowed with extensive properties, during the late eleventh and the twelfth centuries may have provided additional impetus for sustained economic and, possibly, demographic growth not only on the lowlands, but also on the mountainous regions of Cyprus, especially the central Troodos massif.[6]

The origins of the island's relative prosperity during the eleventh and the twelfth centuries are often linked to the renewed political and strategic importance of Cyprus for the Byzantine Empire in its efforts to maintain and advance its interests in the Eastern Mediterranean, especially after the loss of the greatest part of Asia Minor to the Seljuks on the one hand and the establishment of the Crusader States in the Levant on the other. Cyprus' economic development has also been associated with the island's successful integration into the flourishing exchange and communication networks for the transfer of people and goods that connected Western Europe and Byzantium with Egypt and the Syro-Palestinian mainland in the late eleventh and especially in the twelfth century.[7] In terms of material witnesses to these new circumstances, scholars often cite the impressive fortification works along the northern mountain range of Pentadaktylos,[8] as well as the number of churches that were constructed and decorated with frescoes during the eleventh and twelfth centuries due to the generosity and piety of Byzantine officials appointed to Cyprus and of local patrons, lay and ecclesiastic.[9] A relatively small number of icons, manuscripts, and processional crosses probably produced on Cyprus between the tenth and the twelfth century for donation to local shrines has also drawn the attention of historians and art-historians mainly interested in questions of style, piety, and patronage.[10] Beyond these, however, the realities and *realia* of day-to-day existence on the island remain elusive. This is largely the con-

sequence of the lack of systematic archaeological investigation of this period beyond the study of the ecclesiastical monuments and the ecclesiastical portable objects it has bequeathed us. Indeed, not so long ago, in 1982, Hector Catling was entirely justified in claiming, apropos the findings of the survey of the Yialias Valley, that "...the centuries between the end of the Early Christian period (or, perhaps, better — the Early Byzantine period) and the Middle Ages are very largely a blank, due in great part, no doubt, to limited knowledge of the archaeological material belonging to those centuries."[11]

At the dawn of the second decade of the 21st century, however, things are beginning to look less dark. First of all, one needs to acknowledge the significant advances made in the study of ceramic tablewares and coarse wares on Middle Byzantine and Medieval Cyprus thanks to the work of specialists like Demetra Papanikola-Bakirtzē, Marie-Louise von Wartburg, and Smadar Gabrieli.[12] Beyond that, we are now in the exciting position of awaiting the publication of the results of the systematic excavation of three important urban sites with significant late Middle Byzantine and Early Medieval archaeological layers: the ancient theater at Nea Paphos excavated by the University of Sydney under the direction of Prof. Richard Green, and the Hill of Agios Georgios (or PA.SY.D.Y.) and the *Palaion Demarcheion* at Nicosia excavated by the Department of Antiquities of Cyprus, under the direction of Dr. Despo Pilides and Mr. Yiannis Violaris, respectively. At Paphos, over the *orchestra* and stage of the long-abandoned ancient theater, a complex of artisanal installations was established in the twelfth century and continued to function down to the fourteenth.[13] On the other hand, the nature of the remains revealed at Area VIII of the Hill of Agios Georgios is of a different character, comprising four successive phases of ecclesiastical buildings. According to preliminary observations made by Dr. Pilides, there is a strong possibility that the impressive churches associated with the second and third phases of occupation could belong to the period that concerns us here, that is, the eleventh and the twelfth centuries. What makes this site even more important from our own particular point of view are the numerous burials of infants, children, and adults that were associated with the successive churches. Their study, once completed, will provide invaluable information on the life, and death, of the members of the community that worshipped at the Hill of Agios Georgios.[14] As for the site of the *Palaion Demarcheion*, this is located at the very heart of the city of Nicosia and has yielded significant remains of the eleventh and the twelfth century. These include, first of all, two ecclesiastical buildings. Church A, built as a single-aisle chapel in the twelfth century, was enlarged with the addition of a second aisle to the south, possibly in the thirteenth century. A number of burials are associated with the first phase of the chapel. A second, more impressive church of the cross-in-square type, known as Church B, also seems to have been constructed during the twelfth century. Interestingly, a workshop specializing in the manufacture of picrolite (i.e., a variety of serpentine) pendant crosses came to light in close proximity to Church B. The workshop probably catered to the needs of the faithful who came to worship at the church. The site has also yielded a number of sealed pottery deposits that can be securely dated to the Middle Byzantine period.[15] Lastly, in published preliminary reports the excavator makes tantalizing references to "hundreds of objects of everyday life such as tools, jewelry (mainly crosses made of various materials such as picrolite), bracelets made of glass, bells, and so on," which are being studied for publication.[16]

Future prospects, then, for the archaeology of Middle Byzantine Cyprus are indeed promising. Here and now, however, the available information on the material culture of everyday living on the island in terms of published archaeological evidence is limited to say the least. Students of daily life in the lands of the Byzantine Empire — and not just on Cyprus — often find themselves in a comparable predicament, a circumstance which drives them to seek alternative sources to complement the fragmentary and incomplete archaeological evidence at their disposal. The contemporary written record is the obvious first place to turn in search of additional information, though one needs to approach it with due caution, making allowances for limitations imposed by genre and for the biases introduced by the view-point and

objectives of individual authors. We can hardly accept at face value, for example, the claims made by Mouzalon, in his attempt to justify his abandonment of his Cypriot flock in 1110, that most of the Cypriots at his time lived like wild animals dressed in rags and without a roof over their heads because of heavy taxation.[17] As for the story of a Cypriot man reeking of wine and garlic in church, told for the purpose of entertaining a Constantinopolitan audience by Constantine Manasses, who visited Cyprus in 1161/2, this seems to me more informative of Constantinopolitan snobbery than of Cypriot dietary habits.[18] Still, though a wide range of sources — Byzantine, Western, Crusader, and Arabic — refer to political, social, and economic conditions on the island in the period from 965 to 1191, they provide hardly any concrete evidence on aspects that are of interest to us here, such as dress and personal adornment, secular architecture, the organization of domestic space, household furniture and furnishings, tools, implements, and so forth. To my knowledge, the same holds true of the extensive writings of Saint Neophytos the Recluse, active in the late twelfth and early thirteenth century.[19]

The second alternative source to which one could turn in search of information is the artistic record comprising primarily, in the case of Cyprus, a number of monumental iconographic cycles adorning the walls of eleventh-and twelfth-century churches. The indifference of Byzantine art with religious content towards the faithful representation of the trappings of the material world and its preference for the repetition of established iconographic types is well-known. Still, a number of investigations, including the studies by Chrestos Argyrou on aspects of daily life reflected in the painted churches of Cyprus, have argued that contemporary artifacts were depicted side-by-side with fanciful or conventional ones in Byzantine religious pictorial contexts.[20] While the whole would remain "timeless" and unrealistic, certain of its constituent elements could and did refer to contemporary habits at the time of the creation of the artistic work.[21] Identifying these elements is a challenging process, and especially so in the case of Cypriot depictions, since one must factor in the possible use of pictorial formulae disseminated from a major artistic center like Constantinople and, thus, reflecting metropolitan rather than provincial practices and tastes. Furthermore, given that we are dealing with religious paintings, the potential theological symbolism of the items represented in specific iconographic contexts must be taken into account. This is important if we are to avoid misleading conclusions or simplistic interpretations, such as, for instance, considering the attribution of an earring to the Christ-Child on the icon of Panagia Agriotissa (twelfth century) and at Lagoudera (church of the Virgin tou Arakos, 1192) as an early reflection of the much later local custom of firstborn sons to wear an earring as a sign of their birthright.[22]

Pending the results of current and future archaeological research, the following remarks have a very preliminary and tentative character. Of necessity, given the information available, the focus will be on two particular areas of interest, namely dress and household effects, especially kitchen- and tablewares. Questions regarding the character of these facets of Cypriot material culture and the degree to which it reflects the role of Cyprus as a crossroads, where local traditions and practices were fertilized by contacts with metropolitan Byzantium and the neighboring Middle East, Islamic and Crusader, will be tackled to the degree that the extant evidence permits.

We know little regarding the external appearance of the inhabitants of Cyprus during the Middle Byzantine period, other than that the men, like their counterparts in the rest of the Byzantine world, were bearded: in 1191, Richard the Lionheart forced the male members of the local Greek upper class to shave their beards.[23] Surviving portraits which could have shed some light on the question of lay male and female dress on Middle Byzantine Cyprus are practically non-existent. The figures of two supplicants, one male and one female, who appear on the copper-alloy benediction cross from the church of Agia Paraskevi at Temvria, dated to the tenth century, are too schematically rendered to allow any useful observations on their dress.[24] We know from Arab authors such as Ibn Ḥawqal in the tenth century that Cyprus had a well-established textile industry for the production of silk and linen cloths; indeed, silk textiles and precious garments of scarlet and silk were included among the spoils that Richard I took with him when he continued on his journey to the Holy Land in 1191.[25] However, the appearance of the garments made from silk, linen and, one assumes, also from wool is a matter of conjecture.

In anticipation of the publication of the dress accessories such as belt-buckles and buttons from the excavations at the Hill of Agios Georgios and the *Palaion Demarcheion*, one could attempt to glean some information from artistic representations on the island. For instance, it is not improbable that Cypriot men, like men in other parts of the Empire during the twelfth century, wore a combination of a long outer tunic or a coat over a pair of trousers, similar perhaps to the trousers worn by some of the Forty Martyrs in the depiction of their martyrdom at Panagia Phorbiotissa of Asinou in 1105/6.[26] Yet, it is unique representations such as the hooded cape, the hats, and the bags of the shepherds at Trikomo (Church of the Virgin, early twelfth century), Perachorio (church of the Holy Apostles, 1160–1180), and Lagoudera, and the turban-like headdress of the midwife also at Lagoudera that are more likely to reflect local practices.[27] It would seem that the anecdotal character of the episodes of the Bath of the Child and of the Annunciation to the Shepherds, both forming part of the Nativity composition in Byzantine art, made these iconographic contexts suitable for the introduction of charming details inspired from daily life, at the artist's discretion.

At first glance, one would think that the unknown painter of the Holy Apostles at Perachorio introduced an interesting detail in his depiction of the midwife in the scene of Christ's first bath: he showed the long ample sleeves of her dress pulled back and secured between her shoulder-blades, a "realistic" touch highlighting the manual nature of the woman's task that required freedom of movement, while at the same time revealing the adornment of her bare right arm with three dark-colored bands denoting bracelets.[28] Yet, this, as it turns out, was the current way of representing women involved in physical labor in eleventh- and twelfth-century Byzantine pictorial contexts, down to the detail of the bracelets, which, as I have argued elsewhere, were probably meant

FIG. 10.1 *Limassol, Cyprus Medieval Museum, inv. no. MM 516-517 / J. 445. Steatite encolpia with St. Nicholas (Photo: With the permission of the Director of the Department of Antiquities, Cyprus).*

FIG. 10.2 *Nicosia, Excavations of Palaion Demarcheion, inv. no. MTX 2/2004. Picrolite pendant cross (Photo: With the permission of the Director of the Department of Antiquities, Cyprus).*

to demonstrate that pictorial *topoi* were not necessarily devoid of contemporary or local relevance.[31]

Mention of bracelets brings us to the one component of dress on Byzantine Cyprus for which relatively more information is currently available, namely jewelry and, more specifically, encolpia, which are neck-pendants adorned with a sacred image or simply having the shape of the cross. Apart from being expressions of personal piety, the encolpia were meant to protect the bearer from both physical and spiritual evil through life. After death, such pendants would often accompany the bearer in the grave, where he or she lay awaiting the Final Judgment. Two encolpia made of steatite (i.e., soapstone) and bearing a bust-length image of Saint Nicholas are on display at the Cyprus Medieval Museum at Limassol (fig. 10.1).[32] Of unknown provenance, they are ascribed a twelfth-century date and find parallels in comparable arched-top steatite encolpia from elsewhere in the Byzantine world.[33] As for the choice of the sacred figure, Saint Nicholas appears to have been quite popular in Byzantine Cyprus, as suggested, for instance, by the churches dedicated to him and by his regular inclusion in the painted decoration of Cypriot monuments.[34] According to his *Life*, apart from a worker of miracles, Saint Nicholas was also a protector of the weak against the abuses of secular authority.[35] One cannot help but wonder whether this attribute may have contributed to his popularity within the context of Middle Byzantine Cyprus, where instances of cruelty and maltreatment at the hands of state officials are graphically described in the sources, but this is pure conjecture.[36] Much more common were cross-shaped encolpia, which came in a variety of materials, including copper alloy, steatite, and picrolite, and which evidence varying degrees of elaboration meant to satisfy a range of purchasing capabilities and aesthetic preferences (fig. 10.2).[37] Though most were probably locally produced — and the discovery of the workshop next to Church B at the *Palaion Demarcheion* adds support to this assertion — their types and decoration can be paralleled in similar finds from the rest of the Byzantine Empire.[38] On the other hand, another group of encolpia attested on Cyprus, namely copper alloy reliquary crosses bearing rather crude relief or engraved decoration,

to represent glass bangles securely attested in Byzantine archaeological contexts outside Cyprus from the tenth down to the twelfth or thirteenth century.[29] Thus, without other corroborating evidence, the depiction at Perachorio cannot be admitted as proof of the adoption by Cypriot women of the long sleeves, exceedingly wide at the wrists, which were fashionable in Constantinople and other parts of the empire in the eleventh and twelfth centuries, however probable this may be.[30] On the other hand, the glass bracelets unearthed during the excavations at *Palaion Demarcheion*, if found to date to the twelfth century, would serve

were probably imports from centers of production located in Constantinople or, in the case of an eleventh-century cross acquired by the Department of Antiquities in 2003, perhaps from not-so-distant Anatolia (fig. 10.3).[39] Such pendant reliquary crosses enjoyed widespread popularity in all lands of the Empire from the ninth down to the twelfth century, in the cities as well as in the countryside, worn by men and women, laymen and ecclesiastics. Mass-produced and affordable, they were highly desirable because of their increased efficacy, combining as they did the powerful symbol of the cross with the protective powers of sacred images and relics.[40] Cypriot men and women were, thus, following a well-established Byzantine practice when they chose to avail themselves of the protection afforded by these encolpia.

Turning now to the question of household effects, at present we know hardly anything regarding domestic architecture and the organization and use of domestic space on Cyprus during the Middle Byzantine period. Saint Neophytos the Recluse speaks of the impressive houses of the wealthy, which they had to abandon when they left Cyprus trying to escape the tyranny of Isaak Komnenos, but gives no further details as to their appearance and contents.[41] Given the developed Cypriot textile industry at the time, we may assume that such houses would have been equipped with a variety of textile furnishings, including perhaps "the square carpets of Cyprus" that an Arab author of the eleventh century, Muḥammad b. Ahmad Abu'l-Mutahhar al-Azdi, lists as part of the standard equipment of a civilized urban household in the western Islamic world.[42] Elaborate textile furnishings, especially bed valances, are depicted in a number of twelfth-century frescoes on Cyprus, for example at Asinou and at Perachorio, but, considering that such depictions constitute a common feature of Komnenian painting in general, their occurrence in Cypriot contexts does not necessarily reflect local practices.[43] As for actual wooden furniture, particularly beds, their use, it seems, was not unknown. Saint Neophytos in his *Testamentary Rule* of 1214 permitted the use of beds by those infirm due to age or sickness, but forbade it for the remaining members of his monastic community as an unnecessary and harmful luxury that

FIG. 10.3   *Cyprus, Department of Antiquities, inv. no. 2003/ XI-10/38. Copper alloy pendant reliquary cross with St. John (Photo: With the permission of the Director of the Department of Antiquities, Cyprus).*

had no place in the austere monastic world of the *Enkleistra;* the monks were expected to sleep on mats.[44]

Household furnishings, one expects, would have also included lighting devices. Wheel-thrown glazed clay lamps, relatively common in other parts of the Byzantine world during the Middle and Late Byzantine periods, are also attested in Cypriot medieval contexts, as the examples on display at the Medieval Museum demonstrate, but their use may have begun earlier, during the period that concerns us here.[45] On the other hand, the unpublished twelfth-century glass lamp from the church of Panagia Kanakariá at Lythrankomi also at the Medieval Museum was probably intended for ecclesiastical usage.[46] With its tall flaring neck, bulging body, and low foot, it is reminiscent of lamps depicted suspended under ciboria in Middle and Late Byzantine frescoes, though its closest known extant parallels are to be found in contemporary Islamic glass lamps produced, among other places, in neighboring Syria.[47]

FIG. 10.4   *Limassol, Cyprus Medieval Museum, inv. no. MM 514 / 1940/XI-25/1A. Copper-alloy icon with St. Gregory the Miracle-Worker (Photo: With the permission of the Director of the Department of Antiquities, Cyprus).*

Another category of household objects worth mentioning briefly is that of personal icons. I am referring in particular to a small group of relief icons made of steatite and copper-alloy which are dated from the tenth down to the twelfth century.[48] One of these, possibly from Galata or Kakopetria and ascribed a tenth- or eleventh-century date, depicts the popular saintly bishop Saint Gregory the Miracle-Worker (fig. 10.4). According to the supplicatory inscription, it belonged to one Niketas *stratēgos*, i.e., a general Niketas, perhaps, as has been suggested, the selfsame Niketas Chalkoutzes who had reclaimed Cyprus for the Empire in 965.[49] Be this as it may, the small scale of these icons, inviting the viewer to a more intimate contemplation of and interaction with the sacred images they carry, argues in favor of their use in the private setting of the home rather than the public one of the church.

Important and, more significantly, securely dated evidence regarding the storage, preparation, and consumption of food and drink within the Cypriot Middle Byzantine household is provided by the recent publication of a sealed twelfth-century deposit from the *Palaion Demarcheion* site at Nicosia. Beginning with the coarse wares, the array of attested wheel-thrown and hand-made cooking pots and cooking bowls implies a concomitant variety in function for the preparation of dishes cooked in different ways, such as stewing, baking, roasting, or frying. Interestingly, among the finds from the *Palaion Demarcheion* is included a small number of lead-glazed cooking vessels which, according to Wartburg and Violaris, were imported, possibly from the Middle East.[50]

Once the food was prepared, it would have been served for consumption. In poorer households, one assumes, the cooking vessels could have also been used for serving and, in the absence of individual plates, for consumption as well. In more affluent ones, tableware in an array of materials would have been available for serving and consuming food and drink. The most expensive items would have been those made from metal, and gold and silver vessels were included among Richard the Lionheart's booty in 1191.[51] However, to my knowledge, no Middle Byzantine precious metal tablewares have been unearthed on Cyprus thus far. In contrast, a treasure of some ten to fifteen copper alloy dishes and bowls, now dispersed, was discovered around 1960 in the vicinity of the gothic Cathedral of St. Sophia in Nicosia. The bowls and dishes were found along with an estimated 10,000 billon *trachea*, ranging in date from the reign of Alexios I Komnenos (1081–1118) down to that of Isaak II Angelos (1185–1195).[52] One of the bowls of the treasure, with a flat base, flaring walls, and a horizontal lip, is on display at the Leventis Municipal Museum of Nicosia; it bears no decoration.[53] A second member of the group, this time a dish made of brass, forms part of the collection of Mr. Andreas Pitsillides (fig. 10.5).[54] This medium-sized dish, which was created by hammering, has flaring ridged walls and a horizontal rim (diameter 24.5 cm; height 1.8 cm). Its main decoration consists of a broad band of engraved

1997: no. 58; Papacostas 1999a: 196–200; Michaēlidou 2000: nos. 94, 102; Kōnstantinidēs 2005: 454–63; Chotzakoglou 2005: 668–69, 733–35, 741–43; Metcalf 2009: 329–36.

11 Catling 1982: 234. Cf. Gregory 1987: 200.

12 Papanikola-Bakirtzē 1993, 1996, 1997, 1999a, 2004; Maier and Wartburg 1997; Wartburg 2003; Waksman and Wartburg 2006; Wartburg and Violaris 2009; Gabrieli, McCall, and Green 2001; Gabrieli 2008.

13 Hadjisavvas 2000: 689; 2001: 68–71; 2002a: 720–23; Gabrieli, McCall, and Green 2001; Cook and Green 2002; Green, Barker, and Gabrieli 2004: 30–34; Flourentzos 2006: 84–86.

14 Hadjisavvas 2000: 685–88; Flourentzos 2003: 70–75; 2004–2005: 1678–81; 2006: 72–77; Pilides 2003, 2012; Michaelides and Pilides 2012.

15 Hadjisavvas 2002b: 81–84; 2003: 671–73; Flourentzos 2003: 82–84; 2004: 84–86; 2004–2005: 1681–85; 2005: 73–74; 2006: 90–91; Violaris 2004; Wartburg and Violaris 2009.

16 Violaris 2004: 73.

17 Nicholas Mouzalōn, *Verses on His Abdication* 893–95, ed. Doanidou 1934: 136; Karlin-Hayter 1995.

18 Constantine Manasses, *Hodoiporikon*, 90–133, ed. Horna 1904: 344–45.

19 Angelidē et al. 1982; Nerantzē-Varmazē 1996; Mansouri 2001.

20 Argyrou 2001, 2007.

21 Parani 2007.

22 Stylianou 1955: 461; Sophocleous 1992: 45–46, pl. 7; Nikolaïdès 1996: 83; Baltoyianni 1993–1994.

23 Ambroise, *Estoire de la guerre sainte*, verses 1944–48, ed. Ailes and Barber 2003: 31–32, translation by Ailes 2003: 59; *Itinerarium peregrinorum*, ed. Stubbs 1864: 201, translation by Nicholson 1997: 193; Nicolaou-Konnari 2000: 54, 81.

24 Michaēlidou 2000: no. 102; Chotzakoglou 2005: 732–33, fig. 763; Hadjisavvas 2010: no. 186.

25 Ibn Ḥawqal, *Ṣūrat al-ʾArḍ*, 184, translation by Mansouri 2001: 34; Muthesius 2001: 369. Ambroise, *Estoire de la guerre sainte,* verses 1671, 2074–75, ed. Ailes and Barber 2003: 27, 33, translation by Ailes 2003: 54, 61; *Itinerarium peregrinorum*, ed. Stubbs 1864: 194, 204, translation by Nicholson 1997: 187, 195; Hill 1940: 320, n. 2; Nicolaou-Konnari 2000: 59–60.

26 Stylianou 1985: fig. 60; Chatzēchristodoulou and Myriantheus 2002: 26; Parani 2003: 57, 247.

27 Stylianou 1985: fig. 297; Megaw and Hawkins 1962: fig. 32; Winfield 2003: 22, 34, 35.

28 Megaw and Hawkins 1962: fig. 33.

29 Parani 2005: 152–53; Ristovska 2009.

30 Parani 2003: 73–74.

31 Violaris 2004: 73.

32 Kalavrezou-Maxeiner 1985: nos. 97–98; Chotzakoglou 2005: 695–96, fig. 695. Note that Kalavrezou proposes the identification of the saintly figure on the second pendant with St. John Chrysostom, rather than St. Nicholas.

33 Kalavrezou-Maxeiner 1985: nos. 88, 96; Papanikola-Bakirtzē 2002: no. 707.

34 Papacostas 1999a: appendices A.87–89, B.I.76, B.II.29–31. Triantaphyllopoulos 2006.

35 Maguire 1996: 169–86.

36 Nicholas Mouzalōn, *Verses on His Abdication,* ed. Doanidou 1934; Neophytos the Recluse, Περὶ τῶν κατὰ χώραν Κύπρον σκαιῶν, 1–45, ed. Tsiknopoullos 1969: 336–37; Theodosios the Monk, *Life of Leontios Patriarch of Jerusalem,* 70–80, ed. Tsougarakis 1993: 112–27.

37 Flourentzos 2004–2005: 1684, fig. 69; Chotzakoglou 2005: 735, figs. 696, 768. Limassol, Cyprus Medieval Museum, MM 524, 538–542.

38 Papanikola-Bakirtzē 2002: nos. 684, 690, 694–95.

39 Papanikola-Bakirtzē and Iakōvou 1997: no. 59; Michaēlidou 2000: no. 101; Flourentzos 2004–2005: 1643, fig. 23; Chotzakoglou 2005: 735, figs. 769–70; Pitarakis 2006: suppl. 2; Limassol, Cyprus Medieval Museum, MM 525–530, 534–536.

40 Pitarakis 2006.

41 Neophytos the Recluse, Περὶ τῶν κατὰ χώραν Κύπρον σκαιῶν, 33–39, ed. Tsiknopoullos 1969: 337.

42 Serjeant 1951: 76; Papacostas 1999a: 72.

43 Megaw and Hawkins 1962: fig. 42; Chatzēchristodoulou and Myriantheus 2002: 17, 28; Parani 2003: 178, 242, 247.

44 Neophytos the Recluse, Τυπικὴ διαθήκη, canon 9, ed. Tsiknopoullos 1969, repr. 2001: 96; translation Galatariotou 2000: 1364.

45 Parani 2003: 189. Limassol, Cyprus Medieval Museum, MM 428–430.

46 Limassol, Cyprus Medieval Museum, MM 416 (Lythrankomi 66 – A. Papageorghiou): whitish glass, height 12.8 cm, diameter 8.7 cm.

47 Crowfoot and Harden 1931: 205–6, pl. xxx.46–49; Carboni 2001: nos. 38b–c, 99; Parani 2005: 154–55.

48 Kalavrezou-Maxeiner 1985: nos. 62, 76; Chotzakoglou 2005: 695, 743, figs. 711, 748; Campagnolo, Courtois, Martiniani-Reber, and Michaelidou 2006: no. 136.

49 Chatzēdakēs et al. 1964: no. 562; Papacostas 2002: 43; Chotzakoglou 2005: 742, fig. 782.

50 Wartburg and Violaris 2009: 250–55.

51 Ambroise, *Estoire de la guerre sainte*, verses 1666–69, 2068–70, ed. Ailes and Barber 2003: 27, 33, translation by Ailes 2003: 54, 61; *Itinerarium peregrinorum*, ed. Stubbs 1864: 194, 203–4, translation by Nicholson 1997: 187, 195; Hill 1940: 320 n. 2.

52 Chotzakoglou 2005: 741, fig. 789; Metcalf 2009: 209–10.

53 Loizou Hadjigavriel and Theodotou 2009: 43.

54 I am grateful to Mr. Pitsillides for very kindly sharing with me his knowledge of the treasure and for allowing me to examine and photograph the dish in question. For the results of the compositional analysis of the dish carried out by Prof. Vassilike Kassianidou with the assistance of Dr. Maria Dikomitou, see the Appendix on pp. 164–66.

55 Papanikola-Bakirtzē 1999b: nos. 29, 48, 143–144, 199, 202.

56 Megaw and Hawkins 1962: 344, fig. 23.

57 Unpublished. Limassol, Cyprus Medieval Museum, MM 422 (Lythrankomi 66 – A. Papageorghiou): height 9.3 cm; mouth diameter 6.9 cm; base diameter 6.5 cm.

58 Megaw 1968: 89–90, figs. 2–3.

59 Parani 2005: 166, figs. 19–21; Ristovska 2009.

60 Stern 1995: 325 n. 3, 326; Wartburg 2003: 162.

61 Papanikola-Bakirtzē 1993: 121, 123; Papanikola-Bakirtzē and Iakōvou 1997: nos. 60–63; Papanikola-Bakirtzē 1999a: 5–7, figs. 2–5; Wartburg 2003; Campagnolo, Courtois, Martiniani-Reber, and Michaelidou 2006: 116, figs. 35–37; Wartburg and Violaris 2009: 255–63.

62 Chatzēchristodoulou and Myriantheus 2002: 28; Parani 2010: 159, fig. 16. On the ascription of the manuscript, see Gamillscheg 1997: 241.

63 Parani 2010: 156–59.

Chapter 10: Appendix

Compositional Analysis of a Copper Alloy Dish of the Middle Byzantine Period in the A. Pitsillides Collection

by Vasiliki Kassianidou

INTRODUCTION

A literature review of what is known about the techniques and materials used in the Middle Byzantine period to produce metallic vessels and other metal objects reveals that there are hardly any published studies or results of chemical and other analysis on such material, the sole exception perhaps being the publication by M. Lazovic and others in 1977.[1] This was pointed out to me by Maria Parani who, in her chapter here, discusses one such artifact: a copper alloy dish, part of a hoard consisting of coins and dishes, which was found around 1960 in the vicinity of St. Sophia in Nicosia. The artifact is now in the private collection of Mr. Andreas Pitsillides. Since the Archaeological Research Unit of the University of Cyprus recently acquired a portable XRF analyzer (an InnovX Delta Dynamic XRF), which is suitable for the non-destructive compositional analysis of metal artifacts, we decided that it was a great opportunity to analyze this object and gain an insight into the copper alloy used to manufacture it.[2] This brief note presents and discusses the analytical results.

COMPOSITIONAL ANALYSIS USING A P-XRF ANALYZER

As pointed out by Karydas,[3] the X-ray Fluorescence (XRF) technique is a well-established analytical tool used for the non-destructive analysis of a great variety of archaeological materials (e.g., ceramics, glass, pigments, and, especially, metals)[4] in museums, private collections, but also on site.[5] The technique has been used for more than thirty years now, because its basic characteristics render it an ideal choice for work with ancient artifacts.[6] These characteristics include simultaneous quantitative analysis of over 30 elements with high analytical sensitivity, together with the fact that it is non-destructive, as the chemical composition can be determined without sampling and without coming into contact with the object. The recent development of commercially available and affordable instruments has led to its even wider utilization in archaeological projects.

The measurements are performed by illuminating with x-rays a small, flat, and cleaned area on the object for a short time (typically 1–5 minutes).

The x-rays are emitted by a miniaturized x-ray tube. The size of the irradiated area has a diameter of around 3 millimeters. It should be pointed out that this is a surface analysis method and, therefore, one needs to bear in mind that if the object has received any surface treatment (e.g., gilding) then the chemical composition determined is not necessarily characteristic of the whole. Furthermore, if the object is covered by a rough or thick patina, the upper layer should be carefully removed in a very small area in order to guarantee reliable results. Nevertheless, as museum curators and private collectors become more and more reluctant to allow sampling of valuable artifacts, this technique is in reality the only available option for such investigations. In sum, a portable XRF instrument offers a fast, effective, and low-cost performance and is ideal for museum pieces which cannot be sampled.

ANALYSIS OF THE DISH IN THE A. PITSILLIDES COLLECTION

The dish in the Pitsillides Collection (shown in fig. 10.5) has been conserved and, therefore, it is in rather good condition. We took a total of four measurements in the inner surface of the dish at points where the metallic surface looks to be in good condition and there is no visible corrosion. Two were taken in the central circle and two in the outer circle defined by the engraving. The results of the chemical analysis are displayed in Table 1.

The chemical composition shows that the dish is made of brass, the alloy of copper and zinc. Traces of iron (0.12) and lead (0.25) were also detected in the alloy.

DISCUSSION

As zinc is a volatile metal, it can only be produced by distillation, a technique which was introduced to Europe most probably from India after the sixteenth century.[7] In antiquity, therefore, brass, the alloy of copper and zinc, had to be produced in an indirect way: calcined zinc ore was mixed with metallic copper in a closed crucible. The zinc vapor that formed in the crucible because of the high temperature dissolved in the copper to form brass. This process is known as cementation.[8]

Table 1 Chemical composition of dish in weight percentage.

	Cu	Fe	Zn	Pb	Total
Average of 4 measurements	85.99	0.12	12.71	0.25	99.7

Analytical and archaeometallurgical studies on ancient metallic artifacts have shown that although brass was deliberately produced for the first time sometime between the eighth and the seventh century BC in Asia Minor, it is only after the first century BC that it becomes widely available.[9] Initially, its use was restricted to the production of coins, but after the first and second centuries AD it was extended to most other types of bronze work.[10] Nevertheless, bronze, the alloy of copper and tin, remained the preferred alloy. According to Craddock: "…zinc is much more abundant than tin, which only Spain and Britain produced in the Roman Empire; zinc is in nowadays approximately one-tenth of the price of tin and only half the price of copper and its relative pricing was roughly the same in Roman times … therefore, for large scale metal production such as coinage, brass had the obvious advantages of cheapness once viable ways of manufacturing it had been found."[11]

With the collapse of the Roman Empire and the loss of the tin mines of Britannia, Hispania, and Pannonia, it became difficult for the Eastern Mediterranean to obtain tin and thus brass became the preferred alloy.[12] This is reflected in the chemical composition of metallic artifacts of the Roman period when contrasted to those of later periods (sixth–seventh centuries), for example from Coptic Egypt. In the former case, 20% are made of brass, while in the latter the percentage rises to 90%.[13]

Although, as pointed out in the introduction, there is a dearth of analytical data regarding Middle Byzantine metal artifacts, the same is not true of contemporary Islamic metalwork. Analysis of a series of artifacts from the British Museum's Islamic Collection, dating from the tenth to the sixteenth centuries AD, shows that out of 90 analyzed objects, only 3 were made of tin bronze, the rest being made of brass.[14] Two categories of alloy seem to be used in this period for different classes of artifacts. A relatively pure brass, containing between 11% and 23% of zinc with little or no lead, was used for sheet or hammered metalwork, while a more mixed alloy, containing 5–17% zinc and up to 25% lead with a small percentage of tin, was used for large castings.[15] Similar conclusions were reached after the analysis of a series of metal vessels from Jordan dating roughly to the fourteenth century AD.[16] The chemical analysis of the dish in the Pitsillides Collection shows that it falls under the first category of pure brass used for hammered metalwork.

The provenance of the metals used in the manufacture of this object is another interesting question. It is well-known that Cyprus was one of the most important suppliers of copper metal for the Roman Empire.[17] This is attested by the extensive metallurgical remains that have survived in the metalliferous foothills of the Troodos Mountains. Recent fieldwork and systematic recording of the extensive slag heaps have shown that copper production was of an industrial scale throughout the Roman period, but especially so during the Late Roman period.[18] However, currently available evidence indicates that the Cypriot copper industry came to a halt after the seventh–eighth centuries AD.[19] So it is highly unlikely that this object was made of locally-produced copper. It is more likely that the copper came from the one of the neighboring mining regions, namely Anatolia, Feinan in Jordan, and Timna in Israel, all of which were active in this period.

In conclusion, the chemical analysis of the copper dish from the collection of Mr. A. Pitsillides with the help of a portable XRF showed that it was produced from a relatively pure brass, similar to that used by contemporary smiths of the Islamic World for hammered objects. The absence of analytical data of other metal objects of the Middle Byzantine period is noticeable. We hope to continue this collaborative research and address this problem. Hopefully, we will be able to report on more such analysis in the near future.

NOTES

1 Lazovic et al. 1977.

2 I would like to thank my colleague Maria Parani for suggesting the analysis of the object. I hope that this is the first of many Byzantine objects that we will study jointly. We would like to thank Mr. Andreas Pitsillides for allowing us to analyze the object and Maria Dikomitou for assisting with the analysis.

3 Karydas 2007: 419.

4 Ceramics: Papadopoulou et al. 2006; Goren et al. 2009; glass: Tantrakarn et al. 2009; pigments: Aloupi et al. 2000; Karydas et al. 2006; metals: Karydas 2007.

5 Helmig et al. 1989.

6 Hall et al. 1973; Hackens et al 1977.

7 Craddock 1995: 317–21.

8 Ibid.: 294.

9 Craddock 1978: 1.

10 Ibid.: 11.

11 Ibid.: 13.

12 Craddock et al. 1990: 73.

13 Ibid.

14 Craddock 1979: 73.

15 Craddock et al. 1990: 77.

16 Al-Saa'd 2000.

17 Kassianidou 2011: 539–48.

18 Ibid.

19 Ibid.

Chapter 11

The Program of the Panagia Pergaminiotissa: A Narrative in Perspective

by Annemarie Weyl Carr

In the design of this publication, the painted churches of Komnenian Cyprus form the "lived happily ever after" part of the story.[1] Their programs are not only compatible with trends throughout the empire, but numerous enough to have constituted a norm, and they created a bedrock for developments in the ensuing centuries. Especially in the early Komnenian decades, when evidence elsewhere is sparse, the murals of Cyprus are virtually constitutive of our conception of Komnenian artistic developments, and appreciation for their significance has grown steadily since the heady decade of the 1960s when many of the major programs were cleaned and prepared for publication. No longer viewed, as Annabel Wharton and I once did, as belonging to a periphery, they are valued as the very living essence of Byzantine art, their supple iconography and opalescent colors identifying them at once with the Byzantine center.[2] As a way of assessing the art of Cyprus, this remains exclusive, discounting whole categories of evidence like the mural icons in Saint Marina, Rizokarpaso, or the apse at the church of the Holy Cross, Pelendri (dated to 1178), whose forms are not inspired by the capital, and whose implications for the relation of Cypriot art to sources other than Byzantium during the twelfth century, especially the Syro-Palestinian main-land, remain largely unexplored.[3] Nonetheless, it acknowledges the degree to which Komnenian visual culture was defined less by a place than by a variegated and mobile mesh of people, both patrons and painters, who traveled extensively and left behind them a widely dispersed body of inter-related works.

For this volume, the most significant phase of Komnenian painting on Cyprus is the first, produced in the years on either side of 1100. It marks the emergence, after a centuries-long intermission, of sustained artistic activity rooted in metropolitan forms. The factors that conditioned its sudden incandescence, why it occurred only so long after Nikephoros II Phocas had returned the island to Byzantine hegemony in 965, and the degree to which developments in the century after 965 might have been obscured by the vagaries of survival, are open questions whose pursuit has been critically impaired by the inaccessibility of sites in the northern third of the island since 1974. Not only is this region the richest in surviving monuments from the centuries before 1100, but the most informative early Komnenian monuments are in the north. Only one of these — the Holy Trinity chapel adjoining the katholikon of the monastery of St. Chrysostom in Koutsovendis — had been fully cleaned and documented before the invasion;

167

FIG. 11.1   *Panagia Pergaminiotissa. Exterior from the northeast (Photo: author).*

the others, only scantly published, have slowly slipped out of scholarly awareness. Cyril Mango and Tassos Papacostas have succeeded in extracting an exceptionally wide range of insights from the history, fabric, and adornment of the Holy Trinity, and these now dominate our conception of the implantation of Komnenian artistic practices in Cyprus.[4] The narrative, as we understand it, is set in motion by the high military significance assigned to Cyprus in the wake of the Turkish seizure of Antioch and the First Crusade, when Alexios I Komnenos dispatched troops under the command of generals from the inner court circles to fortify the castles of the Kyrenia range. Along with the influx of personnel from the capital, titled Cypriots, too, must have been drawn into the imperial effort.[5] The ranking metropolitan officers, whom Alexios must have endowed with land, included figures like Eumathios Philokales, patron of the chapel of the Holy Trinity, who marked their sojourn on the island with building projects. As exemplified by the Holy Trinity, the characteristic object of such an endeavor was the personal

chapel, attached to or constituting the katholikon of a monastery that could then oversee the religious and memorial needs of the patron and his dependents. Philokales brought one or more accomplished painters to adorn his edifice, and they seem to have disseminated their art in their new setting, establishing a workshop and taking on commissions in other churches, both nearby, as in the katholikon of the Apsinthiotissa monastery,[6] and at considerable distance, as in the monumental icon of St. Nicholas with a donor monk at the south end of the templon in St. Nicholas tis Stegis.[7] Both the services of these painters and the paradigm of the personal church adorned with self-conscious cultivation took root, in turn, among the Cypriot aristocracy, as exemplified by the church at Asinou.

Deservedly, but perhaps too exclusively, the narrative based on the Holy Trinity chapel has dominated our understanding of Cyprus' Komnenian efflorescence. Not to challenge, but to expand it, this article turns to examine the evidence of a second early Komnenian program that survives in the northern portion of the island.

FIG. 11.2 *Panagia Pergaminiotissa. Interior, looking east (Photo: Gerald L. Carr).*

It adorns the bema of the church of the Panagia Pergaminiotissa near Akanthou (fig. 11.1).[8] A cross-in-square structure of somewhat over 12 meters in length, with a long eastern arm and high, fairly narrow dome resting on rectangular piers, the Pergaminiotissa rises on the nave of an Early Christian basilica whose three apses lie just to its east. Surrounded a century ago by other buildings of undetermined function, it now stands alone in a landscape whose vegetation masks traces of an antique acropolis and a number of tombs.[9] Its environs are among the longest-inhabited on the island, with evidence of settlements reaching deep into prehistory.[10] The area was especially densely inhabited in the Hellenistic period, with at least four settlements that lasted into the late Roman era, of which the largest — Pergamon — must be the origin of the church's name.[11] Virtually nothing is known of the site's Byzantine or medieval

history, and despite extensive if scattered signs of settlement throughout the region, there is no evidence that the church was redecorated or altered after the twelfth century. By the Venetian period, a concentration of population seems to have gathered in Akanthou, which Étienne de Lusignan in 1572 speaks of variously as an "estate," or a "town or village."[12] The region's growth during the ensuing Ottoman centuries must have played some role in prompting the construction of the rectangular narthex that now stands at the Pergaminiotissa's western end, and in 1845 Ludwig Ross described the church as "newly refurbished."[13] Doorless and prey to the elements in 2009, the building was taken in charge by USAID-SAVE, which oversaw the cleaning and consolidation of its architectural fabric and remaining frescoes.[14] Thus, it is possible to offer a provisional assessment of its paintings' place in the early Komnenian story, and to compare its testimony with that of Eumathios Philokales' Holy Trinity.

What survives of the Pergaminiotissa's once extensive mural program occupies the upper portion of the two bema walls, the contiguous register on the wall of the central apse, and the soffits of the arches opening from the bema into the pastophories (fig. 11.2). The bema's steep, narrow proportions and considerable depth must have conditioned the choice and distribution of the themes used to decorate it. The narrow hemicylinder of the apse, pierced by a thin window, must have accommodated several horizontal registers of imagery. The sole remaining register, running between the base of the now-vacant apse conch and the top of the window, shows four imperially clad archangels against a deep blue ground, turned with heads bowed and hands extended toward the orant Mother of God at the center (fig. 11.3). The angels' wingtips brush the red border at the top, but Mary's head breaks through it, her halo canted against the projecting cornice that runs under the conch as though literally inclined toward the viewer far below. Both the ripple of the angels' forms and the tilt of her head give the group a striking vitality. An intricately drawn band of red on white vermiculated ornament embroiders the narrow face of the apse opening. The bema walls, in turn, are long enough to accommodate a narra-

FIG. 11.3   *Panagia Pergaminiotissa. View into the bema (Photo: Gerald L. Carr).*

tive cycle of six scenes, three on each side, beneath the now blank surface of the vault. Below them, in the spandrels and upper portions of the wall segments flanking the arched entrances to the pastophories, were once full-length bishop saints, one on each surface. On the intrados of each arch are two monastic saints. The upper borders of the narrative scenes break off before turning the corner into the naos. The dome retains plaster prepared for paint, but no further legible traces remain to suggest how the naos might have been adorned.

To date, the element of the program that has drawn closest attention is the apse wall, for it retains two layers of fresco: the archangels overlie earlier forms. This is most visible at the southern end of the register, where minium contours define the head and shoulders of an alert, frontal youth with short, curly hair and doubly-outlined halo; his lower body vanishes in a scumble of discolored plaster. Remnants of a second head with similarly curly hair, doubly-inscribed halo, and minium underdrawing can be discerned through a gap in the plaster near the northern edge of the register.

Both figures stood against a blue ground, and their haloes, within the inner contour, were painted yellow.[15] The figure on the south, confidently drawn with solid proportions and a radiant frontality, is readily assigned to the eleventh century (fig. 11.4).[16] In the absence of medieval sources documenting the building, this earlier layer of imagery is of critical value, for it shows that the Pergaminiotissa, like Cyprus' other cross-in-square churches with quadrangular piers, belongs to the eleventh century. It is not, then, a product of the early Komnenian efflorescence. It was both built and adorned with competent paintings well before the Komnenian efflorescence began.

The clothing of the youthful figure, which falls in a "v" over his chest, is clearly not the long chlamys of the courtly martyr; rather, it suggests the military chlamys thrown back over the shoulders of a saint in armor, and the figure has accordingly been identified as a young warrior. Holy warriors did flank the apse of Byzantine churches in Cappadocia, though they were generally placed on the piers rather than on the wall itself, at the

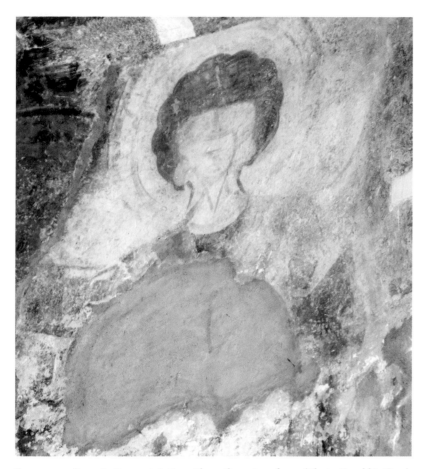

FIG. 11.4 *Panagia Pergaminiotissa. Eleventh-century figure (Photo: Gerald L. Carr).*

The curls along the band's top and the parallel verticals with rounded tips resembling feathers that extend below it suggest instead that it was a wing; an up-swept diagonal behind the figure's left shoulder might be the other. Like armed warriors, symmetrically paired archangels were recurrent guardians of the Mother of God and other saints, and they stood regularly on the walls of apses. Usually they stand near the center, flanking Mary,[18] but in SS. Peter and Paul, Novi Pazar (Serbia), they stand at the outer edge of the upper register, as would have been the case here.[19] If the initial layer indeed included archangels, it may well have prompted the decision to portray archangels in the Komnenian program that replaced it. If so, the latter's dynamism is striking: the frontal stasis of the initial layer would have been strikingly translated here into the dynamism of Komnenian sensibility.

The immediacy with which the archangels impress one as Komnenian is underscored by their remarkably close iconographic kinship with the top tier of the mid-twelfth-century apse mosaic at Cefalù in Sicily, completed in 1148.[20] There, too, a steep, narrow space with multiple registers is topped by a band of paired archangels in imperial vestiture striding toward the orant Mother of God, their hands extended in gestures of honor and acclamation. Two generations after Cefalù, frontal pairs of archangels would flank the orant Mary in the apse wall of the early thirteenth-century church in Ali Reis Street, Ortahisar, Cappadocia.[21] But such coupled ranks are otherwise exceptional. Within the Komnenian century, no apse program echoes that of Cefalù as closely as the Pergaminiotissa. Even the angels' exceptional abandonment of their labara and orbs to extend

level of despotic icons.[17] From the tenth century on, such guardians were portrayed not only in court dress but in armor, their weapons at the ready. In this guise they often guarded the Mother of God and accompanying saints. As an armed guardian of holy figures, then, the youthful saint—and presumably his counterpart on the north side of the apse—would not have been out of place. There was, however, a second type of holy youth with buoyant, bobbed hair whose clothing characteristically fell in a "v" on the chest. These were imperially clad archangels, with the loros crossed on their chest. The gesture of the figure at the Pergaminiotissa, with his left hand raised palm out before his breast, is more amenable to a saint than an archangel, who usually had his hands full with scepter and orb. Nonetheless, the band extending from the figure's right shoulder, suggestive of a spear-bearing arm, must be something else, for the line over the right shoulder shows that the forearm was down.

empty hands in a gesture of veneration is seen in both monuments.[22] The question of their relationship arises inevitably. Ernst Kitzinger's passing suggestion of a bond between Cyprus and Norman Sicily, made on the basis of kindred images in the Martorana and Trikomo,[23] has been more fully explored by Tassos Papacostas, who has demonstrated that mid-twelfth-century Sicilians did own property in Cyprus and proposed that Sicilians from the Principality of Antioch may well have owned and even resided on properties along the northern coast of the island.[24] Under these circumstances, the possibility that Pergaminiotissa could echo the apsidal program of Cefalù cannot be dismissed casually. Given Cefalù's firm date in 1148, such a relationship would have significant implications for the date of the Pergaminiotissa's program. Introduced here as belonging to the early twelfth century, it has also been attributed to its third quarter.[25] The iconography of the archangels suggests the later date; on the other hand, the delicate proportions of the figures, the feathery, flickering highlights on their garments, and the absence of the sinuous, linear fluency of the folds that is seen in Cefalù support the earlier one. The challenge posed by the divergence turns attention to the scenes in the bema. It is to these that the remainder of this chapter is devoted.

The upper walls of the bema recount the initial events of the Protevangelium's narrative of the life of the Mother of God. The cycle was not included in Jacqueline Lafontaine-Dosogne's fundamental compendium of cycles of Mary's infancy, surely because of the Pergaminiotissa's isolation, unpublished, in the wake of 1974.[26] Thus, it deserves attentive study. The theme of the Protevangelium is readily recognized through the three scenes on the south wall of the bema, of which the subjects have been identified several times. Their opening image accords exactly with its title (fig. 11.5), inscribed in white majuscules: Ἡ προσευχὴ τῆς Ἁγίας Ἄννης (the prayer of St. Anne), its final word still legible in the space over Anna's raised hands in the slide

FIG. 11.5   *Panagia Pergaminiotissa. Prayer of Anna (Photo: author).*

of 1979 at Dumbarton Oaks. Full-length in profile orant posture, Anna dominates an exceptionally stark version of the story. A single, schematic tree behind her places the event outdoors; a pink hill beside it takes the place often occupied by the door to Anna's house with her maidservant inside. Anna prays before an upright, rectangular basin of pink masonry. No trees alive with nesting birds rise behind it, though a speckle-breasted bird perches on the upright water spout with what seem to have been two more (chicks?) on the rim below. More notably, no angel bends from the arc of Heaven above to announce Anna's fertility. In the cycle at Hagia Sophia, Kiev (Ukraine), the angel is absent, too, leading Lafontaine-Dosogne to conclude that the scene represented Anna's lament, not her annunciation.[27] In only one monumental cycle, at the Miroz Monastery in Pskov, are lament and annunciation explicitly differentiated, with Anna beneath the arc followed later by a similar composition in which an angel descends toward her.

FIG. 11.6 *Panagia Pergaminiotissa. Joachim and Anna consult the Law (Photo: author).*

Otherwise, one version or the other does service for the whole episode, and it seems plausible, given the frequency with which prayer in itself was an image of prayer responded to, that the Pergaminiotissa's scene was a conflation of the two phases, with the arc of Heaven serving to indicate the success of Anna's invocation.

The sequence of the two events at Pskov poses a question, however, that draws attention onward to the ensuing scene at the center of the Pergaminiotissa's south bema wall. The two episodes of Anna's prayer in the Miroz Monastery are separated by an intervening composition of Anna and her husband Joachim seated at either side of a lectern with an open book. In our cycle, too, Anna's prayer is followed by a composition in which a frontally seated Joachim gestures to a book set open and upright on his lap; Anna stands attentively at his left (fig. 11.6).[28] This presumably represents the consultation with the twelve tribes to see if Joachim was indeed the only one of the righteous without issue. If so, however, it should take its place before the two spouses' prayers, as it

does on the San Marco columns of ambiguous Early Christian or thirteenth-century date,[29] and again in the late twelfth century in the San Marco mosaics.[30] In both, the twelve tribes are summed up as a book open in Joachim's lap, and the mosaic is duly labeled "scripta legit." The cycle at Pskov shows Anna and Joachim sitting at home in the interval between their return from the Temple and their respective retreats into prayer, but no book appears in this scene; their engagement with the book has migrated to a new and different point, between Anna's lament and the annunciation first to her, and then to Joachim, as if the consultation had constituted a turning point. At the Pergaminiotissa, too, it follows Anna's prayer; it is placed yet later in the story in the icon of about 1300 in the church of Joachim and Anna in Kalliana, Cyprus, where it is labeled "Ιοακημ και Ανα διδασκουν τὸ νὸμ[ον] (Joachim and Anna read the law)."[31] In inventorying the scenes at Pskov, Vladimir Sarabianov lists the scene with the book as "Joachim and Anna read the Prophet Isaiah." I know of no Greek text that speaks of their consulting Isaiah, but his great

FIG. 11.7   *Panagia Pergaminiotissa. Meeting of Joachim and Anna (Photo: Gerald L. Carr).*

messianic prophecies of the fertility of the Davidic lineage accord well with the role assigned to the twelve tribes in the Kokkinobaphos manuscripts, summoned not to certify Joachim's shame, but to witness Anna's successful delivery.[32] Thus the relocation of the event in Pskov, the Pergaminiotissa, and later Kalliana suggests that the consultation with the "twelve tribes" had taken on a distinctive life as a confirmation of the place of Joachim's and Anna's fertility in the "Law and the Prophets," instead, and that it had become a sign more of promise than of condemnation.

At Pskov the consultation of the Law was followed by the angel's joyous annunciation to Anna; at the Pergaminiotissa it is followed by the yet more affirmative meeting of Joachim and Anna (figs. 11.3, 11.7). Laconic and without clutter, the scene is legible despite its extensive abrasion. The long-married lovers stride toward one another, their arms entwined and their faces joined in what was clearly a tenderly realized kiss. The setting is minimal: there is no architecture, just a hill with

FIG. 11.8   *Panagia Pergaminiotissa. Prayer of Joachim (Photo: author).*

Fig. 11.9 *Panagia Pergaminiotissa. Rejection of the offerings (Photo: author).*

a tree on either side. With their pom-pom foliage, the trees register their joy.

The three scenes on the south bema wall form an effectively balanced whole, bracketed by the figure of Anna, standing on the left and approaching the meeting from the right, and centered on the white rectangle of the open book. Its sheer centrality begs its interpretation as the assertion of Isaiah 11:1. The scenes on the north wall are more severely damaged, but emerge into clarity as they are read in conjunction with the three on the facing wall. Balancing the prayer of Anna at the apse end of the north wall is the corresponding episode of the prayer of Joachim (fig. 11.8). The curve of the foliage constituting his tent is still legible on the right side of the scene; Joachim himself sits within it, his legs bent, his torso turned to the front, and his ample pallium falling in folds from his lap toward the right. His left elbow rests on his left knee and he cradles his head in his hand. His face is turned

to his right; as in Bertubani, Georgia (1212–13), Joachim twists to look over his shoulder, as if his attention had been captured by something behind him.[33] Just what that was is not clear, but a white inscription, of which a few letters remain legible over his left shoulder,[34] once ran along much of the width of the panel under the frame, leaving room, at best, for an arc of Heaven in the upper left corner. Like Anna, then, Joachim looked from the apse toward an arc of Heaven in his prayer.

The event to which his backward gaze directs us, at the center of the north wall, is almost totally obliterated. A ghost of a pink triangle at the right, a bit of a yellow halo, and two residues of drapery, a pink one beneath the halo and a gray one to its left, suggest that this may have been Joachim's and Anna's return of from the Temple through a landscape signaled by a pink hill akin to the pink hills in the scenes on the bema's south wall. The bits of drapery slant slightly, suggesting movement toward the right. Elsewhere in the cycle Joachim wears gray and Anna pink; this would place Anna in the lead, as is often the case, including the cycle at Pskov. It is hard to give this scene the interpretive centrality on the north wall that the consultation of the Law has on the south; as the moment of deepest dejection, however, it may have formed an effective counterbalance to the ascendant hope of the consultation. In the scene of the return at Ateni, Georgia (ca. 1090), Joachim reproaches his wife for their sterility;[35] if such blamefulness infected the scene at the Pergaminiotissa, it would have found an emphatic rejoinder in the pregnancy foretold in the Law and Prophets.

The final scene on the north wall, like the meeting on the south, shows a striding figure entering the scene from the side of the bema opening (fig. 11.9). On the south it was Anna; on the north, to judge by its sandaled feet, it was a male in a pale garment, with a figure in pink behind him. Their upper bodies, and much of the scene they enter, are gone, but residues of a large halo can still be discerned at the upper right, above a remarkably complicated concentration of ornamental architecture — a domed turret, a taller wall with a bull's eye window over an arched opening with a little balustrade, a sequence of masonry steps, and a further ornamented façade. A fragment of drapery below the halo that is cut off by the steps indicates that the haloed figure stood inside the architecture. This must be the High Priest, approached by the gray-clad Joachim and, behind him, Anna. The scene would then be the rejection of their offerings in the Temple. This is most often composed with the Temple at the left, probably because the bulk of its architecture provided a book-end for the ensuing sequence of scenes; placing it in parallel with the meeting of Joachim and Anna must have recommended its alignment from left to right. Passages in the drapery — the streaky modeling of Joachim's himation, the overlay of a layer of blue above it, the adaptation of a hem to the contour of the turret — are oddly incoherent; both Ludwig Ross and George Jeffery had written of recent intrusive repairs to the painting,[36] and though the bulk of this intervention must have occurred outside the bema, one wonders if these passages might be evidence of it. The architectural forms themselves, though, astonishing as they are after the laconic clarity of the scenes on the south bema wall, can all be paralleled in manuscripts of the decades around 1100, and so must be rooted, at least, in the original composition.

The Pergaminiotissa offers a cogent condensation of the opening of the Protevangelium, arranged in two triplets of events. One triplet is bracketed by Joachim, the other by Anna. The entrance to the bema is flanked with scenes of approach, as the apse is with scenes of prayerful entreaty. The episodes themselves are staple constituents of the Middle Byzantine cycle of Mary's infancy, a body of imagery that became especially widespread and frequent in monumental cycles of the Komnenian period. After four examples from the eleventh century,[37] Lafontaine-Dosogne lists no fewer than eleven monumental cycles in the twelfth, of which seven include at least one scene from the story before Mary's birth.[38] Impressive throughout is how little the monumental cycles have to do with the scenes in the Kokkinobaphos manuscripts.[39] On the other hand, for all their vast geographic dissemination, the murals display a remarkable consistency that makes it difficult to chart a meaningful pattern of chronological development. The scenes at the Pergaminiotissa illustrate this well. Anna's prayer, with its

simple, rectangular fountain adheres to early examples — in the eleventh-century Georgian Shemokmedi icon and, above all, Hagia Sophia in Kiev, where there are once again birds in the fountain,[40] the Panagia church in Trikomo, Cyprus, and the Transfiguration church in the Miroz Monastery, Russia, in the first half of the twelfth.[41] By contrast, the posture of Joachim in the scene of his prayer is best paralleled quite late, at the cave church at Bertubani, Georgia, of 1212–13. Thus, iconographic motifs alone are unlikely to date the cycle within the twelfth century. What stands out in the iconography of the Pergaminiotissa's cycle above all are two factors. One is its selective emphasis on the scenes leading up not to the birth or betrothal, but to the conception of the Mother of God. This is a cycle whose focus lies less with Mary herself than with her parents and their miraculous fertility.[42] The other factor is its kinship to the long cycle at Pskov, above all in its inclusion of the return from the Temple and the consultation of the Law. Lafontaine-Dosogne specifically singles out both of these as scenes alien to the Constantinopolitan tradition.[43] In the Pergaminiotissa, they occupy a central position, literally, at the center of each wall, and Pskov alone of the surviving cycles incorporates both. Thus the Pergaminiotissa seems to have drawn on a model akin to that at Pskov.

Characteristically dated to 1156 and understood as a provincial cycle of the mid-twelfth century, Pskov has been re-evaluated by Olga Etinhof, who has dated its murals to the early 1140s and associated it with the Hellenophile activity of its patron, Archbishop Niphon.[44] She identifies its imagery with a narrative bias, didactic and catechetic in tone, that characterizes programs preceding the theological council of 1156 in Constantinople, and contrasts it with the dogmatic, liturgical emphasis of those that follow. She aligns Pskov especially with the cycle at Trikomo in Cyprus. Even more akin than Trikomo is the cycle of the Pergaminiotissa. Under these circumstances, the imagery of the Virgin's early life seen at the Pergaminiotissa and Pskov would seem to take on a new significance, not as an eccentric (in Lafontaine-Dosogne's word, "oriental") tradition parallel to that of Constantinople, but as representative of Byzantium itself in the first third of the twelfth century. That its imagery continued to circulate into the thirteenth century is indicated by the inclusion of the scene of the consultation of the Law in San Marco (Venice) and the icon at Kalliana. At what point in its extended circulation it was actually adopted at the Pergaminiotissa can only be addressed by style.

To assess the style of murals as abraded as these is challenging. The stark settings, with pink hills and isolated, formulaic trees evoke the schematic hills that enclose and compartmentalize compositional elements in scenes from the middle and third quarter of the twelfth century, like the Nativities in the Cappella Palatina (Sicily) or Perachorio (Cyprus), even hinting in their rosy color at the raspberry-sherbet landscapes of the early Decorative Style codices. Like the archangels in the apse, then, the forms invite alignment with Norman Sicily. Closer inspection, however, shows that these forms had considerable histories of use behind them when they were adopted in mid-twelfth-century Palermo. Thus, the schematic trefoil or pom-pom trees, as Ernst Kitzinger has pointed out, repeat forms already well-established in Byzantine painting, most copiously in manuscript illuminations of the later eleventh and early twelfth centuries.[45] This is equally true of the bird in the prayer of Anna. With its clean contour and smart speckles, it suggests the birds that glitter from the illuminated initials of Mount Sinai codex 339 of 1136 or the mid-century manuscripts of the Kokkinobaphos Master.[46] But such showy, sharply silhouetted birds had festooned the tops of headpieces and canon tables already for decades before being captured for the initials.[47] The hills, in turn, are more impressive for their difference than their similarity, for they do not enclose, but stand aside from the figures, which rise against the blue ground. Rather than being used compositionally to give individual elements a place within a setting, they are used semiotically to signal location. In this, they are more akin to the frothy hummocks that rise between figure groups to punctuate the episodes in the frieze gospels or to locate martyrdoms in eleventh-century menologia.[48] Most indicative of all the elements of setting may be the architecture in the scene of the offerings rejected. With its copious details, it invites comparison with the rich architecture of the Kokkinobaphos manuscripts. But in fact, its oddly aligned collection of incommensurate components, some curiously small, like the domed turret, others curiously large, like the masonry of the steps, is best paralleled in manuscript illuminations from the later eleventh century: the scene of the Presentation of the Virgin in Mount Athos, Panteleimonos 2; the Evangelist portraits in the Florence frieze Gospels; Mount Sinai, codex 205; or the Jaharis Lectionary in The Metropolitan Museum, New York.[49] In each instance, the features of the scenes' settings point to a vocabulary of forms established in the first decades of the Komnenian dynasty, though preserved in manuscripts rather than murals.

The figures themselves retain only episodically the modulations and highlights that defined their formal character, but three elements from the south wall seem still to convey cardinal qualities of the work. One, felt in the detail of the converging faces of Joachim and Anna in the scene of their meeting, is the sensitivity with which contours are drawn to convey character and emotion (fig. 11.7). The event of Anna's and Joachim's reunion is recounted here with utter economy — two figures, two trees, two hills — yet it conveys an impression of intimacy and significance, achieved through the expressive clarity of the two heads, now mere silhouettes, his face raised and expectant, hers bending in welcome.

Clarity of contour is seen again in the episode at the center of the wall, in which Joachim examines the book of the Law. While Anna's figure is muffled in drapery folds that have become hard to interpret in their damaged condition, Joachim's is impressively eloquent (fig. 11.10). Seated frontally, he bends from the hips in a posture of earnest engagement, counterbalancing his movement with the angle of his right leg as he pulls his ankle inward to bear the weight. Neatly turned, the foot brings the pose to an elegant point. Supple and elastic, the pose has a streamlined fluency that seems at first late Komnenian. But in late Komnenian art such fluency characteristically flattens profile postures into silhouettes; by contrast, Joachim's contour conveys the thrust and weight of a posture in depth. Its solidity is summed up in the rounded fullness of the knees. Fine lines of highlighted folds still

FIG. 11.10 *Panagia Pergaminiotissa. Joachim and Anna consult the Law: Joachim (Photo: author).*

FIG. 11.11 *Saint Catherine's Monastery, Mount Sinai, cod. 179, fol. 84v (By permission of Saint Catherine's Monastery, Sinai, Egypt).*

ripple along the rounded edge of his left knee, and a slender cascade of drapery falls past the book. But neither coalesces into the serpentine continuity of late Komnenian linearism. Instead, the hems fall in little frills and the highlights break and feather, producing much the same shimmering play that had made the archangels' forms so light next to their mid-twelfth-century counterparts in Sicily. The nearest parallel for Joachim's pose is not in mid-twelfth-century art, but near 1100, in the figure of Mark in Mount Sinai, codex 179 (fig. 11.11).[50] The elastic mobility of the pose rooted in the hips, the amplitude of the lap, the elegance of the turned foot, and the fineness of the linear highlights along the folds can all be seen there. Sinai 179 is among the manuscripts cited earlier as containing plump, lively birds akin to the one that perches on the fountain head in Anna's prayer. Together, posture and perching bird suggest that

the Pergaminiotissa's painter was familiar with much the same repertoire of late eleventh-century forms that appear in the Sinai miniatures. It may be relevant in this regard that Kurt Weitzmann and George Galavaris tentatively associated the codex with Cyprus rather than Constantinople.[51]

The elastic, elegantly pondered figure of Sinai 179's St. Mark belongs to a particularly refined phase of manuscript painting. Though coincident with the Hellenic humanism that Doula Mouriki singled out also in the roughly contemporary mosaics of Daphni and some of the murals at Veljusa (FYROM) and Ateni (Georgia),[52] it is radically much more delicate in execution and has not been paralleled in wall painting. A pairing like that of the St. Mark with the seated Joachim at the Pergaminiotissa is unprecedented. Certainly the Joachim differs drastically from the comparable examples of seated figures in mural painting of

FIG. 11.12 *Panagia Phorbiotissa, Asinou. Annunciation: Gabriel (Photo: author).*

the period. These are, precisely, in Cyprus itself, in the two Pentecost compositions of Eumathios Philokales' Holy Trinity chapel and Asinou.[53] The contrast is emphatic enough to challenge the very possibility that they could have been painted in the same period. Indeed, the differences between the painters of Koutsovendis and Asinou on the one hand and the Pergaminiotissa on the other are important and will be taken up later. However, a significant piece of evidence suggests that the painter of Asinou was captivated by much the same kind of extremely refined but nonetheless vital and ponderated figure seen in the St. Mark of Sinai 179 and the Pergaminiotissa. This is the figure of the Annunciate Gabriel, discovered in the 1950s beneath thirteenth-century masonry reinforcements in the apse at Asinou (fig. 11.12). A tour de force of complexity from a painter best known for his capacity to clarify and distill, the Gabriel is

an astonishment. It shimmers with doubled and trebled lines of light around abstract balls of mass, and its edges dance with broken folds and ripples of hem jouncing like jingled bells. One wonders what got into the Asinou Master. What got into him seems to have been figures like the Evangelists of Sinai, codex 179, with their immensely refined glitter of fine highlights, delicately shimmering hems, and deftly skillful distribution of the body's volumes in motion. One can see in the Gabriel, the St. Mark, and the Joachim a similar counterpoint of small, delicately executed cadenzas of drapery forms on the one hand, and large, more or less deftly balanced volumes conveying motion on the other. In turn, if one looks ahead to the figures at Perachorio, dated to the third quarter of the twelfth century, one can see how much more fully drapery folds and body parts have been integrated and abstracted.[54] Different as they are from each other, the painters of Asinou and the Pergaminiotissa seem both to have drawn inspiration from the refined, Hellenizing elegance of manuscript painting of the years around 1100.

The figure of the praying Anna points to much the same conclusion (fig. 11.5). Hers is the best-preserved of the figures, and the only one that still retains its face. It is hard to dissociate her slender form in its gracefully draped pink maphorion from the similarly clad figures of Anna in Daphni, and, indeed, the deft, swiftly-brushed slashes of magenta that sketch in the delicate folds of the garment could not be more different from the closed, continuous contours with which the painter of Perachorio traced the long, firm lines of Mary's maphorion. They reflect a fundamentally different approach to form. The most riveting aspect of Anna, however, is her face (fig. 11.13). Here again, we encounter a finely modulated contour that shapes the focused brow, tender cheeks, sweetly pointed chin, and firm jaw. Along with the apples on the cheeks, touches of pink follow the contour, too, lending it warmth and vitality. The cast of the lips, in turn, is expressive. It is hard to speak reliably about the volume of the head, but a comparison with the similarly uplifted head of the Mother of God in the Ascension at Hagia Sophia, Ohrid (1039–56) on the one hand (fig. 11.14), and the head of an angel at Perachorio on the other

FIG. 11.13 *Panagia Pergaminiotissa. Prayer of Anna: Anna (Photo: author).*

FIG. 11.14 *Hagia Sophia, Ohrid. Ascension: Mother of God (Photo: author).*

(fig. 11.15) shows how far still the face of Anna is from the ovoid purity of late Komnenian visages, how much it retains the firm features and rounded solidity of the eleventh-century head. It is hard to place Anna anywhere except in the years around 1100.

As a program from the years around 1100, the cycle at the Pergaminiotissa is striking for its sheer difference from the paintings of the monasteries of St. Chrysostom at Koutsovendis, of the Apsinthiotissa near Sychari, and of the Panagia Phorbiotissa at Asinou. Its painter cannot have been one of the cluster of artists who shared their work in the churches of the Chrysostom monastery, and who seem in turn to have inspired the exceptionally successful Asinou Master. He must have come independently of them, responding as they had to a heightened demand for skilled work on Cyprus, and bringing with him his exceptional capacity to integrate manuscript and mural painting. The very features that allied his work with miniature painting—the sophisticated interplay of depth and contour in his figures, and the deli-

FIG. 11.15 *Holy Apostles, Perachorio. Dome: angel (Photo: Gerald L. Carr).*

cacy of his drapery patterns — must have made it hard to transmit to others, and his style is not readily traced in the surviving mural paintings of the ensuing years. The murals at Trikomo, which adopt many of the same subjects, show this clearly. The Trikomo painter may well have studied the murals at the Pergaminiotissa, for the bird head on his fountain in the prayer of Anna must echo the bird in the Pergaminiotissa. But he reconceptualized the images entirely, filling his backgrounds with garrulous buildings, populating his scenes with angels, servants, and on-lookers, and simplifying his forms. The contrast serves to underscore the independence of the Pergaminiotissa's painter. He belonged to a distinctive initiative, which constitutes a strand of its own within the story of early Komnenian art on Cyprus. Thus he invites us to return to that narrative, to see what his cycle tells us about the way Komnenian initiatives were implanted in Cypriot art.

Certainly his sophistication constitutes one aspect of his importance; linked through his knowledge of manuscript art to the cloistered and courtly world of fine books and demonstrative literacy, he must have been conversant with particularly cultivated centers of artistic production. Thus, he not only joins but amplifies the picture of the excellence available in the years around 1100 in Cyprus. His most valuable addition to our grasp of the period, however, lies at a more basic level. What we know of his work at the Pergaminiotissa is concentrated in his program of scenes from the Protevangelium. This stands out for two features. One is its placement. Scenes of the Protevangelium, as noted, were pervasive in late eleventh- and twelfth-century mural painting, and often they took their place in the eastern end of the church — in the diaconicon, as at Hagia Sophia, Kiev (Ukraine), and the Odalar Camii in Constantinople, or in the prothesis, as in Arkaz, Staraja Ladoga, and Nereditsa (Russia). Their placement in the bema itself, however, stands out. With two exceptions, no counterpart exists until the Palaiologan period, when scenes from the Protevangelium adorn the sanctuary at Gracanića of 1321.[55] The two exceptions are exactly contemporary with the Pergaminiotissa and are on Cyprus itself: the bema at Asinou flanks the apse with scenes of the birth and presentation of Mary, and the apse wall at the Joachim and Anna church in Kalliana seems to have imitated it.[56] In content as in style, the two programs are fundamentally different. That at Asinou extracts from the Marian cycle those events celebrated in the Church as major feasts and builds with them a message whose strongly liturgical character responds in tone if not themes to the "exegesis of the liturgy as concretized in the apse images" that Gordana Babić singled out as distinctively Komnenian.[57] At the Pergaminiotissa, by contrast, not even the apse wall itself seems likely to have adopted the liturgical formulations customary in Komnenian art, and the imagery of the bema walls is narrative, corresponding more closely to the didactic tone that Olga Etinhof had defined as characteristic of monumental programs before the theological controversies of 1156.[58] One is unlikely to have influenced the other. Both, however, devote the imagery of the bema to the apocryphal life of the Mother of God in a way that is not paralleled outside Cyprus. More prominent programs on Cyprus may have done the same, prompting the decision centuries later, by a painter with a retrospective interest in the island's early Komnenian iconography, to fill the apse wall at the Panagia Podithou with a sequence of Protevangelium scenes very like that at the Pergaminiotissa.[59] To this extent, the influx of cosmopolitan painters did more than implant metropolitan conventions; it formulated modes of using them that were distinctive to the island.

The decision to adorn the bema with narrative imagery at the Pergaminiotissa must have been prompted by the depth of the eastern arm, a characteristic feature of Cypriot cross-in-square churches, but one whose implications for figural cycles remains visible only here. The choice of scenes from the advent of Mary rather than of her son may reflect a yet more specifically local devotion: Svetlana Tomeković has argued persuasively and elegantly that the program at Trikomo was devoted to the conception of the Virgin, celebrated as a feast on December 9;[60] the katholikon at Koutsovendis was dedicated on December 9;[61] and the cycle at the Pergaminiotissa, too, whether or not it included scenes beyond those that survive, gave pride of place to the same theme. Whether as a feast of Mary or of Anna, Mary's conception may have had local prominence. [62]

The decision to dwell upon Mary's early life rather than Christ's may illuminate a further and perhaps more pressing question. Aside from the Pergaminiotissa, the cycle of Mary's early life survives in four churches in Cyprus: in Trikomo, in the icon at Kalliana, at the church of the Holy Cross in Pelendri, and in the Panagia Podithou, Galata. Of these, three are village churches; only the fourth was monastic. The original function of the Pergaminiotissa is not known. George Jeffery calls it a monastery church, but no written or archaeological evidence supports this identification, and Papacostas challenges it, suggesting instead that the building must have served a pilgrimage function.[63] It was not, then, the kind of personally sponsored monastic church that the Holy Trinity and Asinou were. It served a different function. As such, its adornment must have been the product of a differently motivated act of patronage. The likely patronage for a program like that installed in it during the years around 1100 remains to be clarified, but it could not have served the essentially self-centered function of an individually sponsored family foundation. Rather, it evokes Tassos Papacostas' reflection that "the numerous clearly non-monastic churches (re)built in this period all over the island ... on venerated pilgrimage sites, associated with episcopal sees and the cult of the latter's early occupants, suggest considerable involvement of the higher clergy."[64] This implies a type of patronage not embraced by the established narrative of early Komnenian Cyprus that was recited at the beginning of this chapter.

The Pergaminiotissa invites us to expand that narrative. It is not, in the first place, an establishment built or even frescoed for the first time in the years around 1100; the church itself may be contemporary with its earlier frescoes, which plausibly predate the late eleventh or early twelfth-century date suggested for it hitherto; the frescoes and architecture alike must belong to the silent interval between Nikephoros II Phokas on the one hand and Alexios I Komnenos on the other. Later, as artistic production burgeoned, the Pergaminioitssa was adorned again: like the monastic foundations that figure in the established narrative, it was frescoed in the years around 1100 by a refined painter of considerable personal originality, who was conversant with very current iconographic and stylistic developments. His imagery, however, was chosen to accommodate both a building resistant to customary Komnenian programs, and a clientele moved by the great stories of divine clemency and sacred birth. The patronage for such imagery, finally, not clearly serviceable to the liturgical purposes of family worship and commemoration, may point instead to the higher clergy. The Pergaminiotissa thus challenges us to a broadened picture of the early Komnenian efflorescence. As such, it shows the importance, in constructing the history of Byzantine Cyprus, of stitching across the rent of 1974.

NOTES

1 This chapter builds upon the paper delivered in the conference of "Cyprus in the Balance of Empires" at the Cyprus American Archaeological Research Institute (CAARI) in Nicosia on 8 January 2011. I thank Dr. Thomas Davis, Director of CAARI, and Dr. Charles A. Stewart for the opportunity to participate in it. I owe my very sincere and special gratitude to Elizabeth Kassinis and her colleagues at USAID/SAVE for the privilege of visiting and photographing the church of the Panagia Pergaminiotissa. I thank the Library at Dumbarton Oaks, as much of the research for this article was pursued there.

2 Wharton 1988: 53–90; Carr 1987.

3 For Rizokarpaso, see Papageorghiou 2010: 342; for Pelendri, see Stylianou and Stylianou 1997: 507–10.

4 Papacostas et al. 2007: 25–156; Mango et al. 1990: 63–94.

5 Thus Grivaud (2013) notes that the Magistros Nikephoros Ischyrios, patron of the church at Asinou and most probably a Cypriot aristocrat, may

have had a role in the military signaling system on Cyprus.

6   Papageorghiou 2010: 395–405.

7   On the fresco icon of St. Nicholas, see Panagiotide 2001: 412; Stylianou and Stylianou 1997: 64, fig. 25.

8   Papageorghiou 2010: 34–42, with earlier bibliography; Chotzakoglou 2005: 1: 590–95, 2: 180–89, figs. 330–37.

9   Goodwin 1978: 653.

10 Hadjisavvas 1991: 12.

11 Thus, Hogarth writes that "The site of the Pergaminiotissa is known as Pergamon, or Ypsilo, because there is a small hill that retains traces of what must have been an acropolis" (1889: 96).

12 Stefano Lusignano (1573), ed. Perdikēs 2004: 1: 52, "Hora è fatto vn casale chiamata Accathu;" 2: 73, "maintenant on le nomme le bourg ou village d'Acanthou."

13 Ross 1852: 134.

14 Sevketoglu et al. 2009.

15 An inspection of the youth at the south side suggests that the halos were first drawn to reach the very top of the wall, and then were redrawn to meet the lower edge of a broad red border that must have been added beneath the conch.

16 More energetic than the warrior saints of Nea Moni from 1042–56 (Mouriki 1985: 2: pls. 58–65), but less nuanced that the St. Demetrios from the church of St. Michael, Kiev, of 1111–12 (Lazarev 1966: pl. 3, 65), he is perhaps most nearly comparable to the frontal saints at Hagia Sophia, Ohrid, of 1039–56 (Bihalji-Merin 1969: fig. 178) or the triconch church of St. Theodore in Tağar, Cappadocia from ca. 1080 (Restle 1967: 3: pl. 355–73), but if it were not so damaged, the frontal saint in the Great Pigeon House, Çavuşin, of 963–69, might be quite as comparable (Restle 1967: 3: pl. 318).

17 Cappadocia is especially rich in examples, especially of warrior saints in armor: see the ninth–century Derin Dere Kilisesi in Jolivet-Lévy 1991: 190, pl. 117; the Great Pigeon House of 963–69 in Çavuşin: Jolivet-Lévy 1991: 21–22, pl. 21; Sümbüllü Kilise of the early eleventh century: Jolivet-Lévy 1991: 306, pl. 167, fig. 2, pl. 168, figs. 1–2; the eleventh-century church of the Hermitage near Çavuşin: Jolivet-Lévy 1991: 13, pl. 20; and the church of St. Theodore at Tağar: Jolivet-Lévy 1991: 213, pl. 130, fig. 3. But see also the imposing warriors flanking the apse of the church of St. Michael, Kiev, of 1111–12: Lazarev 1966: pl. 3, 65.

18 From the tenth century onward, archangels were most often elevated to the apse conch, but examples in Cappadocia include Güllü Dere 3 of the late ninth to early tenth century: Jolivet-Lévy 1991: 34, pl. 29, fig. 2; the Stylite Niketas church near Çavuşin of the early tenth century: Jolivet-Lévy 1991: 9–12, pls. 42, 43, fig. 1; Göreme 13 of the tenth century: Jolivet-Lévy 1991: 117–18; and Sümbüllü Kilise of the early eleventh century: Jolivet-Lévy 1991: 306, pl. 167, fig. 2, pl. 168, figs. 1–2.

19 Babić 1980: 125.

20 Demus 1949: fig. 1. The Pergaminiotissa's apse is called Komnenian here on the basis of its figures' interactive design. Iconographically, it is unlikely to have adhered to the liturgically determined program with the Apostle Communion and officiating bishops that was characteristic of Komnenian churches inspired by the capital. Both the narrowness of the apse itself and the intervention of the window would have precluded an Apostle Communion and favored standing saints. As Babić points out, Latin churches like those of the Normans in Palermo avoided the Byzantine liturgical apse iconography after 1054 in favor of programs still rooted in Ascension imagery (1980: 126–28). But in Cappadocia, Russia, Serbia, and Georgia, too, the more conservative programs of single figures organized beneath an image of theophany continued to be used throughout the twelfth century, especially where the apse wall was tall and narrow. Thus, the Pergaminiotissa and Cefalù share in a broad tradition which was still very much in use. Accordingly, the band of venerating angels may not have been as unusual as it now seems.

21 Jolivet-Lévy 1991: 198–99, pls. 123–24.

22 Though rare, archangels in imperial robes without their orbs were not unique to Sicily and Cyprus. Thus, the adoring angels at the Sion Church in Ateni, Georgia (ca. 1090), are empty-handed like those of the Pergaminiotissa: see Eastmond 1998: pl. VI; for the date, see ibid.: 47–49. The same is true also of the imperially clad archangels in the north apse of the triconch at Tağar in Cappadocia: Jolivet-Lévy 1991: pl. 130, fig. 1.

23 Kitzinger 1990: 236–37. Kitzinger was struck by the close iconographic and formal kinship of the

figures of the Annunciate Virgin in the Martorana and Trikomo (1990: figs. 99, 189). Very nearly the same features, however, are found also in the church of the Birth of the Mother of God in the Antoneva Monastery, Novgorod, painted in 1125: see Sarabianov 2004: 667–68, where he compares all three. Like the kinship between the Pergaminiotissa and Pskov, this widens the circle of works shaped by the early Komnenian capital, setting Cyprus' apparent kinship with Sicily into a broader context.

24 Papacostas 1999b: 482–84.

25 Panagiotide 2001: 416.

26 Lafontaine-Dosogne 1992.

27 Lafontaine-Dosogne 1974: 171 note 50.

28 The book is vigorously but illegibly inscribed with characters that look more like pseudo-Hebrew than Greek. Byzantine painters did differentiate alien scripts in their paintings: see the Evangelist portraits in Mount Athos, Panteleimonos 2, in Pelekanides et al. 1975, where St. Matthew (fig. 274) copies from a codex written in Greek, St. Luke copies from a scroll written in Greek (fig. 275), but Mark (fig. 276) copies from a codex that is inscribed not with Greek letters but with lemmata, clearly intended to indicate an alien tongue. In the Pergaminiotissa, however, the squiggles may indicate that though the painter recognized the importance of what was written in Joachim's book, he had no way to know what it was.

29 Lafontaine-Dosogne 1992: 1: 67 and fig. 4.

30 *The Patriarchal Basilica in Venice* 1990–1991: 2: 97, fig. 2.

31 Ιερά Μητρόπολις Μόρφου 2000: 246–47, no. 3, entry by Kostas Gerasimos and Kyprianos Papaioakeim.

32 See Isaiah 7:14 ("…behold, a Virgin shall conceive, and bear a son, and shall call his name Immanuel") and especially Isaiah 11:1 ("And there shall come forth a rod out of the stem of Jesse, and a Branch shall grow out of his roots"). In both the Kokkinobaphos manuscripts and the Peribleptos at Mistra, the twelve tribes are understood as people, not a book. In the former, the consultation is included in neither the text nor the miniatures; instead, the tribes gather at the Virgin's Nativity; see Hutter and Canart 1991: 28. In Mistra, Joachim meets a group of men: see Lafontaine-Dosogne 1992: 67; Millet 1910: pl. 126, 1.

33 Eastmond 1998: 169–81, color pl. XIX; Lafontaine-Dosogne 1992: fig. 39. The same posture would be adopted centuries later in the church of the Panagia

Podithou, Galata; see Frigerio-Zeniou 1998: fig. 69.

34 The inscription ran in one line along much of the top of the panel, and then at Joachim's right continued into a second. In the upper line, "το Δ" are clear; the delta may be followed by "ΗΚ" (δίκαιος?). In the second line is an "Η." The letters evoke the inscription of Joachim's prayer in the fourteenth-century cycle at the Holy Cross church, Pelendri, Cyprus: "Ὁ Ἰωακὴμ ὁ δίκεος ἐν τὸ δάσι τις Ἠλις," transcribed in Christoforaki 1996: 224. But the "το Δ" of the top line is quite certainly not followed by an alpha, as in δάσι.

35 Lafontaine-Dosogne 1992: 66.

36 Ross saw the church in 1845 and described it as "neu wiederhergestellt" (1852: 134). Jeffery reported that "it has mural paintings of a good style but they have been much destroyed during a recent restoration" (1918: 247).

37 Lafontaine-Dosogne 1992: 1: 38–39. These include cycles in the the diaconicon in Hagia Sophia, Kiev, the narthex at Daphni, the south apsidal arm of the Sion Church at Ateni in Georgia, and the frame of the Georgian Shemokmedi icon.

38 Ibid.: 40–42. The seven are the mosaic cycle in the south arm at San Marco in Venice; that in the naos of the Panagia church, Trikomo, Cyprus; the extensive cycle in the southwest chamber of the Transfiguration church in the Miroz Monastery, Pskov; the surviving scene of the Offerings Rejected at Staraya Ladoga, and the same at the cathedral of Vladimir, Russia; the extensive cycle at the Savior church, Nereditsa, Russia; and the scene of the Offerings Refused at the church in Ahtala, Georgia.

39 There must have been illuminated manuscripts of the Protevangelium, as argued by Westphalen, but Mouriki is surely right that mural painters generally relied on model books; Westphalen 1998: 126; Mouriki 1970: 148. The painter of the scenes at the Pergaminiotissa may complicate the question, however, as he seems to have been conversant with manuscript painting.

40 For Kiev, see Lazarev 1966a: 50, fig. 32. For the Shemokmedi icon, see Lafontaine-Dosogne 1992: 1: fig. 41; Amiranašvili 1971: 118, pls. 73, 74.

41 Sarabianov 2002: 69 and Table X.

42 The bema vault is ample enough to have accommodated further scenes in the Marian narrative. In a similar fashion, Westphalen suggests that the story

of Mary's parents might have occupied the diaconi-con vault at the Odalar Camii in Istanbul, where the scenes from Mary's presentation in the Temple to Joseph's flowering rod are shown on the walls (1998: 130). Even if this proved to be the case, the direction of the narrative with the early part of the story on the more readily visible walls and the choice to stop at the meeting of Joachim and Anna both indicate an interest in emphasizing the Virgin's conception.

43 Lafontaine-Dosogne 1974: 166–67; 1992: 67.

44 Etinhof 2003: 206–7.

45 Kitzinger 1990: 216–17. For examples, see Lowden 2009: 55, fig. 58 (New York, Morgan Library, Ms. M. 639, fol. 49r, St. Matthew); Pelekanides et al. 1975: figs. 106, 107 (Mount Athos, Iveron 463, fol. 100r, 101r), fig. 285 (Pantelemon 2, fol. 210v); Velmans 1971: pl. 8, figs. 16–17 (Florence, Biblioteca Laurenziana, Plut. 6.23, fol. 8r, 8v).

46 Weitzmann and Galavaris 1990: pl. CLVI, figs. 487, 493 (Mount Sinai, Monastery of Saint Catherine, cod. 339); Anderson 1979: 167–85.

47 See Weitzmann and Galavaris 1990: pl. CXXXVI, fig. 438 (Sinai, cod. 179, fol. 210r); Kotzabassi and Ševčenko 2010: 11–12, figs. 16–17 (Princeton, University Libraries, Garrett 2, fol. 36v, 37r) and figs. 226–27 (Princeton, University Libraries, Scheide M 70, fols. 5v-6r); Pelekanides et al. 1975: 31–32, figs. 7–8 (Mount Athos, Iveron 2, fols. 14r, 15r); Lowden 2009: 80, fig. 91 (Venice, Istituto Ellenico, Ms. IE 2, fol. 3v).

48 Velmans 1971: pl. 8 and *passim* (Florence, Biblioteca Laurenziana, Plut. 6.23); Ševčenko 1990: fiches 3D3–3F1 (London, British Library, Additional Ms. 11870).

49 Lowden 1990: 60, fig. 64 (Florence, Biblioteca Laurenziana, Ms. plut. 6.23, 4v, St. Matthew); 42, fig. 30 (Jaharis Lectionary, fol. 43r, St. Matthew);

59, fig. 63 (Sinai, Ms.gr. 205, fol. 45v, St. Matthew); Weitzmann and Galavaris 1990: pl. XCVIII, fig. 277 (Sinai, Ms. gr. 205, 2v, St. John).

50 Weitzmann and Galavaris 1990: 128-30, cat. 48, pl. XXa.

51 Ibid.: 230.

52 Mouriki 1980–81: 94–100; 1980: 176.

53 Mango et al. 1990: fig. 50; Sacopulo 1966.

54 Megaw 1962: especially figs. 5, 6.

55 See Lafontaine-Dosogne 1992: 203–6 on the location of Protevangelium scenes in the church.

56 On the apse at Asinou, see Carr and Nicolaides 2013; on that at Kalliana, see Stylianou and Stylianou 1997: 107.

57 Babić 1980: 127.

58 Etinhof 2003: 207.

59 Frigerio-Zeniou 1998: 9–98, figs. 10, 11, 69, 70.

60 Tomeković 1995–96: 97–104.

61 Papacostas 2007: 56–57. While it is quite possible that December 9 was chosen simply because construction work had drawn to a close at the onset of winter, the date seems to have carried no resonance for the monks on the Syro-Palestinian mainland who adopted the typikon of the Chrysostom monastery, and so may have had local significance.

62 Lafontaine-Dosogne points out that a canon of Nicolas Grammaticus, bishop of Cyprus in the late eleventh to twelfth century, lists four feasts of Mary (the Birth, Presentation, Annunciation, and Koimesis), without the Conception (1992: 33, note 9). Thus the Conception may have been regarded as a feast of Anna on Cyprus. In the *Constitution* of Manuel I it is cited as a Marian feast.

63 Papacostas 1999a: 2: 64, note 92 and Table 1; Jeffery 1918: 247.

64 Papacostas 1999a: 1: 207.

Chapter 12

Decoding Cyprus from Late Antiquity to the Renaissance: Discordant Visions, Saints, and Sacred Topography

by Tassos Papacostas

The most prominent historian of Cyprus in the Ottoman period was the archimandrite Kyprianos who, having moved from his native island to Venice, composed there his Ἱστορία Χρονολογική (published in 1788).[1] In the epilogue to the section dealing with the period of the Lusignan kingdom, he observes that after some three hundred years (since its establishment in the late twelfth century) the island's status reverted to that of a province peacefully administered by Venice; most tellingly, Kyprianos compares that to the Roman and Byzantine periods. Then he goes on to add that

> from that time [since the abolition of the independent kingdom in 1489] until now almost 298 years have passed. Who knows if in another 300 years Cyprus will not be raised to a kingdom once more?[2]

The archimandrite's quasi-sibylline question is worth noting, not so much for its prophetic character as for what it represents in the context of the first theme of this chapter: Kyprianos provides the insider's view, and a well-informed one at that, bringing to the fore a particular aspect of

the complexities involved in the study of the history of post-Classical Cyprus, namely the contrast between views originating within the island and those originating outside it. As we shall see below, all too often there is a surprising and perplexing level of discrepancy that is not always easy to explain. The presentation of the evidence concerning a number of saints' cults will serve to illustrate this point. It will also be used to highlight the second theme of this chapter, namely, the importance of the evidence that the evolution of such cults constitutes for the reconstruction of aspects of the history of settlements.

DISCORDANT VISIONS

The study of the history of Cyprus has made huge leaps in the half century since the island regained its independent status (1960), a change that would have certainly delighted Kyprianos. The publication of both primary material and secondary studies has grown exponentially, as has the number of workshops, conferences, and congresses. Nevertheless, the history of Cyprus is far from being fully decoded. To illustrate some of the problems that historians have to grapple with,

FIG. 12.1   *Kyrenia gate, Nicosia: inner façade with inscriptions (photo: Tassos Papacostas).*

FIG. 12.2   *Famagusta gate, Nicosia: inner façade (photo: Tassos Papacostas).*

FIG. 12.3   *Kyrenia gate, Nicosia: inner façade before 1930 (photo: Haigaz Mangoian, after Marangou 1996, where the photograph is wrongly labeled "The Paphos Gate in Nicosia").*

I will begin with a visual riddle that also requires deciphering in order to become legible and eventually accessible and therefore understandable.

The epigraphically compound inner façade of the Kyrenia gate in Nicosia, quite ingeniously textured as a result of successive adjustments, encapsulates at least half a millennium of Cypriot history (fig. 12.1). The gate, one of three through the Venetian walls erected in 1567 in an ultimately unsuccessful attempt to thwart the Ottoman advance, was called the Porta del Provveditore (possibly the Porta Bemba of contemporary sources, named after Lorenzo Bembo, the *provveditore*, i.e., governor, in office at the time). It was through here that the soldiers defending the nearby bastions escaped on the 9th of September 1570, when they realized that the enemy had already penetrated within the walls, and it was through here also that the Ottoman cavalry made its triumphant entry later on the same day, marking the beginning of a new era in the island's history.[3]

The inscriptions adorning this façade come from different periods. The garbled Venetian inscription carved on three marble panels and bearing the date 1562 does not belong to the original structure that was, of course, not erected until five years later. It was perhaps brought from elsewhere in the early nineteenth century, when the gateway was refurbished, and was employed as the support for something altogether different: the reverse of each panel was carved with koranic verses and placed on the façade in 1820/21 under the *tuğra* (calligraphic monogram) of the reigning sultan, Mahmud II, thus concealing the obverse with the inscription in Latin. The same *tuğra* was also placed on the Famagusta and Paphos gates (Porta Giuliana and Porta San Domenico, respectively), and it was probably at that time that an arched gable (as at the Famagusta gate: fig. 12.2) and a domed chamber were added over the Kyrenia gate (figs. 12.3–4).[4] It is worth noting that these alterations occurred during a period of turmoil, when the repercussions on Cyprus of the Greek War of Independence led to the elimination of the island's Greek leadership in July 1821.

The multi-layered identity of these inscribed slabs is further amplified by their material, the marble itself, adding a probable and unsuspected Byzantine dimension. The soil of Cyprus does not yield this sought-after building material. The Venetian walls of Nicosia, like most of the city's monuments, were built of local limestone. The marble for these panels was surely imported from overseas, either in the sixteenth century or, much more likely, during Late Antiquity, in the fifth- to sixth-century period, when marble imports, most notably from the quarries of Proconnesus in the Sea of Marmara, became common on the island.[5] The use of spolia by the Venetians on Cyprus one millennium later is well-documented, especially at Famagusta; at Nicosia itself the ancient granite column erected a few hundred meters to the south of the Kyrenia gate indeed constitutes a most eloquent nearby witness.[6]

About one century after the gateway's Ottoman reconfiguration, in 1931, openings were cut through the walls on either side in order to facilitate the movement of motorized traffic; mercifully, the gateway itself was spared and demoted to an incongruous centerpiece for a traffic island (the works were carried out between November 1930 and June 1931). At the same time, the inner façade and domed chamber appear to have been at least partly reconstructed, although largely maintaining the earlier layout (fig. 12.5). It was at this juncture that the 1562 inscription on the concealed face of the panels was revealed and proudly displayed within a moulded frame. The sura took its place in the darkness of the masonry, condemned to invisibility and oblivion, as if representing a *damnatio memoriae* of the entire Ottoman period, or at least of Islam, for the *tuğra* above was left in place.[7] These interventions were epigraphically commemorated with King George V's abbreviated name and title, G[eorgius] V R[ex et] I[mperator], using the same language as the newly-discovered Venetian inscription (fig. 12.1). In this way a notional connection with the pre-Ottoman and Christian past of Cyprus was established, only a few years after the island's residual links with its previous status

FIG. 12.4 *Kyrenia gate, Nicosia: outer façade before 1930. Watercolor, Costas and Rita Severis Collection.*

were severed, as it became a crown colony in 1925, but also in the same year that witnessed the most severe riots against colonial rule and a futile declaration of union with Greece by the bishop of Kition (October 1931), a harbinger of developments that eventually led to independence.[8]

Multiple languages, scripts, building materials, functions, contexts, and personalities (the Venetian *provveditore*, the Ottoman sultan, the English monarch) converge on this façade, its panels forming a fascinating palimpsest on which the history of Cyprus is inscribed again and again. The gate's construction was prompted by the Ottoman threat, and its most notable reconfigurations roughly coincided with periods of turmoil (1821, 1931). The gateway was manipulated, appropriated, reinvented, and realigned, largely through the agency of inscribed text, marker and signifier of each of its identity layers. As suggested at the

FIG. 12.5   *Kyrenia gate, Nicosia: view from the south-east (photo: Stefanos Stavridis).*

beginning, deciphering its overlapping messages is not dissimilar to decoding Cyprus as a theater of operations, military, political, diplomatic, social, cultural, artistic, and certainly many others as well.

The Kyrenia gate, despite being located on the island itself, in a way also represents Cyprus seen from without, from Renaissance Venice, Ottoman Istanbul, and London of the Empire at its heyday, perhaps with a nod to Byzantine Constantinople (through the use of marble) and imperial Rome (through the use of Latin). Its inscriptions were put up by the authorities representing these external centers of power. By contrast, its audience, users, and the anonymous masons and craftsmen who worked on its construction, maintenance, and refashioning over the centuries issued from the local population. Yet the Greek element is entirely absent from this monument, or at least invisible, its presence never having been epigraphically sanctioned.

The afore-mentioned musings of Kyprianos on the other hand, although written in Venice, represent that missing element, providing the view of those external powers from within: the islander pondering on his island's long-term fate and future, employing none of the languages of the gate inscriptions, but the prime language of Byzantium instead. This duality, within and without, is both ubiquitous and often unavoidable in the study of everything that has to do with Cyprus. It is imposed by the island's history, by the nature of the evidence, but also by the development of the relevant historiography. This is what the "discordant visions" of this chapter's title refer to.

TALES FROM LATE ANTIQUITY

The cult of saints, the act of pilgrimage, and the veneration of relics have been a perennial concern of modern historians of Cyprus since the seminal article on the island's saints by Hippolyte Delehaye, published more than one century ago.[9] This is the result of the relative abundance of evidence and, indeed, of the same prominence of holy figures in one of the most important primary sources for medieval Cyprus, namely the chronicle of Leontios Machairas. As I will try to show, the dichotomy between views from within and those from without is rarely more pronounced than in this particular area. And in order to be able to exploit this evidence to its full extent, to use it in drawing conclusions about issues broader than pilgrimage and religious practices, we have to be fully aware and take stock of this fact. The study of the cult of saints also brings to the fore another closely related question, which is the fate of such cults over the centuries. The case studies below illustrate to different degrees one or both of these questions.

In the days of Diocletian's persecutions there lived a Christian priest in the city of Laodicea (in Syria), named Artemon. Having joined the local bishop in his attacks against pagan idols, Artemon was arrested by the governor, imprisoned in Caesarea (in Palestine), and tortured, but eventually walked free as the cauldron of boiling pitch prepared for him received instead the governor himself, snatched by two angels turned into eagles and dropped into it; needless to say, he perished immediately. Artemon subsequently moved to Asia Minor where he became a bishop. But after three years only and following accusations of fornication, which were of course miraculously proven false, he escaped to Anemourion on the Isaurian coast. He found no ship to continue his journey across the sea to Cyprus, but in accord with a common hagiographic *topos*, a cloud conveniently lifted the holy man and deposited him safely at Cape Kormakiti.[10] Artemon spent some time in that area but then, hearing of the evil spirits that plagued a place called Avlon, he duly proceeded there, chased them away, and settled on the same spot, building a church next to a holy spring where he baptized many pagans and spent the rest of his days. Soon after his death his fellow Christians from Laodicea traveled to Cyprus where they recorded his deeds in writing. Miracles ensued at the holy spring by the church, and his fame spread accordingly. The only posthumous miracle related in some detail involved the missing child of a prominent senator and his wife, who resolved to sail to Cyprus from Constantinople in order to venerate the saint's relic and have their offspring baptized in the holy spring.[11]

The one and only known manuscript that preserves Artemon's *Vita* (Jer. Saba 259) contains mainly hagiographic material, some with Cypriot associations, and was written on the island in 1089/90 by Gerasimos, a monk who also moved there from the Syro-Palestinian mainland and who may have had links with the region of Antioch and the monasteries of the Judean desert.[12] What is remarkable is that the eleventh-century copyist did not deem it appropriate to enrich the text with more recent miracles. This must be either because he was not aware of any, or because they were no longer occurring, the locus of Artemon's cult having perhaps been forgotten by that time. How and where Gerasimos obtained the text that he copied is unclear. He may well have discovered it on Cyprus or brought it with him from Palestine.

It has been suggested that Artemon's church may have stood at modern Avlona (near Morphou), a village not attested until the late medieval period.[13] In the past, remains of a Late Antique baptistery with mosaic floor were reported there.[14] The village of Ornithi (between Nicosia and Famagusta), where a (late medieval?) church dedicated to Artemon with an ancient subterranean burial chamber is preserved, may be another candidate, although its shrine may also commemorate a different homonymous saint. This uncertainty is largely a result of the fact that, as far as I have been able to ascertain, no surviving later source ever mentions Artemon and his relic or cult again. Leontios Machairas ignores them completely in his long list of holy men and relics venerated on late medieval Cyprus, and no depictions of Artemon are known from the numerous surviving fresco cycles.[15]

The evidence concerning Artemon is instructive in a few ways: it provides a literary counterpart to the archaeological evidence for the close links between Anemourion and Cyprus (the distance to Cape Kormakiti is only 43 miles), for Artemon's celestial journey aside, communications across the sea are well-attested through ceramic evidence.

Excavations at Anemourion have shown that Cypriot sigillata was common in the Roman period, whereas Cypriot red slip was the commonest fine ware later on; in the opposite direction, lamps belonging to a type associated with Anemourion have been recovered at Salamis-Constantia and at the Kornos cave, not far from Artemon's landing place.[16] Thus the route followed by the holy man would have been familiar to many contemporaries (although surely using more conventional means).

Much more important for the purposes of the present discussion, in the context of my second theme, is the evidence concerning cult centers: here we have an early rural cult of a holy man originating and attracting pilgrims from beyond the island's shores that apparently fell into oblivion by the late medieval period. Some of these elements constitute a recurring theme in the holy prosopography and sacred topography of Cyprus. A good example is Hilarion the Great, a native of Gaza, who also spent his last days on the island, which he reached following his protracted peregrinations around the Mediterranean. Our main source, Hilarion's life written by Jerome, tells us that he settled near Paphos, where he died and was buried in AD 371. This is confirmed by slightly later sources, most notably one of the biographies of Epiphanios of Salamis and Sozomen's *Ecclesiastical History*.[17] His tomb became the locus of a cult, and miracles continued even after the removal of the relic by his disciple Hesychius to Palestine. Its location was identified in modern times (though without tangible confirmation) at the village of Episkopi in the Ezousas valley, in the hinterland of Paphos.[18]

Among the most illustrious visitors to what was in fact Hilarion's cenotaph was Gennadios, former patriarch of Constantinople, who resigned his post exactly one century after the death of Hilarion (AD 471). Returning from his pilgrimage to the Holy Land, Gennadios disembarked at Paphos, but died in his attempt to reach the holy man's abode during a severe late November snow storm. Miracles ensued and he was eventually buried at an unspecified location in the wider region, where a church was also erected at the instigation of the (unnamed) bishop of Paphos. We owe our knowledge of all this to Neophytos the Recluse, who himself settled near Paphos in

the mid-twelfth century and composed encomia of both Gennadios and Hilarion.[19] Neither, however, contains any concrete information on shrines linked with their memory or the local cult of these holy men in Neophytos' own times. And once more our principal source for late medieval Cyprus, the chronicle of Machairas, has nothing relevant to say. Machairas and his presumed source for the passage in question do, however, shed light on the vexed issue of Hilarion's association with the homonymous castle on the Pentadaktylos (Kyrenia) mountains, a middle Byzantine structure refurbished as a royal castle in the Lusignan period. They make clear that the Hilarion after whom this is named is not the Palestinian ascetic but a later namesake, thus correcting the assumption of most foreign pilgrims and travelers of this and subsequent periods who regularly make the link, probably based not on any local legends and traditions but on their awareness of Jerome's text (for the link with Cyprus) and the promotion of the cult of Hilarion by the Lusignan court and the Latin church of Cyprus.[20] The discrepancy between these external accounts and Machairas' own internal testimony illustrates again most vividly the aforementioned dichotomy of views from within and without.

Another example of a secondary local cult, better documented, as we shall see, is that of Athanasios Pentaschoinites. According to Anastasius of Sinai, the seventh-century hagiographer from Amathous, Athanasios hailed from the village of Pentaschoinon (by the homonymous stream south of Agios Theodoros) near the south coast. Wrongly accused by his stepmother of stealing from his father's storerooms, he miraculously replenished the oil and wine jars and the wheat containers whose contents he had previously distributed among the poor. Soon after his death at a young age, shortly before the first Arab raid on Cyprus (which occurred in 649), a ship off the nearby coast found herself in grave danger. The crew was saved by the timely and miraculous intervention of a young man who identified himself as Athanasios from Pentaschoinon. Having made it to shore and assuming him to be a local saint, the sailors proceeded to the village intending to offer a gift to the church of their saviour. They quickly realized that no such shrine existed, and upon asking about Athanasios they were eventually led to his tomb by his own father, whence the dead boy spoke to confirm that it was indeed he who had helped them. Anastasius adds that there were numerous witnesses to his story, including the metropolitan of Damascus, who had recently visited the village (in the late seventh century).[21]

This time Leontios Machairas confirms the survival of the cult eight centuries later, for he observes that Athanasios' relic still performed miraculous cures in his own day. The numerous depictions of the saint, curiously as a deacon, testify to his popularity in middle Byzantine times and later on.[22] The now ruinous church where the memory of Athanasios was preserved down to modern times was excavated recently by the Department of Antiquities. The preliminary report places its earliest building phase in the eighth or ninth century. Built as a vaulted pier basilica, it was restored after a severe earthquake in 1491 caused its collapse, and remained in use into the Ottoman period, perhaps as late as the seventeenth century (fig. 12.6).[23] Beneath its nave floor a burial chamber was revealed, accessible through a staircase in the western part of the nave and housing at least two tombs. The northern arcosolium was decorated with imported marble panels and painted crosses, and may represent the original tomb of Athanasios, according to the excavation report. Fragmentary inscriptions and ceramic finds attest to the site's continuous use through the late medieval period. It is thus clear that, unlike the cults of Artemon, Hilarion, or Gennadios, that of Athanasios survived and even flourished beyond Late Antiquity. Why this was so is far from clear; but it must be related at least partly to the development and continuity of occupation of the settlements or sites that housed these shrines. Rural cults were perhaps less likely to remain immutable through the centuries, at least compared to their urban counterparts. The latter, however, were not immune to decline and eventual disappearance either. For

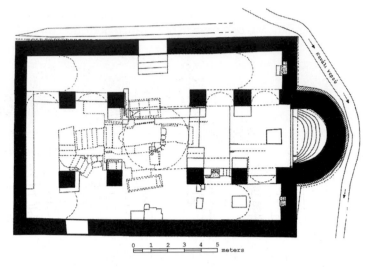

FIG. 12.6   *Church of Saint Athanasios Pentaschoinites: plan of the excavated remains (after Philotheou 2008).*

an example of that we need look no further than nearby Amathous.

We know from the *Life of Saint Tychon*, composed by Patriarch John the Almsgiver of Alexandria, that the local early fifth-century bishop was buried in an oratory that subsequently became the focus of relic veneration and incubation.[24] It was in this same church that the Almsgiver himself was buried, having returned to die in his native Amathous after the Persian occupation of Alexandria in 619.[25] The now ruinous church associated with Tychon has been excavated, showing that the early timber-roof pier basilica (which had replaced a smaller oratory) was damaged probably during the Arab raids of the mid-seventh century. A three-apse funerary chamber to its north recalls the description of the Almsgiver's burial circumstances, when two earlier bishops interred there (including Tychon?) miraculously moved apart in order to make room for their new and august companion (fig. 12.7). In the early medieval period, the church was reconstructed with a dome, and it was rebuilt once more in Lusignan times, leaving out the burial chamber. Like the Pentaschoinites church, it finally collapsed in the course of the Ottoman period and was never rebuilt. The excavation has shown that the remains of the individuals interred therein were carefully removed at some unknown date.[26] If we accept the identification of the shrine with the one in which John

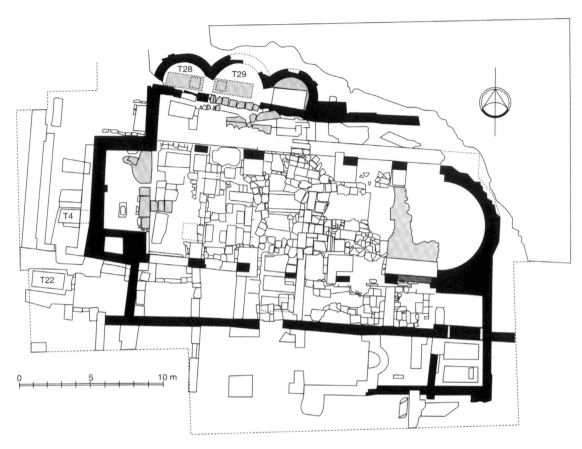

FIG. 12.7 *Church of Saint Tychon, Amathus: plan of the later 5th-century building phase (after Procopiou 1996).*

the Almsgiver had been buried, then this raises the question of the fate of the relics of both the patriarch and Tychon. The latter disappears completely from the record. The patriarch's, however, reappears later on.

In the Late Komnenian period, John the Almsgiver's remains were said to be housed at Constantinople where they were still venerated in Palaeologan times, despite reports that several fragments were taken out of the city in the wake of the Fourth Crusade, ending up in central and western Europe. After 1453, King Matthias Corvinus of Hungary was reportedly sent the patriarch's relic from Constantinople, which he placed in the royal chapel at Buda (it was later transferred to Pressburg/Bratislava). Venetian sources report a different tradition, claiming that in 1249 the patriarch's entire relic was taken to Venice, not from Constantinople, not even Amathous, but from Alexandria, in a sequel to Mark's translation in the same direction five centuries earlier. The archi-

mandrite Kyprianos venerated it at San Giovanni in Bragora, where it is still to be seen today.[27]

The important point here is that although the saint was not forgotten, and indeed the proliferation of relics suggests quite the opposite, on Cyprus itself he barely registered as an important figure. It is yet another case of divergence between local and external sources. Neither Neophytos the Recluse in his *Logos of the Almsgiver*, nor Machairas has anything to say about a local cult. The thirteenth-century *Golden Legend*, the most widespread hagiographic compilation in late medieval western Europe, which does include a life of the patriarch, omits any reference to his links with Cyprus, stressing instead, like the Venetian tradition, his Alexandrian credentials.[28] No wonder then that no pilgrim or visitor to Cyprus ever makes any reference to the saint. What may have conceivably happened is that the relic was transferred from Amathous to Constantinople in the early medieval period. There is nothing unusual about this; the Byzantine capital voraciously hoarded relics from all over the Empire, including those of Lazaros of Bethany, Therapon, Spyridon, and other saints from Cyprus.[29] What remains intriguing, however, is that no memory of the Almsgiver appears to have been preserved at Amathous, unlike Lazaros at Larnaka/Kition and Spyridon at Tremithous. This, in conjunction with the comparable fate of Tychon, is surely indicative of the fate of the city itself that initially housed their relics. But the story of John the Almsgiver also brings to the fore another issue — that of Cyprus as the place of origin of saints venerated abroad, even though in the Almsgiver's case this origin was passed over. Two cases from the medieval period that illustrate this most eloquently will be described in the next section.

MEDIEVAL TALES

The setting for the first case is Genoa, where a new cult appeared at the Benedictine abbey of San Tommaso, probably in the course of the thirteenth century. A saint named Limbania was venerated there, and her skull was kept in the convent's church. Her local Genoese legend claimed that she was born on Cyprus in the twelfth century and had left the island in order to preserve her chastity, threatened by the usual matrimonial plans. Limbania embarked on a ship without sails, drifted across the Mediterranean, and eventually reached Genoa, where she spent the rest of her days and died as a recluse, performing posthumous miracles. Her cult spread beyond the city, and several churches dedicated to the saint were founded in Liguria and Piemonte.[30] Cypriot sources ignore Limbania, although Étienne de Lusignan does mention her as Libonia, making her a Famagustan virgin;[31] but Lusignan probably became aware of her legend while in Italy, although, rather surprisingly, James of Voragine, the Genoese author of the *Golden Legend*, omits any reference to her. Whatever the origin of Limbania's story, what it suggests is that a Cypriot connection was deemed respectable and indeed desirable for holy figures venerated in late medieval Italy. An interestingly different conception of Cyprus appears for another rather obscure female saint, this time in German lands.

Afra was allegedly martyred during the reign of Diocletian, together with her mother Ilaria and three female servants, in Roman Augusta Vindelicorum (Augsburg in Bavaria). Her cult spread throughout southern Germany, and although her legend is first attested in the eighth century, the Cypriot connection does not appear until the thirteenth. According to tradition, Afra was the daughter of the island's king; she had been dedicated by her mother to Venus and worked as a prostitute. She was converted to Christianity by a persecuted bishop who took refuge with the Cypriot women in Augsburg.[32] The most intriguing aspect of this fanciful story is that Cyprus was known in the Crusader period for its ancient association with Venus, and by extension with ritual prostitution, even beyond the Alps; knowledge of this association is reflected in the contemporary account of the northern German Wilbrand of Oldenburg, who was aware of and comments on the ancient link between Venus/Aphrodite and Paphos during his visit to the island in 1211.[33] Contrary to the case of Limbania, Afra's Cypriot origin of course does not bestow respectability, but rather emphasizes her sinful past and glorifies her redemption. Once more Étienne de Lusignan was well aware of Afra's cult, for in 1577 he himself visited Augsburg and the shrine where her relics were kept.[34]

It seems that Cyprus was considered a good place to ascribe saints to, although not always for the same reason. Exactly why this was so is not clear and requires further investigation. But the island's proximity to the Holy Land, and therefore its accessibility to pilgrims, certainly is a factor, while the period when Limbania's cult appeared in Genoa coincides, of course, with the time when merchants from that city settled on Cyprus; and it was in Genoa that a most illustrious relic from the island, the skull of Barnabas, accidentally ended up in 1342 on its way to Catalonia as a royal gift.[35] Similarly, Afra's transalpine cult was enriched with a Cypriot connection at a time when pilgrims and Crusaders from that part of Europe traveled with increasing frequency to the Levant. Needless to add, Leontios Machairas never seems to have heard of either Limbania or Afra. Much more surprisingly, however, he fails to mention other much better-known saints associated with Cyprus.

FIG. 12.8 *Map of Cyprus: episcopal sees listed by Leontios Machairas with, in light gray, those not represented in the synaxarion of Consantinople (Tassos Papacostas).*

RELICS, CULTS, AND TOPOGRAPHY

The fifteenth-century chronicler, after enumerating the most prominent occupants of the island's fourteen episcopal sees since early Christian times, proceeds with a list of relics venerated locally. In addition to five fragments of the True Cross and a miraculous icon (that of Kykko), he gives 54 names of holy figures. Only three are identified as bishops (and their sees are not given), the rest being martyrs or ascetics of whom most belong to the group referred to in later sources as the 300 Alaman saints.[36] This contrasts sharply with some 30 Cyprus-related saints commemorated in the *synaxarion* of Constantinople: only four or five of those are ascetics, all the others being bishops representing, like Machairas' *synodikon*, most of the sees of Late Antique Cyprus.[37] In that respect, they closely match the evidence from medieval monumental decorations, where, as Doula Mouriki observed many years ago, bishops predominate.[38] The resulting distribution maps could not be more different (figs. 12.8-9). Most notably, whereas the Troodos massif is devoid of episcopal sees (and

therefore centers linked with the memory of early bishops), Machairas cites several saints' cults associated with localities within this mountainous region (Koilani, Vasa, Marathasa, Plakontoudi).

It is therefore rather disconcerting that, despite this wide geographical coverage, there is no reference whatsoever in Machairas to cults known definitively from other sources to have been popular in this period. Those centered on relics long taken away, like that of Lazaros, the best documented case, can be excused. But what about the cults of Barnabas, Epiphanios, and Catherine of Alexandria in and around Salamis-Constantia? And the numerous relics of the Passion, or of John the Baptist, Luke the Evangelist, Cosmas and Damian, and Saint George attested in the churches of Famagusta and Nicosia? The existence and veneration of all these in Lusignan and Venetian Cyprus are reported solely by foreign pilgrims and visitors.[39] And here must lie the clue, for the latter moved primarily between the urban centers of Nicosia and Famagusta, and usually ventured beyond their walls only in order to visit prominent shrines such as Staurovouni and sometimes Saint

FIG. 12.9   *Map of Cyprus: distribution of named saints' and other holy relics according to Leontios Machairas (Tassos Papacostas).*

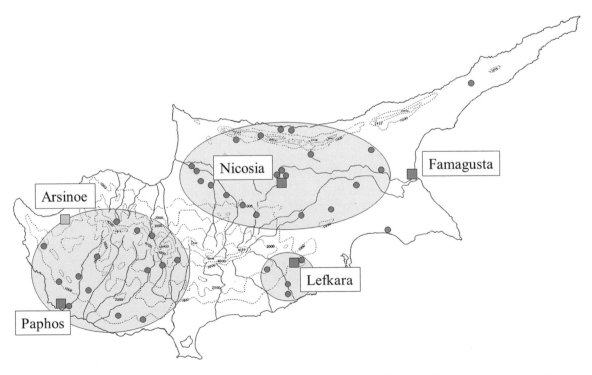

FIG. 12.10   *Map of Cyprus: concentrations of named saints' and other holy relics according to Leontios Machairas (Tassos Papacostas).*

Mamas at Morphou. Machairas, on the other hand, focuses on rural cults. His sacred topography is centered on often obscure holy figures from the post-Roman centuries whose memory was maintained in the village communities of Lusignan Cyprus.

If we look at his distribution, certain patterns emerge: there are two large areas of concentration, around Nicosia and the central plain on the one hand, and in the west of the island, from the central Troodos down to the coast of Paphos, on the other. A smaller cluster occurs around the area of Helena Augusta's alleged activity in the fourth century, mostly represented by fragments of the True Cross (fig. 12.10). Limassol and its region, but most importantly Famagusta and its immediate hinterland, are left a blinding blank on the map. Why does Machairas ignore Famagusta's shrines? Most were of course Latin, but the chronicler does not shy away from listing the Latin Saint John of Montfort, venerated in Nicosia. In the fifteenth century, when he was writing, Famagusta was in Genoese hands, yet this fact alone cannot possibly explain his silence; nor can his reliance on his presumed source, an earlier, perhaps thirteenth- or fourteenth-century compilation.[40]

It is tempting to argue that the distribution pattern of cults may be related to the proximity of the settlements where the four Greek bishops had their base in the later Lusignan period (at Nicosia, Famagusta, Lefkara, and either Paphos or Arsinoë). The promotion of some of these cults may have resulted from the new map of dioceses. But this yet again leaves Famagusta, also the seat of a Greek bishop, unaccounted for and totally invisible.

FINAL REMARKS

This preliminary comparison of sources on cults and pilgrimage raises many questions. I have already mentioned a few; their answers require sustained investigation and further study. But I do believe that this is a valid and fruitful approach that contributes to our scholarly tools, in which an apparent disadvantage (that is, the perplexing duality that pervades the source material) can be turned into a springboard for further progress in decoding Cyprus. I also hope that I have demonstrated how we can use most profitably the evidence for the growth, decline, revival, or abandonment of cults, to the extent that all this can be indeed reconstructed, as an instrument for the investigation of aspects of the history and, especially, the fate of the settlements that hosted them. The study of Late Antique Amathous and Salamis-Constantia, as well as medieval Nicosia and Famagusta stands to gain a lot from this approach. The vanishing of the Almsgiver's brief cult at Amathous soon after his burial there, in conjunction with the apparent survival or perhaps revival of the more ancient cult of Tychon on the same spot, will have to be taken into account when trying to determine when the city declined and was abandoned after the Arab raids of the mid-seventh century. Similarly, the history of the veneration of Barnabas and Epiphanios at Salamis-Constantia after the decline of the city in the early medieval period surely has to be seen within the context of not only the stature of the two saints within the Church of Cyprus, but also in the context of medieval Famagusta's rise nearby. The subsequent population increase provided, once more, a regular audience for their shrines. It eventually led to the growth of new cults, most notably that of Catherine of Alexandria, offering a uniquely explicit example of how the veneration of a saint can be customized and adapted to a new environment.[41]

NOTES

1 Kitromilides 2001: 54–55, 174–77.

2 Archimandrite Kyprianos, Ἱστορία χρονολογική 264: "Καὶ ἡ Κύπρος μετὰ τριακοσίους χρόνους περίπου πάλιν κατέστη ἐπαρχία ὑπ᾽ αὐτῶν, ὡς καὶ ἐπὶ τοῦ καιροῦ τῶν ʽΡωμάνων, καὶ ʽΡωμαίων. Ἔκτοτε δὲ καὶ μέχρι νῦν 1788, παρῆλθον χρόνοι 298 σχεδόν. Τίς ἄρα οἶδεν, εἰ μετὰ πάλιν τριακοσίους χρόνους ἀναστηθήσεται εἰς βασίλειον."

3 Angelo Calepio, *Vera et fidelissima narratione,* in Steffano Lusignano, *Chorograffia* 105r, and in Étienne de Lusignan, *Description,* 260v; Pietro Valderio, *La Guerra di Cipro,* ed. Grivaud and Patapiou 1996: 56, 60; Hill 1940–52: 3:848 n.1; Leventis 2005: 327; list of *provveditori generali* in Aristeidou 1990: 176.

4 Jeffery 1918: 29 and 1931: 9–12; Gunnis 1936: 46; Imhaus 2004: 1:367; Bağışkan 2009: 489–90.

5 Papacostas 2001: 115, with further bibliography.

6 Langdale 2010 and Papacostas 2010 on spolia; Jeffery 1918: 59–60 on the column.

7 Gunnis 1936: 46; Pilides 2009: 1:288–301.

8 Hill 1940–52: 4:540–51.

9 Delehaye 1907.

10 *The Life of Artemon,* eds. Abicht and Reichelt 1898: 185–97.

11 Ibid.: 196–97.

12 On the manuscript, see Constantinides and Browning 1993: 63–68; on Gerasimos, see Papacostas 2007: 34–36.

13 *Le livre des remembrances,* ed. Richard 1983: 90; Grivaud 1998b: 467.

14 Chotzakoglou 2005: 497 note 237, 506, 537; Charalambous 2012: 234.

15 Leontios Makhairas, ed. Dawkins 1980: 1:30–38, eds. Pieris and Konnari 2003: 82–88; Mouriki 1993.

16 Williams 1989: 1, 27–28; Russell 2002: 225; on the Kormakiti region, see Quilici 1989.

17 Jerome, *Vita sancti Hilarionis,* ed. Migne 1912: 23.50–52; *Vita Epiphanii,* ed. Migne 1912: 91.65; Sozomenus, *Historia Ecclesiastica,* ed. Hansen 1960: 121–22, 206.

18 Stylianou and Stylianou 1977.

19 Delehaye 1907: 221–28, 296; Neophytos the Recluse, eds. Stephanēs and Sōteroudēs 1996–2005: 3:285–301, 408–19.

20 Leontios Makhairas, ed. Dawkins 1980: 1:30, eds.

21 Pieris and Konnari 2003: 82; and Papadopoullos 1952: 29; Kyrris 1993: 230–31; Schabel 2005: 212.

21 Greek text in Philotheou 2008: 494.

22 Leontios Makhairas, ed. Dawkins 1980: 1:36; eds. Pieris and Konnari 2003: 84–86; Philotheou 2008: 229–32.

23 Philotheou 2008: 234–42; Stavrides 1998: 125, 143; the church is also mentioned in a sixteenth-century portolan: Delatte 1947: 123.

24 John the Almsgiver, *Life of Saint Tychon,* ed. Delehaye 1907: 141–45.

25 Leontios of Neapolis, *Life of John the Almsgiver,* eds. Festugière and Rydén 1974: 404–5, 408–9.

26 Procopiou 1996; Lehman 2005: 36–38.

27 Majeska 1984: 43, 153, 165, 308; *Acta Sanctorum, Ianuarii II,* 530–33; Corner 1758: 29–31; Archimandrite Kyprianos, Ἱστορία χρονολογική, ed. Stephanou 1971: 349; for a more detailed discussion, see Papacostas, forthcoming b.

28 Neophytos the Recluse, eds. Stephanēs and Sōteroudēs 1996–2005: 3:369–90; and Delehaye 1907: 229–32; James of Voragine, *Legenda aurea* 1:188–97.

29 Delehaye 1907: 240, 247, 257.

30 *Acta Sanctorum, Septembris II,* 784–800; *Bibliotheca Sanctorum* 8:54; Polonio 2001: 382.

31 Étienne de Lusignan, *Description,* 56v.

32 *Acta Sanctorum, Augustii II,* 37–59; *Bibliotheca hagiographica latina* 1:19–21, and *Novum supplementum,* 15–16; *Bibliotheca Sanctorum* 1:283–87; see also Karras 1990: 15–16 (I owe particular thanks to Ioanna Christoforaki for bringing this article to my attention).

33 *Peregrinatores medii aevi,* ed. Laurent 1873: 182; *Excerpta Cypria,* ed. Cobham 1908: 14; Calvelli 2009: 257–58.

34 Étienne de Lusignan, *Description,* 49r–50r; Hieronymos Tragoudistes (flour. 16th c.), the Cypriot composer, music theorist, and copyist who settled in Augsburg a few years earlier, must have also been aware of Afra's cult and Cypriot connections.

35 Georgii et Iohannis Stellae, *Annales Genuenses,* ed. Petti Balbi 1975: 136–37; Golubovich 1906–27: 2:210–11; see also Polonio 2001: 375–76.

36 Leontios Makhairas, ed. Dawkins 1980: 1:30–38, eds. Pieris and Konnari 2003: 82–88; on the "Alaman" saints, see Kyrris 1993.

37 Delehaye 1907: 257–61.

38 Mouriki 1993.

39 Numerous mentions in *Excerpta Cypria* (Cobham 1908) and *Excerpta Cypria Nova* (Grivaud 1990).

40 Papadopoullos 1952: 25–26; on the presumed source's date, see Kyrris 1993: 203–4, and Grivaud 1998a: 47–48.

41 Calvelli 2009: 157–245.

Bibliography

NOTE: *In collating the various primary and secondary sources for each chapter, a modified referencing system was adopted for this volume, since each contributor used a different system. It was important to the editorial committee that the historical sources were clearly cited. As a result, the entries here begin with the original author's forename. If the text's original author was unknown, then the secondary editor (ed.) or translator (transl.) is listed. For a primary source published more than once, the first editor/translator is listed, and subsequent editions are noted afterwards. For the sake of referencing, the dates of subsequent publications are paired with the editors' names.*

PRIMARY SOURCES

Abicht, R., and Reichelt, C. (eds.)
  1898   *The Life of Artemon*, in "Quellennachweise zum Codex Suprasliensis," *Archiv für Slavische Philologie* 20: 181–200.

Acta conciliorum oecumenicorum
  ed. E. Schwartz, J. Straub, and R. Schieffer (Berlin: de Gruyter, 1914–2008).

Acta sanctorum
  (Paris and Rome: Apud Victorem Palme, intermittently 1643–1940).

Agapius of Manbij, *Kitāb al-'Unwān* [Universal History]
  ed. and transl. by A. Vasiliev, *Patrologia Orientalis* 8 (1912); partial French transl. Mansouri (2001a), *see entry below*.

Al-Balādhuri, Ahmad bn. Yahyā bn. Jābir. *Kitāb Futūh al-Buldān* [Book of the Conquests of Lands] English transl. by P. Hitti and F. Murgotten, *The Origin of the Islamic State* [Studies in History, Economics and Public Law 68] (New York: Columbia University, 1916 and 1924); partial French transl. Mansouri (2001a), *see entry below*.

Alexander Monachus, *Laudatio Barnabae*
  ed. and German transl. B. Kollmann, *Alexander Monachus, Laudatio Barnabae (Lobrede auf Barnabas)* (Turnhout: Brepols, 2007).

Al'Idrīsi, Abū 'Abd Allāh Muhammad. *Nuzhat al-Mushtāq fī Iktirāq al-Āfāq* [The Book of Pleasant Journeys into Faraway Lands]
  ed. E. Cerulli, *Opus geographicum* (Naples: Brill, 1970–75); Partial French transl. by Mansouri (2001a), *see entry below*.

Ambroise, *Estoire de la guerre sainte*
  ed. and transl. M. Ailes and M. Barber, *The History of the Holy War* (Woodbridge: The Boydell Press, 2003).

Anna Komene, *Alexiad*
  Engl. transl. E. Sewter, revised P. Frankopan (London: Penguin, 2009).

Antonini Placentini Itinerarium
  in *Itineraria et Alia Geographica*, ed. P. Geyer [*Corpus Christianorum, Series Latina* 175] (Turnhout: Brepols, 1966), 127–74.

Antony of Choziba, *Vita sancti Georgii Chozibitae*
ed. C. Houze, "Sancti Georgii Chozebitae confessoris et monachi vita auctore Antonio eius discipulo," *Analecta Bollandiana* 7 (1888): 95–144, 336–359.

Basil of Caesarea, *Epistulae*
ed. Y. Courtonne, *Saint Basile. Lettres* (Paris: Firmin-Didot, 1966).

Bibliotheca hagiographica latina antiquae et media aetatis
(Brussels: Société des Bollandistes, 1898–1900)

Bibliotheca Sanctorum
(Rome: Instituto Giovanni XXIII nella Pontificia Università lateranense, 1961–70).

Brightman, F.E., and Hammond, C.
1896   *Liturgies, Eastern and Western; Being the texts, original or translated, of the principal liturgies of the church* (Oxford: Clarendon).

Constantine Manasses, *Hodoiporikon*
ed. K. Horna, "Das Hodoiporikon des Konstantin Manasses," *Byzantinische Zeitschrift* 13 (1904): 313–55.

Cobham, C. D.
1908   *Excerpta Cypria* (Cambridge: Cambridge University; repr. New York, 1969).

Dagron, G.
1978   *Vie et miracles de Sainte Thècle* (Brussels: Société des Bollandistes).

Delehaye, H. (ed.)
1902   *Synaxarium ecclesiae Constantinopolitanae e codice Sirmondiano nunc Berolinensi* (Brussels: Société des Bollandistes).
1907   in "Saints de Chypre," *Analecta Bollandiana* 26:
   Laudatio SS. Andronici et Athanasiae, pp. 178–80.
   Laudatio S. Arcadii ep. Arsinoes, pp. 197–206.
   Laudatio S. Diomedis, pp. 212–20.
   Laudatio S. Gennadii archiep, pp. 221–28.
   Laudatio S. Polychronii, pp. 175–78.
   Laudatio S. Theosebii Arsinoitae, pp. 181–96.

Le Panegyricon de Néophyte le Reclus, p. 274.
Narratio de monacho Palaestinensi, pp. 162–74.
Oratio de terrae motibus, pp. 207–11.
Vita S. Tychonis, pp. 229–32.
1927   "Une vie inédite de saint Jean l'Aumonier," *Analecta Bollandiana* 45: 5–74.

Deun, P. van, and Noret, J. (eds.)
1993   *Hagiographica Cypria: Sancti Barnabae Laudatio auctore Alexandro monacho et Sanctorum Bartholomaei et Baranabae Vita e menologio imperiali deprompta* [Corpus Christianorum Series Graeca 26] (Turnhout: Brepols).

Epiphanius, *Panarion*
ed. K. Holl, *Epiphanius, Ancoratus und Panarion* (Leipzig: Hinrichs, 1915); transl. F. Williams, *The Panarion of Epiphanius of Salamis. Book I* (Leiden: Brill, 1987).

Étienne de Lusignan (Stefano Lusignano)
1573   *Chorograffia et breve historia universale dell'Isola de Cipro principiando al tempo di Noè per in sino al 1572* (Bologna: Alessandro Benaccio); revised French transl. *Description de toute l'isle de Chypre* (Paris: G. Chaudiere, 1580); reprinted (Famagusta: Les Editions L'Oiseau, 1968); modern Greek transl. S. K. Perdikēs, *Λογίζου Σκευοφύλακος κρονικα(χ): ήγουν χρονογραφία του νησσίου της Κύπρου: παράρτημα / Chronograffia: dell' isola de Cipro* (Nicosia: Politistikon Idryma Trapezēs, 2004).

Festugière, A.-J.
1970   *Vie de Theodore de Sykeon* (Brussels: Société des Bollandistes).

Flusin, B.
1992   *Saint Anastase le Perse et l'Histoire de la Palestine au Début du VIIe Siècle* I, *Les Textes* (Paris: CNRS).

Fros, H.
1986   *Bibliotheca hagiographica latina antiquae et media aetatis, Novum supplementum,* (Brussels: Société des Bollandistes).

Halkin, F.
1964 "Les Actes apocryphes de saint Héraclide de Chypre, disciple de l'apôtre Barnabé," *Analecta Bollandiana* 82: 133–69.

Halkin, F., et al.
1969 *Bibliotheca hagiographica graeca* (Brussels: Société des Bollandistes, 3rd ed.).

Hierokles, *Synekdemos*
ed. J. von Arnim. *Hierokles. Ethische Elementarlehre (Papyrus 9780)* [Berliner Klassikertexte 4] (Berlin:Weidmann, 1906), 7–47.

Gascou, J.
2006 *Sophrone de Jérusalem, Miracles des saints Cyr et Jean (BHG 477–479)* (Paris: De Boccard).

Georgii et Iohannis Stellae (Giorgio and John Stella), *Annales Genuenses*
ed. G. Petti Balbi, *Rerum Italicarum Scriptores* 17.2 (Bologna: Zanichelli, 1975).

George of Pisidia
Italian transl. A. Pertusi, *Giorgio di Pisidia poemi* (Ettal: Buch-Kunstverlag Ettal, 1959)
Bellum Avaricum, pp. 176–200.
Heraclias, pp. 240–61.
Expeditio Persica, pp. 84–136.
In Bonum patricium, pp. 163–70.
In restitutionem S. Crucis, pp. 225-230.

Georgius Monachus, *Vita Theodori Syceorae*
French transl. by A.-J. Festugière, *Vie de Theodore de Sykeon* (Brussels: Société des Bollandistes, 1970).

Golubovich, P.G.
1906–27 *Biblioteca bio-bibliografica della Terra Santa e dell'oriente francescano* (Florence: Collegio di S. Bonaventura).

Grivaud, G.
1990 *Excerpta Cypria Nova, I. Voyageurs occidentaux à Chypre au XVème siècle* (Nicosia: Cyprus Research Centre).

Ibn A'tham al-Koufi, Ahmad. *Kitāb al-Futuh* [Book of Conquest]
(Hyderabad: al-Dakkan, Matba'at Majlis Dairat al-Ma'arif al-'Uthmaniyah, 1968); partial French transl. Mansouri (2001a), *see entry below.*

Ibn Ḥawqal, Abū'l-Qāsim. *Kitāb al-Masālik wa'l Mamālik* or *Kitāb Ṣūrat al-'Arḍ* [The Face of the Earth]
ed. J.H. Kramers (Leiden: Brill, 1938–1939); French transl. by J.H. Kramers and G. Wiet, *Ibn Hauqal, Configuration de la terre* (Paris: Maisonneuve et Larose, 1964); partial French transl. Mansouri (2001a), *see entry below.*

Ibn Manẓūr, Muḥammad ibn Mukarram. *Lisān al-'Arab* [The Arab Tongue]
(Beirut: Dār Ṣādir, 1956–1955).

Ibn Sallām, Abū-'Ubayd al-Qāsim. *Kitāb al-Amwāl* [The Book of Finances]
ed. M. Haras (Beirut: Dār al-Jīl, 1988); partial French transl. Mansouri (2001a), *see entry below.*

Ibn Taġrībirdī, Abu-'l-Maḥāsin. *Al-Nujūm al-zāhirah fī mulūk Miṣr wa-al-Qāhirah*
ed. I.A. Tarhān (Cairo: al-Hai'a al-Misrīya al-'Āmma, 1963–1971); partial French transl. Mansouri (2001a), *see entry below.*

Itinerarium Egeriae
in *Itineraria et Alia Geographica*; ed. A. Francheschini and R. Weber [*Corpus Christianorum, Series Latina* 175] (Turnhout: Brepols, 1965), 35–103; Engl. transl. M.L. McClure and C. L. Feltoe, *The Pilgrimage of Etheria* (London: Society for Promoting Christian Knowledge, 1919).

James of Voragine, *Legenda aurea*
ed. G.P. Maggioni, *Iacopo da Varazze, Legenda aurea* (Tavarnuzze: Sismel, 1998)

Jerome, *Vita sancti Hilarionis*
ed. J.-P. Migne, *Patrologiae cursus completus,*

Series latina (Paris: Fratres Garnier) 23: 29–54.

John of Euboia, *Sermone*
German transl. and commentary F. Dölger, "Johannes 'von Euboia,' *Anhang* Die Predigt des Johannes 'von Euboia' auf die Erweckung des Lazaros," *Analecta Bollandiana* 68: 5–26.

John of Nikiu, *Chronikon*
English transl. R.H. Charles, *The Chronicle of John, Bishop of Nikiu* (Oxford: Oxford University, 1916).

John Scylitzes
Historiae, ed. H. Thurn, *Ioannis Scylitzae Synopsis historiarum* (Berlin: de Gruyter, 1973); ed. I. Bekker, *Georgius Cedrenus, Joannis Scylitzae opera* (Bonn: Weber, 1839).
Synopsis Historiarum; Engl. transl. J. Wortley in *John Skylitzes: A Synopsis of Byzantine History, 811–1057* (Cambridge: Cambridge University, 2010).

John the Almsgiver, *Life of Saint Tychon*
ed. H. Usener, *Der Heilige Tychon* (Berlin: Teubner, 1907).

Kyprianos, Archimandrite
1788   Ἱστορία χρονολογικὴ τῆς νήσου Κύπρου (Venice; repr. Nicosia: Stephanou, 1971).

Laurent, J.C.M.
1873   *Peregrinatores medii aevi quator: Burchardus de Monte Sion, Ricoldus de Monte Crucis, Odoricus de Foro Julii, Wilbrandus de Oldenborg* (Leipzig: Hinrichs, 1864; second ed. Leipzig, 1873).

Leontios Makhairas, *Recital concerning the Sweet Land of Cyprus entitled 'Chronicle'*
ed. and Engl. transl. R.M. Dawkins (Oxford: Clarendon, 1932; repr. New York: AMS, 1980); Diplomatic edition by M. Pieris and A. Nicolaou-Konnari. Λεοντίου Μαχαιρά, Χρονικό της Κύπρου. Παράλληλη

διπλωματική ἔκδοση των χειρογράφων (Nicosia: Cyprus Research Centre, 2003).

Leontius of Neapolis
Vita et miracula sancti Symeonis Sali
ed. A.-J. Festugière and L. Rydén, *Léontius de Néapolis, Vie de Syméon le Fou et Vie de Jean de Chypre* (Paris: Geuthner, 1974).
Vita S. Johannis Ellemosynarii
ed. A.-J. Festugière and L. Rydén, *Léontius de Néapolis, Vie de Syméon le Fou et Vie de Jean de Chypre* (Paris: Geuthner, 1974); ed. K. Chatzioannou, Λεοντίου Ἐπισκόπου Νεαπόλεως Κύπρου, Βίος Του Αγίου Ιωάννου Του Ελεήμονος (Nicosia, 1988); English transl. E. Dawes (with N. Baynes), *Three Byzantine Saints: Contemporary Biographies of St. Daniel the Stylite, St. Theodore of Sykeon and St. John the Almsgiver* (Oxford: Blackwell, 1948).

Majeska, G.P.
1984   *Russian Travelers to Constantinople in the Fourteenth and Fifteenth Centuries* (Washington, DC: Dumbarton Oaks Research Library and Collection).

Mansouri, M.T.
2001a   *Chypre dans les sources arabes médiévales* (Nicosia: Centre de Recherche Scientifique de Chypre).

Maximus the Confessor
1931   *Mystagogia.* Italian transl. R. Cantarella in *Massimo Confess., La mistagogia ed altri scritti,* (Florence: Edizioni Testi cristiani).

Migne, J.-P. (ed.)
1912   *Vita Epiphanii,* in *Patrologiae cursus completus, Series graeca* (Paris: Fratres Garnier) 91: 24–116.

Müller, K. (ed.)
1855–1882   *Geographi graeci minores* (Paris: Firmin Didot).

Nerantzē-Varmazē, V.
1996 Σύνταγμα βυζαντινῶν πηγῶν κυπριακῆς
      ιστορίας, 4ος–15ος αιώνας [Πηγές και
      μελέτες της ιστορίας της Κύπρου 23]
      (Nicosia: Kentro Epistēmonikōn Ereunōn)

Neophytos the Recluse
      Αγίου Νεοφύτου του Εγκλείστου, Συγγράμματα
      eds. I. Stephanēs and P. Sōteroudēs (Paphos:
      Ieras Vasilikē kai Stauropēgiakē Monē
      Agiou Neophytou, 1996–2005).
      Περὶ τῶν κατὰ χώραν Κύπρον σκαιῶν
      ed. with commentary I.P. Tsiknopoullos,
      "Τὰ ἐλάσσονα τοῦ Νεοφύτου πρεσβυτέρου
      μοναχοῦ καὶ ἐγκλείστου," Byzantion 39
      (1969): 336–43.
      Τυπικὴ διαθήκη
      ed. with commentary I.P. Tsiknopoullos,
      Κυπριακὰ τυπικά [Πηγὲς καὶ Μελέτες τῆς
      Κυπριακῆς Ἱστορίας 2] (Nicosia: Κέντρο
      Ἐπιστημονικῶν Ἐρευνῶν, 1969), 69–122;
      photographic reproduction I.P. Tsikno-
      poullos, Κυπριακὰ τυπικά [Πηγὲς καὶ
      Μελέτες τῆς Κυπριακῆς Ἱστορίας 37]
      (Nicosia: Kentro Epistēmonikōn Ereunōn,
      2001); english transl. by Galatariotou 2000,
      see entry in Secondary Sources.

Nicholas I, Patriarch, Epistulae.
      English transl. by R. Jenkins and L. Wester-
      ink, Nicholas I Patriarch of Constantinople:
      Letters (Washington, DC: Dumbarton
      Oaks, 1973).

Nicholas Mesarites, Seditio Joanni Comneni
      ed. and transl. A. Heisenberg, Nikolaos
      Mesarites, Die Palastrevolution des Johannes
      Komnenos. Programm des K. Alten Gym-
      nasiums zu Würzburg für das Studienjahr
      1906–1907 (Würzburg: Königliche Univer-
      sitätsdruckerei von H. Stürzt, 1907).

Nicholas Mouzalōn, Verses on His Abdication
      ed. with commentary S.I. Doanidou "Η
      παραίτησις Νικολάου τοῦ Μουζάλωνος
      ἀπὸ τῆς ἀρχιεπισκοπῆς Κύπρου," Ἑλληνικά
      7 (1934): 109–50.

Palladius of Helenopolis, Dialogus de vita
s. Joannis Chrysostomi
      ed. A.-M. Malingrey, Sources chrétiennes 341
      (Paris: Les Éditions du Cerf, 1988); ed. R.
      Meyer, Ancient Christian Writers 45 (New
      York: Paulist Press, 1985).

Pietro Valderio, La Guerra di Cipro
      ed. G. Grivaud and N. Patapiou (Nicosia:
      Centre de Recherches Scientifiques, 1996)

Pseudo-Epiphanius, Notitia episcopatum
      ed. J. Darrouzès, Notitiae episcopatuum Ec-
      clesiae Constantinopolitanae (Paris: Institut
      Français d'Études Byzantines, 1981).

Qudama ibn Ja'far, al-Kharaj wa sina'at al-Kitaba
      ed. M.H. al-Zubaydi (Baghdad: al-Jumhuri-
      yah al-'Iraqiyah, 1981); partial French transl.
      Mansouri (2001a), see entry above.

Sophronius, Vita SS. Cyri et Joannis. Miracula
      ed. J.-P. Migne, Patrologia Graeca 87.3
      (Paris: Migne, 1865): 3423; ed. J. Gascou,
      Sophrone de Jérusalem, Miracles des saints
      Cyr et Jean (BHG 477–479) (Paris: De Boc-
      card, 2006).

Sozomen, Historia Ecclesiastica
      ed. J. Bidez and G.C. Hansen, Kirchenge-
      schichte (Berlin: Akademie-Verlag, 1960).

Silverstein, T., and Hilhorst, A.
1997 Apocalypse of Paul. A New Critical Edition
      of the Three Long Latin Versions [Cahiers
      d'Orientalisme 21] (Geneva: Cramer).

Stephanus of Byzantium, Ethnika
      ed. A. Meinecke, Stephani Byzantii Ethni-
      corvm quae svpersvnt (Berlin: Reimer; repr.
      Graz: Akademische Druck- u. Verlagsan-
      stalt, 1958).

Stephen Mansūr, The Passio of St. Romanos
the Neomartyr
      ed. P. Peeters, "Saint Romain le Néomartyr (+
      1er mai 780) d'après un document géorgien,"
      Analecta Bollandiana 30 (1911): 393–427.

Strabo, *Geographica*
　　ed. K. Müller, *Geographi graeci minores* (Paris: Firmin Didot, 1855–1882).

Stubbs, W.
1864　*Itinerarium peregrinorum et gesta Regis Ricardi*, in *Chronicles and Memorials of the Reign of Richard I*, vol. 1, [Rerum Britannicarum medii aevi scriptores 38] (London, 1864); English transl. H. Nicholson, *Book Chronicle of the Third Crusade* (Brookfield: Ashgate, 1997).

Richard, J.
1983　*Le livre des remembrances de la secrète du royaume de Chypre (1468–1469)*, ed. J. Richard, with the collaboration of Th. Papadopoullos (Nicosia: Centre de Recherches Scientifiques).

Tabari, Muhammad bn. Jarīr. *Taʿrīkh al-Rusul waʾl Mulūk* [Annals of Prophets and Kings]
　　ed. M. Ibrāhīm (Cairo: Dar al-Maʿarif, 1960–1969); partial French transl. Mansouri (2001a), *see entry above.*

Theodore Lector, *Historia ecclesiastica*
　　ed. G.C. Hansen, *Theodoros Anagnostes. Kirchengeschichte* (Berlin: Akademie-Verlag, 2nd ed. 1995).

Theodosios the Monk, *Vita Leontii patriarchae hierusalemi*
　　ed.and transl. D. Tsougarakis, *The Life of Leontios Patriarch of Jerusalem. Text, Translation, Commentary* (Leiden: Brill, 1993).

Theophanes the Confessor, *Chronographia*
　　ed. C. de Boor, *Theophanis Chronographia* (Leipzig: Teubner, 1885); Engl. transl. and commentary C. Mango and R. Scott, *The Chronicle of Theophanes Confessor: Byzantine and Near Eastern History AD 284–813* (Oxford: Oxford University, 1997).

Theophylact Simocatta, *Historiae*
　　ed. C. De Boor and P. Wirth (Stuttgart, 1972); Engl. Transl. M. and M. Whitby, *The History of Theophylact Simocatta: An English Translation, with Introduction* (Oxford: Oxford University, 1986).

Thomas, J., and Hero, A.
2000　*Byzantine Monastic Foundation Documents*, ed. in 5 vols. (Washington, DC: Dumbarton Oaks Research Library and Collection).

Whitby, Michael, and Whitby, Mary
1989　*Chronicon Paschale 284–628 AD*, Engl. Transl. (Liverpool: Liverpool University).

Yaqut ibn ʿAbd Allāh al-Ḥamawī, *Kitāb muʾjam al-buldān* [Dictionary of Writers]
　　(Beirut: Dār Ṣādir, 1955–1957)

SECONDARY SOURCES

NOTE: For ease of referencing, authors with Modern Greek names and publishers were transliterated, unless they had an established Latinized name. Titles were left in Modern Greek.

Abicht, R., and Reichelt, C.
1898 "Quellennachweise zum Codex Supra-sliensis," *Archiv für Slavische Philologie* 20: 181–200.

Adovasio, J.; Fry, G.; Gunn, J.; and Maslowski, R.
1975 "Prehistoric and Historic Settlement Patterns in Western Cyprus," *World Archaeology* 6: 339–364.

Ailes, M.
2003 *The History of the Holy War. Ambroise's Estoire de la Guerre Sainte* (Woodbridge: Boydell).

Aloupi, E.; Karydas, A.; and Paradellis, T.
2000 "Pigment Analysis of Wall Paintings and Ceramics from Greece and Cyprus. The Optimum Use of X-Ray Spectrometry on Specific Archaeological Issues," *X-Ray Spectrometry* 29: 18–24.

Alpago-Novello, A.; Berize, V.;
and Lafontaine-Dosogne, J.
1980 *Art and Architecture in Medieval Georgia* (Louvain-la-Neuve: Collège Érasme).

Al-Saad, Z.
2000 "Technology and Provenance of a Collection of Islamic Copper-based Objects as Found by Chemical and Lead Isotope Analysis," *Archaeometry* 42.2: 385–97.

Amiranašvili, S.
1971 *Georgian Metalwork from Antiquity to the 18th Century* (London: Hamlyn).

Anderson, J.
1979 "The Illustration of Cod. Sinai Gr. 339," *Art Bulletin* 61: 167–85.

Angelidē, Ch. et al.
1982 Παράλιος κυπριακὸς χῶρος. Ἀποδελτίωση πηγῶν καὶ καταγραφὴ μνημείων (μέσα 11ου–τέλη 13ου αἰ.) (Athens: Ethnikon Idryma Ereunōn).

Argoud, G.; Callot, O.; and Helly, B.
1980 *Une Residence Byzantine "L'Huilerie"* [Salamine de Chypre 11] (Paris: De Boccard).

Argyrou, Ch.
2001 "Παραστάσεις μουσικών οργάνων στις τοιχογραφημένες εκκλησίες της Κύπρου (12ος–16ος αιώνας). Η βυζαντινή παράδοση και δυτικές επιδράσεις," *Ἐπετηρίδα Κέντρου Μελετῶν Ἱερᾶς Μονῆς Κύκκου* 5: 215–43.
2007 "Όψεις του καθημερινού βίου μέσα από τη μνημειακή τέχνη της Κύπρου." Pp. 232–59 in *Κύπρος. Από την αρχαιότητα έως σήμερα*, edited by A. Maragkou, G. Georgēs, T.E. Sklavenitēs, and K.S. Staikos (Athens: Kotinos).

Aristeidou, A.
1990 *Ανέκδοτα έγγραφα της κυπριακής ιστορίας από το αρχείο της Βενετίας, τόμος Α' (1474-1508)* (Nicosia: Cyprus Research Centre).

Aristeidou, E.
1982 *The Tekke of Hala Sultan.* 2nd ed. (Nicosia: Cyprus Historical Museum).

Armstrong, P.
2006 "Rural Settlement in Lycia in the Eighth Century: New Evidence." Pp. 19–29 in *Proceedings of the 3rd Symposium on Lycia, 07-10 November 2005, Antalya* I, ed. K. Dörtlük et al. (Antalya: Suna & Inan Kiraç Research Institute on Mediterranean Civilizations).

2009   "Trade in the East Mediterranean in the 8th Century." Pp. 157–78 in *Byzantine Trade, 4th–12th Centuries. The Archaeology of Local, Regional and International Exchange. Papers of the Thirty-eighth Spring Symposium of Byzantine Studies, St John's College, Unviersity of Oxford, March 2004,* ed. M.M. Mango (Farnham: Ashgate).

Arnaud, P.
2005   *Les routes de la navigation antique. Itinéraires en Méditerranée* (Paris: Editions Errance).

Arthur, J., et al.
1891   "Excavations in Cyprus, 1890. Third Season's Work. Salamis," *The Journal of Hellenic Studies* 12: 59–198.

Asdracha, A.
2005a   "Θέμα Κύπρου." Pp. 199–233 in *Ἱστορία τῆς Κύπρου. Τόμος Γ'. Βυζαντινὴ Κύπρος,* ed. Th. Papadopoullos (Nicosia: Archbishop Makarios III Foundation).
2005b   "Ἡ Κύπρος ὑπὸ τοὺς Κομνηνούς (Α')." Pp. 293–347 in *Ἱστορία τῆς Κύπρου. Τόμος Γ'. Βυζαντινὴ Κύπρος,* ed. Th. Papadopoullos (Nicosia: Archbishop Makarios III Foundation).
2005c   "Ἡ Κύπρος ὑπὸ τοὺς Κομνηνούς (Β')." Pp. 349–412 in *Ἱστορία τῆς Κύπρου. Τόμος Γ'. Βυζαντινὴ Κύπρος,* ed. Th. Papadopoullos (Nicosia: Archbishop Makarios III Foundation).

Asgati, N.
1995   "The Proconnesian Production of Architectural Elements in Late Antiquity, Based on Evidence from the Marble Quarries." Pp. 263–88 in *Constantinople and its Hinterland, Papers from the Twenty-seventh Spring Symposium of Byzantine Studies, Oxford, April 1993,* ed. C. Mango and G. Dagron [Society for the Promotion of Byzantine Studies 3] (Aldershot: Variorum).

Ault, B.A., and Leonard, J.
forthcoming   "The Akrotiri-*Dreamer's Bay,* Ancient Port Project: Ancient Kourias

found?" In *The Ancient Kourion Area: Penn Museum's Legacy and Recent Research in Cyprus. Proceedings of a Conference held at the University of Pennsylvania Museum of Archaeology and Anthropology, March 27–29, 2009,* ed. E. Herscher (Philadelphia: The University Museum of Archaeology and Anthropology).

Aupert, P.
1996   *Guide de l'Amathonte* [Sites et monuments 15] (Paris: École Française d'Athènes).

Aupert, P., and Flourentzos, P.
2008   "Helios, Adoni et Magie: Les Tresors d'une Citerne d'Amathonte" *Bulletin de Correspondance Hellénique* 132: 311–46.

Aupert, P., and Leriche, P.
1994   "Fortifications et Histoire a Amathonte," *Revue des Études Anciens* 96: 1–2, 337–348.

Avenarius, A
2000   *Die byzantinische Kultur und die Slawen. Zum Problem der Rezeption und der Transformation (6. bis 12. Jahrhundert)* [Veröffentlichungen des Instituts für Österreichische Geschichtsforschung 34] (Vienna: Oldenbourg).

Aviam, M.
1993   "Horvat Hesheq: A Church in Upper Galilee." Pp. 54–65 in *Ancient Churches Revealed,* ed. Y. Tsafrir (Jerusalem: Israel Exploration Society).

Avigad, N.
1993   "The Nea: Justinian's Church of St. Mary, Mother of God Discovered." Pp. 128–35 in *Ancient Churches Revealed,* ed. Y. Tsafrir (Jerusalem: Israel Exploration Society).

Babić, G.
1969   *Les Chapelles Annexes des Églises Byzantines, Fonction Liturgique et Programmes Iconographique* (Paris: Klincksieck)
1980   "Les programmes apsidaux en Géorgie et dans les Balkans entre le XIe et le XIIIe

siècle." Pp. 117–36 in *L'Arte Georgiana dal IX al XIV secolo, Atti del Terzo simposio internazionale dell'arte Georgiana, Bari-Lecce, 14–18 ottobre 1980*, ed. M. Mariani (Galatina: Congedo Editore).

Bagatti, B.
1952–53 "Espressioni bibliche nelle antiche iscrizioni cristiane della Palestina," *Liber Annuus* 3: 111–48.

Bağışkan, T.
2009 *Ottoman, Islamic and Islamised Monuments in Cyprus* (Nicosia: Cyprus Turkish Education Foundation).

Baird, D.
1985 "Survey in Peyia Village Territory, Paphos, 1983," *Report of the Department of Antiquities Cyprus*: 340–49.

Bakirtzis, Ch.
1976 "Παλαιοχριστιανική Βασιλική στους Γιορκούς ΒΑ της Αγηαίνου," *Report of the Department of Antiquities Cyprus* 1976: 260–66.
1995 "The Role of Cyprus in the Grain Supply of Constantinople in the Early Christian Period." Pp. 247–53 in *Cyprus and the Sea: Proceedings of the International Symposium, Nicosia, 25–26 September 1993*, ed. V. Karageorghis and D. Michaelides (Nicosia: University of Cyprus).
1997 "Η θαλάσσια διαδρομή Κύπρου-Αιγαίου στα παλαιοχριστιανικά χρόνια." Pp. 327–32 in *Η Κύπρος και το Αιγαίο στην Αρχαιότητα* [Proceedings of the International Archaeological Conference "Cyprus and the Aegean in Antiquity" from the Prehistoric Period to the 7th Century AD, Nicosia, 8–10 December 1995] (Nicosia: Department of Antiquities).
1999 "Early Christian Rock Cut Tombs at Hagios Georgios, Peyia, Cyprus." Pp. 35–41 in *Medieval Cyprus*, ed. N. Ševčenko and C. Moss (Princeton: Princeton University).
2001 "Αποτελέσματα ανασκαφών στον Αγιο Γεώργιο Πέγειας (Ακρωτήριον Δρέπανον),

1991–1995." Pp. 155–70 in *Πρακτικά τοθ Γ΄ Διεθνούς Κυπρολογικού Συνεδρίοθ* (Λεθκωσία, 16–20 Απριλίου 1996).
2002 "Pilgrimage to Thessalonike: The Tomb of St. Demetrios," *Dumbarton Oaks Papers* 56: 175–92.

Balance, M.; Boardman, J.; Corbet, S.; and Hood, S.
1989 *Excavations in Chios 1952–1955, Byzantine Emporio* [British School of Archaeology Supplement 20] (London: Thames and Hudson).

Balderstone, S.
2007 *Early Church Architectural Forms: A Theologically Contextual Typology for the Eastern Churches of the 4th–6th centuries* (Melbourne: Australian Institute of Archaeology).

Baldini Lippolis, I.
1999 *L'oreficeria nell'impero di Costantinopoli fra IV e VII secolo* (Bari: Edipuglia).

Baldovin, J.F.
1987 *The Urban Character of Christian Worship. The Origins, Development, and Meaning of Stational Liturgy* [Orientalia Christiana Analecta 228] (Rome: Pontificium Institutum Studiorum Orientalium).

Baltoyianni, Ch.
1993–94 "Christ the Lamb and the ἐνώτιον of the Law in a Wall Painting of Araka on Cyprus," *Δελτίον της Χριστιανικής Αρχαιολογικής Εταιρείας* 17: 53–58.

Balty, J.
1984 "Les mosaïques de Syrie au Ve siècle et leur répertoire," *Byzantion* 54: 437–68.

Baratte, F., and Bejaoui, F.
2001 "Églises urbaines, églises rurales dans la Tunisie paléochrétienne: Nouvelles recherches d'architecture et d'urbanisme," *Comptes rendus des séances de l'Académie des Inscriptions et Belles-Lettres* 145.4: 1447–98.

Barla, Ch.
1965 "Ἀνασκαφὴ Κεφάλου Ἀμβρακικοῦ,"
      Πρακτικὰ τῆς ἐν Ἀθήναις Ἀρχαιολογικῆς
      Ἑταιρείας 1965: 78–84.

Bartl, K., and al-Razzaq Moaz, A. (eds.)
2008 Residences, Castles, Settlements. Transfor-
      mation Processes from Late Antiquity to
      Early Islam in Bilad al-Sham. [Proceedings
      of the International Conference held at
      Damascus, 5–9 November 2006] (Rahden:
      Leidorf).

Bellinger, A.; Grierson, P.; and Hendy, M.
1966–99) Catalogue of the Byzantine Coins in the
      Dumbarton Oaks Collection and in the
      Whittemore Collection (Washington, DC:
      Dumbarton Oaks Research Library and
      Collection).

Belting, H.
1996 Likeness and Presence. A History of the
      Image before the Era of Art (Chicago: Uni-
      versity of Chicago).

Bihalji-Merin, O. (ed.)
1969 Art Treasures of Yugoslavia (New York:
      Abrams).

Blue, L.
1997 "Cyprus and Cilicia: The Typology and
      Paleogeography of Second Millennium
      Harbors." Pp. 31–43 in Res Maritimae, Cy-
      prus and the Eastern Mediterranean from
      Prehistory to Late Antiquity, Proceedings of
      the Second International Symposium "Cities
      and the Sea," Nicosia, October 8–22, 1994, ed.
      S. Swiny, R. Hohlfelder, and H. Swiny [ARS
      4/CAARI Monograph 1] (Atlanta: Scholars).

Bormpoudakis, M.
2004 "Ἀνασκαφή Μητροπόλεως." Pp. 617–36 in
      Creta Romana e Protobizantina, Atti del
      Congresso Internazionale, Iraklion 23–30
      Settembre 2000, vol. 2 (Padova: Bottega
      d'Erasmo).

Bouras, Ch.
1977–79 "Twelfth and thirteenth century varia-
      tions of the single domed octagon plan,"
      Δελτίον τῆς Χριστιανικῆς ἀρχαιολογικῆς
      ἑταιρείας 9: 21–32.
1981 Η Νέα Μονή της Χίου, Ιστορία και αρχι-
      τεκτονική (Athens: Emporikē Trapeza tēs
      Ellados) [english transl. D. Hardy, 1982].
2006 Byzantine and Post-Byzantine Architecture
      in Greece (Athens: Melissa).

Bowden, W.
2001 "A New Urban Elite? Church Builders and
      Church Building in Late-Antique Epirus."
      Pp. 57–68 in Recent Research in Late-
      Antique Urbanism, ed. L. Lavan [Journal
      of Roman Archaeology Supplement 42]
      (Portsmouth: JRA).

Bowersock, G.W.
2000 The International Role of Late Antique Cy-
      prus, 14th Annual Lecture on the History
      and Archaeology of Cyprus (Nicosia: Bank
      of Cyprus Cultural Foundation).

Bowersock, G., and Brown, P.
1999 Late Antiquity: A Guide to the Postclassical
      World (Cambridge: Belknap).

Boyd, S.
1999 "Champlevé Production in Early Byzantine
      Cyprus." Pp. 49–62 in Medieval Cyprus:
      Studies in Art, Architecture, and History in
      Memory of Doula Mouriki, ed. N. Ševčenko
      and C. Moss (Princeton: Princeton Univer-
      sity).
2007 "The Champlevé Revetments." Pp. 235–301
      in Kourion. Excavations in the Episcopal
      Precinct, eds. A.H.S. Megaw et al. [Dumbar-
      ton Oaks Studies 38] (Cambridge: Harvard
      University).

Brandes, W., and Haldon, J.
2000 "Towns, Tax and Transformation: States,
      Cities, and their Hinterlands in the East
      Roman World, c. 500–800." Pp. 141–72 in
      Towns and their Territories between Late

Antiquity and the Early Middle Ages, eds. G. Broglioglo et al., [Transformation of the Roman World 9] (Leiden: Brill).

Briois, F.; Petit-Aupert, C.; and Péchoux, P.-Y.
2005 *Histoire de campagnes d'Amathonte* I. *L'occupation du sol au néolithique* [Études chypriotes 16] (Athens: École Francaise d'Athènes).

Brock, S.
1973 "An Early Syriac Life of Maximus the Confessor," *Analecta Bollandiana* 91: 299–346.

Brouskari, E., et al.
2008 *EGERIA: Monuments of Faith in the Medieval Mediterranean* (Athens: Hellenic Ministry of Culture).

Brown, P.
1978 *The Making of Late Antiquity* (Cambridge: Harvard University).

Browning, R.
1977–79 "Byzantium and Islam in Cyprus in the Early Middle Ages," *Επετηρίς της Κυπριακή Εταιείας Ιστορικόν Σπούδων* 9: 101–16.

Brubaker, L., and Haldon, J.
2001 *Byzantium in the Iconoclast Era (ca. 680–850)* [Birmingham Byzantine and Ottoman monographs 7] (Aldershot: Ashgate).

Bryer, A.A.M., and Georghallides, G.S.
1993 *'The Sweet Land of Cyprus.' Papers Given at the Twenty-Fifth Jubilee Spring Symposium of Byzantine Studies (Birmingham, March 1991)* (Nicosia: Birmingham, Cyprus Research Centre and the Society for the Promotion of Byzantine Studies).

Buchwald, H.
2009 "Western Asia Minor as a Generator of Architectural Forms in the Byzantine Period, Provincial Backwash or Dynamic Center of Production?" Pp. 199–234 in *Forms, Style and Meaning in Byzantine Church Architecture* (Aldershot: Variorum).

Buckler, W.
1933 "Frescoes at Galata, Cyprus," *The Journal of Hellenic Studies,* 53: Part 1: 105–10.
1946 "Tour in Cyprus, 1934," *The Journal of Hellenic Studies* 66: 61–65.

Butzer, K., and Harris, S.
2007 "Geoarchaeological Approaches to the Environmental History of Cyprus: Explication and Critical Evaluation," *Journal of Archaeological Science* 34: 1932–52.

Buxton, H., et al.
1933 "The Church of Asinou, Cyprus and its Frescoes," *Archaeologia* 83: 327–50.

Byzantios, D.
1890 *Η Κωνσταντινούπολις Περιγραφή* (Athens: Estias).

Cadogan, G.
2004 "Hector Catling and the Genesis of the Cyprus Survey." Pp. 17–22 in *Archaeological Field Survey in Cyprus, Past History, Future Potentials,* ed. M. Iacovou [British School at Athens Supplement 11] (London: British School at Athens).

Callot, O.
2004 *Les monnaies. Fouilles de la ville 1964–1974* [Salamine de Chypre 16] (Paris: De Boccard).

Calvelli, L.
2009 *Cipro e la memoria dell'antico fra Medioevo e Rinascimento. La percezione del passato romano dell'isola nel mondo occidentale* (Venice: Istituto Veneto di Scienze, Lettere ed Arti).

Cameron, A.
1992 "Cyprus at the Time of the Arab Conquests." Pp. 27–49 in *Επετηρίς της Κυπριακή Εταιείας Ιστορικόν Σπούδων* 1; reprinted in A. Cameron, *Changing Cultures in Early Byzantium* (Aldershot: Variorum, 1996).

Campagnolo, M.; Courtois, C.; Martiniani-Reber, M.; and Michaelidou, L.
2006　*Chypre. D'Aphrodite à Mélusine* [Exhibtion catalogue] (Milan: Skira).

Caraher, W.; Moore, S.; Noller, J.; and Pettegrew, D.
2005　"The Pyla-Koutsopetria Archaeological project: First Preliminary Report (2003–2004 Seasons)," *Report of the Department of Antiquities Cyprus* 2005: 245–67.
2007　"The Pyla-Koutsepetria Archaeological Project," *Report of the Department of Antiquities Cyprus* 2007: 293–306.

Caraher, W.; Moore, S.; and Pettegrew, D.
2008　"Surveying Late Antique Cyprus," *Near Eastern Archaeology* 71: 81–89.

Carboni, S.
2001　*Glass from Islamic Lands: The al-Sabah Collection* (New York: Thames & Hudson).

Carr, A.W.
1987　*Byzantine Illumination, 1150–1250: The Study of a Provincial Tradition* (Chicago: University of Chicago).
2008　"Dumbarton Oaks and the Legacy of Byzantine Cyprus" *Near Eastern Archaeology* 71.1–2: 95–103.
forthcoming　"Images in Place: The Presentation of the Virgin in Asinou and Lagoudera," in *Proceedings of the 4th International Cyprological Congress, Lefkosia, 29 April–3 May 2008: B. Medieval* 2, ed. Ch. Chotzakoglou (Nicosia: Etaireīa Kypriakōn Spoudōn).

Carr, A.W., and Morrocco, L.
1991　*A Byzantine Masterpiece Recovered: The Thirteenth-Century Murals of Lysi, Cyprus* (Austin: University of Texas and the Menil Collection).

Carr, A.W., and Nicolaides, A. (eds.)
2013　*Asinou across Time: Studies in the Architecture and Murals of the Panagia Phorbiotissa, Cyprus* (Washington, DC: Dumbarton Oaks and Harvard University).

Catling, H.W.
1962　"Patterns Of Settlement in Bronze Age Cyprus," *Opuscula Atheniensia* 4: 129–69.
1972　"An Early Byzantine Pottery Factory at Dhiorios," *Levant* 4: 1–82.
1980　*Cyprus and the West, 1600–1050 B.C.* (Sheffield: Sheffield University).
1982　"The Ancient Topography of the Yialias Valley," *Report of the Department of Antiquities Cyprus* 1982: 227–36.
2008　"Appearance and Reality: Thoughts on the Interpretation of Archaeological Field Surveys." Pp. 200–215 in *Dioskouroi. Studies Presented to W. G. Cavanagh and C. B. Mee on the Anniversary of their 30-Year Joint Contribution to Aegean Archaeology*, ed. C. Gallou et al. [BAR-IS 1889] (Oxford: British Archaeological Reports).

Catling, H., and Dikigoropoulos, A.
1970　"The Kornos Cave: an Early Byzantine site in Cyprus," *Levant* 2: 43–59.

Cayla, J.-B.
2007　"Chypre," *L'Année Epigraphique 2004* (Paris, Presses Universitaires de France)

Chadwick, H.
1974　"John Moschus and His Friend Sophronius the Sophist," *Journal of Theological Studies* 25: 41–74.

Chalkia, E.
1991　*Le mense paleocristiane: tipologia e funzioni delle mense secondarie nel culto paleocristiano* (Vatican: Pontificio Istituto di archeologia cristiana).

Chaniotaki-Starida, L., and Marē, M.
2004　"Παλαιοχριστιανική Χερσόνησος." Pp. 288–99 in *Creta Romana E Protobizantina, Atti Del Congresso Internazionale* 2 (Padova: Bottega d'Erasmo).

Charalambous, E.N.
2012　*Τεχνολογία κατασκευής των επιδαπέδιων ψηφιδωτών της Κύπρου* (Nicosia: Ziti).

Charles-Gaffiot, J.
1991   *La France aux portes de l'orient. Chypre
        XIIème-XVème siècle* (Paris: Centre Culturel
        du Panthéon).

Chatzēchristodoulou, Ch.,
and Chatzēchristodoulou, D.
2002   *Ο ναός της Παναγίας της Ασίνου* [Οδηγοί
        Βυζαντινών Μνημείων Κύπρου] (Nicosia:
        Politistiko Idryma Trapezēs Kyprou).

Chatzēchristophē, Ph.
1997   "Το δάπεδο του Αγίου Προκοπίου στη
        Συγκραση," *Report of the Department of
        Antiquities Cyprus* 1997: 277–83.

Chatzēdakēs, M.
1948   "Ἀνασκαφαί ἐν Ἀθῆναις Κατά Τήν
        Βασιλικήν Τοῦ Ἰλισσοῦ," *Πρακτικὰ τῆς ἐν
        Ἀθήναις Ἀρχαιολογικῆς Ἑταιρείας,* 69–86.
1951   "Remarques sur la basilique de L'Ilissos,"
        Cahiers Archéologiques 5: 61–74.

Chatzēdakēs, M., et al.
1964   *Ἡ βυζαντινὴ τέχνη, τέχνη εὐρωπαϊκή.Ἐνάτη
        ἔκθεσις ὑπὸ τὴν αἰγίδα τοῦ Συμβουλίου τῆς
        Εὐρώπης.* Exhibition catalogue (Athens:
        Upēresia Archaiotētōn kai Anastēlōseōn).

Chatzēpaschales, A., and Iakovou, M.
1989   *Χάρτες Καὶ Ἄτλαντες* (Nicosia: Politistiko
        Idryma Trapezēs Kyprou).

Chatzētryphonos, E.
2004   *Το Περίστωo Στην Υστεροβυζαντινή
        Εκκλησιαστική Αρχιτεκτονική, Σχεδια-
        σμός-Λειτουργία* (Thessalonike: Europaiko
        Kentro Vyzantinon kai Metavyzantinon
        Mnemeion).

Chatzioannou, K.
1973   *Ἡ ἀρχαία Κύπρος Εἰς Τάς ἑλληνικάς Πηγάς*
        2 (Nicosia).
1988a   *Λεοντίου Επισκόπου Νεαπόλεως Κύπρου,
        Βίος Του Αγίου Ιωάννου Του Ελεήμονος*
        (Nicosia).
1988b   "Τα Μοναστηριακά Ιδρύματα Του Αγίου
        Ιωάννου Του Ελεήμονος Στην Αμαθούντα

Και Οι Ανασκαφές Του Τμήματος
Αρχαιοτήτων," *Report of the Department
of Antiquities Cyprus* 1988.2: 235–38.

Cheynet, J.-C.
1994   "Chypre à la veille de la conquête franque."
        Pp. 67–77 in *Les Lusignans et l'Outre-
        Mer* [Actes du colloque. Poitiers-Lusignan,
        20–24 Octobre 1993] (Poitiers: Université
        de Poitiers).

Chotzakoglou, Ch.
2005   "Βυζαντινή ἀρχιτεκτονική Και Τέχνη Στήν
        Κύπρο." Pp. 464–787 in *Ιστορία Τῆς Κύπρου*
        3, ed. Th. Papadopoulos (Nicosia: Archbi-
        shop Makarios III Foundation).

Christides, V.
2006   *The Image of Cyprus in the Arabic Sources*
        (Nicosia: Archbishop Makarios III Founda-
        tion).

Christodoulou, D.
1959   *The Evolution of the Rural Land Use Pattern
        in Cyprus* [Regional Monograph 2] (Bude,
        Cornwall: Geographical Publications).

Christoforaki, I.
1996   "Cyprus between Byzantium and the Le-
        vant: Eclecticism and Interchange in the
        Cycle of the Life of the Virgin in the Church
        of the Holy Cross at Pelendri," *Επετηρίδα*
        22: 215–55.

Christou, D.
1993   *Annual Report of the Department of An-
        tiquities Cyprus* (Nicosia: Department of
        Antiquities).
1998   "Chypre L'Ile aux Cent Basiliques: Kourion.
        La Basilique Portuaire," *Le Monde de la
        Bible* 112: 50–51.
2008   *Kourion: its Monuments and Local Museum*
        [Guide, 10th edition] (Nicosia: Philokipros).

Chronopoulos, I.
2010   *Ηράκλειος ως ο Μέγας Αλέξανδρος του
        Βυζαντίου* (Athens: Periskopio).

Chrysos, E.
1984 "Ὁ Ἡράκλειος Στην Κύπρο." Pp. 53–62 in Πρακτικά Συμποσίου Κυπριακής Ιστορίας (Λευκωσία 2–3 Μαΐου 1983), ed. N. Constaninides, (Ioannina: Ekdosē Tomea Istorias Panepistemiou Ioanninon).
1993 "Cyprus in Early Byzantine Times." Pp. 3–14 in 'The Sweet Land of Cyprus.' Papers Given at the Twenty-Fifth Jubilee Spring Symposium of Byzantine Studies (Birmingham, March 1991) eds. A. Bryer and G. Georghallides (Nicosia: Cyprus Research Centre).
1999 "Ἀπὸ Τὴν ἱστορία Τοῦ Μοναχισμοῦ Στὴν Κύπρο Τὸν 7ο Αἰῶνα," Ἐπετηρὶς Κέντρου Μελετῶν Ἱερᾶς Μονῆς Κύκκου 4: 205–18.

Chrysostomos, Abbot of Kykkos Monastery
1969 Η Ιερά Βασιλική και Σταυροπηγιακή Μονή του Κύκκου (Nicosia: Mouseion Ieras Monēs Kykkou).

Coche de la Ferté, É.
1957 Collection Hélène Stathatos: Les Objets byzantins et post-byzantins (Limoges: Bontemps).

Committee for the Protection
of the Cultural Heritage of Cyprus
1998 Cyprus: A Civilization Plundered (Athens: The Hellenic Parliament).

Constantinides, C.N., and Browning, R.
1993 Dated Greek Manuscripts from Cyprus to the Year 1570 (Nicosia: Cyprus Research Centre).

Cook, H.K.A., and Green, J.
2002 "Medieval Glazed Wares from the Theatre Site at Nea Pafos, Cyprus: Preliminary Report," Report of the Department of Antiquities Cyprus 2002: 413–26.

Consolino, F.E.
1982 "Usener e l'agiografia: Legenden der Heiligen Pelagia e Der heilige Tychon." Pp. 161–80 in Aspetti di Hermann Usener, filologo della religione, ed. G. Arrighetti and A. Momigliano (Pisa: Giardini).

Corner, F.
1758 Notizie storiche delle chiese e monasteri di Venezia, e di Torcello tratte dalle chiese veneziane e torcellane (Padova: Nella stamperia del Seminario appresso G. Manfrè).

Corrie, R.W.
1997 "Icon with the Virgin and Child (front) and Saint James the Persian (back)." Pp. 127–29 (no. 75) in The Glory of Byzantium: Art and Culture of the Middle Byzantine Era, A.D. 843–1261 (New York: Metropolitan Museum of Art).

Corrigan, K.
1995 "Text and Image on an Icon of the Crucifixion at Mount Sinai." pp. 45–62 in The Sacred Image: East and West, ed. R. Ousterhout and L. Brubaker (Chicago: University of Illinois).

Craddock, P.T.
1978 "The Composition of the Copper Alloys Used by the Greek, Etruscan and Roman Civilizations," Journal of Archaeological Science 5: 1–16.
1979 "The Copper Alloys of the Medieval Islamic World – Inheritors of the Classical Tradition," World Archaeology 11.1: 68–79.
1995 Early Metal Mining and Production (Edinburgh: Edinburgh University).

Craddock, P.T.; La Niece, S.; and Hook, D.R.
1990 "Brass in the Medieval Islamic World." Pp. 73–101 in 2000 Years of Zinc and Brass, ed. P.T. Craddock [British Museum Occasional Paper, 50] (London: British Museum).

Croddy, S.
1999 "Gothic Architecture and Scholastic Philosophy," British Journal of Aesthetics 39.3: 263–72.

Crowfoot, J.W.
1931 Churches at Jerash, A Preliminary Report of the Joint Yale-British School Expeditions at Jerash, 1928–1930 (London: Beccles).

Crowfoot, G., and Harden, D.
1931 "Early Byzantine and Later Glass Lamps," *Journal of Egyptian Archaeology* 17: 196–208.

Cuming, G.J.
1990 *The Liturgy of St. Mark* (Rome: Pontificium Institutum Studiorum Orientalium).

Ćurčić, S.
1977a "Domed Bemas in Byzantine Churches: Architecture vs. Iconography," *Byzantine Studies Conference Abstracts of Papers* 3: 49–51.
1977b "Architectural Significance of Subsidiary Chapels in Middle Byzantine Churches," *Journal of the Society of Architectural Historians* 36.2: 94–110.
1996 "From the Temple of the Sun to the Temple of the Lord: Monotheistic Contribution to Architectural Iconography in Late Antiquity." Pp. 56–59 in *Architectural Studies in Memory of Richard Krautheimer*, ed. C.L. Striker (Mainz: von Zabern).
1999 "Byzantine Architecture on Cyprus: An Introduction to the Problem of the Genesis of a Regional Style." Pp. 71–94 in *Medieval Cyprus. Studies in Art, Architecture, and History in Memory of Doula Mouriki*, eds. N. Patterson-Ševčenko and C. Moss (Princeton: Princeton University).
2000 *Middle Byzantine Architecture on Cyprus: Provincial or Regional?* [13th Annual Lecture on the History and Archaeology of Cyprus] (Nicosia: Bank of Cyprus Cultural Foundation).
2010 *Architecture in the Balkans* (New Haven: Yale University).

Curta, F.
2000 Review of A. Avenarius, *Die byzantinische Kultur und die Slawen. Zum Problem der Rezeption und der Transformation,* in *Bryn Mawr Classical Review* 2000.12.04, online at http://bmcr.brynmawr.edu/2000/2000-12-04.html.

Curzon, R.
1849 *A Visit to the Monasteries in the Levant* (London: Murray).

Dalton, O.M.
1911 *Byzantine Art and Archaeology* (Oxford: Clarendon).

Dauphin, C.
1993 "A Byzantine Ecclesiastical Farm at Shelomi." Pp. 43–48 in *Ancient Churches Revealed*, ed. Y. Tsafrir (Jerusalem: Israel Exploration Society).

Dauphin, C., and Edelstein, G.
1993 "The Byzantine Church At Nahariya." Pp. 49–53 in *Ancient Churches Revealed*, ed. Y. Tsafrir (Jerusalem: Israel Exploration Society).

Davis, T.
2008 "What's in a Name: CAARI at 30," *Near Eastern Archaeology* 71.1–2: 16–20.
2010 "Earthquakes and the Crises of Faith: Social Transformation in Late Antique Cyprus," *Buried History* 46: 3–14.
forthcoming "An Amateur's Dream: McFadden at Kourion." In *The Ancient Kourion Area: Penn Museum's Legacy and Recent Research in Cyprus,* ed. E. Herscher (Philadelphia: The University Museum of Archaeology and Anthropology).

Deckers, K.
2005 "Post-Roman History of River Systems in Western Cyprus: Causes and Archaeological Implications," *Journal of Mediterranean Archaeology* 18: 155–81.

Delatte, A.
1947 *Les portulans grecs* (Liège: Faculté de Philosophie et Lettres).

Delehaye, H.
1907 "Les sources de l'hagiographie cypriote," *Analecta Bollandiana* 26: 233–73.

Deligiannakis, G.
2008   "The Economy of the Dodecanese in Late Antiquity." Pp. 209–33 in *Sailing in the Aegean. Readings on the Economy and Trade Routes*, eds. Ch. Papageorgiadou-Banis and A. Giannnikouri [Research Centre for Greek and Roman Antiquity Meletemata 53] (Athens: National Hellenic Research Foundation).

Delvoye, C.
1972   "La place de Chypre dans l'architecture paléochrétienne de la Méditerranée." Pp. 17–21 in *Πρακτικά του Πρώτου Διεθνούς Κυπρολογικού Συνέδριου, Λευκωσία, 14–19 Απρίλιου 1969* 2 (Nicosia).
1976   "L'art paléochrétien de Chypre." Pp. 2–60 in *XVe Congrès international d'études Byzantines: rapports et co-rapports* 4 [Chypre dans le Monde Byzantine 5] (Athens).
1978   "La place des grandes basiliques de Salamine de Chypre dans l'architecture paléochrétienne," *Bulletin de l'Académie Royale de Belgique*, ser. 5, 64: 75–89.
1980   "La place des grandes basiliques de Salamine de Chypre dans l'architecture paléochrétienne." Pp. 313–27 in *Salamine de Chypre. Histoire et archéologie*, ed. M. Yon (Paris: Déroche).

Demesticha, S.
2003   "Amphora Production on Cyprus during the Late Roman Period." Pp. 469–76 in *VIIe Congrès international sur la céramique médieévale en Méditerranée, Thessaloniki, 11–16 Octobre 1999*, ed. Ch. Bakirtzis (Athens: Archaeological Receipts Fund).

Demosthenous, A.
2007   "Interpreting Byzantine Cyprus: Two Essays," *Byzantinoslavica* 65.1: 153–66.

Demus, O.
1949   *The Mosaics of Norman Sicily* (London: Routledge and Kegan Paul).

Der Parthog, G.
2006   *Medieval Cyprus: A Guide to the Byzantine and Latin Monuments* (Nicosia: Moufflon).

Diamanti, Ch.
2010   "Stamped Late Roman/Proto-Byzantine Amphoras from Halasarna of Kos," *Rei Cretariae Romanae Fautorum, Acta* 41: 1–8.

Diederichs, C.
1980   *Céramiques hellénistiques, romaines et Byzantines* [Salamine de Chypre 9] (Paris: De Boccard).

Dikigoropoulos, A.I.
1940–48   "The political status of Cyprus A.D. 648–965," *Report of the Department of Antiquities Cyprus* 1940–48: 94–114.
1956   "A Byzantine Hoard from Kharcha, Cyprus," *The Numismatic Chronicle* 16: 255–65.
1961   "Cyprus 'betwixt Greeks and Saracens,' A.D. 647–965." Unpublished D.Phil. dissertation, Oxford University (Lincoln College) [MSS.D.Phil.d.2530-1].
1965–66   "The Church of Cyprus during the Period of the Arab Wars," *The Greek Orthodox Theological Review* 11: 237–79.
1978   "Agrarian Conditions and the Demography of Cyprus during the period of the Arab Wars AD 648–965," *Γεωγραφικά Χρονικά (Bulletin of the Cyprus Geographical Association)* 8.13: 3–14.

Dix, G.
1945   *The Shape of the Liturgy* (London: Dacre).

Djobadze, W.
1984   "Observations on the Georgian monastery of Yalia (Galia) in Cyprus," *Oriens Christianus* 68: 196–209.

Donceel-Voûte, P.
1995   "L'inévitable chapelle des martyrs: identification." Pp. 179–96 in *Martyrium In Multidisciplinary Perspective: Memorial Louis Reekmans*, eds. M. Lamberigts and P. Van Deun (Leuven: Peeters).
1998   "Le Fonctionnement des lieux de culte aux VIe–VIIe siècles: Monuments, textes et images." Pp. 97–156 in *Acta XIII Congressus Internationalis Archaeologiae Christianae: Split-Poreč 25.9–1.10.1994*, vol. 2 (Vatican:

Pontificio Istituto de Archeologia Cristiana).

Downey, G.
1958 "The Claim of Antioch to Ecclesiastical Jurisdiction over Cyprus," *Proceedings of the American Philosophical Society* 102: 224–28.

Drosogianni, Ph.
1963 "Μεσαιωνικά Μακεδονίας," *Αρχαιολογικόν Δελτίον* 18.2: 235–54.

Ducellier, A.
1990 *L'Église byzantine entre pouvoir et esprit (313-1204)* (Paris: Desclée).

Dunn A.W.
1998 "Heraclius, 'Reconstruction of Cities,' and their Sixth Century Balkan Antecedents." Pp. 705–806 in *Acta XIII Congressus Internationalis Archaeologiae Christianae: Split-Poreč 25.9-1.10.1994*, vol. 2 (Vatican: Pontificio Istituto de Archeologia Cristiana).
2007 "Rural Producers and Markets: Aspects of the Archaeological and Historiographical Problem." Pp. 101–9 in *Material Culture and Well-Being in Byzantium (400-1453). Proceedings of the International Conference (Cambridge, 8-10 September 2001)*, ed. M. Grünbart et al. [Österreichische Akademie der Wissenschaften, philosophisch-historische Klasse, Denkschriften 356] (Vienna: Österreichische Akademie der Wissenschaften).

Du Plat Taylor, J.
1933 "A Water Cistern with Byzantine Paintings, Salamis, Cyprus," *The Antiquaries Journal* 13.2: 97–108.

Du Plat Taylor, J., and Megaw, A.H.S.
1980 "Excavations at Ayios Philon, the Ancient Carpasia, Part 1," *Report of the Department of Antiquities Cyprus* 1980: 152–216.
1981 "Excavations at Ayios Philon, the Ancient Carpasia, Part 2," *Report of the Department of Antiquities Cyprus* 1981: 209–50.

Duval, N.
1989 "Les Monuments D'Époque Chrétienne en Cyrénaïque." Pp. 2743–806 in *Actes Du XIe Congrès International d'Archéologie Chrétienne: Lyon, Vienne, Grenoble, Genève et Aoste 21.-28.9.1989*, vol.2, (Vatican: Pontificio Istituto di Archeologia Cristiana).

Dvornik, F.
1958 *The Idea of Apostolicity in Byzantium and the Legend of the Apostle Andrew* (Cambridge: Harvard University).

Dyggve, E.
1934 "Salona Christiana." Pp. 237–54 in *Atti del III Congresso Internationale di Archeologia Cristiana, Ravenna 1932* (Rome: Pontificio Istituto di Archeologia Cristiana).

Eastmond, A.
1998 *Royal Imagery in Medieval Georgia* (University Park: Pennsylvania State University).

Edwards, R.
1987 *The Fortifications of Armenian Cilicia* (Washington, DC: Dumbarton Oaks Research Library and Collection).

Efthymiadis, S.
2011 *The Ashgate Research Companion to Byzantine Hagiography: Periods and Places* (Aldershot: Ashgate).

Elton, H.
2006 "Church Decoration in Late Roman Lycia." Pp. 239–42 in *Proceedings of the 3rd Symposium on Lycia, 07–10 November 2005 I, Antalya*, ed. K. Dörtlük et al. (Antalya: Suna & Inan Kiraç Research Institute on Mediterranean Civilizations).

Englezakēs, V.
1979–80 "Ὁ ὅσιος Νεόφυτος ὁ Ἔγκλειστος καὶ αἱ ἀρχαὶ τῆς ἐν Κύπρῳ Φραγκοκρατίας," *Ἐπετηρὶς τοῦ Κέντρου Ἐπιστημονικῶν Ἐρευνῶν* 10: 31–83.
1995a "Epiphanius of Salamis, the Father of the Cypriot Autocephaly." Pp. 29–39 in *Studies*

on the History of the Church of Cyprus, 4th–20th Centuries (Aldershot: Variorum).

1995b "Cyprus Nea Justinianoupolis." Pp. 63–79 in Studies on the History of the Church of Cyprus, 4th–20th Centuries (Aldershot: Variorum).

Enlart, C.
1899 L'art gothique et la Renaissance en Chypre (Paris: Thorin); Gothic Art and the Renaissance in Cyprus, transl. D. Hunt (London: Trigraph, 1987).

Epalza, M. de
1991 "Mallorca bajo la autoridad compartida de Bizantinos y Arabes (siglos VIII–IX)." Pp. 145–48 in Homenaje a Juan Nadal, ed. J. Nadal Cañellas [Anuario de 1989] (Athens: Asociación Hispano-Helénica).

Esbroek, M. van
1985 "Les actes arméniens de saint Héraclide de Chypre," Analecta Bollandiana 103: 115–62.

Etinhof, O.
2003 "On the Date of the Wall Paintings of the Transfiguration Katholikon in the Miroz Monastery (Pskov)." Pp. 205–10 in Λαμπηδών. Αφιέρωμα στην μνήμη της Ντούλας Μουρίκης, ed. M. Aspra-Varvadake (Athens: Panespistemiakēs).

Evangelides, D.
1930–31 "Πρωτοβυζαντινὴ Βασιλικὴ Μυτιλήνης," Αρχαιολογικόν Δελτίον 13: 1–40.

Falkenhausen, V. von
1999 "Bishops and Monks in the Hagiography of Byzantine Cyprus." Pp. 21–33 Medieval Cyprus: Studies in Art, Architecture, and History in Memory of Doula Mouriki, eds. N. Patterson-Ševčenko and C. Moss (Princeton: Princeton University).

Farioli, R.O.
1969 Corpus de la Scultura di Ravenna 3 (Rome: De Luca).

Feissel, D.
1987 "Bulletin épigraphique-Chypre," Revue Études Greques 100: 380–81.

Fejfer J.
1995 Ancient Akamas I, Settlement and Environment (Aarhus: Aarhus University).

Fejfer, J., and Hayes, P.
1995 "Ancient Akamas and the Abandonment of Sites in 7th century A.D. Cyprus." Pp. 62–69 in Visitors, Immigrants, and Invaders in Cyprus, ed. P. Wallace (Albany: University of New York).

Felle, A.E.
2006 Biblia Epigraphica. La sacra scrittura nella documentazione epigrafica dell' Orbis christianus antiquus (III-VIII secolo) (Bari: Edipuglia).

Fergusson, J.
1874 A History of Architecture in All Countries (London: Mead).

Ferrazzoli, A., and Ricci, M.
2010 "Un centro di produzione delle anfore LR1: Elaiussa Sebaste in Cilicia (Turchia). Gli impianti, le anfore." Pp. 815–26 in LRCW 3. Late Roman Coarse Wares, Cooking Wares and Amphorae in the Mediterranean, Archaeology and Archaeometry, Comparison between Western and Eastern Mediterranean, eds. S. Menchelli et al. [British Archaeological Reports IS-2185] (Oxford: Archaeopress).

Flourentzos, P.
1996 Excavations in the Kouris Valley II: The Basilica of Alassa (Nicosia: Department of Antiquities Cyprus).

2003 Annual Report of the Department of Antiquities for the Year 2003 (Nicosia: Ministry of Communications and Works 2005).

2004 Annual Report of the Department of Antiquities for the Year 2004 (Nicosia: Ministry of Communications and Works 2006)

2004–5 "Chronique des fouilles et découvertes archéologiques à Chypre en 2003 et 2004," *Bulletin de Correspondance Hellénique* 128–29: 1635–1708.

2005 *Annual Report of the Department of Antiquities for the Year 2005* (Nicosia: Ministry of Communications and Works 2007)

2006 *Annual Report of the Department of Antiquities for the Year 2006* (Nicosia: Ministry of Communications and Works 2008)

2008 "The Swedish Cyprus Expedition and the Results of 15 Campaigns at the Site of Amathous Lower Town." Pp. 119–47 in *The Swedish Cyprus Expedition, 80 Years*, eds. P. Åström and K. Nys [Studies in Mediterranean Archaeology-Pocket-book 175] (Sävedalen: Åström).

Foerster, G.
1989 "Decorated Marble Chancel Screens in Sixth Century Synagogues in Palestine and their Relation to Christian Art and Architecture." Pp. 1809–20 in *Actes du XIe Congrès International D' Archéologie Chrétienne, (Lyon, Vienne, Grenoble, Genève et Aoste 21.–28.9.1989*, vol. 2 (Vatican: Pontificio Istituto di Archeologia Cristiana).

Forsyth, G., and Weitzmann, K.
1973 *The Monastery of Saint Catherine at Mount Sinai: The Church and Fortress of Justinian* (Ann Arbor: University of Michigan).

Foss, C.
1991 "Charsianon," *The Oxford Dictionary of Byzantium* 1 (Oxford: Oxford University).

Foulias, A.
2004 "Η Ανεικονική Ζωγραφική στην Αγία Παρασκευή Γεροσκήπου," *Κυπριακαί Σπουδαί* 67–68: 123–45.

2005 "Άγιοι Σαράντα/Kirklar Tekke: Μια νέα παλαιοχριστιανική βασιλική," *Κυπριακαί Σπουδαί* 69: 3–24.

2006 *The Church of Our Lady Angeloktisti at Kiti, Larnaca* [guidebook] (Nicosia).

2008a "The church of Agia Paraskevi." Pp. 61–73 in *Geroskipou from Antiquity to the Present* (Nicosia: Municipality of Geroskipou).

2008b "Churches, Hermitages, Chapels and Cemeteries." Pp. 95–118 in *Geroskipou from Antiquity to the Present* (Nicosia: Municipality of Geroskipou).

2011 "Ανεικονικός διάκοσμος και μια πρώιμη βυζαντινή επιγραφή από τον ναόν της Αγίας Αθανασίας στο Ριζοκάρπασο," *Βυζαντινά* 31: 203–29.

Frend, W.H.C.
1996 *The Archaeology of Early Christianity* (London: Chapman).

Frigerio-Zeniou, S.
1998 *L'art "Italo-byzantin" à Chypre au XVIe siècle* (Venice: Institut Hellénique de Venise).

Gabrieli, S.
2008 "Towards a Chronology – The Medieval Coarse Ware from the Tomb in Icarus Street, Kato Pafos," *Report of the Department of Antiquities Cyprus* 2008: 423–54.

Gabrieli, R.; McCall, B.; and Green, J.
2001 "Medieval Kitchen Ware from the Theatre Site at Nea Pafos," *Report of the Department of Antiquities Cyprus* 2001: 335–56.

Gabrieli, R.; Jackson, M.; and Kaldelli, A.
2007 "Stumbling into the Darkness: Trade and Life in Post-Roman Cyprus." Pp. 791–80 *LRCW 2: Late Roman Coarse Wares, Cooking Wares and Amphorae in the Mediterranean: Archaeology and Archaeometry*, eds. M. Bonifay and J.-C. Treglia [British Archaeological Reports IS-1662] (Oxford: British Archaeological Reports).

Gagniers, J. des, and Tinh, T.T.
1985 *Soloi: Dix campagnes de fouilles (1964–1974)* (Sainte-Foy: Université Laval).

Gagoshidze, G.
2009 "Georgian Monastery in Gialia (Cyprus)." Pp. 254–55 in *Georgian Art. Proceedings of*

the 1st International Congress of Georgian Art June 21–29, ed. V. Beridze (Tblisi: Georgian Arts and Culture Center).

Galatariotou, C.
1991   (reprint 2004) *The Making of a Saint: The Life, Times and Sanctification of Neophytos the Recluse* (Cambridge: Cambridge University).
2000   "Neophytos: *Testamentary Rule* of Neophytos for the Hermitage of the Holy Cross near Ktima in Cyprus." Pp. 1338–73 in *Byzantine Monastic Foundation Documents* 4 (Washington, DC: Dumbarton Oaks Research Library and Collection).

Galavaris, G.
1970   *Bread and the Liturgy. The Symbolism of Early Christian and Byzantine Stamps* (Madison: University of Wisconsin).

Gamillscheg, E.
1997   "Zypern oder nicht Zypern? Methodische Überlegungen zu einer wichtigen Neuerscheinung," *Jahrbuch der Österreichischen Byzantinistik* 47: 239–43.

Gelzer, H.
1893   *Leontios' von Neapolis Leben des heiligen Iohannes des Barmherzigen, Erzbischofs von Alexandrien* (Freiburg: Mohr Siebeck).
1901   "Ungedruckte und ungenügend veröffentlichte Texte der Notitiae Episcopatuum, ein Beitrag zur byzantinischen Kirchen- und Verwaltungsgeschichte," *Abhandlungen der königlich bayerischen Akademie der Wissenschaften, Philosophisch-philologische und Historische Klasse* 21.3: 534–45.
1995   (reprint) *Patrum Nicaenorum nomina* (Leipzig: Teubner, 1898).

Georghallides, G.
1985   *Cyprus and the Governorship of Sir Ronald Storrs* [Texts and Studies of the History of Cyprus 13] (Nicosia: Cyprus Research Centre).

Georgiou, S.
2007   "Μερικές παρατηρήσεις για την οικονομία της Κύπρου κατά την περίοδο των Κομνηνών," *Επετηρίδα Κέντρου Επιστημονικών Ερευνών* 33: 21–75.
2010   "Η Κύπρος τὸν ΙΑ'καὶ τὸν ΙΒ'αἰώνα: ὄψεις μίας βυζαντινῆς ἐπαρχίας," *Ἐπετηρίδα Κέντρου Μελετῶν Ἱερᾶς Μονῆς Κύκκου* 9: 129–48.

Gerasimou, K.
2002   *Holy Bishopric of Morphou. 2000 Years of Art and Holiness* (Nicosia: Bank of Cyprus Cultural Foundation), pp. 242–43.

Ghazarian, J.
2000   *The Armenian Kingdom in Cilicia during the Crusades* (Surrey: Curzon).

Giangrande, C., et al.
1987   "Cyprus Underwater Survey, 1983–1984. A Preliminary Report," *Report of the Department of Antiquties Cyprus* 1987: 185–97.

Gill, M.A.V.
2002   *Amorium Reports, Finds I: The Glass (1987–1997)* [BAR International Series 1070] (Oxford: British Archaeological Reports).

Given, M.
2000   "Agriculture, Settlement and Landscape in Ottoman Cyprus," *Levant* 32: 215–36.
2007   "Mountain Landscapes on Early Modern Cyprus." Pp. 137–50 in *Between Venice and Istanbul. Colonial Landscapes in Early Modern Greece*, eds. S. Davies and J. L. Davis [*Hesperia* Supplement 40] (Princeton: American School of Classical Studies).

Given, M., et al.
1999   "The Sydney Cyprus Survey Project: An Interdisciplinary Investigation of Long-term Change in the North Central Troodos, Cyprus," *Journal of Field Archaeology* 26: 19–39.

Given, M.; Corley, H.; and Sollars, L.
2007 "Joining the Dots: Continuous Survey, Routine Practice and the Interpretation of a Cypriot Landscape (with interactive GIS and integrated data archive)," *Internet Archaeology* 20 [http://intarrch.ad.uk/journal/issue20/taesp_index.html].

Given, M.; Kassianidou, V.; Knapp, A.B.; and Noller, J.
2002 "Troodos Archaeological and Environmental Survey Project, Cyprus: Report on the 2001 Season," *Levant* 34: 25–38.

Given, M., and Knapp, A.B.
2003 *The Sydney Cyprus Survey Project: Social Approaches to Regional Archaeological Survey* [Monumenta Archaeologica 21] (Los Angeles: Cotsen Institute of Archaeology).

Gkioles, N.
2003 *Η χριστιανική τέχνη στην Κύπρο* (Nicosia: Mouseion Ieras Monēs Kykkou).

Gnoli, R.
1971 *Marmora Romana* (Roma: Edizioni dell'Elefante).

Goodwin, J.
1978 *A Historical Toponymy of Cyprus* (Nicosia: Goodwin, 3rd edition).

Goren, Y.; Mommsen, H.; and Klinger, J.
2009 "Non-destructive Provenance Study of Cuneiform Tablets Using Portable X-ray Fluorescence (pXRF)," *Journal of Archaeological Science* 38.3: 684–96.

Gounaridis, P.
1996 "The Economy of Byzantine Cyprus: Cyprus, an Ordinary Byzantine Province." Pp. 175–83 in *The Development of the Cypriot Economy. From the Prehistoric Period to the Present Day*, eds. V. Karageorghis and D. Michaelides (Nicosia: University of Cyprus and Bank of Cyprus).

Gounaris, G.
2000 *Εισαγωγή Στην Παλαιοχριστιανική Αρχαιολογία, Α΄ Αρχιτεκτονική* (Thessaloniki: University Studio).

Grabar, A.
1949 "Christian Architecture, East and West: From the Martyrium to the Church," *Archaeology* 2: 95–104.
1972 *Martyrium. Recherches sur le Culte des Reliques et l'Art Chrétien Antique* (London: Variorum, originally published in 1946).

Graham, A.; Winther Jacobson, K.; and Kassianidou, V.
2006 "Agia Marina-*Mavrovouni*. Preliminary Report of the Roman Settlement and Smelting Workshop in the Central Northern Foothills on the Troodos Mountains," *Report of the Department of Antiquities Cyprus* 2006: 345–66.

Graham, S.
2008 "Justinian and the Politics of Space." Pp. 53–77 in *Constructions of Space II: The Biblical City and Other Imagined Spaces*. eds. J. Berquist and C. Camp (New York: Clark).

Green, R.; Baker, G.; and Gabrieli, S.
2004 *Fabrika. An Ancient Theatre of Paphos* (Nicosia: Moufflon).

Gregory, T.E.
1987 "Circulation of Byzantine and Medieval Pottery in southwestern Cyprus." Pp. 199–213 in *Western Cyprus: Connections. An Archaeological Symposium held at Brock University, St. Catharines, Ontario, Canada, March 21–22, 1986*, ed. D.W. Rupp, [Studies in Mediterranean Archaeology 77] (Göteborg: Åström).
1993 "Byzantine and Medieval Pottery." Pp. 157–75 in *The Land of the Paphian Aphrodite 2, The Canadian Palaipaphos Survey Project, Artifact and Ecofactual Studies*, eds. L. Sørensen and D. Rupp [Studies in Mediterranean Archaeology 104.2] (Göteborg: Åström).

2001 "Cities of Late Roman Cyprus: Preliminary thoughts of Urban Change and Continuity." Pp. 715–26 in *Πρακτικά του Τρίτου Διεθνούς Κυπρλογικού Συνεδρίου (Λευκοσία, 16–20 Απριλιου 1996)*, vol. 2 (Nicosia: Society of Cypriot Studies).

Greifenhagen, A.
1974 *Schmuckarbeiten in Edelmetall*, vol. 2 (Berlin: Staatliche Museen Preussischer Kulturbesitz, Antikenabteilung).

Grierson, P.
1968 *Catalogue of the Byzantine Coins in the Dumbarton Oaks Collection and the Whittemore Collection*. Vol. 2: *Phocas to Theodosius III* (Washington, DC: Dumbarton Oaks Research Library and Collection).

Grivaud, G.
1998a "Formes et mythe de la *strateia* à Chypre," *Études Balkaniques* 5: 33–54.
1998b *Villages désertés à Chypre (fin XIIe–fin XIXe siècle)* [Μελέται καὶ Ὑπομνήματα 3] (Nicosia: Archbishop Makarios III Foundation).
2013 "Fortunes and Misfortunes of a Small Byzantine Foundation." Pp. 13–36 in *Asinou Across time: Studies in the Architecture and Murals of the Panagia Phorbiotissa, Cyprus*, eds. A.W. Carr and A. Nicolaïdès [Dumbarton Oaks Studies 43] (Cambridge: Harvard University).

Grossman, P.
1984 "Neue Funde aus dem Gebiet von Abu Mina." Pp. 141–51 in *Πρακτικά Του 10ου Διεθνούς Συνεδρίου Χριστιανικής Αρχαιολογίας Θεσσαλονίκη 1980*, vol. 2 (Vatican: Studi di Antichità Cristiana).
1989 *Abu Mina I. Die Gruftkirche und die Gruft* [Archäologische Veröffentlichungen 44] (Mainz: von Zabern).
2007 "Early Christian Architecture in Egypt and Its Relationship to the Architecture of the Byzantine World." Pp. 103–36 in *Egypt in the Byzantine World, 300–700*, ed. R. Bagnall (Cambridge: Cambridge University).

Guidobaldi, A.G.
2000 "Gli arredi liturgici: botteghe e produzioni." Pp. 265–73 in *Christiana Loca: Lo Spazio Cristiano Nella Roma del Primo Millennio*, ed. L. Pani Ermini (Rome: Palombi).
2002 "La Sculptura di Arredo Liturgico nelle Chiese di Roma: Il Momento Byzantino." Pp. 1479–524 in *Ecclesiae urbis* [*Atti del Congresso internazionale di studi sulle chiese di Roma (IV–X secolo), Roma, 4–10 settembre 2000*], vol. 3 (Vatican: Pontificio Istituto di Archeologia Cristiana).

Guidobaldi, A.G., and Barsanti, C.
2004 *Santa Sofia di Costantinopoli. L'arredo marmoreo della Grande Chiesa Giustinianea* (Vatican: Pontificio Istituto di Archeologia Cristiana).

Guillou, A.
1998 "La géographie historique de l'île de Chypre pendant la période byzantine (IVe–XIIe s.)," *Études Balkaniques* 5: 9–32.

Guimier-Sorbets, A.-M.
2005–6 "Perles et pirouettes: diverses formes, divers emplois du motif en mosaïque." Pp. 333–46 in *ΚΑΛΑΘΟΣ. Studies in Honour of Asher Ovadiah*, ed. by S. Mucznik [Assaph 10–11] (Tel Aviv: Tel Aviv University.

Gunnis, R.
1936 *Historic Cyprus. A Guide to its Towns, Villages, Monasteries and Castles* (Nicosia: Rustem),

Hackens, T.; McKerrell, H.; and Hours, M.
1977 *X-Ray Microfluorescence Analysis Applied to Archaeology* [PACT 1] (Strasbourg: Conseil de l'Europe).

Hackett, J.
1901 *A History of the Orthodox Church of Cyprus* (London: Methuen; reprint New York, Franklin, 1972).

Hadad, S.
1998 "Glass Lamps from the Byzantine through Mamluk Periods at Bet Shean, Israel," *Journal of Glass Studies* 40: 63–76.

Hadjichristophi, F.
2000 "Les pavements du VIe siècle à Chypre." Pp. 531–44 in Πρακτικά του Τρίτου Διεθνούς Κυπρλογικού Συνεδρίου (Λευκοσία, 16–20 Απριλίου 1996) I (Nicosia: Society of Cypriot Studies).

Hadjicosti, M.
1993 "Excavations At Pyla-*Koutsopetria*," *Annual Report of the Department of Antiquities*: 70–72.

Hadjisavvas, S.
1977 "The Archaeological Survey of Paphos. A Preliminary Report," *Report of the Department of Antiquities Cyprus* 1977: 222–31.
1991 Καταβολές I. Η αρχαιολογική επισκόπηση 20 κατεχομένων σήμερα χωριών της επαρχίας Αμμοχώστου (Nicosia: Department of Antiquities).
2000 "Chronique des fouilles et découvertes archéologiques à Chypre en 1999," *Bulletin de Correspondance Hellénique* 124: 665–99.
2001 *Annual Report of the Department of Antiquities for the Year 2001* (Nicosia: Ministry of Communications and Works 2007).
2002a "Chronique des fouilles et découvertes archéologiques à Chypre en 2001," *Bulletin de Correspondance Hellénique* 126: 691–728.
2002b *Annual Report of the Department of Antiquities for the Year 2002* (Nicosia: Ministry of Communications and Works, 2007).
2003 "Chronique des fouilles et découvertes archéologiques à Chypre en 2002," *Bulletin de Correspondance Hellénique* 127: 643–82.
2010 *Cyprus: Crossroads of Civilizations* (Nicosia: Government of the Republic of Cyprus).

Haldon, J.
1990 *Byzantium in the Seventh Century: The Transformation of a Culture* (Cambridge: Cambridge University).

2010 *Money, Power and Politics in Early Islamic Syria. A Review of Current Debates* (Farnham: Ashgate).

Hall, E.; Schweizer, F.; and Toller, P.
1973 "X-Ray Fluorescence analysis of Museum Objects: A New Instrument," *Archaeometry* 15: 53–78.

Hamidullah, M.
1953 "Embassy of Queen Bertha of Rome to Caliph al-Muktafi Billah in Baghdad, 293H/906," *The Journal of the Pakistan Historical Society* 1: 272–300.

Hardy, K. (ed.)
2010 *Archaeological Invisibility and Forgotten Knowledge. Conference Proceedings, Lódź, Poland, 5th–7th September 2007* [British Archaeological Reports IS-2183] (Oxford: Archaeopress).

Harper, N.K., and Fox, S.
2008 "Recent Research in Cypriot Bioarchaeology," *Bioarchaeology of the Near East* 2: 1–38.

Hayes, J.W.
1980 "Problèmes de la céramique des VIIème–IXème siècles à Salamine et à Chypre." Pp. 375–87 in *Salamine de Chypre. Histoire et archéologie. État des recherches, Lyon, 13–17 mars 1978*, ed. M. Yon [Colloques internationaux du CNRS 578] (Paris, Centre National de la Recherche Scientifique).
2003 "Hellenistic and Roman Pottery Deposits from the 'Saranda Kolones' Castle Site at Paphos," *Annual of the British School at Athens* 98: 447–516.
2007 "Pottery." Pp. 435–75 in A.H.S. Megaw, *Kourion. Excavations in The Episcopal Precinct* [Dumbarton Oaks Studies 38] (Washington, DC: Dumbarton Oaks).

Helmig, D.; Jackwerth, E.; and Hauptmann, A.
1989 "Archaeometallurgical Fieldwork and the Use of a Portable X-ray Spectrometer," *Archaeometry* 31: 181–91.

Hill, G.
1940   *A History of Cyprus* 1, *To the Conquest by Richard Lion Heart* (Cambridge: Cambridge University, reprinted 2010).
1948a   *A History of Cyprus* 2, *The Frankish Period, 1192–1432* (Cambridge: Cambridge University, reprinted 2010).
1948b   *A History of Cyprus* 3, *The Frankish Period, 1432–1571* (Cambridge: Cambridge University, reprinted 2010).
1952   *A History of Cyprus* 4, *The Ottoman Province. The British Colony, 1571–1948* (Cambridge: Cambridge University, reprinted 2010).

Hill, S.
1996   *The Early Byzantine Churches of Cilicia and Isauria* (Aldershot: Variorum).

Hirschfeld, Y.
1992   *The Judean Desert Monasteries in the Byzantine Period* (New Haven, Yale University).
1993   "Churches in Judea and in the Judean Desert." Pp. 147–54 in *Ancient Churches Revealed*, ed. Y. Tsafrir (Jerusalem: Israel Exploration Society).

Hizmi, H.
1993   "The Byzantine Church at Khirbet el-Beiyudat in the Lower Jordan Valley." Pp. 155–63 in *Ancient Churches Revealed*, ed. Y. Tsafrir (Jerusalem: Israel Exploration Society).

Hoddinott, R.F.
1963   *Early Byzantine Churches in Macedonia and Southern Serbia: A Study of the Origins and the Initial Development of East Christian Art* (New York: St. Martin's).

Hogarth, D.G.
1889   *Devia Cypria: Notes of an Archaeological Journey in Cyprus in 1888* (London: Frowde).

Hopkins, K.
1998   "Christian Number and Its Implications," *Journal of Early Christian Studies* 6/2: 185–226.

Hörmann, H.
1951   *Die Johanneskirche* [Forschungen in Ephesos 4.3] (Vienna: Österreichisches Archäologisches Institut).

Hutter, I., and Canart, P.
1991   *Das Marienhomiliar des Mönches Jakobos von Kokkinobaphos. Codex Vaticanus Graecus 1162* (Zürich: Belser).

Iacomi, V.
2010   "Some Notes on Late-Antique Oil and Wine Production in Rough Cilicia (Isauria) on the Light of Epigraphic Sources." Pp. 19–32 in *Olive Oil and Wine Production in Anatolia during Antiquity* [Symposium Proceedings, 06–08 November 2008, Mersin, Turkey] eds. Ü. Aydinoğlu and A.K. Şenol (Istanbul: Research Center of Cilician Archaeology).

Iakovou, M. (ed.)
2004   *Archaeological Field Survey in Cyprus: Past History, Future Potentials* [Proceedings of a Conference held by the Archaeological Research Unit of the University of Cyprus, 1–2 December, 2000] (London: British School at Athens).

Imhaus, B.
2004   *Lacrimae Cypriae. Les larmes de Chypre, ou Recueil des insciptions lapidaires pour la plupart funéraires de la période franque et vénitienne de l'île de Chypre* (Nicosia: Department of Antiquities).

Jacopi, G.
1925   *Edifici bizantini di Scarpanto, mosaici ed iscrizioni* (Rhodes: Tipogr. editr. Rodia).

Janin, R.
1953   "Chypre." Pp. 791–820 in *Dictionnaire d'histoire et de géographie ecclésiastique* 12 (Paris: Letouzey et Ané).

Jasink, A.M.
2010   "The Kouris River Valley Project: An Introduction." Pp. 1–8 in *Researches in Cypriote*

History and Archaeology. Proceedings of the Meeting held in Florence April 29th–30th, 2009, eds. A. Jasink and L. Bombardieri (Florence: Firenze University).

Jeffery, G.

1915–16 "Byzantine Churches of Cyprus," *Proceedings of the Society of Antiquaries of London* 28: 106–34.

1918 *A Description of the Historic Monuments of Cyprus: Studies in the Archaeology and Architecture of the Island* (Nicosia: Government Office; reprint: London: Zenon, 1983).

1928 "A Basilica of Constantia, Cyprus," *The Antiquaries Journal* 8: 344–49.

1931 *Cyprus Monuments. Historical and Architectural Buildings. The Present Condition of the Historical Monuments of Cyprus* (Nicosia: Government Office).

Jelčić, J.

1979 "Le Narthex dans l'Architecture Paléochrétienne sur le Territoire Oriental de l'Adriatique," *Prilozi Povijesti Umjetnosti U Dalmaciji* 23: 23–39.

Jolivet-Lévy, C.

1991 *Les églises byzantines de Cappadoce. Le programme iconographique de l'abside et de ses abords* (Paris: CNRS).

Jurković, M.

1998 "La Sculpture Post-Justinien en Istrie et la Problème de Continuité." Pp. 1121–30 in *Acta XIII Congressus Internationalis Archaeologiae Christianae: Split-Poreč 25.9–1.10.1994*, vol. 2 (Vatican: Pontificio Istituto de Archeologia Cristiana).

Kaegi, W.

2003 *Heraclius, Emperor of Byzantium* (Cambridge: Cambridge University); transl. D. Konstaninakou, Ἡράκλειος, Αὐτοκράτορας Τοῦ Βυζαντίου (Athens: Indiktos, 2007).

Kalavrezou-Maxeiner, I.

1985 *Byzantine Icons in Steatite* [Byzantina Vindobonensia 15.1–2] (Vienna: Österreichische Akademie der Wissenschaften).

Kallinikos, P.

1969 Ὁ Χριστιανικός Ναός Καὶ Τὰ Τελούμενα ἐν Αὐτῷ (Athens: Gregori).

Kapitän, G.

1969 "The Church Wreck of Marzamemi," *Archaeology* 22.2: 122–33.

1980 "Elementi Architectonici per una Basilica dal Relitto Navale del VI Secolo di Marzamemi," *Corso di Cultura sull'Arte Ravennate e Bizantina* 27: 71–136.

Karač, Z.

1998 "The Problem of the Exploration of 6th and 7th Century Urban Planning on Croatian Soil within the Context of General Byzantine Urban Studies." Pp. 959–974 in *Acta XIII Congressus Internationalis Archaeologiae Christianae, Split-Poreč 25.9–1.10.1994* (Vatican: Pontificio Istituto di Archeologia Cristiana).

Karageorghis, V.

1960 "Chroniques des fouilles en 1959," *Bulletin de Correspondance Hellénique* 84: 242–99.

1965 "Chronique des fouilles et découvertes archéologiques à Chypre en 1964," *Bulletin de Correspondance Hellénique* 89: 231–300.

1966 *Annual Report of the Director of the Department of Antiquities for 1965* (Nicosia: Department of Antiquities).

1967 "Chroniques des fouilles en 1966," *Bulletin de Correspondance Hellénique* 91: 275–370.

1968 "Chroniques des fouilles en 1967," *Bulletin de Correspondance Hellénique* 92: 261–358.

1969 "Chroniques des fouilles en 1968," *Bulletin de Correspondance Hellénique* 93: 431–569.

1985 "The Cyprus Department of Antiquities, 1935–1985." Pp. 1–10 in *Archaeology in Cyprus, 1960–1985* (Nicosia: Department of Antiquities).

2007 *A Lifetime in the Archaeology of Cyprus* (Stockholm: Medelhavsmuseet).

2011   *Cypriote and Other Antiquities in the Collec-
        tion of Angelos and Emily Tsirides* (Nicosia:
        En Tipis).

Karlin-Hayter, P.
1995   "The Tax-collector's Violence Drove the
        Archbishop into the Cloister?" *Byzantino-
        slavica* 56: 171–82.

Karras, R.M.
1990   "Holy Harlots: Prostitute Saints in Medieval
        Legend," *Journal of the History of Sexuality*
        1: 3–32.

Karydas, A.G.
2007   "Application of a Portable XRF Spectrom-
        eter for the Noninvasive Analysis of Mu-
        seum Metal Artefacts," *Annali di Chimica*
        97: 419–32.

Karydas, A.; Brecoulaki, H.; Bourgeois, B.;
Jockey, P.; and Zarkadas, C.
2006   "In-situ XRF analysis of Raw Pigments and
        Traces of Polychromy on Marble Sculpture
        Surfaces: Possibilities and Limitations." Pp.
        48–62 in in *The 28th International Sympo-
        sium on the Conservation and Restoration
        of Cultural Property*, "Non-destructive
        Examination of Cultural Objects – Recent
        Advances in X-ray Analysis" *Tokyo, Japan,
        1–3 December 2004* (Tokyo: Tokyo National
        Research Institute of Cultural Properties).

Kassianidou, V.
2011   "The Production of Copper in Cyprus dur-
        ing the Roman Period." Pp. 539–48 in *Pro-
        ceedings of the Fourth International Cypro-
        logical Conference (Nicosia, 29 April–3 May
        2008). A. Ancient Section*, ed. A. Demetriou
        (Nicosia: Etaireīa Kypriakōn Spoudōn).

Kazhdan, A. (ed.)
1991   *The Oxford Dictionary of Byzantium* (Ox-
        ford: Oxford University).

Killian, K.L.
2008   "Hellenistic, Roman, and Medieval Phla-
        moudhi." Pp. 87–97 in *Views from Phla-

moudhi, Cyprus*, ed. J.S. Smith [Annual of
        the American Schools of Oriental Research
        63] (Boston: American Schools of Oriental
        Research).

Kitromilides, P.M.
2001   *Κυπριακή λογιοσύνη 1571–1878. Προσω-
        πογραφική θεώρηση* (Nicosia: Cyprus
        Research Centre).

Kitzinger, E.
1990   *The Mosaics of St. Mary's of the Admiral
        in Palermo* [Dumbarton Oaks Studies
        27] (Washington, DC: Dumbarton Oaks
        Research Library).

Kleinbauer, W.E.
1992   *Early Christian and Byzantine Architecture:
        An Annotated Bibliography and Historiog-
        raphy* (Boston: Hall).

Koch, G.
1998   "Sarkophage des 5. und 6, Jahrhunderts
        im Osten des Römischen Reiches." Pp.
        439–78 in *Acta XIII Congressus Internatio-
        nalis Archaeologiae Christianae: Split-Poreč
        25.9–1.10.1994*, vol. 2 (Vatican: Pontificio
        Istituto de Archeologia Cristiana).

Koder, J.
1998   "Παρατηρήσεις Στην Οικιστική Διάρθρωση
        Της Κεντρικής Μικράς Ασίας Μετά Τον 6°
        Αιώνα, Μία Προσέγγιση Από Την Οπτική
        Γωνία Της Θεωρίας Των Κεντρικών Τόπων."
        Pp. 245–65 in *Η Βυζαντινή Μικρά Ασία,
        Διεθνή Συμπόσια, Αθήνα 1998*, ed. S. Lam-
        pakis [Εθνικό Ίδρυμα Ερευνών 6] (Athens:
        Institouto Byzantinōn Ereunōn).

Kolia-Dermitzaki, A.
1991   *Ο Βυζαντινός Ιερός Πόλεμος, Η Έννοια Και
        Η Προβολή Του Θρησκευτικού Πολέμου Στο
        Βυζάντιο* (Athens: Basilopoulos).

Kōnstantinidēs, K.
2005   "Η παιδεία καὶ τὰ γράμματα στὴ βυζαντινὴ
        Κύπρο." Pp. 413–63 in *Ἱστορία τῆς Κύπρου.
        Τόμος Γ΄. Βυζαντινὴ Κύπρος*, ed. Th. Papa-

dopoullos (Nicosia: Archbishop Makarios III Foundation).

Korol, D.
2000 "Die spätantik-christlichen Wand- und Gewölbemosaiken Zyperns (5.–7. Jh.) und ihre neuere Geschichte." Pp. 159–201 in *Zypern—Insel im Brennpunkt der Kulturen*, ed. S. Rogge [Schriften des Instituts fur Interdisziplinäre Zypern-Studien 1] (Münster: Waxmann).

Kotzabassi, S., and Patterson-Ševčenko, N.
2010 *Greek Manuscripts at Princeton, Sixth to Nineteenth Century* (Princeton, Princeton University).

Kotzias, N.
1952 "Ἀνασκαφαὶ Τῆς Βασιλικῆς Τοῦ Λαυρεωτικοῦ Ὀλύμπου," *Πρακτικὰ τῆς ἐν Ἀθήναις Ἀρχαιολογικῆς Ἑταιρείας* 1952: 92–128.

Kountoura, A.
1996 *Τα Αρχαία Μέτρα, Ελληνικά, Ρωμαϊκά, Βυζαντινά* (Thessaloniki: Pournaras).

Koutellas, M.
1998 *Κάλυμνος, Ιστορία-Αρχαιολογικοί Χώροι-Μνημεία* (Athens: Demos Kalymnion).

Knapp, A.B., and Antoniadou, S.
1998 "Archaeology, Politics and the Cultural Heritage of Cyprus." Pp. 13–43 in *Archaeology under Fire: Nationalism, Politics and Heritage in the Eastern Mediterranean and Middle East*, ed. L. Meskell (London: Routledge).

Krautheimer, R.
1960 "Mensa, coemeterium, martyrium," *Cahiers archéologiques* 11: 15–40.
1964 "A Note on Justinian's Church of the Holy Apostles in Constantinople." Pp. 265–70 in *Mélanges Eugene Tisserant* 2 (Vatican: Studi e Testi).
1969 "Introduction to an 'Iconography of Medieval Architecture.'" Pp. 115–50 in *Studies in Early Christian, Medieval, and Renaissance Art* (New York: New York University).

1986 *Early Christian and Byzantine Architecture* (New Haven: Yale University, 4th edition); transl. of 3rd edition by Ph. Mallouchou-Touphano, *Παλαιοχριστιανική Και Βυζαντινή Αρχιτεκτονική* (Athens: Morphotkio Idryma Ethnikēs Trapezēs).

Krautheimer, R. et al.
1937–80 *Corpus Basilicarum Christianarum Romae*, 5 vols. (Vatican: Pontificio Istituto di Archelogia Cristiana).

Kresten, O.
1977 "Leontius von Neapolis als Tachygraph? Hagiographische Texte als Quellen zu Schriftlichkeit und Buchkultur im 6. und 7. Jahrhundert," *Scrittura e civiltà* 1: 155–75.

Krueger, D.
1996 *Symeon the Holy Fool. Leontius's* Life *and the Late Antique City* (Berkeley: University of California).

Kyprianos, Archimandrite
1788 *Ἱστορία χρονολογικὴ τῆς νήσου Κύπρου* (Venice; repr. Nicosia: Stephanou, 1971).

Kyriazēs, N.
1936 "Παλαιογραφικά," *Κυπριακά Χρονικά* 12.4: 96–131.

Kyrris, C.
1970 "Military Colonies in Cyprus in the Byzantine Period," *Byzantinoslavica* 31: 157–81.
1982 "The Nature of Arab-Byzantine Relations in Cyprus from the Middle of the 7th to the middle of the 10th century A.D.," *Graeco-Arabica* 1: 144–75.
1984 "Characteristics of Cypriote History during Early Byzantine period." Pp. 17–40 in *Πρακτικά Συμποσίου Κυπριακής Ιστορίας (Λευκωσία 2–3 Μαΐου 1983)*, ed. N. Constaninides (Ioannina: Ekdosē Tomea Historias Panepistemiou Ioanninon).
1985 *History of Cyprus, with an Introduction to the Geography of Cyprus* (Nicosia: Nicocles).
1987 *The Kanakaria Documents 1666–1850* (Nicosia: Cyprus Research Centre).

1993   "The 'Three Hundred Alaman Saints' of
        Cyprus: Problems of Origin and Identity." Pp.
        203–35 in 'The Sweet Land of Cyprus.' Papers
        Given at the Twenty-Fifth Jubilee Spring Sym-
        posium of Byzantine Studies (Birmingham,
        March 1991) eds. A. Bryer and G. Georghal-
        lides (Nicosia: Cyprus Research Centre).
1994–98 "Cyprus, Byzantium and the Arabs from the
        7th to the early 8th century," Τόμου
        τις επετηρίδας τις εταιρείας βυζαντινών
        σπουδών 49: 185–236.
1996   History of Cyprus (Nicosia: Lampousa).
1997   "Cyprus, Byzantium, and the Arabs from the
        Mid-7th century to the Early 8th century."
        Pp. 625–74 in Oriente e Occidente tra Me-
        dioevo ed età moderna: studi in onore di Geo
        Pistarin, ed. by L. Balletto (Genoa: Brigati).

Labbas, G.
2009   Ο Πανίερος Ναός της Αναστάσεως στα
        Ιεροσόλυμα (Athens: Akadēmia Athēnōn),

Laiou, A.E.
2005   "The Byzantine Village (5th–14th Centu-
        ry)." Pp. 31–54 in Les villages dans l'empire
        byzantin (IVe–XVe siècle), eds. J. Lefort,
        C. Morrisson, and J.-P. Sodini [Réalités
        Byzantines 11] (Paris: Lethielleux).

Lafontaine-Dosogne, J.
1974   "Iconography of the Cycle of the Life of
        the Virgin." Pp. 161–94 in The Kariye Djami,
        Volume 4: Studies in the Art of the Kariye
        Djami and its Intellectual Background, ed.
        P.A. Underwood (Princeton: Princeton
        University).
1992   Iconographie de l'enfance de la Vierge dans
        l'Empire byzantine et en Occident (Brussels:
        Palais des Académies, 2nd ed.)

Langdale, A.
2010   "At the Edge of Empire: Venetian Archi-
        tecture in Famagusta, Cyprus," Viator 41:
        155–98.

L'Anson, E., and Vacher, S.
1883   "Medieval and other Buildings in the Is-
        land of Cyprus," Transactions of the Royal

Institute of British Architects (May 1883):
        13–32.

Lappa-Zizicas, E.
1970   "Un épitomé inédit de la Vie de S. Jean
        l'Aumônier," Analecta Bollandiana 88: 265–78.

Laskaris, P.
1970   "Ἀνασκαφαὶ Νέας Ἀγχιάλου (Βασιλικὴ Γʹ),"
        Πρακτικὰ τῆς ἐν Ἀθήναις Ἀρχαιολογικῆς
        Ἑταιρείας 1970: 36–49.
1996   "Παλαιοχριστιανικά και Βυζαντινά Ταφικά
        Μνημεία της Ελλάδος," Βυζαντιακά 16:
        295–350.
2000   Monuments Funéraires Paléochrétiens (et
        Byzantins) de Grèce (Athens: Basilopoulos).

Lazarev, V.N.
1966a   Михайловские Мозаики (Moscow:
        Iskusstvo).
1966b   Old Russian Murals and Mosaics (London:
        Faber and Faber).

Lazović, M.; Durr, N.; Durand, H.; Houriet, C.;
and Schweitzer, F.
1977   "Objets byzantins de la collection du Musée
        d'art et d'histoire," Genava 25: 5–62.

Lefort, J.
2002   "The Rural Economy, Seventh–Twelfth
        Centuries." Pp. 231–310 in The Economic
        History of Byzantium: From the Seventh
        through the Fifteenth Century, ed. A.E.
        Laiou, [Dumbarton Oaks Studies 39] (Was-
        hington, DC: Dumbarton Oaks).

Lehmann, T.
2005   "Die spätantiken Kirchenbauten von
        Amathous und die Wunderheilungen am
        Grab des Bischofs Tychon." Pp. 23–40 in
        Beiträge zur Kulturgeschichte Zyperns von
        der Spätantike bis zur Neuzeit, Symposium,
        München 12.–13. Juli 2002, eds. J.G. Deckers,
        M.-E. Mitsou, and S. Rogge [Schriften des
        Instituts fur Interdisziplinäre Zypern-Stu-
        dien 3] (Münster: Waxmann).

Leidwanger, J.
2005 "The Underwater Survey at Episkopi Bay: Preliminary Report," *Report of the Department of Antiquities Cyprus* 2005: 270–75.
2007 "Two Late Roman Wrecks from Southern Cyprus," *International Journal of Nautical Archaeology* 36: 308–16.

Lemerle, P.
1945 *Philippes et La Macédoine Occidentale à l'Époque Chrétienne et Byzantine* (Paris: De Boccard).

Leonard, J.
1995 "Evidence for Roman Ports, Harbours and Anchorages In Cyprus." Pp. 227–45 in *Cyprus and the Sea: Proceedings of the International Symposium, Nicosia, 25–26 September 1993*, eds. V. Karageorghis and D. Michaelides (Nicosia: University of Cyprus).
1997 "Harbor Terminology in Roman Periploi." Pp. 163–90 in *Res Maritimae, Cyprus and the Eastern Mediterranean from Prehistory to Late Antiquity* (Atlanta: Scholars).

Leonard, J., and Demesticha, S.
2004 "Fundamental Links in the Economic Chain: Local Ports and International Trade in Roman and Early Christian Cyprus." Pp. 189–202 in *Transport Amphorae and Trade in the Eastern Mediterranean*, eds. J. Eiring and J. Lund [Monographs of the Danish Institute at Athens 5] (Athens: Danish Institute at Athens).

Leventis, P.
2005 *Twelve Times in Nicosia, Cyprus, 1192–1570: Topography, Architecture and Urban Experience in a Diversified Capital City* (Nicosia: Cyprus Research Centre).

Lewin, A.S., and Pellegrini, P.
2006 *Settlements and Demography in the Near East in Late Antiquity, Proceedings of the Colloquium, Matera 27–29 Oct 2005*, (Rome: Instituti editoriali e poligrafici internazionali).

Limberis, V.
1994 *Divine Heiress, the Virgin Mary and the Creation of Christian Constantinople* (London: Routledge).

Loizou-Hadjigavriel, L., and Theodotou, D.
2009 *A Guide to the History of Nicosia through the Leventis Municipal Museum* (Nicosia: Leventis Municipal Museum of Nicosia).

Lokin, J.
2005 "Ο πολίτικος και διοικητικός θεσμός της Κύπρου από τον μεγάλο Κωνσταντίνο έως τον Ιουστινιανό." Pp. 155–98 in *Ιστορία της Κύπρου – Βυζαντινή Κύπρος*, vol. 4, ed. T. Papadopoullos (Nicosia: Archbishop Makarios III Foundation).

Lowden, J.
2009 *The Jaharis Gospel Lectionary. The Story of a Byzantine Gospel Book* (New York: Metropolitan Museum of Art).

Lund, J.
2006 "Writing Long-Term History with Potsherds: Problems – Prospects." Pp. 213–27 in *Old Pottery in a New Century: Innovating Perspectives on Roman Pottery Studies. Atti del convegno internatzionale di studi, Catania, 22–24 Aprile 2004*, eds. D. Malfitana, J. Poblome, and J. Lund (Catania: Istituto per i beni archeologici e monumentali).

Lutz, J., and Pernicka, E.
1996 "EDXRF Analysis of Ancient Copper Alloys," *Archaeometry* 38.2: 313–23.

Macridy, T.
1964 "The Monastery of Lips and the Burials of the Palaeologi," *Dumbarton Oaks Papers* 18: 253–77.

Magen Y.
1993 "The Monastery Of St Martyrius At Maale Adummin." Pp. 170–96 in *Ancient Churches Revealed*, ed. Y. Tsafrir (Jerusalem: Israel Exploration Society).

1991) eds. A. Bryer and G. Georghallides (Nicosia: Cyprus Research Centre).

1994 "Τὸ Magenta Ware στὴν Κύπρο." Pp. 311–22 in *Γ΄ Ἐπιστημονικὴ Συνάντηση γιὰ τὴν Ἑλληνιστικικὴ Κεραμική: "Χρονολογημένα Σύνολα-Ἐργαστήρια". Θεσσαλονίκη, 24–27 Σεπτεμβρίου 1991* [Bibliothekē tēs en Athēnais archaiologikēs Etaireīas 137] (Athens: Archaiologikē Etaireia).

1996 "The Economy of Cyprus during the Hellenistic and Roman Periods." Pp. 139–52 in *The Development of the Cypriot Economy from the Prehistoric Period to the Present Day*, eds. V. Karageorghis and D. Michaelides (Nicosia: Leventis Foundation).

1997 "Magenta Ware in Cyprus once more." Pp. 137–44 in *"Four Thousand Years of Images on Cypriote Pottery,"* Proceedings of the Third International Conference on Cypriot Studies. Nicosia, 3–4 May 1996, ed. V. Karageorghis et al. (Nicosia: Leventis Foundation).

1998 "Du paganisme au christianisme." Pp. 12–15 in *Chypre: L'île aux cent basiliques* [Le Monde de la Bible 112] (Lausanne).

2000 "The *opus sectile* of the Southern Church of the Monastery of Ayios Chrysostomos at Koutsoventis and Jacques Georges Desmeules." Pp. 223–28 in *Philokypros. Mélanges de Philologie et d'Antiquités Grecques et Proche-Orientales dédiés à la Memoire d'Olivier Masson*, eds. L. Dubois and E. Masson (Salamanca: Universidad de Salamanca).

2001a "Some Characteristic Traits of a Mosaic Workshop in Early Christian Cyprus." Pp. 314–25 in *Actes du VIIIéme Colloque International sur la Mosaïque Antique et Médiévale, Lausanne, 6–11 October*, eds. D. Paunier and C. Schmidt [Cahiers d'Archéologie Romaine 86] (Lausanne).

2001b "Archeologia Paleocristiana a Cipro," *Corso di Cultura sull'Arte Ravennate e Bizantina* 44: 179–239.

2002 "The Ambo of Basilica A at Cape Drepanon." Pp. 43–56 in *Mosaic. Festschrift for A.H.S. Megaw* (London: British School at Athens).

2004 "'Ayioi Pente' at Yeroskipou, a New Early Christian Site in Cyprus," *Musiva & Sectilia* 1: 185–98.

2005a "Geroskipou-*Agioi Pente*." Pp. 77–79 in *Annual Report of the Department of Antiquities for the Year 2003*, ed. P. Flourentzos (Nicosia: Government Office).

2005b "Two New 'Cypriot' Mosaics." Pp. 399–404 in *Actes du IXe Colloque international pour l'Etude de la Mosaïque antique et médiévale. Association Internationale pour l'Etude de la Mosaïque Antique (AIEMA), Rome, 5–10 November 2001*, ed. H. Morlier (Rome: Ecole Française de Rome).

2006 "Geroskipou-*Agioi Pente*." Pp. 83–84 in *Annual Report of the Department of Antiquities for the year 2004*, ed. P. Flourentzos (Nicosia: Government Office).

2008a "Yeroskipou-*Agioi Pente*," in P. Flourentzos, "Chronique des fouilles et découvertes archéologiques a Chypre en 2003 et 2004," *Bulletin de Correspondance Hellénique* 128–29: 1700-1703.

2008b "The Archaeology of Geroskipou, from Earliest Times to the Early Christian Period." Pp. 27–60 in *Geroskipou from Antiquity to the Present*, collective volume (Nicosia: Municipality of Geroskipou).

2013 The Excavations of the University of Cyprus at 'Ayioi Pente' of Yeroskipou." Pp. 87–95 in *The Insular System of the Early Byzantine Mediterranean. Archaeology and History*, eds. D. Michaelides, P. Pergola and E. Zanini [Limina/Limites 2, BAR International Series 2523] (Oxford: Archaeopress).

Michaelides, D., and Bakirtzis, C.

2003 "Αραβικοί αμφορείς στην Κύπρο." Pp. 125–36 in *7º Διεθνές Συνέδριο Μεσαιωνικής Κεραμικής της Μεσογείου, Πρακτικά 11–16 Οκτωβρίου 1999* (Athens), 125-136.

2010 "Byzantine Cyprus." Pp. 207–13 in *Cyprus: Crossroads of Civilizations* ed. S. Hadjisavvas (Nicosia: Government of the Republic of Cyprus).

Michaelides, D.; Herz, N.; and Foster, G.V.
1988 "Marble in Cyprus: Classical Times to Middle Ages." P. 159 in *Classical Marble: Geochemistry, Technology, Trade,* eds. N. Herz and M. Waelkens (Dordrecht: Kluwer Academic).

Michaelides, D., and Pilides, D.
2012 "Nicosia: From the Beginnings to Roman Ledroi." Pp. 1–76 in *Historic Nicosia,* ed. D. Michaelides (Nicosia: Rimal).

Michaelides, M.
1963 "Ἔδεσσα, Βασιλικὴ Α᾽ Λόγγου," *Ἀρχαιολογικὸν Δελτίον* 18.2.2: 251–52.
1965 "Παλαιοχριστιανικὴ Βασιλικὴ Α᾽ Λόγγου Ἐδέσσης," *Ἀρχαιολογικὸν Δελτίον* 20.2.3: 475–76.
1968 "Παλαιοχριστιανικὴ Ἔδεσσα, Ἀνασκαφὴ Βασιλικῆς Α᾽," *Ἀρχαιολογικὸν Δελτίον* 23: 195–220.

Michaēlidou, L.
2000 *Ἱερὰ Μητρόπολις Μόρφου. 2000 Χρόνια Τέχνης καὶ Ἁγιότητος* [Exhibition catalogue] (Nicosia: Politistiko Idryma Trapezēs Kyprou).

Michel, A.; Duval, N.; and Piccirillo, M.
2001 *Les Eglises d'Epoques Byzantine et Umayyade de la Jordanie: Ve–VIIIe Siècle* [Bibliothèque de L'Antiquité Tardive 2] (Turnhout: Brepols).

Millet, G.
1910 *Monuments byzantins de Mistra* (Paris: Leroux).

Mitford, T.B.
1950 "Some new Inscriptions from Early Christian Cyprus," *Byzantion* 20: 105–75.

Mitford, R.B.
1980 "Roman Cyprus," *Aufstieg und Niedergang der römischen Welt* II.7.2: 1285–1384.

Morrisson, C., and Sodini, J.-P.
2006 "The Sixth-Century Economy." Pp. 171–220 in *The Economic History of Byzantium:* *From the Seventh through the Fifteenth Century,* ed. A.E. Laiou [Dumbarton Oaks Studies 39] (Washington, DC: Dumbarton Oaks).

Mouriki, D.
1970 "Περὶ βυζαντινοῦ κύκλου τοῦ βίου τῆς Παναγίας εἰς φορητὴν εἰκόνα τῆς Μονῆς τοῦ Ὄρους Σινᾶ," *Ἀρχαιλογικὴ Ἐφημερίς 1970*: 125–53. (English summary as "A Byzantine Cycle from the Life of the Virgin Depicted on an Icon at Mount Sinai," pp. 151–53.)
1980 "Observations on the Style of the Wall Paintings of the Sion Church at Ateni, Georgia." Pp. 173–85 in *L'arte Georgiana dal IX al XIV secolo, Atti del Terzo simposio internazionale dell'arte Georgiana, Bari-Lecce, 14–18 ottobre 1980,* ed. M.S. Calo' Mariani (Galatina: Congedo).
1980–81 "Stylistic Trends in Monumental Painting of Greece During the Eleventh and Twelfth Centuries," *Dumbarton Oaks Papers* 34–35: 76–124.
1985 *The Mosaics of Nea Moni on Chios* (Athens: Commercial Bank of Greece).
1986 "Thirteenth-Century Icon Painting in Cyprus," *The Griffon (Gennadius Library)* 1–2: 9–80 (pls. 1–65).
1990 "Εικόνες από τον 12° ως τον 15° αιώνα." Pp. 101–24 in *Σινά. Οι Θησαυροί της Μονής,* ed. K. Manaphes (Athens: Athēnōn).
1993 "The Cult of Saints in Medieval Cyprus as Attested in Church Decoration and Icon Painting." pp. 238–45 in *'The Sweet Land of Cyprus.' Papers Given at the Twenty-Fifth Jubilee Spring Symposium of Byzantine Studies (Birmingham, March 1991)* eds. A. Bryer and G. Georghallides (Nicosia: Cyprus Research Centre).

Mullaly, T.
1990 "Art and Architecture in Byzantine Cyprus." Pp. 71–84 in *Cyprus: The Legacy,* ed. J. Koumoulides (Bethesda: University of Maryland).

Muthesius, A.M.
2001   "The Question of Silk in Medieval Cyprus."
        Pp. 369–84 in Πρακτικά του Τρίτου Διε-
        θνούς Κυπρολογικού Συνεδρίου (Λευκωσία,
        16-20 Απριλίου 1996). Τόμος Β'. Μεσαιωνικό
        Τμήμα, ed. A. Papageorghiou (Nicosia:
        Etaireīa Kypriakōn Spoudōn).

Nau, F.
1907   "La légende des saints évêques Héraclide,
        Mnason et Rhodon, ou l'apostolicité de
        l'église de Chypre," Revue de l'Orient Chré-
        tien 12: 125–36.

Nautin, P.
1963   "Épiphane." Cols. 617–31 in Dictionnaire
        d'histoire et de géographie ecclésiastiques 15
        (Paris: Letouzey et Ané).

Neal, D.
2010   The Basilica at Soloi, Cyprus: A Survey of the
        Buildings and Mosaics (Nicosia: IRG Group
        for SAVE/USAID).

Nerantzē-Varmazē, V.
1995   "Η Κύπρος βασικός σταθμός επικοινωνίας
        Βυζαντινών και Φράγκων της Παλαιστίνης
        το 12ο αιώνα." Pp. 19–27 in Cyprus and the
        Crusades. Papers Given at the International
        Conference "Cyprus and the Crusades," Nico-
        sia, 6–9 September, 1994, eds. by N. Coureas
        and J. Riley-Smith (Nicosia: Cyprus Re-
        search Centre).
1997   "The Identity of the Byzantine Province in
        the 12th Century," Επετηρίδα του Κέντρου
        Επιστημονικών Ερευνών 23: 9–14.

Nersessian, S. Der
1960   "Two Images of the Virgin in the Dumbar-
        ton Oaks Collection," Dumbarton Oaks
        Papers 14: 69–86.

Nicholson, H.
1997   Chronicle of the Third Crusade. A Trans-
        lation of the Itinerarium Peregrinorum
        et Gesta Regis Ricardi [Crusade Texts in
        Translation 3] (Aldershot: Ashgate).

Nicolaou, I.
1990   "The Jewellery of Cyprus from Neolithic
        to Roman Times," Archaeologia Cypria 2:
        117–20.

Nicolaou, I., and Metcalf, D.M.
2007   "The Limassol (Molos) Hoard of Byzantine
        gold, t.p.q. 641," Report of the Department
        of Antiquities Cyprus 2007: 399–433.

Nicolaou, K.
1983   "A Late Cypriote Nekropolis at Yeroskipou,
        Paphos," Report of the Department of An-
        tiquities Cyprus 1983: 142–50.

Nicolaou-Konnari, A.
2000   "The Conquest of Cyprus by Richard the
        Lionheart and Its Aftermath: A Study of
        Sources and Legend, Politics and Attitudes
        in the Year 1191–1192," Επετηρίδα Κέντρου
        Επιστημονικών Ερευνών 26: 25–123.

Nikolaïdès, A.
1996   "L'église de la Panagia Arakiotissa à Lagou-
        dera, Chypre: étude iconographique des
        fresques de 1192," Dumbarton Oaks Papers
        50: 1–137.

Nordiguian, L., and Voisin, J.-C.
1999   Châteaux et Eglises du Moyen Age au Liban
        (Beirut: Terre du Liba).

Noret, J.
1986   "L'expédition canadienne à Soli et ses ré-
        sultats pour l'intelligence et la datation de
        la Vie de S. Auxibe," Analecta Bollandiana
        104: 445–52.

Öhler, M.
2003   Barnabas. Die historische Person und ihre
        Rezepetion in der Apostelgeschichte (Tübin-
        gen: Mohr Siebeck).

Olster, D.
1993   "The Construction of a Byzantine Saint:
        George of Choziba, Holiness, and the
        Pilgrimage Trade in Seventh-Century Pal-

estine," *Greek Orthodox Theological Review* 38: 309–22.

Orlandos, A.K.

1928–33 "Παλαιοχριστιανικοί καὶ Βυζαντινοί Ναοί τῶν Καλυβίων Κουβαρᾶ," *Ἀθηνᾶ* 21: 165–90.

1929 "Αἱ Παλαιοχριστανικαὶ Βασιλικαὶ τῆς Λέσβου," *Ἀρχαιολογικὸν Δελτίον* 12: 1-72.

1933 "Βασιλική Σικυῶνος", *Πρακτικὰ τῆς ἐν Ἀθήναις ρχαιολογικῆς Ἑταιρείας* 1933: 31–90.

1948 "Παλαιοχριστιανικὰ Λείψανα τῆς Ρόδου," *Ἀρχεῖον τῶν βυζαντινῶν μνημείων τῆς Ἑλλάδος* 3: 1–227.

1951 "Ἡ Σταυρική Βασιλική τῆς Θάσου," *Ἀρχεῖον τῶν βυζαντινῶν μνημείων τῆς Ἑλλάδος* 7: 3–61.

1957 "Rapports sur les Monuments Paléochrétien Découvertes ou Étudiés en Grèce de 1938 à 1954." Pp. 109–16 in *Actes du Ve Congrès international d'archéologie chrétienne, Aix-en-Provence, 13–19 septembre 1954* (Paris: Congresso Internazionale di Archeologia Cristiana).

1964–65 "Ἡ ἀπὸ τοῦ Νάρθηκος Πρὸς τὸ ἱερόν Μετακίνησις τοῦ Διακονικοῦ εἰς τὰς Ἑλληνιστικὰς βασιλικάς," *Δελτίον τῆς Χριστιανικῆς ἀρχαιολογικῆς ἑταιρείας* 4: 353–72.

1965 *Ἡ πρόσφατος ἀναστήλωσις της Καταπολιανής της Πάρου* (Athens: Kypraios).

1973 "Παλαιοχριστιανικὰ καὶ Βυζαντινὰ Μνημεῖα Τεγέας-Νυκλίου," *Ἀρχεῖον τῶν βυζαντινῶν μνημείων τῆς Ἑλλάδος* 12: 1–171.

1994 *Ἡ Ξυλόστεγος Παλαιοχριστιανικὴ Βασιλικὴ τῆς Μεσογειακῆς Λεκάνης*, 2nd ed. (Athens: Athēnais Archaiologikē Etaireia).

1998 *Βυζαντινή Ἀρχιτεκτονική* (Athens: Athēnais Archaiologikē Etaireia).

Ousterhout, R.

1992 "Originality in Byzantine Architecture: The Case of Nea Moni," *Journal of the Society of Architectural Historians* 51.1: 48–60.

1998 "The Holy Space: Architecture and the Liturgy." Pp. 81–121 in *Heaven on Earth*, ed. L. Safran (University Park: Pennsylvania State University).

2001 "The Architecture of Iconoclasm." Pp. 5–25 in *Byzantium in the Iconoclast Era (ca. 680–850): The Sources. An Annotated Survey*, eds. L. Brubaker and J. Haldon (Aldershot: Ashgate).

2007 "Pilgrimage Architecture." Pp. 47–57 in *Egeria, Monuments of Faith in the Medieval Mediterranean* (Athens: Hellenic Ministry of Culture).

2008 *Master Builders of Byzantium* (Philadelphia, University of Pennsylvania).

Ovadiah, A.

1970 *Corpus of the Byzantine Churches in the Holy Land* (Bonn: Hanstein).

2005 "Liturgical Modifications in the Early Byzantine Church in Eretz Israel," *Liber Annuus* 55: 363–76.

Pallas, D.

1950 "Ἀρχαιολογικά-Λειτουργικά," *Ἐπετηρὶς ἑταιρείας βυζαντινῶν σπουδῶν* 20: 283–89 [Reprinted in *Συναγωγή Μελετῶν Βυζαντινῆς Ἀρχαιολογίας* I (Athens: 1987–88), 49–97].

1952 *Ἡ Θάλασσα τῶν ἐκκλησιῶν. Συμβολὴ εἰς τὴν Ἱστορίαν τοῦ Χριστιανικοῦ Βωμοῦ καὶ τὴν Μορφολογίαν τῆς Λειτουργίας* [Ekdoseis tou Gallikou Institoutou Athēnōn 68] (Athens).

1954 Αἱ Παρ᾽ Εὐσεβίῳ ἐξέδραι τῶν ἐκκλησιῶν τῆς Παλαιστίνης," *Θεολογία* 25: 470–83 [Reprinted in *Συναγωγή Μελετῶν Βυζαντινῆς Ἀρχαιολογίας* I (Athens, 1987–88), 49–97].

1960 "Ἀνασκαφαὶ ἐν Λεχαίῳ," *Πρακτικὰ τῆς ἐν Ἀθήναις Ἀρχαιολογικῆς Ἑταιρείας* 1960: 144–70.

1963 "Μεσαιωνικὰ Ἀργολιδοκορινθίας," *Ἀρχαιολογικὸν Δελτίον* 17: 69–83.

1969 "Νεκρικὸν ὑπόγειον ἐν Κορίθῳ. Συντήρησις Τοιχογραφιῶν," *Πρακτικὰ τῆς ἐν Ἀθήναις Ἀρχαιολογικῆς Ἑταιρείας* 1969: 121–34.

1976–77 "Ἡ Παναγία τῆς Σκριποῦς ὡς Μετάπλαση τῆς Παλαιοχριστιανικῆς ἀρχιτεκτονικῆς σε Μεσαιωνική Βυζαντινή," *Ἐπετηρίς Ἑταιρείας Στερεοελλαδικῶν Μελετῶν* 6: 1–70 [Reprinted in *Συναγωγή Μελετῶν Βυζα-*

ντινῆς Ἀρχαιολογίας I (Athens, 1987–88), 567–640]

1977 *Les Monuments Paléochrétiens de Grèce Découverts de 1959 à 1973* [Sussidi allo studio delle antichità christiane 5] (Vatican: Pontificio Istituto).

1981 "Ἡ Παναγία τοῦ Ἡρωδίωνος στὴν Ὑπάτη," Ἀντίδωρον Πνυματικόν Εἰς τόν Καθηγητήν Γεράσιμον Κονιδάρην, Ἀθῆναι, 1–30 [Reprinted in Συναγωγή Μελετῶν Βυζαντινῆς Ἀρχαιολογίας I (Athens, 1987–88), 641–67].

2007 Ἀποφόρητα, eds. E. Chalkia and D. Triantaphyllopoulos (Athens: Potamos).

Panagiotide, M.
2001 "Ἡ ζωγραφική του 12ου αιώνα στην Κύπρο και το πρόβλημα των τοπικών εργαστηρίων." Pp. 411–39 in Πρακτικά του τρίτου κυπρολογικού Συνεδρίου (Λευκωσία, 16–20 Απριλίου 1996), Τόμος Β' Μεσαιωνικό τμήνα, ed. A. Papageorghiou (Nicosia: Ministry of Education and Culture.

Panofsky, E.
1951 *Gothic Architecture and Scholasticism* (Latrobe: Archabbey).

1972 *Renaissance and Renascences in Western Art* (New York: Harper and Row).

Papalexandrou, N.
2008 "Hala Sultan Tekke, Cyprus: An Elusive Landscape of Sacredness in a Liminal Context," *Journal of Modern Greek Studies* 26.2: 251–81.

Papacostas, T.
1995 "Medieval Byzantine Urban Churches in Cyprus," unpublished M.Phil. thesis, University of Oxford.

1999a "Byzantine Cyprus. The Testimony of its Churches, 650–1200," Ph.D. dissertation, University of Oxford.

1999b "Secular Landholdings and Venetians in 12th-Century Cyprus," *Byzantinische Zeitschrift* 92.2: 479–501.

2001 "The Economy of Late Antique Cyprus." Pp. 107–28 in *Economy and Exchange in the East Mediterranean during Late Antiquity*, eds. S. Kingsley and M. Decker (Oxford: Oxbow).

2002 "A Tenth-Century Inscription from Syngrasis, Cyprus," *Byzantine and Modern Greek Studies* 26: 42–64.

2005 "In Search of a Lost Byzantine Monument: Saint Sophia of Nicosia," Ἐπετηρίδα Κέντρου Επιστημονικών Επευνωήν 31: 11–37.

2006a "Architecture et communautés étrangères à Chypre aux XIème et XIIème siècles." Pp. 223–40 in *Actes du colloque 'Identités croisées en un milieu méditerranéen: Le cas de Chypre'*, eds. S. Fourrier and G. Grivaud (Rouen).

2006b "Gothic in the East: Western Architecture in Byzantine Lands." Pp. 510–30 in *A Companion to Medieval Art: Romanesque and Gothic in Northern Europe*, ed. C. Rudolph [Blackwell Companions to Art History] (Oxford: Blackwell).

2007 "The Architecture and History of the Monastery of St. John Chrysostom, Cyprus," *Dumbarton Oaks Papers* 61: 25–155 [with contributions from C. Mango and M. Grünbart].

2010 "Echoes of the Renaissance in the Eastern Confines of the *Stato da mar*: Architectural Evidence from Venetian Cyprus," *Acta Byzantina Fennica* 3: 136–72.

2012 "Byzantine Nicosia." Pp. 77–109 in *Historic Nicosia*, ed. D. Michaelides (Nicosia: Rimal).

forthcoming a "From Late Antique Salamis to Medieval Famagusta." In *Medieval Famagusta*, eds. C. Schabel and A.W. Carr (Leiden: Brill).

forthcoming b "Neapolis – Nemesos – Limassol: From Late Antiquity to Richard Lionheart." In *Tale of a City: Limassol from Antiquity to 1878*, eds. C. Schabel and A. Nicolaou-Konnari (Nicosia: University of Cyprus).

Papadopoullos, T.
1952 "Ἐκ τῆς ἀρχαιοτάτης ἱστορίας τοῦ πατριαρχείου Ἱεροσολύμων. Ἡ ἐπίσκεψις τῆς ἁγίας Ἑλένης εἰς Παλαιστίνην καὶ Κύπρον," Νέα Σιών 1952: 1–30.

2005 *Ιστορία της Κύπρου – Βυζαντινή Κύπρος*, vol. 4 (Nicosia: Archbishop Makarios III Foundation).

Papadopoulou, D.; Zachariadis, G.; Anthemidis, A.; Tsirliganis, N.; and Stratis, J.
2006 "Development and Optimisation of a Portable micro-XRF Method for in situ Multi-element Analysis of Ancient Ceramics," *Talanta* 68.5: 1692–99.

Papaevangelou, P.
1970 *Ο Χριστιανικός Ναός εξ επόψεως Ορθοδόξου* (Thessaloniki).

Papageorghiou, A.
1963a "Η Μονή Αψινθιωτίσσης," *Report of the Department of Antiquities Cyprus* 1963: 73–83.
1963b "Η Βασιλική Μαραθοβούνου," *Report of the Department of Antiquities Cyprus* 1963: 84–101.
1964a "Η Παλαιοχριστιανική και βυζαντινή αρχαιολογία και Τέχνη εν Κύπρω, κατά το 1963," *Απόστολος Βαρνάβας* 25: 153–62, 209–16, 274–84, 349–53.
1964b "Les premières incursions arabes à Chypre et leurs conséquences." Pp. 152–58 in *Αφιέρωμα εις τον Κωνσταντίνον Σπυριδίκιν* (Nicosia).
1965a "Η παλαιοχριστιανική και βυζαντινή αρχαιολογία και τέχνη εν Κύπρω κατά το 1964," *Απόστολος Βαρνάβας* 26: 91–96.
1965b *Masterpieces of Byzantine Art of Cyprus* (Nicosia: Government Office).
1966a "Η παλαιοχριστιανική και βυζαντινή αρχαιολογία και τέχνη εν Κύπρω κατά το 1965," *Απόστολος Βαρνάβας* 27: 151–73, 220–42, 269–81.
1966b "Ερευνά εις τον ναών του αγίου Σπυρίδωνος εν Τρεμετουσιά," *Κυπριακαί Σπουδαί* 30: 17–33.
1968 "Η Παλαιοχριστιανική και βυζαντινή αρχαιολογία και Τέχνη εν Κύπρω, κατά τα έτη 1965–1966," *Απόστολος Βαρνάβας* 29: 77–82.
1969 "Η Παλαιοχριστιανική και βυζαντινή αρχαιολογία και τέχνη εν Κύπρω κατά το 1968," *Απόστολος Βαρνάβας* 30: 280–90.

1970 "Η παλαιοχριστιανική και βυζαντινή αρχαιολογία και τέχνη εν Κύπρω κατά τα ετη 1967–1968," *Απόστολος Βαρνάβας* 31: 3–96.
1975 *Οι Ξυλόστεγοι ναοί της Κύπρου* (Nicosia: Government Printing Office).
1974 "Recently discovered Wall-Paintings in the 10th–11th Century Churches of Cyprus." Pp. 411–14 in *Actes du XIVe Congrès International des Études Byzantines, Bucarest, 6–12 Septembre 1971* (Bucarest: Editura Academiei Republiciis).
1976 *Βυζαντινές Εικόνες της Κύπρου* (Athens: Benaki Museum).
1981 "Η Κύπρος κατά τους Βυζαντινούς χρόνους." Pp. 33–78 in *Κύπρος Ιστορία, προβλήματα και αγώνες του λαού της*, eds. G. Tenekides and G.Kranidiotes (Athens: Vivliopoleion tes Hestias, Kollarou & Sia).
1982a "Constantinopolitan Influence on the Middle Byzantine Architecture of Cyprus," *Jahrbuch der Österreichischen Byzantinistik* 32.4: 468–78.
1982b "The Narthex of the Churches of the Middle Byzantine Period in Cyprus." Pp. 437–48 in *Rayonnement Grec*, eds. L. Hadermann-Misguich and G. Raepsaet (Brussels: Université de Bruxelles).
1982c "L'art byzantin de Chypre et l'art des croisés influences réciproques," *Report of the Department of Antiquities Cyprus* 1982: 217–26.
1984 "Αλύπου Παναγίας Μοναστήρι." Pp. 384–85 in *Μεγάλη Κυπριακή Εγκυκλοπαίδεια* 1 (Nicosia: Philokypros).
1985a "Βαρνάβα και Ιλαρίωνος εκκλησία." Pp. 151–52 in *Μεγάλη Κυπριακή εγκυκλοπαίδεια* 3 (Nicosia: Philokypros).
1985b "L'Architecture Paléochrétienne de Chypre," *Corsi di cultura sull'arte Ravennate e Bizantina* 22: 299–324.
1985c "L'Architecture de la Période Byzantine à Chypre," *Corsi di cultura sull'arte Ravennate e Bizantina* 22: 325–29.
1985d "Βαρβάρας Άγιας βασιλική, Κορόβια." P. 145 in *Μεγαλη Κυπριακή εγκυκλοπαίδεια* 3 (Nicosia: Philokypros).
1985e "Άγιος Λάζαρος, Λάρνακα." Pp. 174–75 in *Μεγαλη Κυπριακή εγκυκλοπαίδεια* 8 (Nicosia: Philokypros).

1985f "Βαρνάβα Αποστόλου Θρόνος." Pp. 157–59 in *Μεγαλη Κυπριακή εγκυκλοπαίδεια* 3 (Nicosia: Philokypros).

1985g "Αχειροποιήτου Μοναστήρι." Pp. 96–97 in *Μεγάλη Κυπριακή Εγκυκλοπαίδεια* 3 (Nicosia: Philokypros).

1986 "Foreign Influences on the Early Christian Architecture." Pp. 490–504 in *Acts of the International Archaeological Symposium: Cyprus between the Orient and the Occident. Nicosia, 8–14 September 1985* (Nicosia: Department of Antiquities).

1986–88 "Μια σύγχρονη πηγή για τις δύο πρώτες αραβικές επιδρομές κατά της Κύπρου," *Stasinos* 9: 167–75.

1989 "Παρασκευής Αγίας εκκλησία, Γεροσκήπου." Pp. 106–9 in *Μεγαλη Κυπριακή εγκυκλοπαίδεια* 11 (Nicosia: Philokypros).

1991 *Εικόνες της Κύπρου* (Nicosia: Holy Archbishopric of Cyprus).

1992 *Icons of Cyprus* (Nicosia: Holy Archbishopric of Cyprus).

1993 "Cities and Countryside at the End of Antiquity and the Beginning of the Middle Ages in Cyprus." Pp. 27–51 in *'The Sweet Land of Cyprus.' Papers Given at the Twenty-Fifth Jubilee Spring Symposium of Byzantine Studies (Birmingham, March 1991)* eds. A. Bryer and G. Georghallides (Nicosia: Cyprus Research Centre).

1995a *The Autocephalous Church of Cyprus: A Catalogue of the Exhibition* (Nicosia: Byzantine Museum).

1995b "Crusader Influence on Byzantine Art in Cyprus." Pp. 275–94 in *Cyprus and the Crusades. Papers Given at the International Conference "Cyprus and the Crusades," Nicosia, 6–9 September, 1994,* eds. by N. Coureas and J. Riley-Smith (Nicosia: Cyprus Research Centre).

1996 *Ιερά Μητρόπολις Πάφου, Ιστορία και τέχνη* (Nicosia: Imprinta).

1997 "Θεοτόκος με τον Χριστό - Αδιάγνωστος άγιος," *Βυζαντινή Μεσαιωνική Κύπρος (κατάλογος έκθεσης στο Πολιτιστικό Ίδρυμα Τραπέζης Κύπρου)* (Nicosia: Politistiko Idyma Trapezēs Kyprou).

1998 "Ο ναός του Αγίου Λάζαρου στη Λάρνακα," *Report of the Department of Antiquities Cyprus* 1998: 205–24.

2002a "Η Χριστιανική Τέχνη Στήν Κύπρο Κατά Τήν Α΄ Χριστιανική Χιλιετία." Pp. 322–23 in *Πρακτικά Επιστημονικού Συνεδρίου: Εκκλησία Κύπρου. 2000 Χρόνια Χριστιανισμοῦ (Λευκωσία 9–11.6.2000)* (Nicosia: Praktika Synedriou).

2002b "Byzantine Architecture (Fourth–Twelfth Century)." Pp. 63–70 in *Holy Bishopric of Morphou: 2000 Years of Art and Holiness,* ed. L. Michaelidou (Nicosia: Bank of Cyprus).

2010 *Christian Art in the Turkish-Occupied Part of Cyprus* (Nicosia: The Holy Archbishopric of Cyprus).

Papageorghiou, A., and Eliades, I.

2008 *Guide to the Byzantine Museum and Art Gallery of the Archbishop Makarios III Foundation* (Nicosia: Archbishop Makarios III Foundation).

Papanikola-Bakirtzē, D.

1993 "Cypriot Medieval Glazed Pottery: Answers and Questions." Pp. 115–30 in *'The Sweet Land of Cyprus.' Papers Given at the Twenty-Fifth Jubilee Spring Symposium of Byzantine Studies (Birmingham, March 1991)* eds. A. Bryer and G. Georghallides (Nicosia: Cyprus Research Centre).

1996 *Μεσαιωνικὴ ἐφυαλωμένη κεραμικὴ τῆς Κύπρου. Τὰ ἐργαστήρια Πάφου καὶ Λαπήθου* (Thessaloniki: Leventis Foundation).

1997 "Η ἐφυαλωμένη κεραμικὴ στὴ βυζαντινὴ μεσαιωνικὴ Κύπρο (12ος–15ος αἰώνας)." Pp. 129–57 in *Βυζαντινή Μεσαιωνική Κύπρος: Βασίλισσα στην Ανατολή καὶ Ρήγαινα στη Δύση,* eds. D. Papanikola-Bakirtzē and M. Iakōvou (Nicosia: Bank of Cyprus Cultural Foundation).

1999a *Επιτραπέζια καὶ μαγειρικά σκεύη από τη μεσαιωνική Κύπρο* (Nicosia: Leventis Foundation).

2004 *Colours of Medieval Cyprus. Through the Medieval Ceramic Collection of the Leventis Municipal Museum of Nicosia* (Nicosia:

Leventis Foundation and Leventis Municipal Museum).

Papanikola-Bakirtzē, D. (ed.)
1999b Βυζαντινά εφναλωμένα κεραμικά. Η τέχνη των εγχαράκτων (Athens: Tameio Archaiologikōn Porōn kai Apallotriōseōn).
2002 Καθημερινή ζωή στο Βυζάντιο (Thessaloniki: Ministry of Culture of Greece).

Papanikola-Bakirtzē, D., and Iakōvou, M.
1997 Βυζαντινὴ Μεσαιωνικὴ Κύπρος. Βασίλισσα στὴν Ἀνατολὴ καὶ Ρήγαινα στὴ Δύση (Nicosia: Bank of Cyprus Cultural Foundation).

Parani, M.
2003 Reconstructing the Reality of Images. Byzantine Material Culture and Religious Iconography (11th–15th Centuries) [The Medieval Mediterranean 41] (Leiden: Brill).
2005 "Representations of Glass Objects as a Source on Byzantine Glass: How Useful Are They?" Dumbarton Oaks Papers 59: 147–71.
2007 "Byzantine Material Culture and Religious Iconography." Pp. 181–92 in Material Culture and Well-Being in Byzantium (400–1453), eds. M. Grünbart, E. Kislinger, A. Muthesius, and D. Stathakopoulos (Vienna: Österreichische Akademie der Wissenschaften).
2010 "Byzantine Cutlery: An Overview," Δελτίον της Χριστιανικής Αρχαιολογικής Εταιρείας 31: 139–64.

Parks, D.
1996 "Excavations at Kourion's Amathus Gate Cemetery, 1995" Report of the Department of Antiquities Cyprus 1996: 127–33.
1997 "Excavations at Kourion's Amathus Gate Cemetery, 1996" Report of the Department of Antiquities Cyprus 1997: 271–76.

Parks, D., and Chapman, N.
1999 "Preliminary Report of the 1998 Excavations at Kourion's Amathus Gate Cemetery," Report of the Department of Antiquities Cyprus 1999: 259–67.

Parks, D.; Given, M.; and Chapman, N.
1998 "Excavations at Kourion's Amathus Gate Cemetery, 1997" Report of the Department of Antiquities Cyprus 1998: 171–85.

Patrich, J.
1993 "The Early Church of the Holy Sepulchre in the Light of Excavations and Restoration." Pp. 101–17 in Ancient Churches Revealed, ed. Y. Tsafrir (Jerusalem: Israel Exploration Society).

Pazaras, T.
1977 "Κατάλογος Χριστιανικῶν ἀναγλύφων Πλακῶν ἐκ Θεσσαλονίκης Με Ζωομόρφους Παραστάσεις," Βυζαντινά 9: 23–95.

Peacock, D.P.S.
1982 Pottery in the Roman World: An Ethnoarchaeological Approach (London: Longman).

Pelekanides, S.
1955 "Ἡ ἔξω Τῶν Τειχῶν Παλαιοχριστιανικὴ Βασιλικὴ Τῶν Φιλίππων," Αρχαιολογική Εφημερίς 1955: 114–79.

Pelekanides, S.; Christou, P.; Mauropoulou-Tsioume, C.; and Kadas, S.
1975 The Treasures of Mount Athos: Illuminated Manuscripts, 2: The Monasteries of Iveron, St. Panteleimon, Esphigmenou, and Chilandari (Athens: Athēnōn).

Peña, T.J.
2007 Roman Pottery in the Archaeological Record (Cambridge: Cambridge University).

Perdikis, S. (ed.)
2004 Λογίζου Σκευοφύλακος Κρόνικα, ἤγουν χρονογραφία τοῦ νησιοῦ τῆς Κύπρου. Παράρτημα: Steffano Lusignano, Chorografia dell'isola di Cipro (Bologna 1573), Τόμος Ά. (Nicosia: Μουσεῖον Ἱερᾶς Μονῆς Κύκκου).

Perna, R.
2004 "L'Acropole di Cortina in età Romana e Protobizantina." Pp. 545–56 in Creta Romana e Protobizantina, Atti del Congresso

Internazionale, Iraklion 23–30 Settembre 2000, vol. 2 (Padova: Bottega d'Erasmo).

Petermann, H.
1860 *Reisen im Orient* (Leipzig: Veit).

Petinos, C.
1999 "L'église de Chypre entre Constantinople et Antioche (IVème–Vème siècle)," *Byzantinische Forschungen* 25: 131–41.

Petit, C.; Péchoux, P.-Y.; and Dieulafait, Ch.
1996 "Amathonte et son territoire à travers les ages." Pp. 173–82 in *Guide d'Amathonte,* ed. P. Aupert [Sites et monuments 15] (Paris: École Française d'Athènes).

Pettegrew, D.
2010 "Regional Survey and the Boom-and-Bust Countryside: Re-reading the Archaeological Evidence for Episodic Abandonment in the Late Roman Corinthia," *International Journal of Historical Archaeology* 14: 215–29.

Philadelpheus, A.
1918 "Νικοπόλεως Ἀνασκαφαὶ," *Ἀρχαιολογικὴ ἐφημερίς*: 34-41.

Philias, G.
2006 *Παράδοση καὶ Ἐξέλιξη στη Λατρεία τῆς Ἐκκλησίας* (Athens: Gregorēs).

Philotheou, G.
2006 "Τα Εκκλησιαστικά Μνημεία της Φραγκοκρατίας Ενετοκρατίας." Pp. 129–50 in *Λεμεσός, Ταξίδι στους Χρόνους Μιας Πόλης,* ed. A. Marangou (Limassol: Demou Lemesou).
2008 "The Church and Tomb of Aghios Athanasios Pentaschoinitis: A Significant Place of Pilgrimage on Cyprus." Pp. 227–42, 493–97 in *Routes of Faith in the Medieval Mediterranean. History, Monuments, People, Pilgrimage Perspectives. Proceedings of an International Symposium, Thessalonike 7–10/11/2007* (Thessaloniki: European Centre of Byzantine and Post-Byzantine Monuments).

Phountoules, I.
2007 *Κείμενα Λειτουργικῆς, Τεῦχος 3: Θεία Λειτουργίαι* (Thessaloniki).

Piccirillo, M.
1993 *The Mosaics Of Jordan,* eds. P. Bikai and T. Dailey (Amman: American Center of Oriental Research).

Pierides, A.
1971 *Jewellery in the Cyprus Museum* [Picture Book 5] (Nicosia: Department of Antiquities).

Pilides, D.
2003 "Excavations at the Hill of Hagios Georgios (PA.SY.D.Y.), Nicosia: 2002 Season – Preliminary Report," *Report of the Department of Antiquities Cyprus* 2003: 181–200.
2009 *George Jeffery: His Diaries and the Ancient Monuments of Cyprus* (Nicosia: Department of Antiquities).
2012 "A Short Account of the Recent Discoveries Made on the Hill of Ayios Yeoryios (PA.SY.D.Y.)." In *Historic Nicosia,* ed. D. Michaelides (Nicosia: Rimal).

Pitarakis, B.
2006 *Les croix-reliquaires pectorales byzantines en bronze* [Bibliothèque des Cahiers Archéologiques 16] (Paris: Picard).

Platon, N.
1955 "Αἱ Ξυλόστεγαι Παλαιοχριστιανικαὶ Βασιλικαὶ Τῆς Κρήτης." Pp. 415–32 in *Πεπραγμένα Τοῦ Θ´ Διεθνοῦς Βυζαντινολογικοῦ Συνεδρίου (Θεσσαλονίκη, 12–19 Ἀπριλίου 1953),* vol. 1 (Athens).

Poblome, J., and Zelle, M.
2002 "The Table Ware Boom. A Socio-Economic Perspective from Western Asia Minor." Pp. 275–87 in *Patris und Imperium. Kulturelle und politische Identität in den Städten der römischen Provinzen Kleinasiens in der frühen Kaiserzeit. Kolloquium Köln, November 1998,* eds. Ch. Berns et al., [Babesch Supplementa 8] (Leuven: Peeters).

Polonio, V.
2001   "Devozioni di lungo corso: lo scalo geno-
       vese." Pp. 349–94 in *Genova, Venezia, il Le-
       vante nei secoli XII–XIV. Atti del Convegno
       Internazionale di Studi, Genova–Venezia,
       10–14 marzo 2000*, eds. G. Ortalli and D.
       Puncuh (Genoa: Società ligure di storia
       patria).

Poulou-Papadimitriou, N., and Dimioumi, S.
2010   "Nouvelles données sur la production de
       l'atelier céramique protobyzantin à Karda-
       maina (Cos-Grèce)." Pp. 741–49 in *LRCW3.
       Late Roman Coarse Wares, Cooking Wares
       and Amphorae in the Mediterranean. Ar-
       chaeology and Archaeometry. Comparison
       between Western and Eastern Mediterranean*,
       eds. S. Menchelli, S. Santoro, M. Pasquinucci,
       and G. Guiducci [British Archaeological Re-
       ports IS-2185 (II)] (Oxford: Archaeopress).

Pralong, A.
1994   "La Basilique de l'Acropole d'Amathonte
       (Chypre)," *Rivista di archeologia cristiana*
       70.1–2: 411–55.

Procopiou, E.
1996   "Église d'Ayios Tykhonas (Saint-Tykhon)."
       Pp. 153–60 in *Guide d'Amathonte*, ed. P.
       Aupert [Ecole Française d'Athènes, Sites et
       Monuments 15] (Paris: De Boccard).
1997   "Λεμεσός Οδός ζικ-ζακ," *Report of the
       Department of Antiquities Cyprus* 1997:
       285–317.
2006   "Τα Μνημεία Της Πόλης Και Επαρχίας
       Λεμεσού Κατά Την Παλαιοχριστιανική,
       Πρωτοβυζαντινή Και Μεσοβυζαντινή
       Περίοδο 324–1191." Pp. 113–28 in *Λεμεσός,
       Ταξίδι στους Χρόνους Μιας Πόλης*, ed. A.
       Marangou (Limassol: Demou Lemesou).
2007a "Ο Συνεπτυγμένος Σταυροειδής Εγγε-
       γραμμένος Ναός στην Κύπρο (9ος–12ος
       αιώνας)," *Κυπριακί Σπουδαί* 31–36: 187–207.
2007b *Ο Συνεπτυγμένος Σταυροειδής Εγγεγραμ-
       μένος Ναός στην Κύπρο (9ος–12ος αιώνας)*
       (Nicosia: Museum of Kykko Monastery).
2007c "Excavations at Germasogeia-*Kalogeroi*."
       P. 71 in *Annual Report of the Director of

the Department of Antiquities 2001*, ed. P.
       Flourentzos (Nicosia).
2008   "Ιερός Ναός Αρχαγγέλου Μιχαήλ, Κελλάκι:
       Συμβολή στη Μελέτη των Καμαροσκέπα-
       στων Μεσοβυζαντινών Ναών της Επαρχίας
       Λεμεσού," *Κυπριακαί Σπουδαί* 72: 13–17:
       219–28.

Pulgher, D.
1878   *Les anciennes églisés byzantines de Constan-
       tinople* (Vienna).

Quilici, L.
1989   "Poleografia e popolamento della pen-
       isola di Kormakiti a Cipro," *Felix Ravenna*
       137–38: 7–23.

Rapp, C.
1991   "The Vita of Epiphanius of Salamis: An
       Historical and Literary Study," D.Phil. dis-
       sertation (Oxford: Oxford University).
1993   "Epiphanius of Salamis: The Church Father
       as Saint." Pp. 169–87 in *'The Sweet Land of
       Cyprus.' Papers Given at the Twenty-Fifth
       Jubilee Spring Symposium of Byzantine Stud-
       ies (Birmingham, March 1991)* eds. A. Bryer
       and G. Georghallides (Nicosia: Cyprus
       Research Centre).
2004   "All in the Family: John the Almsgiver,
       Nicetas and Heraclius." Pp. 121–34 in *Nea
       Rhome. Rivista di ricerche bizantinistiche* 1
       (*Studi in onore di Vera von Falkenhausen*)
       (Rome: Universita degli Studi di Roma "Tor
       Vergata").
2005   *Holy Bishops in Late Antiquity: The Nature
       of Christian Leadership in an Age of Transi-
       tion* (Berkeley: University of California).
2008   "Hellenic Identity, Romanitas, and Chris-
       tianity in Byzantium." Pp. 127–47 in *Helle-
       nisms: Culture, Identity, and Ethnicity from
       Antiquity to Modernity*, ed. K. Zacharia
       (Aldershot: Ashgate).
2012   "Hagiography and the Cult of Saints in
       the Light of Epigraphy and Acclamations."
       Pp. 291–311 in *Byzantine Religious Culture.
       Studies in Honor of Alice-Mary Talbot*, eds.
       D. Sullivan, E. Fisher, and E. Papaioannou
       (Leiden: Brill).

Rapp, S.
2003 *Studies in Medieval Georgian Historiography* (Leuven: Peeters).

Raptes, K., and Vasileiadou, S.D.
2005 "Διαχρονική χρήση, διαδοχικές θέσεις και απόπειρα επαν-ένταξης των μαρμάρινων αρχιτεκτονικών μελών των βασιλικών Α, Β, Β Αγίος Γεωργίος (Πάφος)," *Report of the Department of Antiquities Cyprus* 2005: 199–224.

Raptou, E.
2007a "Agia Paraskevi Square, Geroskipou." P. 72 in *Annual Report of the Department of Antiquities for the Year 2007*, ed. P. Flourentzos (Nicosia: Government Office).
2007b "Les amphores orientales d'un bâtiment religieux de Yeroskipou." Pp. 695–703 in *Amphores d'Egypte de la Basse Époque à l'époque Arabe*, vol. 2, eds. S. Marchand and A. Marangou [Cahiers de la Céramique égyptienne 8] (Cairo: IFAO).

Rautman, M.
1998 "Handmade Pottery and Social Change: The View from Late Roman Cyprus," *Journal of Mediterranean Archaeology* 11: 81–104.
2000 "The Busy Countryside of Late Roman Cyprus," *Report of the Department of Antiquities of Cyprus* 2000: 317–31.
2001a "Rural Society and Economy in Late Roman Cyprus." Pp. 241–62 in *Urban Centers and Rural Contexts in Late Antiquity*, eds. J. Eadie and T. Burns (East Lansing: Michigan State University).
2001b "The Context of Rural Innovation: An Early Monastery at Kalavasos-Sirmata," *Report of the Department of Antiquities Cyprus* 2001: 307–18.
2003 *A Cypriot Village of Late Antiquity: Kalavasos-Kopetra in the Vasilikos Valley* [JRA Supplement 52] (Ann Arbor: Journal of Roman Archaeology).
2004 "Valley and Village in late Roman Cyprus." Pp. 189–218 in *Recent Research on the Late Antique Countryside*, eds. W. Bowden et al. (Leiden: Brill).

2007 "The Villages of Byzantine Cyprus." Pp. 453–64 in *Les villages dans l'empire byzantin*, eds. J. Lefort et al. (Paris: Lethielleux).

Rautman, M., and McClellan, M.C.
1992 "Excavations at Late Roman Kopetra, Cyprus," *Journal of Roman Archaeology* 5: 265–71.
1994 "The 1991–1993 Field Seasons at Kalavasos-Kopetra," *Report of the Department of Antiquities Cyprus* 1994: 289–307.

Rautman, M., and Neff, H.
2002 "Compositional Analysis of Ceramics from Maroni-Petrera." Pp. 55–57 in *The Late Roman Church at Maroni-Petrera*, eds. S. Manning et al. (Nicosia: Leventis Foundation).

Rautman, M.; Gomez, B.; Neff, H.; and Glascock, M.D.
1993 "Neutron Activation Analysis of Late Roman Ceramics from Kalavasos-Kopetra and the Environs of the Vasilikos Valley," *Report of the Department of Antiquities Cyprus* 1993: 233–64.
1995a "Neutron Activation Analysis of Cypriot and Related Ceramics at the University of Missouri." Pp. 331–49 in *Hellenistic and Roman Pottery in the Eastern Mediterranean. Advances in Scientific Studies*, eds. H. Meyza and Y. Młynarczyk (Warsaw: Polish Academy of Sciences).
1995a "Clays Related to the Production of White Slip Ware," *Report of the Department of Antiquities Cyprus* 1995: 113–18.
1996 "Clays Used in the Manufacture of Cypriot Red Slip Pottery and Related Ceramics," *Report of the Department of Antiquities Cyprus* 1996: 69–82.
1999 "Amphoras and Rooftiles from Late Roman Cyprus: A Compositional Study of Calcareous Fabric Ceramics from Kalavasos-Kopetra," *Journal of Roman Archaeology* 12: 377–91.
2002 "Source Provenance of Bronze Age and Roman Pottery from Cyprus," *Archaeometry* 44: 23–36.

Reese, D.
1989 "Tracking the Extinct Pygmy Hippopotamus of Cyprus," *Field Museum of Natural History Bulletin* 60.2: 22–29.

Reese, D.; Mienis, H.K.; and Woodward, F.R.
1986 "On the Trade of Shells and Fish from the Nile River," *Bulletin of the American Schools of Oriental Research* 264: 79–84.

Reinink, G.J.
1985 "Die Entstehung der syrischen Alexanderlegende als politisch-religiöse Propagandaschrift für Herakleios Kirchenpolitik." Pp. 263–81 in *After Chalcedon. Studies in Theology and Church History. Offered to Professor Albert van Roey for his Seventieth Birthday*, eds. C. Laga, J.A. Munitiz, and L. Van Rompay [Orientalia Lovaniensia Analecta 18] (Leuven: Peeters).
2002 "Apocalyptic Prophesies during the Reign of Heraclius." Pp. 81–94 in *The Reign of Heraclius (610–641), Crisis and Confrontation*, eds. G. Reinink and B.H. Stolte (Paris: Dudley).

Regan, G.
2006 Ἡράκλειος: Ὁ Πρῶτος Σταυροφόρος, transl. K. Anastasopoulou (Athens: Enalios); originally published in English as *First Crusader: Byzantium's Holy Wars* (New York: Palgrave Macmillan, 2001).

Remsen, W.
2010 "The Survey of the Church." Pp. 71–102 in *The Canopy of Heaven: The Ciborium in the Church of St. Mamas, Morphou*, eds. M. Jones and A.M. Jones (Nicosia: USAID/SAVE).

Restle, M.
1967 *Byzantine Wall Painting in Asia Minor* (Recklinghausen: Bongers).

Reuther, O.
1912) *Ocheïdir: Nach Aufnahmne von Mitgliedern der Babylon-Expedition der Deutschen Orientgesellschaft* (Leipzig: Hinrichs).

Rey, E.G.
1871 *Etude sur les monuments de l'architecture militaire des Croisés en Syrie et dans l'île de Chypre* (Paris: Imprimerie nationale).

Reynolds, P.
2003 "Pottery and the Economy in 8th Century Beirut: An Umayyad Assemblage from the Roman Imperial Bath (BEY 045)." Pp. 725–34 in *VIIe Congrès international sur la céramique médiéévale en Méditerranée, Thessaloniki, 11–16 Octobre 1999*, ed. C. Bakirtzis (Athens: Archaeological Receipts Fund).

Reynolds Brown, K.
1979 "306. Pair of Earrings." Pp. 327–28 in *Age of Spirituality. Late Antique and Early Christian Art, Third to Seventh Century*, ed. K. Weizmann (New York: The Metropolitan Museum of Art).

Richter, J.-P.
1897 *Quellen der byzantinischen Kunstgeschichte* (Vienna: Graeser).

Ristovska, N.
2009 "Distribution Patterns of Middle Byzantine Painted Glass." Pp. 199–220 in *Byzantine Trade, 4th–12th Centuries. The Archaeology of Local, Regional and International Exchange*, ed. M. Mundell Mango [Society for the Promotion of Byzantine Studies Publications 14] (Farnham: Ashgate).

Ross, L.
1852 *Reisen nach Kos, Halykarnassos, Rhodos und der Insel Cypern* (Halle: Schwetschke und Sohn).

Ross, M.C.
1959 "A Byzantine Treasure in Detroit," *Art Quarterly* 22: 229–37.

Rosser, J.
1985 "Excavations at Saranda Kolones, Paphos, Cyprus, 1981–1983," *Dumbarton Oaks Papers* 39: 81–97.

Rouerché, C.
2001 "The Prehistory of the Cyprus Department of Antiquities." Pp. 155–66 in *Mosaic. Festschrift for A.H.S. Megaw* [British School at Athens Studies 8] (London: British School at Athens).

Roux, G.
1998 *La Basilique de la Campanopetra* [Salamine de Chypre 15] (Paris: De Boccard).

Ruggieri, V.
1991 *Byzantine Religious Architecture (582–867): Its History and Structural Elements* (Rome: Pontificium Institutum Studiorum Orientalium).
1993 "The IV Century Greek Episcopal Lists in the Mardin. Syriac. 7 (olim Mardin. Orth. 309/9)," *Orientalia Christiana Periodica* 59: 315–56.

Runciman, S.
1990 "The Byzantine Period." Pp. 134–62 in *Footprints in Cyprus: An Illustrated History,* ed. D. Hunt (London: Trigraph).

Rupp, D.W.
1986 "The Canadian Palaipaphos (Cyprus) Survey Project. Third Preliminary Report, 1983–1985," *Acta Archaeologica* 57: 27–45.
1997 "'Metro' Nea Paphos: Suburban Sprawl in Southwestern Cyprus in the Hellenistic and Earlier Roman Periods." Pp. 236–62 in *Urbanism in Antiquity from Mesopotamia to Crete,* eds. W.E. Aufrecht et al. [Journal for the Study of the Old Testament, Suppl. 244] (Sheffield: Sheffield Academic).

Russell, J.
2002 "Anemourion." Pp. 221–28 in *The Economic History of Byzantium: From the Seventh through the Fifteenth Century,* vol. 1, ed. A. Laiou (Washington, DC.: Dumbarton Oaks Research Library and Collection).

Ryden, L.
1993 "Cyprus at the Time of the Condominium as Reflected in the Lives of Sts Demetrianos and Constantine the Jew." Pp. 189–202 in *'The Sweet Land of Cyprus.' Papers Given at the Twenty-Fifth Jubilee Spring Symposium of Byzantine Studies (Birmingham, March 1991)* eds. A. Bryer and G. Georghallides (Nicosia: Cyprus Research Centre).

Sacopoulo, M.
1962 "La fresque chrétienne la plus ancienne de Chypre," *Cahiers Archéologiques* 13: 61–83.
1966 *Asinou en 1106 et sa contribution à l'iconographie* (Brussels: Éditions de Byzantion).

Sader, Y.
1987 *Peintures murales dans des églises maronites médiévales* (Beirut: Dar Sader).

Sarbianov, V.D.
2002 *Transfiguration Cathedral of the Mirozh Monastery* (Moscow: Severny Palomnik).
2004 "Собор Богоматери Антонива Монастыря." Pp. 531–789 in *Монументальая Живопись Великого Новгорода, Конец XI – первая четверть XII века,* eds. L.I. Lifshitz, V.D. Sarbianov, and T. Tsarevskaia (St. Petersburg: Bulanin).

Savvidēs, A.
1993 "Προσωπογραφικό σημείωμα για τον απελευθερωτή της Κύπρου Νικήτα Χαλκούτζη και για τη χρονολογία ανακατάληψης της μεγαλονήσου (965 μ.Χ.)," *Επετηρίδα Κέντρου Μελετών Ιεράς Μονής Κύκκου* 2: 371–78.

Schabel, C.
2005 "Religion." Pp. 157–218 in *Cyprus. Society and Culture 1191–1374,* eds. A. Nicolaou-Konnari and C. Schabel (Leiden: Brill).

Scholem, G.
2007 "Magen, David." Pp. 336–39 in *Encyclopaedia Judaica,* eds. F. Skolnik and M. Berenbaum (Detroit: Macmillan Reference).

Schulz, H.J.
1997 *Η Βυζαντινή Λειτουργία,* transl. D. Tzerpos (Thessaloniki: Akritas).

Serjeant, R.B.
1951 "Materials for a History of Islamic Textiles up to the Mongol Conquest," *Ars Islamica* 15–16: 29–85.

Ševčenko, I.
1979–80 "Constantinople Viewed from the Eastern Provinces in the Middle Byzantine Period." Pp. 712–47 in *Eucharisterion: Essays Presented to Omeljan Pritsak, Harvard Ukrainian Studies,* 3/4, part 2; reprinted in *Ideology, Letters and Culture in the Byzantine World* (London: Variorum, 1982).

Ševčenko, N. Patterson
1990 *Illustrated Manuscripts of the Metaphrastian Menologion* (Chicago: University of Chicago).
1991 "Agiosoritisa" and "Virgin Hagiosoritissa." P. 2171 in *The Oxford Dictionary of Byzantium,* vol. 3, eds. A.P. Kazhdan et al. (Oxford: Oxford University).
1999 "The 'Vita' Icon and the Painter as Iconographer," *Dumbarton Oaks Papers* 53: 149–65.

Sevketoğlu, M.; Kucukso, H.; and Aslier, A.
2009 *Church of the Panagia Perghamiotissa* (Nicosia: USAID/SAVE).

Shoemaker, S.J.
2008 "The Cult of Fashion. The Earliest 'Life of the Virgin' and Constantinople's Marian Relics," *Dumbarton Oaks Papers* 62: 53–74.

Sijpesteijn, P.M.
2007 "New Rule over Old Structures: Egypt after the Muslim Conquest." Pp. 183–200 in *Regime Change in the Ancient Near East and Egypt,* ed. H. Crawford [Proceedings of the British Academy 136] (Oxford: British Academy).

Simmons, A.H.
1988a "Test Excavations at Acrotiri-*Aetokremnos* (Site E). An Early Prehistoric Occupation in Cyprus. Preliminary Report," *Report of the Department of Antiquities Cyprus* 1988: 15–24.

1988b "Extinct Pygmy Hippopotamus and Early Man in Cyprus," *Nature* 333. 6173: 554–57.

Simmons, A.H.; Held, S.; and Reese, D.
1988 "Extinct Pygmy Hippopotamus, Early Man, and the Initial Human Occupation of Cyprus." P. 81 in *International Conference "Early Man in Island Environments, Oliena, Sardinia).* ed. M. Sanges (Sassari: Industria Grafica Stampacolor).

Silogava, V.
1994 *Kumurdo – Tazris epigrapika* (Tbilisi: Mecniereba).

Smirnov, J.
1897 "Хрйстанскія Мозайкй Кйпра (Christian Mosaics in Cyprus)," *VizVrem* 4: 1–93.

Smith, R.H., and Day, L.
1989 *Pella of the Decapolis 2. Final Report on the College of Wooster Excavations in Area Ix, the Civic Complex, 1979–1985* (Wooster, OH: College of Wooster).

Sodini J.-P.
1998 "Les inscriptions de l'aqueduct de Kythrea à Salamine de Chypre," *Byzantina Sorbonensia* 16: 619–34.
2004 "La Naissance de l'Habitat Médiéval en Méditerranée Byzantine le Cas de Gortyne." Pp. 669–86 in *Creta Romana e Protobizantina, Atti del Congresso Internazionale, Iraklion 23–30 Settembre 2000,* vol. 2 (Padova: Bottega d'Erasmo).
2006 "Η Χρήση Μαρμάρου Και Πέτρας (7ος–15ος Αιώνας)." Pp. 223–48 in *Οικονομική Ιστορία του Βυζαντίου από τον 7ο Ως τον 15ο Αιώνα* 1, ed. A. Laïou (Athens: Morphotiko Idryma Ethnikēs Trapezēs).

Sodini, J.-P.; Barsanti, C.; and Guidobaldi, A.
1998 "La Sculpture Architecturale en Marbre au VIe Siècle à Constantinople et dans les Régions sous Influence Constantinopolitaine." Pp. 301–76 in *Acta XIII Congressus Internationalis Archaeologiae Christianae:*

Split-Poreč 25.9–1.10.1994, vol. 2 (Vatican: Pontificio Istituto de Archeologia Cristiana).

Sodini, J.-P., and Villeneuve, E.
1992   "Le passage de la céramique byzantine à la céramique omeyyade en Syrie du nord, en Palestine et en Transjordanie." Pp. 195–228 in *La Syrie de Byzance à l'Islam, VIIe–VIIIe siècles, Actes du colloque international, Lyon, Paris, 11–15 Septembre 1990*, eds. P. Canivet and J-P. Rey-Coquais (Damascus: Institut Français de Damas).

Sollars, L.H.
2005   "Settlement and Community: Their Location, Limits and Movement through the Landscape of Historical Cyprus," unpublished Ph.D. dissertation, University of Glasgow [http://theses.gla.ac.uk/231/].

Sondaar, P. Y.
1986   "The Island Sweepstakes," *Natural History* 95.9 (September): 50–57.

Sophocleous, S.
1992   *Οι Δεσποτικές Εικόνες της Μονής του Μεγάλου Αγρού* (Nicosia: Museum Publications).
1994   *Icons of Cyprus* (Nicosia: Museum Publications).
2000   *Cyprus, the Holy Island. Icons through the Centuries* (Nicosia: Leventis Foundation).
2006   *Icones de Chypre: Diocese de Limassol, 12e–16e siècle* (Nicosia: Centre du patrimoine culturel).

Soren, D., and James, J.
1988   *Kourion: The Search for a Lost Roman City* (New York: Anchor).

Sørensen, W.L., and Rupp, D.W.
1993   *The Land of the Paphian Aphrodite 2, The Canadian Palaipaphos Survey Project, Artifact and Ecofactual Studies* [Studies in Mediterranean Archaeology 104.2] (Göteborg: Åström).

Sørensen, W.L., et al.
1987   "Canadian Palaepaphos Survey Project: Second Preliminary Report of the Ceramic Finds 1982–1983," *Report of the Department of Antiquities Cyprus* 1987: 259–78.

Soteriou, G.A.
1920a   "Παλαιά Χριστιανική Βασιλική Ἰλισσοῦ" (Reprint from *Ἀρχαιολογικὴ ἐφημερίς* 1919) 1–31.
1920b   *Χριστιανικὰ Μνημεῖα τῆς Μικρᾶς Ἀσίας* (Athens: Syllogos pros Diadosin Ophelimon Vivlion).
1924   "Ἀνασκαφαὶ Τοῦ Βυζαντινοῦ Ναοῦ Ἰωάννου Τοῦ Θεολόγου ἐν Ἐφέσῳ" [Reprint from *Ἀρχαιολογικοῦ Δελτίου* 7 (1921–22)].
1929   "Αἱ Παλαιοχριστιανικαί Βασιλικαί Τῆς Ἑλλάδος," *Ἀρχαιολογικὴ ἐφημερίς* 1929: 161–248.
1929–30 "Αἱ Χιστιανικαί Θῆβαι Τῆς Θεσσαλίας," *Ἀρχαιολογικὴ ἐφημερίς* 3: 1–150 (Reprint 1993).
1931   "Τα παλαιοχριστιανικά και βυζαντινά μνημεία της Κύπρου," *Πρακτικά της Ακαδημίας Αθηνών* 1931: 477–90.
1935   *Τα Βυζαντινά Μνήματα της Κύπρου* (Athens: Athens Academy).
1937   "Ήώ ναός και τάφος του Απόστολου Βαρνάβα παρά την Σαλαμίνα τες Κύπρου," *Κυπριακαί Σπουδαί* 1: 175–87.
1940   "Les églises byzantines de Chypre à trois et à cinq coupoles et leur place dans l'histoire de l'architecture byzantine." Pp. 401–9 in *Atti del V Congresso Internazionale di Studi Bizantini [Rome, 20–26 Sept. 1936]*, vol. 2 (Rome: Tipografia del Senato).
1942   *Χριστιανική και Βυζαντινή Αρχαιολογία* 1: *Χριστιανικά Κοιμητήρια – Εκκλησιαστική Αρχιτεκτονική* (Athens: Athēnais Archaiologikē Etaireia).

Soteriou, G.A., and Soteriou, M.
1952   *Ἡ Βασιλικὴ Τοῦ Ἁγίου Δημητρίου Θεσσαλονίκης* (Athens: Athēnais Archaiologikē Etaireia).

Spain Alexander, S.
1977 "Heraclius, Byzantine Imperial Ideology, and the David Plates," *Speculum* 52: 217–37.

Spanou, C.
2002 "Η Τέχνη στην Μητροπολιτική Περιφέρεια Κιτίου από τον 6ον έως τον 15ον αιώνα. Μνημειακή ζωγραφικκή και φορητές εικόνες." Pp. 19–45 in *Η κατά Κίτιον γιογραφική τέχνη*, eds. K. Gerasimou, K. Papaioakeim and C. Spanou (Larnaka: Hiera Metropolis Kitiou).

Stavrides, T.
1998 "Ο σεισμός του 1491 στην Κύπρο," *Επετηρίδα Κέντρου Επιστημονικών Ερευνών* 24: 125–44.

Stern, E.
1995 "Export to the Latin East of Cypriot Manufactured Glazed Pottery in the 12th–13th Century." Pp. 325–35 in *Cyprus and the Crusades. Papers Given at the International Conference "Cyprus and the Crusades," Nicosia, 6–9 September, 1994*, eds. N. Coureas and J. Riley-Smith (Nicosia: Cyprus Research Centre and Society for the Study of the Crusades and the Latin East).
2008 "Chronological Tables," in *The New Encyclopedia of Archaeological Excavations in the Holy Land*, vol. 5 (Jerusalem: Israel Exploration Society).

Stewart, C.A.
2008 *Domes of Heaven: The Domed Basilicas of Cyprus*, Ph.D. dissertation (Ann Arbor, ProQuest/UMI).
2010 "The First Vaulted Churches in Cyprus," *Journal of the Society of Architectural Historians* 69.2: 162–90.
2012 "Flying Buttresses and Pointed Arches in Byzantine Cyprus," in *Masons at Work*, eds. R. Ousterhout, R. Holod and L. Haselberger (Philadelphia: University of Pennsylvania) [http://www.sas.upenn.edu/ancient/publications.html].
forthcoming a "The Barrel-Vaulted Basilicas of Cyprus," in *Proceedings of the 4th International Cyprological Congress, Lefkosia, 29 April–3 May 2008: B. Medieval* 2, ed. Ch. Chotzakoglou (Nicosia: Etaireīa Kypriakōn Spoudōn).
forthcoming b "Early Byzantine Military Architecture in Cyprus," in *The Archaeology of Late Antique and Byzantine Cyprus(4th–12th centuries AD): Recent Research and New Discoveries*, eds. M. Parani and D. Michaelides [Cahiers du Centre d' Etudes chypriotes 43] (Paris: De Boccard).
forthcoming c "The Fortification of Cyprus within the Grand Strategy of the Byzantine Empire (965–1185)," in *'Byzantium' in Transition*, Volume 2: *Middle to Late Byzantine or Early Frankish Era, 12th–13th Centuries*, eds. A. Vionis and M. Parani (Cambridge: Cambridge University).
forthcoming d "Architectural Innovation during the Reign of Emperor Heraclius," *Architectural History* 57 [SAHGB, London].

Stefanidis, I.
1999 *Isle of Discord: Nationalism, Imperialism and the Making of the Cyprus Problem* (New York: New York University).

Stoufi-Poulimenou, I.
1999 *Τὸ Φράγμα τοῦ Ιεροῦ Βήματος στὰ Παλαιοχριστιανικά Μνημεῖα τῆς Ελλάδος* (Athens: National and Kapodistrian University of Athens).

Strube, C.
1973 *Die Westliche Eingangsseite der Kirchen von Konstantinopel in Justinianischer Zeit* (Wiesbaden: Harrassowitz).

Strzygowski, J.
1918 *Die Baukunst der Armenier und Europa* (Vienna: Schroll).

Stylianou, A.
1955 "Αἱ τοιχογραφίαι τοῦ ναοῦ τῆς Παναγίας τοῦ Ἀράκου, Λαγουδερά, Κύπρος." Pp. 459–67 in *Πεπραγμένα τοῦ Θ' Διεθνοῦς Βυζαντινολογικοῦ Συνεδρίου, Θεσσαλονίκη, 12-19 Ἀπριλίου 1953*, vol.1, ed. St. Kyriakidēs,

A. Xyngopoulos, and P. Zepos (Athens: Etaireīa Makedonikōn Spoudōn).

1963   *Cyprus, Byzantine Mosaics and Frescoes* [UNESCO World Art Series] (Greenwich, CT: New York Graphic Society).

Stylianou, A., and Stylianou, J.
1977   "St. Hilarion the Great in Paphos, Cyprus," *Κυπριακαὶ Σπουδαί* 41: 1–5.
1985   *The Painted Churches of Cyprus* (Nicosia: Leventis Foundation, 2nd revised ed. 1997).

Sweetman, R.
2010   "The Christianization of the Peloponnese: The Topography and Function of Late Antique Churches," *Journal of Late Antiquity* 3.2: 203–61.

Swiny, H.W.
1982   *An Archaeological Guide to the Ancient Kourion Area and the Akrotiri Peninsula* (Nicosia: Department of Antiquities).

Swiny, S.
1988   "The Pleistocene Fauna of Cyprus and Recent Discoveries on the Akrotiri Peninsula," *Report of the Department of Antiquities Cyprus* 1988: 1–14.

Swiny, S., and Mavromatis, C.
2000   "Land behind Kourion. Results of the 1997 Sotira Archaeological Project Survey," *Report of the Department of Antiquities Cyprus* 2000: 433–52.

Symeonoglou, S.
1972   "Archaeological Survey in the Area of Phlamoudhi, Cyprus," *Report of the Department of Antiquities Cyprus* 1972: 187–98.

Taft, R.F.
1980   "The Pontifical Liturgy of the Great Church According to a Twelfth-Century Diataxis in Codex British Museum Add. 34060," *Orientalia Christiana Periodica* 46: 105–15.
1980–81 "The Liturgy of the Great Church: An Initial Synthesis of Structure and Interpre-

tation on the Eve of Iconoclasm," *Dumbarton Oaks Papers* 34–35: 49–52.
1992   *The Byzantine Rite. A Short History* (Collegeville, MN: Liturgical).
1997   *Beyond East and West: Problems in Liturgical Understanding* (Washington, DC: Pastoral).
2004   *A History of the Liturgy of St. John Chrysostom*, 5 vols. (Rome: Pontificium Institutum Studiorum Orientalium).

Talbert, R.J.
2010   *Rome's World. The Peutinger Map Reconsidered* (Cambridge: Cambridge University).

Tantrakarn, K.; Kato, N.; Hokura, A.; Nakai, I.; Fujii, Y.; and Gluščević, S.
2009   "Archaeological Analysis of Roman Glass Excavated from Zadar, Croatia, by a Newly Developed Portable XRF Spectrometer for Glass," *X-Ray Spectrometry* 38.2: 121–27.

Tatton-Brown, V.
2001   *Cyprus in the 19th Century AD – Fact, Fancy and Fiction: Papers of the 22nd British Museum Classical Colloquium, December 1998* (Oxford: Oxbow).

Thiel, A.
2005   *Die Johanneskirche in Ephesos* (Wiesbaden: Reichert).

Thierry, N.
1984   "Matériaux Nouveaux en Cappadoce (1982)," *Byzantion* 54: 315–57.

Thirgood, J.V.
1987   *Cyprus. A Chronicle of its Forests, Land, and People* (Vancouver: University of British Columbia).

Thonemann, P.
2012   "Abercius of Hierapolis: Christianization and Social Memory in Late Antique Asia Minor." Pp. 257–82 in *Historical and Religious Memory in the Ancient World*, eds. B. Dignas and R.R.R. Smith (Oxford: Oxford University).

Todd, I.A.

2004   *The Field Survey of the Vasilikos Valley*
        1 [Vasilikos Valley Project 9 / Studies in
        Mediterranean Archaeology 71.9] (Göte-
        borg: Åström).

forthcoming   *The Field Survey of the Vasilikos*
        Valley 2 [Vasilikos Valley Project 10 / Stud-
        ies in Mediterranean Archaeology 71.10]
        (Göteborg: Åström).

Tolotti, F.

1982   "Le basiliche cimiteriali con deambulatorio
        del suburbio romano: Questione ancora
        aperta," *Römische Mitteilungen* 89.1: 153–211.

Tomeković, S.

1995–96   "Quatre illustrations rares, au XIIe siècle,
        des événements precedent la naissance de
        la Vierge à Trikomo," *Δελτίον τῆς Χριστια-*
        νικῆς ἀρχαιολογικῆς Ἑταιρείας 18: 97–104.

Touma, M.

2001   "Chypre: Céramique et problèmes." Pp.
        267–91 in *The Dark Centuries of Byzantium*
        (7th–9th c.), ed. E. Kountoura-Galake
        [International Symposium 9] (Athens:
        National Hellenic Research Foundation).

Trempelas, P.

1993a   *Λειτουργικοί Τύποι Αἰγύπτου καῖ Ἀνατολῆς.*
        Συμβολαὶ εἰς τὴν Ἱστορίαν τῆς Χριστιανικῆς
        Λατρείας 2 (Athens: Soter).

1993b   *Ὁ Προφήτης Ἰωνᾶς*, 3rd ed. (Athens: Soter).

1997   *Αἱ Τρεῖς Λειτουργίαι Κατὰ τοὺς ἐν Ἀθῆναις*
        Κώδικας (Athens: Soter).

Triantaphyllopoulos, D.D.

2006   "Il culto e l'immagine di san Nicola a Cipro."
        Pp. 117–26 in *San Nicola. Splendori d'arte*
        d'Oriente e d'Occidente, ed. M. Bacci (Mi-
        lan).

Trombley, F.R.

1998   "War, Society and Popular Religion in
        Byzantine Anatolia (6th–13th Centuries)."
        Pp. 97–139 in *Η Βυζαντινή Μικρά Ασία,*
        Διεθνή Συμπόσια, ed. S. Lampakis (Athens:
        Ethniko Idryma Ereunōn).

Trygonaki, C.

2004   "Εισηγμένα Αρχιτεκτονικά Γλυπτά και
        Τοπικά Εργαστήρια στην Πρωτοβυζαντινή
        Κρήτη." Pp. 1147–59 in *Creta Romana e*
        Protobizantina, Atti del Congresso Interna-
        zionale, Iraklion 23–30 Settembre 2000, vol.
        2 (Padova: Bottega d'Erasmo).

Tsafrir, Y.

1993   "Monks and Monasteries in Southern Sinai."
        Pp. 315–33 in *Ancient Churches Revealed*,
        ed. Y. Tsafrir (Jerusalem: Israel Exploration
        Society).

2000   "Procopius and the Nea Church in Jerusa-
        lem," *Antiquité Tardive* 8: 149–164.

Tsiknopoulos, I.

1971   *Ἱστορία τῆς Ἐκκλησίας τῆς Πάφου* (Nicosia:
        Holy Bishopric of Paphos).

Tsirpanlis, C.N.

1993   "The Origins of Cypriot Christianity," *The*
        Patristic and Byzantine Review 12.1–3: 25–31.

Tzaferis, V.

1993   "The Early Monastery at Kursi" and "The
        Early Christian Holy Site at Shepherds'
        Field." Pp. 77–79 and 204–6 in *Ancient*
        Churches Revealed, ed. Y. Tsafrir (Jerusa-
        lem: Israel Exploration Society).

Unger, F.

1878   *Quellen der byzantinischen Kunstgeschichte*
        (Vienna: Braumüller).

Usener, H.

1907   *Der heilige Tychon* (Leipzig: Teubner).

Vailhé, S.

1910   "Formation de l'église de Chypre (431),"
        Échos d'Orient 13: 5–10.

Vanhaverbeke, H.; Vionis, A.; Poblome, J.;
and Waelkens, M.

2009   "What Happened after the 7th Century AD?
        A Different Perspective on Post-Roman
        Rural Anatolia." Pp. 177–90 in *Archaeology*
        of the Countryside in Medieval Anatolia,

eds. T. Vorderstrasse and J. Roodenberg (Leiden: Nederlands Instituut voor het Nabije Oosten).

Varalis, I.
2001 "Η Επίδραση της Θείας Λειτουργίας και των Ιερών Ακολουθιών στην Εκκλησιαστική Αρχιτεκτονική του Ανατολικού Ιλλυρικού 395–753," unpublished Ph.D. dissertation, Aristotle University of Thessaloniki.
2004 "Παρατηρήσεις Στην Παλαιοχριστιανική Ναοδομία Της Κρήτης." Pp. 813–38 *Creta Romana e Protobizantina, Atti del Congresso Internazionale, Iraklion 23–30 Settembre 2000,* vol. 2 (Padova: Bottega d'Erasmo).

Varinlioglu, G.
2008 "Living in a Marginal Environment: Rural Habitat and Landscape in Southeastern Isauria," *Dumbarton Oaks Papers* 61: 287–317.

Varnava, A.
2005 "Punch and the British Occupation of Cyprus in 1878," *Byzantine and Modern Greek Studies* 29.2: 167–86.

Veikou, M.
2009 "'Rural Towns' and 'In-Between' or 'Third' Spaces. Settlement Patterns in Byzantine Epirus (7th–11th Centuries) from an Interdisciplinary Approach," *Archaeologia medievale* 36: 43–54.

Velmans, T.
1971 *Le Tétraévangile de la Laurentienne, Florence, Laur. VI.23* [Bibliothèque des Cahiers archéologiques 6] (Paris: Klincksieck).

Vicelja, M.
1998 "The Justinianic Sculpture at Pula; A Reconsideration." Pp. 1037–46 in *Acta XIII Congressus Internationalis Archaeologiae Christianae: Split-Poreč 25.9–1.10.1994,* vol. 2 (Vatican: Pontificio Istituto de Archeologia Cristiana).

Vikan, G.
1988 "Saint Spyridon" and "Archangel Gabriel," in *Holy Image. Holy Space. Icons and Frescoes from Greece* [Exhibition Catalogue] ed. M. Acheimastou-Potamianou (Athens: Byzantine Museum of Athens), nos. 10 and 11, pp. 84–85, 174–76.

Violaris, Y.
2004 "Excavations at the Site of *Palaion Demarcheion,* Lefkosia," *Cahier du Centre d'Études Chypriotes* 34: 69–80.

Vionis, A.K.; Poblome, J.; and Waelkens, M.
2009 "The Hidden Material Culture of the Dark Ages. Early Medieval Ceramics at Sagalassos (Turkey): New Evidence (AD 650–800)," *Anatolian Studies* 59: 147–65.

Vita, A. di
2004 "Gortina." Pp. 459–76 in *Creta Romana e Protobizantina, Atti del Congresso Internazionale, Iraklion 23–30 Settembre 2000,* vol. 2 (Padova: Bottega d'Erasmo).

Vlysidou, V.; Kountoura-Galake, E.; Lampakis, S.; Loungis, T.; and Savvidēs, A.
1998 *Η Μικρά Ασία Των Θεμάτων* (Athens: Ethniko Idryma Ereunōn).

Vroom, J.
2003 *After Antiquity. Ceramics and Society in the Aegean from the 7th to the 20th Century A.C. A Case Study from Boeotia, Central Greece* (Leiden: Leiden University).
2007 "Limyra in Lycia: Byzantine/Umayyad Pottery Fines from Excavations in the Eastern Part of the City." Pp. 261–92 in *Les produits et les marchés. Céramique antique en Lycie (VIIe s. av. J.-C.–VIIe s. ap. J.-C.), Actes de la table-ronde de Poitiers (21–22 mars 2003),* ed. S. Lemaître (Bordeaux: Ausonius).

Waksman, S.Y., and von Wartburg, M.-L.
2006 "'Fine-Sgraffito Ware', 'Aegean Ware', and Other Wares: New Evidence for a Major Production of Byzantine Ceramics," *Report*

of the Department of Antiquities Cyprus
2006: 369–88.

Walmsley, A.
2008   "Economic Developments and the Nature
        of Settlement in the Towns and Country-
        side of Syria-Palestine, ca. 565–800 CE,"
        Dumbarton Oaks Papers 61: 319–52.

Walter, C.
1969   "Lazarus a Bishop," *Revue des Études By-
        zantines* 27: 197–208.

Wander, S.
1973   "The Cyprus Plates: The Story of David and
        Goliath," *Metropolitan Museum Journal* 8:
        89–104.

Ward-Perkins, J.B.
1972   "Recent Work and Problems in Libya." Pp.
        219–36 in *Acta Del VII Congresso Interna-
        zionale Di Archaeologia Christiana, Bar-
        celona 1969* (Vatican: Pontificio Istituto di
        Archeologia Cristiana).

Wartburg, M.-L. von
2003   "Cypriot Contacts with East and West as
        Reflected in Medieval Glazed Pottery from
        the Paphos Region." Pp. 153–66 in *Actes du
        VIIe Congrès International sur la Céramique
        Médiévale en Méditerranée, Thessaloniki,
        11–16 octobre 1999*, ed. C. Bakirtzis (Athens:
        Archaeological Receipts Fund).

Wartburg, M.-L. von, and Violaris, Y.
2009   "Pottery of a 12th Century Pit from the
        Palaion Demarcheion Site in Nicosia: A
        Typological and Analytical Approach
        to a Closed Assemblage." Pp. 249–64 in
        *Actas del VIII Congreso Internacional de
        Cerámica Medieval en el Mediterráneo,
        Ciudad Real-Almagro del 27 de febrero al
        3 de marzo de 2006*, vol. 1, ed. J. Zuzaya et
        al. (Ciudad Real: Asociacion Espanola de
        Arqueologia Medieval).

Weitzman, K.
1975   "A Group of Early Twelfth-Century Sinai
        Icons attributed to Cyprus." Pp. 47–63 in
        Studies in Memory of David Talbot Rice,
        eds. G. Robertson and G. Henderson (Ed-
        inburgh: Edinburgh University).
1976   *The Monastery of Saint Catherine at Mount
        Sinai. The Icons* 1: *From the sixth to the tenth
        Century* (Princeton: Princeton University).
1981   "Les icônes de Constantinople," in *Les
        Icônes*, eds. K. Weitzman, G. Alibegasvili,
        et al. (Milan: Mondadori).

Weitzmann, K., and Galavaris, G.
1990   *The Monastery of Saint Catherine at Mount
        Sinai. The Illuminated Greek Manuscripts*,
        1: *From the Ninth to the Twelfth Centuries*
        (Princeton: Princeton University).

Wessel, K., and Restle, M.
1966   *Reallexikon zur byzantinischen Kunst* 1:
        Abendmahl–Dura-Europos (Stuttgart: Hierse-
        mann).
1972   *Reallexikon zur byzantinischen Kunst* 3:
        Himmelsleiter–Kastoria (Stuttgart: Hierse-
        mann).
2005   *Reallexikon zur byzantinischen Kunst* 5:
        Kreuz–Maltechnik (Stuttgart: Hiersemann).

Westphalen, S.
1998   *Die Odalar Camii in Istanbul. Architektur
        und Malerei einer Mittelbzyantinischen
        Kirche* [Istanbuler Mitteilungen, Beiheft 21]
        (Tübingen: Wasmuth).

Wharton, A.
1977   "The 'Iconoclast' Churches of Cappadocia."
        Pp. 103–12 in *Iconoclasm: Papers given at
        the 9th Spring Symposium of Byzantine
        Studies, University of Birmingham, March
        1975* (Birmingham: Centre for Byzantine
        Studies).
1986   *Tokali Kilise. Tenth Century Metropolitan
        Art in Byzantine Cappadocia* (Washington,
        DC: Dumbarton Oaks, Trustees of Harvard
        University).

1988   *Art of Empire: Painting and Architecture of the Byzantine Periphery* (University Park: Pennsylvania State University).

1991   "Cyprus." Pp. 567–70 in *The Oxford Dictionary of Byzantium* 1(Oxford: Oxford University).

1995   *Refiguring the Post Classical City: Dura Europos, Jerash, Jerusalem and Ravenna* (New York: Cambridge University).

Williams, C.

1989   *Anemurium. The Roman and Early Byzantine Pottery* (Toronto: Pontifical Institute of Mediaeval Studies).

Winfield, D., and Winfield, J.

2003   *The Church of the Panaghia tou Arakos at Lagoudhera, Cyprus: The Paintings and Their Painterly Significance* [Dumbarton Oaks Studies 37] (Washington, DC: Dumbarton Oaks Research Library and Collection).

Winther-Jacobsen, K.

2010   *From Pots to People: A Ceramic Approach to the Archaeological Interpretation of Ploughsoil Assemblages in Late Roman Cyprus* [Babesch Supplementa 17] (Leuven: Peeters).

Wright, G.R.

1992   *Ancient Building in Cyprus* [Handbuch der Orientalistik 8] (Leiden: Brill).

Wroth, W.

1908   *Catalogue of the Imperial Byzantine Coins in the British Museum* (London: British Museum; reprinted Chicago, 1970, 2nd ed.).

Yannopoulos, P.A.

1983   "Les couches populaires de la société chypriote au VIIe siècle selon les sources locales et contemporaines," *Επετηρίς του Κέντρου Επιστημονικών Ερευνών Κύπρου* 12: 79–85.

Zibawi, M.

1995   *Orients Chrétiens – Entre Byzance et l'Islam* (Paris: Desclée de Brouwe).

Contributors

DR. DEMETRIOS MICHAELIDES is Director of the Archaeological Research Unit at the University of Cyprus. Besides his excavation activity, he is considered the foremost specialist in Hellenistic through Byzantine mosaic floors and marble pavements. His publications include *Cypriot Mosaics* (1992) and *Egypt and Cyprus in Antiquity* (2009).

DR. CLAUDIA RAPP, at the time of the conference, was Professor of History at the University of California at Los Angeles. Her most recent book is *Holy Bishops in Late Antiquity* (2005). She is currently Professor of Byzantine Studies at the University of Vienna.

DR. MARCUS RAUTMAN is Professor of Art History and Archaeology at the University of Missouri. He has directed numerous field surveys and excavations in Cyprus and Turkey. His publications include *A Cypriot Village of Late Antiquity. Kalavasos-Kopetra in the Vasilikos Valley* (2003) and *Daily Life in the Byzantine Empire* (2006).

DR. D.M. METCALF is currently retired, after a distinguished career as Professor and Keeper of the Heberden Coin Collection at the Ashmolean Museum, Oxford University. He is an expert in numismatics and Byzantine sigillography. His recent books are *Byzantine Lead Seals from Cyprus* (2004) and *Byzantine Cyprus: 491–1191* (2009).

DR. ELENI PROCOPIOU is a Senior Archaeological officer at the Department of Antiquities, Cyprus. Her expertise lies in Late Roman and Byzantine archaeology. Her book *The 'Compressed Cross-in-Square' Church in Cyprus* (2007), in Greek, is an important contribution to architectural history.

DR. M. TAHAR MANSOURI, at the time of the conference, was Professor at the University of Dammam, Saudi Arabia. His specialty lies in Byzantine and Arab relations during the Middle Ages. He is currently Professor of Medieval History at the University of Manouba, Tunisia. His book *Chypre dans les sources arabes médiévales* (2001) analyzed key Arabic texts for understanding Byzantine politics.

DR. SOPHOCLES SOPHOCLEOUS is Director of the Centre of Cultural Heritage and Professor of Art History at the University of Nicosia. He is a professional conservator of Byzantine frescos and icons. His recent books include *Icones De Chypre* (2006) and *Paralimni: The Church of Agios Georgios* (2009).

DR. MARIA PARANI is Assistant Professor of Byzantine and Post-Byzantine Art and Archaeology at the Department of History and Archaeology of the University of Cyprus. Her research focuses mainly on the study of material culture and daily life in Byzantium with an interdisciplinary approach that makes use of written and artistic evidence, as well as archaeological data.

DR. VASILIKI KASSIANIDOU is Associate Professor in the Department of History and Archaeology at the University of Cyprus. She is a recognized expert in the study of ancient metallurgy. Her forthcoming book (with G. Papasavvas) *Eastern Mediterranean Metallurgy and Metalwork* is in print.

DR. TASSOS PAPACOSTAS is Lecturer in Byzantine Material Culture at King's College, University of London. His many publications have made significant contributions to our understanding of Eastern Mediterranean economic, settlement, and architectural history.

DR. ANNEMARIE WEYL CARR is Distinguished Professor of Art History Emerita at Southern Methodist University (Dallas). Her most recent publications are *Imprinting the Divine: Byzantine and Russian Icons from The Menil Collection* (2011) and *Asinou Across Time* (2013).

DR. THOMAS W. DAVIS, at the time of the conference, was director of the Cyprus American Archaeological Research Institute. He has excavated many ancient sites throughout the Eastern Mediterranean. His book *Shifting Sands* (2004) examined the history of archaeological research in the Near East. He is currently Professor of Archaeology at Southwestern Baptist Theological Seminary, Dallas.

DR. CHARLES ANTHONY STEWART is Assistant Professor of Art and Architectural History at the University of St. Thomas, Houston. He has conducted fieldwork throughout the Europe and the Near East, focusing on Early Christian and Byzantine art and architectural history.

Index

NOTE: *Historical persons are listed with their titles after their names in order to distinguish between them and toponyms or monuments. Proper names in Arabic begin with their definite article or patronym. In the subject index, religious buildings in Cyprus begin with their Greek descriptors (i.e., "Agia"), whereas sites outside begin with the English "Saint" or "Hagia."*

HISTORIC PERSONS AND PLACES

SUBJECTS, MONUMENTS, AND EVENTS